# The Black Sea

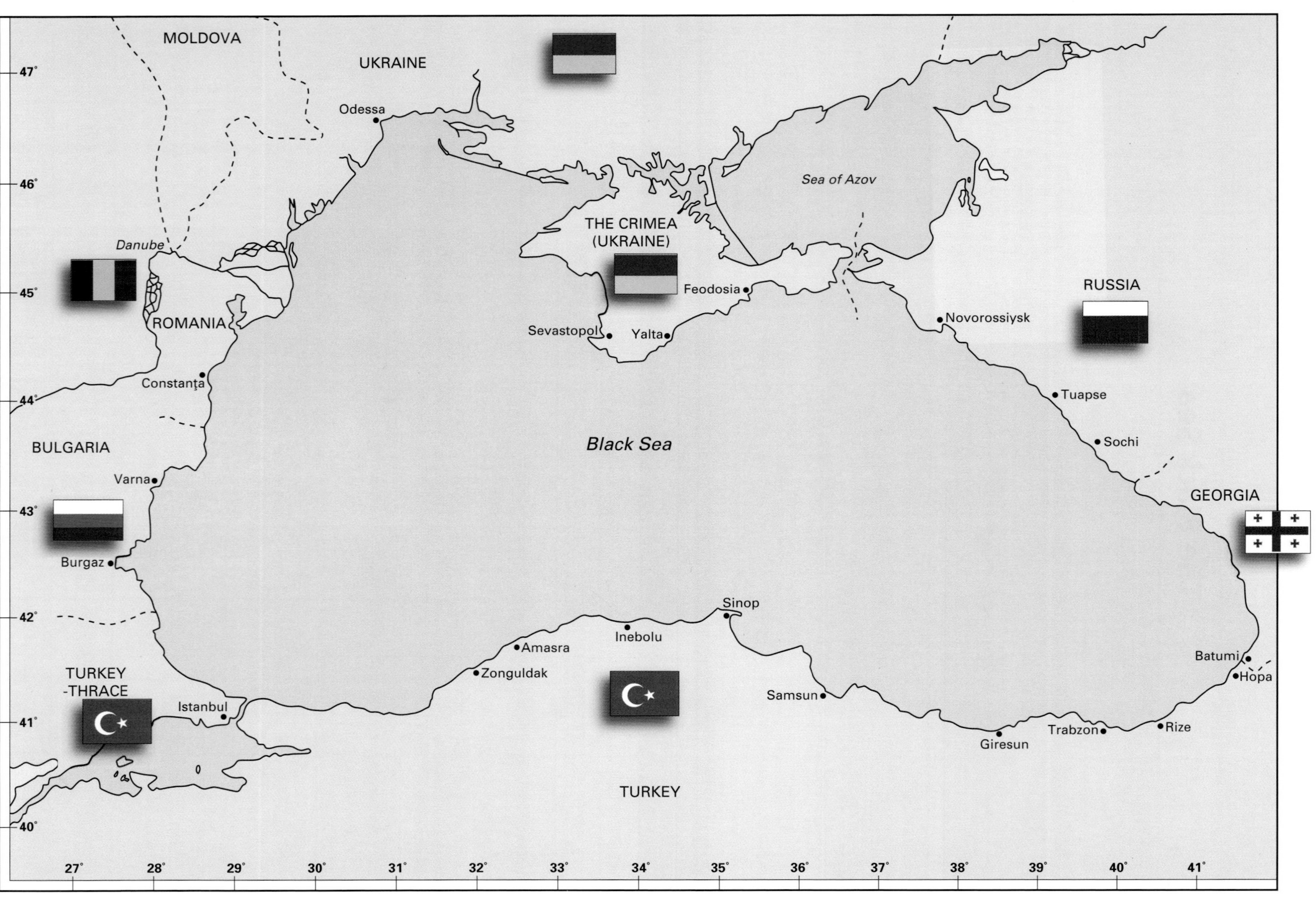
MOLDOVA
UKRAINE
Odessa
Danube
ROMANIA
Constanța
BULGARIA
Varna
Burgaz
TURKEY
-THRACE
Istanbul
THE CRIMEA
(UKRAINE)
Sevastopol
Yalta
Feodosia
Sea of Azov
RUSSIA
Novorossiysk
Tuapse
Sochi
GEORGIA
Batumi
Hopa
Rize
Trabzon
Giresun
Samsun
Sinop
Inebolu
Amasra
Zonguldak
Black Sea
TURKEY
47°
46°
45°
44°
43°
42°
41°
40°
27°
28°
29°
30°
31°
32°
33°
34°
35°
36°
37°
38°
39°
40°
41°

# The Black Sea

David Read Barker and Lisa Borre

Imray Laurie Norie & Wilson Ltd

Published by
**Imray Laurie Norie & Wilson Ltd**
Wych House The Broadway St Ives Cambridgeshire PE27 5BT
England
✆ +44 (0)1480 462114 *Fax* +44 (0)1480 496109
*Email* ilnw@imray.com
www.imray.com
2012



First edition 2012



ISBN 978 184623 412 5

British Library Cataloguing in Publication Data.
A catalogue record for this title is available from the British Library.

Printed in Singapore by Star Standard Industries

## CORRECTIONAL SUPPLEMENTS

This pilot book may be amended at intervals by the issue of correctional supplements. These are published on the internet at our website www.imray.com (and also via www.rccpf.org.uk) and may be downloaded free of charge. Printed copies are also available on request from the publishers at the above address. Like this pilot, supplements are selective. Navigators requiring the latest definitive information are advised to refer to official hydrographic office data.

## ADDITIONAL INFORMATION

Additional information may be found under the Publications page at www.rccpf.org.uk. This includes a downloadable waypoint list, links to Google maps, additional photographs and mid-season updates when appropriate. Passage planning information may also be found on that website.

## CAUTION

Whilst the RCC Pilotage Foundation, the authors and the publishers have used reasonable endeavours to ensure the accuracy of the content of this book, it contains selected information and thus is not definitive. It does not contain all known information on the subject in hand and should not be relied on alone for navigational use: it should only be used in conjunction with official hydrographical data. This is particularly relevant to the plans, which should not be used for navigation. The RCC Pilotage Foundation, the authors and the publishers believe that the information which they have included is a useful aid to prudent navigation, but the safety of a vessel depends ultimately on the judgment of the skipper, who should assess all information, published or unpublished. The information provided in this pilot book may be out of date and may be changed or updated without notice. The RCC Pilotage Foundation cannot accept any liability for any error, omission or failure to update such information. To the extent permitted by law, the RCC Pilotage Foundation, the authors and the publishers do not accept liability for any loss and/or damage howsoever caused that may arise from reliance on information contained in these pages.

### POSITIONS

All positions in the text are to WGS 84 datum. They are supplied as aids to help orientation and to assist in locating and maintaining transits referred to in the book. As always, care must be exercised to work to the datum of the chart in use.

### WAYPOINTS

This edition of *The Black Sea* pilot includes waypoints. The RCC Pilotage Foundation consider a waypoint to be a position likely to be helpful for navigation if entered into some form of electronic navigation system for use in conjunction with GPS. In this pilot they have been derived from electronic charts and direct observation. They must be used with caution. All waypoints are given to datum WGS 84 and every effort has been made to ensure their accuracy. Nevertheless, for each individual vessel, the standard of onboard equipment, aerial position, datum setting, correct entry of data and operator skill all play a part in their effectiveness. In particular it is vital for the navigator to note the datum of the chart in use and apply the necessary correction if plotting a GPS position on the chart.
Our use of the term 'waypoint' does not imply that all vessels can safely sail directly over those positions at all times. Under appropriate conditions some may be linked to form recommended routes but this is the skipper's responsibility. Verification by observation, or use of radar to check the accuracy of a waypoint, may sometimes be advisable and reassuring.
We emphasise that we regard waypoints as an aid to navigation for use as the navigator or skipper decides. We hope that the waypoints in this pilot will help ease that navigational load.

### PLANS

The plans in this guide are not to be used for navigation – they are designed to support the text and should always be used together with navigational charts. It should be borne in mind that the characteristics of lights may be changed during the life of the book, and that in any case notification of such changes is unlikely to be reported immediately. All bearings are given from seaward and refer to true north. Symbols are based on those used by the British Admiralty – users are referred to *Symbols and Abbreviations* (*NP 5011*).

# Contents

**Forword** *vii*

**Introduction** *1*

1. **Cruising the Black Sea** *5*

2. **Preparations for cruising the Black Sea by yacht** *12*

3. **History and human life** *20*

4. **Turkey east of the Bosphorus** *33*
   Section1: Bosphorus to Amasra, *39*
   Section 2: Amasra to Bafra Burnu, *58*
   Section 3: Bafra Burnu to Çam Burnu, *81*
   Section 4: Çam Burnu to the Georgian border, *97*

5. **Georgia** *119*

6. **Russian Federation** *130*

7. **Ukraine** *134*
   Section 1: Yalta to Feodosia and the Kerch Straits, *138*
   Section 2: Yalta to the Romanian border, *146*

8. **Romania** *161*

9. **Bulgaria** *171*

10. **Turkey west of the Bosphorus** *195*

**Appendix** *199*

**Index**, *202*

## THE RCC PILOTAGE FOUNDATION

The overall management of the RCC Pilotage Foundation is entrusted to Trustees appointed by the Royal Cruising Club, with day to day operations being controlled by the Hon Director as Chief Executive. All these appointments are unpaid. In line with its charitable status, the Foundation distributes no profits; any surpluses are used to finance new publications and developments and to subsidise research into those regions where pilotage information is sparse.

The object of the Foundation is to collect and research information relating to small boat pilotage, navigation and operations (including information relating to remote areas where other sources of information are scarce or non-existent) and to disseminate this information through the production of books, charts, lectures, meetings, internet or such media or means as appropriate.

We aim to produce and maintain high-quality pilotage information and advice on how to obtain more specific details. In recent years we have concentrated on presenting our books in an easy-to-use manner as well as making them relevant in the electronic age. Our range of publications is steadily increasing with many books available in French, Spanish, Italian or German editions. We currently issue 24 books, 11 ebooks and also Passage Planning Guides for all the oceans of the world.

## PUBLICATIONS OF THE RCC PILOTAGE FOUNDATION

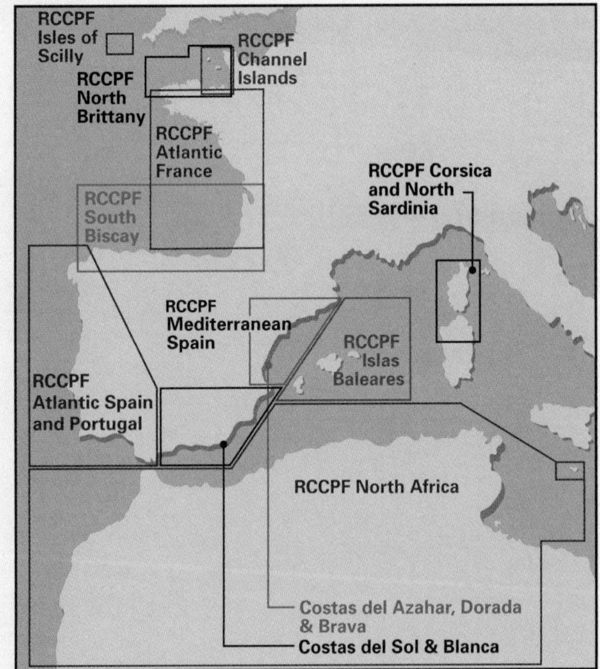


***Imray***
Faroe, Iceland and Greenland
Norway
The Baltic Sea
Channel Islands
North Brittany and the Channel Islands
Isles of Scilly
North Biscay
South Biscay
Atlantic Islands
Atlantic Spain & Portugal
Mediterranean Spain
  Costas del Sol and Blanca
  Costas del Azahar, Dorada & Brava
Islas Baleares
Corsica and North Sardinia
North Africa
Chile
Black Sea

***Adlard Coles Nautical***
Atlantic Crossing Guide
Pacific Crossing Guide

***On Board Publications***
South Atlantic Circuit
Havens and Anchorages for the South American Coast

***The RCC Pilotage Foundation***
Supplement to Falkland Island Shores
Guide to West Africa
Argentina

***RCCPF Website www.rccpf.org.uk***
Supplements
Support files for books
Passage Planning Guides
ePilots - from the Arctic to the Antarctic Peninsula

## Foreword

Having been fortunate enough to join KAYRA* 2001 to cruise the Black Sea with yachts of 19 nations under the leadership of Teoman Arsay I was delighted when, 10 years later, David Barker and Lisa Borre offered to produce a pilotage guide to the Black Sea following their cruise there in 2010. Although more boats are venturing into the waters of the Black Sea each year, no comprehensive pilotage notes for yachtsmen had been published since Dorren and Archie Annan's book *Cruise the Black Sea* was produced 10 years before in conjunction with Ataköy Yacht Club in Istanbul. In 2011 the Annans generously granted the Pilotage Foundation the sole right to use their material, including all their originally researched and detailed plans. This book now allows their work to live on and reach a wider audience than before.

This guide is more than a pilot book, although that remains the prime object. David and Lisa's studies of all aspects of the Black Sea provide a fascinating backdrop to the area from ancient history to modern times as well as discussing current environmental concerns and pressures and it offers yachtsmen a deeper insight into the Black Sea than hitherto. The authors have consulted widely but write a personal account in a highly easy to read and factual manner. The Pilotage Foundation is most grateful for all their efforts and asks that subsequent sailors send in their findings as text or photograph so that this work may be updated and expanded in the years to come. Thanks also go to Imray who, with their usual professional standards, have quickly turned our ePilot into this book.

Political changes affecting the leisure sailor cruising the Black Sea are possible and may happen rapidly. The advice from Russia in mid-2011 was that inland waterways will soon be opened to foreigners, and with simpler procedures than hitherto; such action would greatly enhance cruising opportunities through to the White Sea as well as to the borders of the Black Sea.

Details of how to contribute to this work may be found on www.rccpf.org.uk. This website includes considerable pilotage information to assist yachtsmen plan their approach through the Mediterranean Sea to the Black Sea as well as worldwide. Updates to this guide will be published as supplements by the publisher or via the website.

*Martin Walker*
*Hon Director RCCPF*
*December 2011*

* KAYRA was the Karadeniz Yat Rallisi (Black Sea Yacht Rally) and is mentioned later by the authors. Teoman Arsay, who conceived and led KAYRA, has continued as Commodore of the ever-popular EMYR (East Mediterranean Yacht Rally). See www.emyr.org.

## Preface

We first became attracted to visiting the Black Sea by its ancient tales, particularly Tim Severin's *The Jason Voyage*. But thoughts of the harsh climate and ecological problems, as well as the challenges of dealing with former Communist bureaucracies made us wonder, 'Who in their right mind would want to visit the Black Sea?' The break came from Al Duda, a former colleague and senior advisor for the International Waters portfolio at the Global Environmental Facility. He introduced us to Dr Ahmet Kideyş, who opened doors for us among scientists.

Through Ahmet, the Black Sea Commission (BSC) 'sponsored' our voyage and brought us into contact with the BSC's network of scientists, technicians and policymakers. Wanting to visit Wetlands Convention sites, we received guidance from Tobias Salathe at the Ramsar Secretariat in Switzerland.

The Black Sea is one of the most isolated of all the world's great water bodies. Although it suffers from significant environmental damage, it is teeming with dolphins, and it supports millions of families with fish. It is an exciting and very interesting place to sail, as we discovered in the summer of 2010 cruising on the Black Sea in our 37ft Tayana cutter sailboat. We found that there was a serious lack of good up-to-date information about what a private yacht might experience on the Black Sea, and consequently most visiting yachtsmen had one or more bad experiences. We undertook our voyage with the intention of providing up-to-date advice based on experience, and this guide is the result.

Finding information about sailing on the Black Sea was not easy, especially because we hoped to sail all the way round it. The guides were often out of date and the information was scattered among numerous books, several of which are out of print. We managed to locate copies of each published guide and to interview and/or obtain cruising notes from a couple of dozen cruising sailors who visited the Black Sea in recent years. During the winter months we found one of the last copies of Rick and Sheila Nelson's guide, Nicky Allardice's guide *Cruising Bulgaria and Romania*, and the Admiralty Pilot. We had to be especially persistent to locate a copy of *Cruise the Black Sea* by Doreen and Archie Annan, which has served as the basis for this book.

Our luck continued to improve upon arrival in Istanbul in May 2010. We decided to stay in the Setur Kalamis and Fenerbaçe Marina on the Asian side because it seemed like the most convenient place to moor our boat *Gyatso* while we prepared for our voyage, rather than at the Ataköy Marina. To our surprise we found little interest in the Black Sea when we contacted Ataköy Marina, despite it having sponsored the KAYRA Black Sea Rallies and published the Annans' guide. By chance we found ourselves in the same marina where the former

KAYRA rally organiser, Teoman Arsay, berths his yacht. Within hours of our arrival, he and other members of the club were well on the way to becoming our fast friends, and he shared his enthusiasm, wealth of knowledge and numerous contacts around the Black Sea.

In 2010 we circumnavigated the Black Sea, visiting five of the six countries beginning in Turkey and continuing in a counter-clockwise direction to Georgia, Ukraine, Romania and Bulgaria before returning to Turkey again. We decided not to visit Russia. Even with all of our experience and contacts we could not make it happen – not for lack of trying, or because it is explicitly prohibited, but because officials there could not give assurances regarding clearance procedures and the safety of our vessel and crew. For us it was a disappointment not to be able to visit by yacht the site of the next Winter Olympics in Sochi, Russia. In the end prudence prevailed, and Russia was removed from our cruising itinerary.

### About the authors

David Barker and Lisa Borre sailed together on Chesapeake Bay, the Atlantic coast of the US, and on all five of the Great Lakes in the US and Canada before setting out on an extended voyage aboard their Tayana 37ft cutter *Gyatso* in 2005. Since then they have covered nearly 20,000 miles while living aboard and cruising full-time in the Caribbean, Mediterranean and Black Seas and they crossed the Atlantic in 2007 with the ARC Europe Rally. They continue to chronicle their sailing adventures and contribute to cruising and pilotage information as members of the Ocean Cruising Club (OCC) and through their extensive website (www.gyatso.net).

David is retired from a career in international development in which he worked for the United Nations, as a management consultant, and as an NGO executive. Lisa's 20-year career in the field of environmental management includes working on lake and wetland conservation issues as co-founder of LakeNet, a world lakes network, and as the coordinator of the Lake Champlain Basin Program.

## Acknowledgements

It would have been inconceivable for us to have completed the Black Sea voyage without the generous help of many people who deserve acknowledgement. In Turkey, we benefitted from long conversations in Istanbul with Teoman Arsay; Professor Dr Bayram Öztürk; and Dr Ahmet Kideyş and the staff of the Black Sea Commission. Elsewhere, we met with Professor Levent Bat and Habeş Kaptan in Sinop; Professor Ilhan Altinok in Çamburnu; Hüseyin Göktürk in Doğanyurt; Hasan Tecimer in Rize; Dr Ertuğ Düzgüneş, Dr Recep Kizilcik, Avtandil Mikatsadze, Yahya Saka, Taner Demirbulut and Merve Yazicoğlu in Trabzon; Özer Akbaşli, M. Volkan Türkyılmaz and Osman Aker in Giresun; and Ali İhsan Dumlu in Terme. In Georgia we received the hospitality of David Pirtskhalaishvili in Batumi; Jumber (Juki) Tsomaia at Poti Yacht Club; Marika Nadaraia at Poti Seaport; and Khatuna Katsarava at Kolkheti, in Poti. In the Ukraine we received help and advice from Volodymyr R Papakin in Yalta; Natasha Marskovskaya in Balaclava; Professor Dr Borys Aleksandrov in Odessa; and Vasiliy Kostyushin in Kiev. In Romania Cornel Ciucu, Dumitru Bucureşteanu and Magdalena Ion in Constanţa went out of their way to guide us. In Bulgaria Hristo Tzvetkov in Sozopol extended a warm welcome. In Europe and North America we were helped by Al Duda and Ivan Zavadsky in Washington DC, and by Mary Lou Baker in Annapolis, Maryland; Tobias Salathe in Gland, Switzerland; Robin Waterfield, Aidan Liddle, and Neal Ascherson in Great Britain; and Tim Severin in Ireland. Finally, yachtsmen on 21 yachts offered advice and charts, and shared adventure stories: Nick Martin and Jo Crooks on *Kiwi Spirit*; Bert and Lorraine Bramble on *Twist of Fate*; John and Vanessa Ross on *Meand'er*; Felix and Monika Seidel on *Makani*; Chuck and Alison Spinney on *ChaliVentures*; Keith and Jean Nicholson on *La Liberté*; Fred and Jane Hoette on *Escape Key*; Nout and Jolanda Goverse on *Atlantis*; Robert Sprung and Karin Fehlau on *Huibuh*; Clive Garner on *Santuzza*; Rudolf H Gwalter on *Moira DMM*; Henry and Julie Danielson on *Tapestry*; Robert and Susanne Meggle on *Cherokee*; Heinz and Käthi Dietel on *Peppermint*; Jürgen CW Schröder on *Mien Chip*; Mike Yendell on *Cooya*; Margaret Reichenbach and Matt Rollberg on *Santana*; Alan Logan on *Katy II*; Peter Ogilvy-Stuart on *Cougar*; Steve Anderson on *Eirenic*; and Sally Humphreys on *Kalypso*. Heartfelt thanks to all.

Having completed the Black Sea voyage, it would have been inconceivable for us to have brought this book into print without the encouragement and guidance of Martin Walker.

We dedicate this cruising guide to Teoman Arsay, President, Marmara Offshore Yacht Club and to Professor Ahmet E Kideyş, Executive Director, Commission on the Protection of the Black Sea Against Pollution.

*David Read Barker and Lisa Borre*
*December 2011*
*www.gyatso.net*

# Introduction



### *Gyatso's* voyage to the Black Sea

The Black Sea is ecologically unique and, because comparatively few yachts visit it, a cruise there is a pretty big adventure. *Gyatso* is a Tayana 37ft cutter-rigged sailboat with a 30-horsepower diesel engine, constructed of fibreglass in 1985 in Taiwan. Throughout five years of living aboard, the boat proved to be comfortable even in bad weather and relatively easy to handle by a husband-and-wife crew.

*Gyatso's* Black Sea voyage in 2010 took 111 days, beginning with a departure from Istanbul on 29 May and returning again to the Bosphorus on 15 September. We visited five of the six countries during the 2,118-mile counter-clockwise circumnavigation, including Turkey, Georgia, the Ukraine, Romania and Bulgaria. We were unable to visit the Russian Federation, so to avoid entering Russian waters, we made a 330-mile offshore passage from Georgia to the Crimean Peninsula in the Ukraine.

During our cruise we were not required to use an agent for entrance or exit formalities except in Yalta, on the Crimean Peninsula. We were glad to have the name and contact of a reputable agent in Yalta, and elsewhere in Ukraine the port control authorities were a hassle, but everywhere else we encountered only professionalism and efficiency.

Contrary to published guides about the Black Sea, we found it teaming with life. Dolphins and porpoises made regular appearances in our bow wave. We met with many experts and scientists about the environmental conditions and were encouraged to learn of some signs of improvement to this highly degraded ecosystem.

It was an arduous voyage at times, but not because of the notorious Black Sea storms. Other than relatively short-lived severe thunderstorms and high wind events, the gales occur primarily during winter months. By keeping a close eye on the weather and with the abundance of protected harbours, especially along the exposed Turkish coast, we managed to avoid getting caught out in bad weather most of the time.

The sweltering summer heat sapped our energy. We deployed our sun awnings more frequently than

*Gyatso* under sail in passage to Şile, Turkey

we expected and felt lucky to be near the water. We limited our travel to inland destinations, in part because of the heat and humidity, but also because of the huge task of gathering pilotage information for the updated cruising guide, which took much more effort than we anticipated.

The lack of wind along the Turkish coast in June and early July required more motoring days than we would like, but in comparison, it was not very different from our experience in Spain and Italy during the months of July and August. It is somewhat more frustrating on the Black Sea because the persistent swell seemed to indicate that the wind was blowing somewhere not too far away.

We were awed by the sheer beauty of the mountainous Black Sea coastline in Eastern Turkey, especially near the border with Georgia, on the Crimean Peninsula, and in the foothills of the Balkan Mountains in Bulgaria. We were mesmerised by the long stretches of sandy beach on either side of the Bosphorus, stretching along the western shore of the Black Sea to Odessa, and along the shore of the 80-mile long sand spit known as Djarilgach Island in the Ukraine. It was off this coast that we experienced the most glorious sailing conditions of the summer.

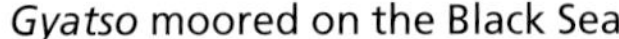

*Gyatso* moored on the Black Sea

Georgia, near Batumi

Bafra Burnu, Turkey, wetlands of the Kizilirmak Delta

In the end we had the kind of experiences that happen when you get off the beaten path, some of which are captured in *Gyatso's* online logbook (see www.gyatso.net). We certainly had no shortage of lasting memories.

### About this guide

We found an excellent guide in Archie and Doreen Annans' book *Cruise the Black Sea*, published by the Ataköy Marina, Istanbul, in association with the Ataköy Marina Yacht Club (AMYC), in 2001. The AMYC had strongly promoted Black Sea yachting by conducting the KAYRA rallies, but during the decade following the publication of *Cruise the Black Sea* the marina was sold to new owners and the yacht club moved to new quarters and was renamed the Marmara Offshore Yacht Club. The book may still be obtained in the UK – refer to www.rccpf.org.uk for contact details – or from a few outlets in Turkey. Copyright lies with the Annans, who have generously granted rights to use its information to the RCC Pilotage Foundation who sponsor and hold copyright of this publication.

The Annans' guide served us very well during the Black Sea voyage. A great many changes have

Inebolu, Turkey

occurred in the Black Sea since their visit, but most of Archie Annan's excellent plans of 180 anchorages and harbours are still accurate; they have been used throughout this guide. Without them, it would have been more difficult to produce this update. We have made every effort to update everything, based on what we found in 2010. In about a dozen cases we have prepared new chartlets for yacht harbours that did not exist or were in the planning stage at the time of the Annans' visits.

At the same time, we were able to gain a greater appreciation of the Black Sea through some understanding of its natural history, so we have included information about this and especially about three of the wetlands of international importance that encircle the Sea.

This cruising guide begins at the Bosphorus, where most yachts enter the Black Sea, and moves in a counterclockwise (anticlockwise) direction. It starts with the Turkish coast and continues to Georgia, Russia, the Ukraine, Romania and Bulgaria and back to Turkey along the Thracian coast to the Bosphorus again. As it follows the direction of the rim current, this is the direction that most sailors go, or are advised to go, unless they plan to visit only the Bulgarian and/or Romanian coasts.

The guide covers almost the entire body of the Black Sea, but it excludes the shallow and relatively isolated Sea of Azov and the narrow Kerch Strait which connects the Sea of Azov and the Black Sea. This whole area is within what we describe as a 'yachting caution zone' extending NE of the line between Poti, Georgia and Feodosia, Ukraine. Private yachts are discouraged from attempting to visit Abkhazia because of ongoing efforts by Georgia to blockade the region and by the Russian naval patrols to keep Abkhazian waters open.

The guide also excludes the great rivers that flow in from the north the Don and Kuban, flowing into the Sea of Azov, and the Dnieper, Dniester and Bug, entering the Black Sea through vast deltas. For the Ukraine, political changes make previous cruising guides now seem overly optimistic about the extent of bureaucracy involved in visiting more than just a handful of ports.

Although we had hoped to give balanced attention to each country, we (like almost every other yacht) were unable to visit the Russian Federation and therefore are able to write much less about what sort of experience one might have there. We have included such information that we judge to be accurate, though we had no opportunity to verify it in person.

Ports located on the major rivers are excluded, except for Sulina, Romania, on the Danube, because this is a convenient port of entry for yachts entering or leaving Romania on the Black Sea. Upstream ports and anchorages in the Danube Delta are described in other cruising guides, but it should be noted that procedures for foreign yachts visiting Romania and Bulgaria have improved tremendously since their publication.

Any visit to the Black Sea will be enhanced by reading standard tour guides such as those published by Lonely Planet, Rough Guides and DK Guides, as well as from the internet and local tourism offices. We have tried to provide information about those places not covered in standard tourist guides or for which good information is not readily available. Throughout the Black Sea mobile phones and wireless internet connectivity have revolutionised information to the point that so many street maps, tour packages and shopping guides can be viewed online that there is little need to include them in a cruising guide.

We have not included detailed descriptions of inland excursions, except to make reference to suggested itineraries, travel logistics for people arriving by yacht, and sites of interest accessible from the individual ports.

### Future updates and revisions

Plans for the future: the countries of the Black Sea are changing, some rapidly, so we would welcome any updating information being sent the RCCPF through their website so that this can be published on that site or promulgated further as necessary. Please refer to www.rccpf.org.uk.

### How to use this guide

Basic directions for sailing on the Black Sea are given in Chapter 1, which also includes a list of harbours suitable for yachts. Preparations for Cruising are summarised in Chapter 2. Sketches of the natural history and modern life are provided in Chapter 3. Chapters 4–10 cover individual countries, beginning with Asian Turkey (E of Bosphorus), Georgia, Russia, the Ukraine, Romania, Bulgaria and European Turkey (W of Bosphorus).

Harbours are described in more or less detail depending on their suitability for yachts and/or their potential interest to people visiting by yacht. More detailed write-ups are organised into sections about 'Approach', 'Mooring', 'Facilities' and 'General' information. A plan and/or photo of every important harbour, anchorage or town is provided. Most harbour plans were originally prepared by the Annans during research they conducted in 2000 and 2001. Where needed, we have updated plan information or prepared new harbour plans based on our observations in 2010.

All plans should be used with prudence. We have made every effort to verify the accuracy of the information contained in this cruising guide, but it is just that, a guide. As we observed, things change rapidly, and it is occasionally difficult for foreign yachts to obtain information, especially about Russia.

Doğanyurt, Turkey

Lat/Long co-ordinates were gathered using GPS (WGS84) while cruising and verified against published sources. Except where noted, the GPS position given for the individual harbour summaries is the position of the outer (seaward) breakwater at the entrance to the harbour or a safe approach mark. All GPS coordinates are rounded to nearest tenth of a minute of N latitude or E longitude (e.g. Şile 41°10'·7N 29°36'·0E). Note should be taken of the datum of any charts used when using this GPS derived information. All bearings are given as True. All depths are in metres. On the harbour plans, yachts are shown as solid black and other vessels as an outline only.

Information about entrance and exit formalities for each country is provided in the individual chapters. This has changed rapidly, mostly for the better.

Istanbul, tall shps

# 1. Cruising the Black Sea


1.1 Two routes to enter
1.2 Prevailing winds and currents
1.3 Shoreline
1.4 National ports of entry
1.5 Caution zone
1.6 Cruising routes
1.7 Harbours suitable for yachts
1.8 Cruise ships


As *Gyatso's* voyage and those of many other yachtsmen demonstrate, a private solo yacht can sail all the way around the coast of the Black Sea entirely on its own, without any official sponsorship and without joining a rally. KAYRA rallies have ceased, but it seems that every year an informal network develops among yachts visiting the Black Sea, bound by email and SMS communication and by travelling in company on the longer legs.

In the 8th century BC, when the ancient Greeks began establishing colonies all along the Black Sea coasts, there were really only two choices after passing the Clashing Rocks at the mouth of the Bosphorus: turning left and heading north along the west coast, or turning right and heading east along the south coast. Today there are more choices, and yachts' sailing routes are conditioned by the sort of destination sought, the point of entry into the Black Sea, the prevailing winds and currents, and the ports of entry in the surrounding countries.

## 1.1 Two routes to enter

In 2010 two international water bodies provided yachts with access to the Black Sea: the Danube River and the Bosphorus. Hopefully, changes to regulations being discussed by the Russian Duma in 2011 will allow the route through Russia from the White Sea – or the Baltic – to once more be open to yachts.

View of Bosphorus from Istanbul

A ship passes on the Danube

From the NW it is more than 1,600M down the Danube River from Germany to the port of Sulina, Romania, near the Black Sea coast. We understand that in 2010 fewer than 10 yachts made this entire trip, and all of them continued on down the west coast to the Bosphorus and onward to the Aegean Sea; the alternative of battling the current back up the Danube is not attractive. Most yachts head for the Mediterranean. For those in a hurry, shipping back to European waters from there is an option.

From the SW it is about 200M from the Aegean, up the Dardanelles, through the Sea of Marmara, and up the Bosphorus to the fishing port of Poyrazköy, at the juncture with the Black Sea. About 20 foreign yachts visited the Black Sea via this route during 2010.

## 1.2 Prevailing winds and currents

One of the major questions facing a yachtsman planning an extended Black Sea voyage is whether to go in a clockwise or an anticlockwise (counterclockwise) direction. The rim currents flow anticlockwise, and the winds are generally N, so it can be challenging for a low-powered yacht to travel directly from the Bosphorus to the middle of the W coast in the face of both the prevailing wind and a current. *See also 3.6 for details on currents.*

The longer the planned voyage, the stronger becomes the rationale for voyaging in an anticlockwise direction in order to move with the rim currents. The KAYRA rallies sailed clockwise, but this was due to logistical considerations for the organisers.

Intermittent counter-currents are sometimes encountered along the coast, and all coastal currents are affected by wind events. The Black Sea is notorious for creating swells larger than the local

Western Black Sea coast in windier conditions

winds can account for. Windy days along the N shore can send swell all the way to the Turkish coast.

## 1.3 Shoreline

The shoreline of Turkey starts low and sandy on both sides of the Bosphorus. It is rocky, with 'working' towns, no resorts but several tourist-oriented towns (Amasra and inland Safronbolu, Amasya). Heading E, the mountains generally rise higher and higher almost to the Georgian border. The climate of Georgia is sub-tropical, with a beach resort at Batumi. There is a yacht club and friendly people in Poti but little in the way of tourist amenities in this large commercial port.

Highlights of the Ukraine are the Crimean Peninsula, with dramatic coastline and summer resorts, and Odessa, the large, interesting city of what was formerly called New Russia.

On the W coast, Bulgaria and Romania offer beaches and summer resorts. The central stretch of the W coast, from Constanţa, Romania (44°10'N 28°40'E) to Tsarevo, Bulgaria (42°10'N 27°51'E), contains far more sandy beaches and associated beach resorts than anywhere else on the Black Sea. These resort beaches occupy a substantial portion of the 579km European Union shoreline and offer more than a dozen yacht marinas.

## 1.4 National ports of entry

With six countries surrounding the Black Sea, planning a cruise requires careful consideration of which ports of entry can be used reliably by yachts. There are a total of 26 official ports of entry on the Black Sea. Of these, 14 are ports of entry through which a yacht can reliably check in or out of the five yacht-friendly countries.

**Turkey (from W to E)**: Sinop, Trabzon and Hopa. Other official ports of entry where a yacht should be able to clear in and out are: Ereğli, Zonguldak, Inebolu, Samsun, Giresun and Rize.

**Georgia**: Batumi and Poti.

**Russia**: There are no reliable ports of entry for yachts. Sochi, Tuapse and Novorossiysk are ports of entry for commercial vessels only.

**Ukraine**: Yalta and Odessa. Sevastapol in the Crimea and Izmail on the Danube are ports of entry but not reliable for yachts.

**Romania**: Sulina, Constanţa and Mangalia. Tulcea, on the Danube, is an upstream port of entry but not recommended for yachts on the Black Sea because of problems with clearing in and out of the Ukraine at Izmail.

**Bulgaria**: Balchik, Varna, Burgas and Tsarevo.

Ideal ports of entry for yachts are located near international borders so that clearance in and out can occur promptly after entering national territory. Hopa (Turkey) and Batumi (Georgia) are examples of ports of entry conveniently situated for yachts. At the other extreme are European Turkey and the eastern Crimea, where the absence of a port of entry at Iğneada (Turkey) and Feodosia (Ukraine) necessitates yachts anchoring without clearance and deprives them of the opportunity to legally and conveniently visit intermediate ports. This cruising guide contains information on 16 such 'stranded' ports, eight in each of these two locations, which cannot be visited conveniently.

As is noted in the discussion below about Cruising Routes, Yalta turns out to be a key port of entry for yachts making an anticlockwise extended Black Sea voyage. It is very easy, but not necessary, to have a

Shoreline near Akçakale, Turkey

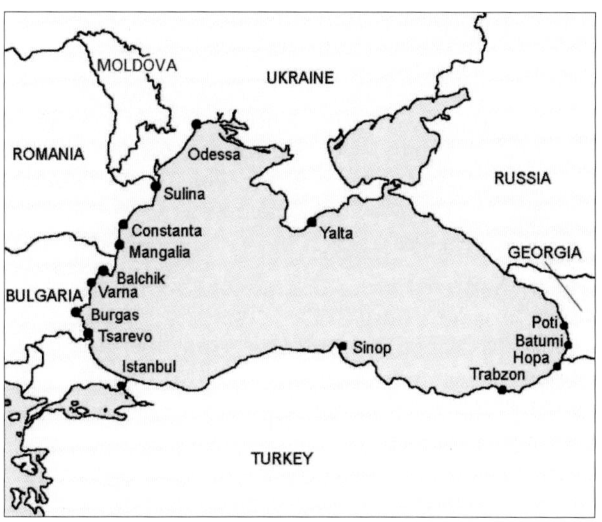


**Reliable ports of entry 2010**

Border control guard in Odessa

bad experience with officialdom in Yalta. If you use the right agent to clear in to the Ukraine at Yalta it is possible to receive permission to visit the intermediate ports on the Crimean Peninsula by yacht, from Feodosia in the E to Chernomorskoe in the W. This permission can only be granted in Yalta. If sailing W, you can arrange to leave the Crimean Peninsula and sail to Odessa from Yevpatoria instead.

If you want to visit the Crimea by yacht, plan to spend the going rate of $200 (agent fees are set by regional law in the Crimea and quoted in USD) whether clearing in or out here. Some yachts have departed the Ukraine without properly clearing out. Whether out of ignorance or frustration with authorities, the owner or captain runs the risk of serious penalties and fines and also makes it more difficult for the crews of future cruising yachts. Problems have been reported with corrupt agents looking to drum up business, or when clearing in or out of the Ukraine in Sevastopol. It should also be noted that Balaclava is not (and never was) a port of entry and, contrary to the information in three previous cruising guides, Feodosia is no longer a port of entry. The key pieces of advice here is to use Yalta as the port of entry and to arrange a good agent in advance. (Volodymyr Papakin's firm, Yalmar, is recommended.)

When entering Turkey from Bulgaria, Romania or the Ukraine on the W coast of the Black Sea, yachts are usually allowed to stay in the intermediate harbours such as Iğneada, Karaburun and Poyrazköy before officially clearing into the country. However, officials may request to see boat documents and passports and may refuse permission to go ashore.

When entering or leaving Turkey in the east, a certain amount of patience and preparation may help smooth the way. If checking in to Turkey at one of the Black Sea ports, be sure to have a new transit log with you. Because so few yachts make it this far east, the port authorities may not have one on-hand. If you arrive in Turkey at Hopa, the authorities may pass you along to Trabzon. Upon arrival in Sinop, Trabzon or Hopa, you are likely to be approached by an agent looking for business. Familiarise yourself with the clearance procedures and avoid being taken advantage of. Some problems have been reported with yachts clearing out of Turkey in Sinop, a process that should not require an agent or special 'fee' to the harbourmaster. See the Sinop harbour detail for a helpful local contact.

The difficult and often expensive process of clearing in or out at Istanbul deserves some consideration in route planning. Yachts headed up the Bosphorus to Bulgaria, for example, must clear out in Istanbul because there is no longer a port of entry nor can special arrangements be made to clear in or out in Iğneada as earlier guides suggested was possible. Clearing out at Istanbul is not as difficult as clearing back in to Turkey in Istanbul. (Elsewhere in Turkey staff at marinas, or local agents, generally help with clearance in and out of Turkey and it tends to be a straight forward process.) Many yachtsmen in Istanbul have had a difficult time completing the formalities or have had to hire an agent. In 2010, the going rate was €200. To avoid this hassle and expense, some yachts chose to continue straight from the Black Sea to Çanakkale or Ayvalik to clear into Turkey or to continue on to Greece, avoiding the need for a Turkish transit log altogether.

The best news about formalities for foreign yachts visiting the Black Sea is the improved clearance procedures in Bulgaria and Romania, described in Chapters 8 and 9. The process is much easier than it used to be.

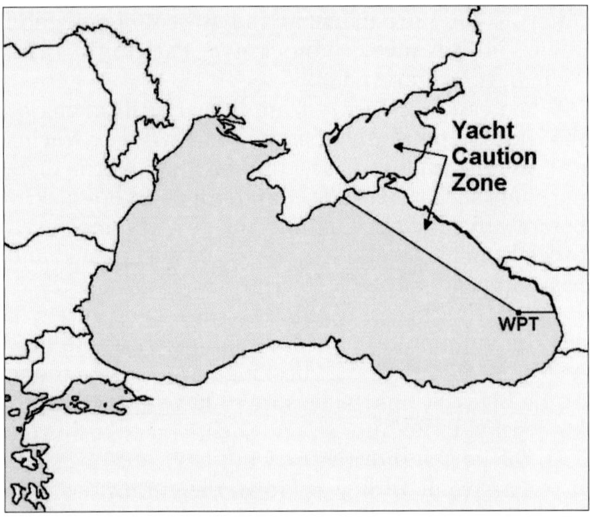


**Yachting Caution Zone**

## 1.5 Caution Zone

The map of the Black Sea shows that ports are not evenly distributed around the shoreline. There is a gap at the NE quadrant which can be visited by only the most risk-loving yachtsmen. But this still leaves abundant opportunities to create a cruising route to suit almost any taste.

Departing from Poti, yachts are advised to head 289° for 55M, to a point S and W of 42°27′N 40°26′E. This is the SW corner of 'Area 740', marked 'Occasionally Dangerous to Navigation' on Admiralty Chart *2236*, Tirebolu to Tuapse. This point is more than 30M from the coast and outside the Abkhazian coastal area patrolled by Russian naval vessels. Until relationships and cooperation improve, yachts should consider the area N and E of the line from Poti to Yalta to be a 'Yachting Caution Zone'. Change might happen as quickly as 2012; supplements via www.imray.com and www.rccpf.org.uk will cover this if appropriate.

## 1.6 Cruising routes

Taken as a whole, the 20 ports of entry offer a very large number of potential cruising routes, but just four routes, of increasing length, serve to exemplify the basic alternatives. These routes can be termed the West coast, the Turkish coast, the Middle Circuit, and the Whole Way 'Round.

### Route 1: The West Coast

The five top yachting destinations along the West Coast are: (1) Burgas Bay (Bulgaria) (2) Danube Delta (Romania) (3) Odessa (Ukraine) (4) Port Tomis (Constanţa) (Romania) and (5) the Blue Flag Marinas: Dinevi Marina, Sveti Vlas (Bulgaria) and Ana Yacht Club, Eforie Nord (Romania).

Each of these destinations is described by its geographic location in Chapters 7, 8 and 9. Burgas Bay is the only 'cruising ground' on the Black Sea. The Danube Delta is a World Heritage Site. Odessa offers a glimpse into the extraordinary achievement of New Russia. Constanţa is both an ancient city and Romania's largest port. The Blue Flag marinas are perfect for those wanting the best and willing to pay for it.

Starting from the Bosphorus, some yachts choose to visit only the West Coast of the Black Sea. Yachts wait in Poyrazköy for a suitable weather window to sail N from the Bosphorus to Bulgaria, Romania, or in some cases, all the way to Odessa or Yalta in the Ukraine. Itineraries can be planned to visit just one or all of these countries. Most yachts arriving from the Danube visit the West Coast only, heading S from Romania to Bulgaria and then the Bosphorus. Others leave their yachts in the water or on land at one of several suitable harbours (see chapters on these countries) before continuing their onward voyage.

Another possible way to reach the West Coast is to begin by heading E to Ereğli, about 135M, with sheltered stops at Şile, Kefken and Akçakoca before clearing out of Turkey and sailing offshore to Bulgaria or Romania. This involves crossing the busy shipping lanes N of the Bosphorus, which is probably why we could not find any first-hand accounts.

Beach resorts are common on the west coast

Black Sea architecture on the Turkish coast

Black Sea coast near Sinop

## Route 2: The Turkish Coast

From the Bosphorus many yachts choose to remain along the Turkish coast. With this route it is not necessary to clear out and then back into Turkey. One of the few foreign yachts we know to have made four visits to the Black Sea has explored only the Turkish coast. Many others have had enjoyable cruises venturing E as far as Amasra, Sinop and Trabzon. The five top 'turn around' destinations on the northern coast of Turkey are, from W to E: Amasra, Sinop, Samsun, Giresun and Trabzon.

**Amasra** is the harbour nearest to the Bosphorus that is among the favourites of yachtsmen on this coast. The anchorage is challenging and very busy but the town somehow retains a very ancient appearance and feel, making it a major tourist spot. Sailing to Amasra passes many interesting spots along the coast, including anchoring at Kefken, Ereğli and Filyos.

**Sinop** is tucked under Boztepe Burnu, the eastern promontory of Ince Burun, the northernmost point on the Turkish coast. From Amasra the route passes two (Gideros and Akliman) of the Black Sea's three natural harbours and the port town of Inebolu, noted for its distinctive architecture. Sinop is popular as the jumping-off point for Yalta.

**Samsun** is a step beyond the fairly well-worn path that most yachts follow. Although it is not really very far from Sinop, the route passes around Bafra Burnu, the vast delta of the Kizilirmak River. The Samsun Yacht Club is a secure, although somewhat expensive, place to leave a yacht for inland travel. A less expensive alternative place to leave a yacht is Yakakent.

**Giresun**, the centre of the hazelnut-growing region, has a small yacht club and an interesting castle. The route from Samsun passes the delta of the Yeşilirmak River, Yasun Burnu (Jason's Cape), and the interesting small city of Ordu.

**Trabzon** was the most important city on the Black Sea for most of the past 2,500 years. The city and its surroundings are fascinating. The route from Giresun passes Tirebolu with its two Genoese forts. The Trabzonspor Yacht Club may agree to watch a yacht for a few days. This is the least expensive and most secure place to leave a yacht during a trip inland.

## Route 3: The Middle Circuit

The shape of the Black Sea is distinctive because large peninsulas project from the N and the S shores almost opposite each other. The cities of Yalta, near the S tip of the Crimean Peninsula, and Sinop, at the end of the 'Nose' peninsula (Ince Burun), are in the

Crimean coastline between Balaclava and Sevastopol

top rank of appeal for yachtsmen. Sinop is about 215M beyond Ereğli, or 310M from the Bosphorus, with sheltered stops at Filyos, Amasra, Cide, Doğanyurt, Inebolu, Çaylioğlu and Akliman.

From Sinop to Yalta is an overnight sail of about 155M on a course of 342°. Clear into Yalta at the Customs Dock at the passenger port, using Volodymyr Papakin as Agent (see Ukraine chapter for contact information).

From Yalta you can sail to Balaclava, 37M, and return to Yalta to clear out for Romania, about 200M W, or Bulgaria, about 270M SW. Or you can continue E along the Crimean coast, as far as Feodosia. Alternately, continue onwards, around the W coast of the Crimean Peninsula, and cross to Odessa, the largest city on the Black Sea. After clearing out from Odessa it is an overnight sail of 105M to Sulina, Romania, a river port town at the mouth of the most navigable course of the Danube. Due to difficulties with clearance formalities in Izmail, it is recommended that yachts clear out of the Ukraine in Odessa.

Hopping among the many yacht-friendly harbours in Romania and Bulgaria along the W coast, it is about 380M from Sulina to the Bosphorus.

Lighthouse in Poti, Georgia

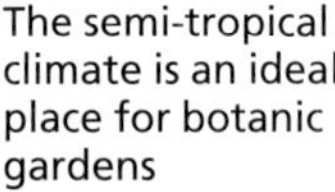

The semi-tropical climate is an ideal place for botanic gardens

### Route 4: The Whole Way 'Round

In Arrian's time, during the 2nd century AD, sailing the whole way 'round the Black Sea was to skirt the outer frontier of the Roman Empire. For his *Periplus Ponti Euxini* he visited Sebastopolis, modern Sukhumi (Abkhazia). Sailing off what is now the coast of Russia, Arrian visited Stachemphax, King of the Zilchoi. From there he visited the city of Pantikapaion, at what is now the Kerch Straits, connecting the Black Sea to the Maiotis Lake, known today as the Sea of Azov. Entering the Maiotis Lake, Arrian came to the river Tanaïs (now the Don) which divided Asia from Europe.

However, it is no longer possible for a yacht to follow this portion of Arrian's route. Based on *Gyatso*'s 2010 judgement of acceptable risks, it is recommended that yachts stay out of the 'Yachting Caution Zone' delimited by the line between Poti, Georgia and Feodosiya, Ukraine.

For yachts one main consequence of the ports of entry and the caution zone is that the 'Middle Circuit' and the 'Whole Way 'Round' both reach the Crimean Peninsula at Yalta. Indeed, the attraction of the 'Whole Way 'Round' depends entirely on the lure of eastern Turkey and Georgia. By the time you get to Sinop you will certainly know whether you want to continue. By then sailors will be gaining the experience of receiving the unique hospitality of the eastern Black Sea.

## 1.7 Harbours suitable for yachts

The Black Sea has several different types of place where a yacht might find a safe mooring. A simple way to categorise these places is in four groups: commercial harbours, multi-purpose harbours, fishing harbours and yacht marinas. Commercial harbours are constructed primarily for large ships to tie up and load and unload, and they are normally served with good road and rail connections. Multi-purpose harbours can normally serve large ships but are also used by other types of vessels including naval and coastguard, ferries, tour boats and fishing boats. Fishing harbours are constructed to serve fishing boats. Yacht marinas, of which there are presently six on the Black Sea, are constructed specifically to serve yachts; the piers are lower, water and electricity is normally available, and there may be additional facilities immediately ashore.

A total of 48 harbours on the Black Sea are suitable for general use by yachts under a wide variety of winds and seas. A very considerable number more are suitable under calm and stable conditions but may be vulnerable or untenable with certain seas or winds.

A total of 18 harbours on the Black Sea have been designed and constructed specifically to serve yachts. These are the most important places that a yacht might anchor or tie up for the night. They are:

**Turkey:** Giresun, Samsun yacht harbour and Trabzonspor Marina, Trabzon

**Georgia:** Batumi and Poti

Turkish fishing boats

Cruising yacht anchored in Turkish fishing harbour

**Ukraine:** Yalta Passenger Harbour, Sevastopol, Odessa and Balaclava

**Romania:** Mangalia, Port Tomis (Constanţa), Ana Yacht Club (Eforie Nord)

**Bulgaria:** Varna, Burgas, Balchik, Sozopol, Dinevi Marina (Sveti Vlas) and Yacht's Port (Nessebar)

Of the 20 commercial harbours described in this guide seven of them, all in Turkey, offer a safe place for a yacht to anchor or tie up and spend the night. First among these is Giresun, where the yacht facility consists of a designated pier within the larger facility. Other harbours that can accommodate yachts are: Ereğli, Zonguldak, Inebolu, Ünye, Bartin Commercial Harbour and Hopa.

All seven multi-purpose harbours with no special yacht facilities are nevertheless suitable for yachts under most weather conditions:

**Turkey:** Amasra, Kurucaşile, Cide, Tirebolu and Terme

**Ukraine:** Yevpatoria and Chernomorskoe

In addition to these 25 harbours there are 16 fishing harbours that yachts can also use:

**Bulgaria:** Pomorie

**Turkey:** Şile, Kefken, Akçakoca, Filyos, Doğanyurt, Çaylioğlu, Akliman, Sinop, Gerze, Yakakent, Yaliköy, Ordu, Akçakale, Rize Fishing Harbour and Pazar.

Fishermen normally raft-up as many as four or five deep, with the largest boat inside and the successively smaller ones outside. Yachts are invariably welcome to tie alongside the outermost fishing boat. No matter how crowded it gets, there's always room for one more.

In addition to the modern harbours, a fairly large number of piers were constructed to serve commercial shipping on the Black Sea in past decades, before harbour construction became common. A few of these piers are still in regular use, but many have fallen into ruin. None of them provide a safe place for yachts to tie up, even when they have been surrounded by modern breakwaters.

## 1.8 Cruise ships

Two distinct types of cruise ships ply the waters of the Black Sea: ocean-going ships with high freeboard and river ships, long and low to meet the lock system and with generally much lower freeboard. The ocean-going ships typically carry up to 2,000 passengers and stop at six to eight ports over the course of 7–12 days. The river cruise ships are most commonly found in Ukrainian ports and frequently begin or end at Kiev, reaching the Black Sea along the Dnieper River. If you want to take a break from cruising then consider leaving your boat at the marina in Odessa, take the overnight train to Kiev and, after a day exploring the beautifully restored churches, underground tombs and art and craft displays, join a river cruise ship for a 4/5-day meander down the River Dnieper and see a glimpse of inland Ukraine.

The 11 Black Sea ports that receive ocean-going cruise ships are: Istanbul, Sinop and Trabzon (Turkey); Batumi (Georgia); Sochi (Russia); Yalta, Sevastopol and Odessa (Ukraine); Constanţa (Romania); and Varna and Nessebar (Bulgaria). At least six major cruise lines offer Black Sea excursions: Costa Cruises, Oceana Cruises, Regent, Seabourn, Silversea, and Voyages of Discovery.

River cruise ship in Yalta

# 2. Preparations for cruising the Black Sea by yacht

2.1 Recent experience of yachts
2.2 Cruising guides
2.3 Preparing the yacht
2.4 Personal preparation
2.5 Entrance, travel and exit formalities
2.6 Navigation and charts
2.7 Communications
2.8 Weather forecasts

A private yacht can sail solo all the way around the Black Sea entirely on its own and without any official sponsorship and without belonging to an organised rally. Every year informal networks develop among yachts visiting the Black Sea; recent experience is summarised in Section 2.1. Cruising Guides improve safety and enhance enjoyment and these are described Section 2.2. By the time a yacht reaches the Black Sea it will normally be well-prepared. Specific considerations are highlighted in Section 2.3. Issues of personal preparation are taken up in Section 2.4

## 2.1 Recent experience of yachts

Although yachting on the Black Sea is not quite the novelty it was 20 years ago after the break-up of the Soviet Union and the fall of communism in Eastern Europe, the number of cruising yachts venturing N of the Bosphorus or sailing down the Danube remains small in comparison to the cruising grounds of the Aegean and Mediterranean. The Black Sea remains an off-the-beaten-path cruising destination for at the most a few dozen foreign cruising yachts every year. Many changes have occurred, including greatly improved facilities for visiting yachts, especially in Bulgaria and Romania. Changes are sure to continue.

One of the first modern accounts of a foreign-flagged yacht cruising on the Black Sea was by Alan Logan, an Ocean Cruising Club member who visited the Black Sea in 1989 and 1991 and wrote about it in *Flying Fish 1990/1* and *1991/1*. Oddly enough, he had some of the most privileged access to the Black Sea by a private yacht that has been recounted since. *Gyatso* also found a rich body of experience in the published and unpublished accounts, email correspondence and interviews with individual yachtsmen. These accounts total in the dozens: stories of people's experience on KAYRA Rallies, with informally organised flotillas or as a solo yacht. Many of these individuals are recognised in the Acknowledgements.

The KAYRA Rallies were the work of Teoman Arsay, sponsored by the Ataköy Marina, just S of Istanbul, and by the Ataköy Marina Yacht Club. (The Ataköy Marina Yacht Club has subsequently moved to a new location and re-organised itself as the Marmara Offshore Yacht Club.) The rallies were held five times between 1997 and 2004. The first rally simply followed the Turkish coast. In 1998 Bulgaria and Ukraine were added. In 1999 the KAYRA rally visited all six countries, and in 2001 a trip up the Danube River was added. The last rally, in 2004, was composed of 37 yachts from 12 countries.

*Gyatso* at anchor on the Black Sea coast in Amasra, Turkey

By then Doreen and Archie Annan had already completed *Cruise the Black Sea*, the publication of which made available pilotage for yachts.

In 2010 *Gyatso* encountered 16 other foreign yachts and heard of a handful of others. Of these, five visited only the Turkish coast; three of these ventured past Sinop. Four yachts entered from the Danube and visited only the Romanian and Bulgarian coasts. Another four made a 'short loop' which did not include Georgia or Russia (one excluded the Ukraine too). Three, including *Gyatso*, sailed all the way around (excluding a stop in Russia); of these, two went counterclockwise and one went clockwise and attempted to enter three different Russian ports, without success. The foreign yachts on the Black Sea hailed from ports in North America and Europe: Germany (6), United States (2), United Kingdom (2), Switzerland (2), Sweden (1), Austria (1), France (1) and the Netherlands (1).

Authorities in Sulina, Romania, noted that 32 foreign yachts had checked in or out of the Danube port during the first three weeks of August 2010. In Mangalia, Romania, the harbourmaster said that 92 yachts (foreign and local) had visited the new marina that far in the 2010 cruising season. In contrast, it is thought that only two other yachts visited Georgia in 2010.

Yachts cruising the Black Sea are of various makes and sizes. In 2010, 12 were fibreglass production yachts, four were custom-designed steel, wooden or fibreglass yachts and one was an experimental solar-powered catamaran which traveled down the Danube to the Black Sea. Two were less than 30 feet, five were between 30 and 40 feet, and 10 were longer than 40 feet.

## 2.2 Cruising guides

While preparing for the cruise of the Black Sea, *Gyatso* relied on a number of previous guides as well as published and unpublished accounts of other cruising sailors. They encountered only three other yachts with the Annans' guide onboard; a few were using second-hand copies of the Nelson's guide. For those visiting just the Turkish coast, many made do with the basic detail of Rod Heikell's chapter in his *Turkish Waters & Cyprus Pilot*. Likewise for the Bulgarian and Romanian coast, English-speaking yachtsmen used Allardice's guide.

A most useful book to have on board is the Admiralty Sailing Directions, *NP24*, *Black Sea and Sea of Azov Pilot*. Its greatest value is that the Admiralty Pilots are among the global standards for commercial ship captains. Moreover, rather than having little relevance to yachting, it is crammed with accurate passage information. It also opens a window to the big ships' navigation and helps in the practice of collision avoidance.

Two previous guides were published which cover the entire coastline of the Black Sea:

*Black Sea Cruising Guide* by Rick and Sheila Nelson (Imray Laurie Norie and Wilson) 1995. The first comprehensive guide to cruising in the six countries around the Black Sea is this now out of print guide by American sailors Rick and Sheila Nelson based on information gathered by the authors during a cruise in 1993. While most of the cruising information is now out of date, the guide contains a wealth of information about history, culture and tourist sites, as well as beautiful sketches by Sheila Nelson of scenes from around the Black Sea. The knowledge is now 20 years old and the book is difficult to obtain.

*Cruise the Black Sea* by Scottish sailors Doreen and Archie Annan was published by Ataköy Marina Yacht Club in 2001. The guide was developed by veterans of KAYRA rallies based on information they gathered as participants and during extensive exploratory cruises of their own in the summers of 2000 and 2001. It also contains information they compiled for *Cruise Ukraine*, which was published by Ataköy Marina in 2000. In the preparation of their guide, the Annans made good use of a network of local contacts who were involved in organising the KAYRA rallies. The guide provides tremendous detail about 80 harbours and anchorages along the Turkish coastline. In 2010 it remained the most up-to-date and complete guide covering all six countries around the Black Sea. It may still be obtained – visit www.rccpf.org.uk for more information.

Key changes which have occurred since the publication of these guides include: ongoing construction of new harbours and completion of main sections of the coastal highway on the Turkish coastline E of Sinop; advances and temporary set-backs (e.g. brief war with Russia in 2008) for yachts visiting Georgia; greater administrative difficulties for yachts wanting to visit Russia; changes to the entrance formalities and further restrictions on harbours that foreign cruising yachts can visit in the Ukraine; rapid expansion of yachting facilities and improvements to entrance and exit formalities in Romania and Bulgaria, both of which joined the European Union in 2007.

Two other guides cover sections of the Black Sea coastline:

*Cruising Bulgaria and Romania* by Nicky Allardice was published in 2007 by Imray Laurie Norie & Wilson, based on a trip the British sailor took down the Danube to the Black Sea and subsequent cruises made along the Black Sea coast. The author makes note of reading Rod Heikell's *The Danube, A River Guide* which was written in 1991, and of purchasing the *Black Sea Cruising Guide* by the Nelsons, to which his guide was intended to provide supplemental information. The guide includes detailed passage notes, historical information about each harbour covered, data about even the smallest anchorage for those with sufficient time to explore the coastline, and a section for those wishing to explore the Danube Delta. Clearance procedures are now very much simpler than in 2007 as there have been considerable changes for the better since both countries joined the EU.

*Turkish Waters & Cyprus Pilot* by well-known cruising guide author Rod Heikell is published by Imray Laurie Norie & Wilson Ltd (see www.imray.com). 'Unlike the rest of the pilot,' the author explains, 'the final chapter gives only a brief resume of pilotage information...' While he goes on to caution his readers about using the plans and abbreviated pilotage information, many people who have come to rely on Heikell's pilots and have difficulty finding any other pilotage information for the Turkish coast have used the skeleton chapter as their main source of pilotage information along the coast.

## 2.3 Preparing the yacht

By the time it nears the Black Sea almost every yacht will have travelled far enough, and through enough varied conditions, to be reasonably well prepared. As was noted in the Introduction, the Black Sea has no unique characteristics which demand special layout, rigging or equipment. Whether it reaches the sea by sailing down the Danube or up the Bosphorus, the chances are good that the yacht and its crew will have acquired everything it needs in the normal course of cruising.

Nevertheless, there are some considerations that can be satisfied quite easily in Istanbul or the Aegean but are more challenging in many Black Sea harbours. These are:

Fenders, as large in diameter and as long as can be carried. Three for each side is optimal. In addition, one or two ball fenders can be particularly helpful against large fishing boats and rough concrete piers.

Large fenders should be carried

Fuel cans and ball fenders are helpful on the Black Sea

Long docklines for rafting and/or taking ashore. In addition to a standard dockline inventory, *Gyatso* carried two strong 15m docklines which found almost daily use.

Depending on the size of the main fuel tank(s), as many fuel jerry cans – typically holding 20 litres – as can be conveniently carried. *Gyatso* carried two 20-litre fuel jerry cans made of polyethylene (plastic) for occasional use when refuelling by jerry can and taxi.

A clean fuel tank and good fuel filtering system is particularly important. Several yachts with dirty fuel tanks have experienced problems with clogged fuel filters after getting caught in rough conditions on the Black Sea. *Gyatso* had no problems with a new stainless steel tank and excellent (Racor 5000) in-line fuel filtering and water separation system. A pre-filter was rarely used when filling the tank except when filling by jerry can or when the source was questionable (see note regarding fuel below).

Carrying seawater pump impellers – or preferably a complete ready to fit seawater pump – is recommended.

A good water strainer, easy to check and clean, is essential to keep the water intake on the engine, water maker, etc. free of jellyfish and also other debris washed in by rivers after heavy rain.

Several long water hoses with connection adapters, ideally totalling up to 50m.

Both a 2-pin 'European' electrical plug and a typical 3-pin plug commonly found in marinas in the Mediterranean and Aegean. A long 220V electrical cable, up to 50m, is occasionally needed to bring electrical power aboard.

An anchor light which can be hung about 2m above deck level is almost essential in fishing harbours, where fishermen are not accustomed to noticing masthead anchor lights.

### Marine supplies

Chandlery, spare parts, maintenance items such as filters and most marine supplies are not available everywhere along the Black Sea coast, but there are good marine suppliers and ships' chandlers in all the larger coastal cities. If you need spare parts or repairs and are not sure where to find them, ask the harbourmaster, fishermen or other yachtsmen for assistance. They should be able to help you arrange for repairs and tell you where to find the needed part or how to import it.

Because of the lack of repair facilities on the Black Sea compared to other cruising grounds, a yacht's crew should be reasonably self-sufficient and the yacht itself in good repair. Spares, such as impellers or fuel filters, are readily available in Istanbul and the cities and large towns on the Romanian and Bulgarian coast, but they are almost completely unavailable on the Turkish Black Sea coast and in Georgia and the Ukraine. See below for marine suppliers which may be helpful while preparing for or during your Black Sea voyage.

In Turkey several yacht chandlers can be found at or near the Setur Kalamis and Fenerbaçe Marina on the Asian side of Istanbul:

**Horizon Ltd** is the onsite chandlers in the boatyard at the marina. The manager, Aysun Orhon, speaks English and is willing to ship parts and supplies to locations in Turkey.
✆ +90 216 550 3313/3314 *Fax* +90 216 550 3315
*GSM* +90 537 886 5458 *Email* aysun@horizon-mart.com or info@horizon-mart.com www.horizon-mart.com

**West Marine** has a small shop just outside the marina entrance and a larger store accessible by bus between Kalamis and Pendik. The staff speak English and prices are quoted in US dollars.
Kumlar Cad. No 8, Istanbul Kartal, 34862
✆ +90 216 517 3242 www.westmarine.com

Several other good marine supply stores can be found within a few blocks of the marina with helpful staff, but limited English is spoken. On the European side, a number of marine supply stores operate in the several-block area behind the fish market near the Karaköy ferry dock in Istanbul.

In Georgia, 'Smart One' ship chandlers is located in Batumi (see harbour detail for more information). Georgian courtesy flags (sized for large ships) and other supplies may be available or specially ordered.

In Bulgaria and Romania, marine chandlers, several catering to the yachting community, can be found in the larger ports: Burgas, Varna and Constanţa (Port Tomis). Most of the modern marinas have yacht chandlers located onsite or nearby: Sozopol, Nesebar, Sveti Vlas, Balchik, Mangalia, Eforie Nord and Constanţa (Port Tomis). See the corresponding harbour detail for more information.

**Marina Store** is a Greek-owned chain (Lalizas Ltd) with convenient and locally operated yacht chandlery outlets in Constanţa (near the marina in Port Tomis) and Varna (next to the yacht club).

### Fuel

Good quality fuel is available by tanker truck (in all but the smallest harbours) or at a dedicated fuel dock (Balaclava and Odessa in the Ukraine, Sulina and Eforie Nord in Romania, and Balchik, Nessebar, Sveti Vlas and Sozopol in Bulgaria). In Georgia the Euro-diesel grade is recommended because it is the highest quality and has no additives, but fuel must be obtained by jerry can and taxi in order to avoid harbour fees (in Poti the yacht club will lend you extra jerry cans). Fuel prices are most reasonable in Georgia and the Ukraine and most expensive in Turkey.

## 2.4 Personal preparation

### Money

It is no longer necessary to carry local or foreign currency with you. Cash can be obtained from ATMs in all but the smallest communities in every country or with a VISA or Mastercard at banks and money changing offices. The only place where a credit card can be used to purchase provisions is in large cities with international supermarket chains such as Migros and Carrefour (the locations of these are noted in harbour details). On *Gyatso*, it was found useful to have a small amount of cash currency (US dollars or euros) on hand when arriving in Georgia and the Ukraine because it can easily be exchanged for local currency if needed. (However, check the latest rules about bring large sums of money into the individual countries; Ukraine was sensitive about this in 2011.)

Fuel is everywhere paid in cash using local currency. Credit cards are not accepted to pay for fuel. It is best to use or exchange all local currency before leaving the country because you may have difficulty exchanging it in another country.

### Local currency

| *Country* | *Currency* |
|---|---|
| Turkey | Lira (TL) |
| Georgia | Lari (GEL) |
| Russia | Rouble (RUB) |
| Ukraine | Hryvnia (Grivna) (UAH) (pronounced *Hreevna*) |
| Romania* | Leu (pl. Lei) (RON) |
| Bulgaria* | Lev (BGN) |

* Romania and Bulgaria had applied but not yet joined the Euro Zone in 2010. Until accepted, the Leu and Lev remain the local currency in these countries.

### Laundry

Laundry service (wash only or wash-dry-fold) can be easily arranged in Amasra, Sinop, Samsun, Trabzon, Balaclava (temporarily out of service in 2010), Constanţa, Balchik and Sozopol. Self-service laundromats seem not to have reached the Black Sea yet or are well-kept secrets. The only self-service facility identified convenient to a marina was at the Poti Yacht Club in Georgia. The supply of clothing onboard therefore determines how frequently laundry will be washed by hand. A good plastic washtub is a big help for hand-washing laundry when needed.

### Local customs

In summertime, the beaches of the Ukraine, Romania and Bulgaria are packed with sunbathers in swimsuits, and the dress code is very casual even in large cities such as Odessa and Varna. The situation is very different in Turkey (where dress is much more conservative, especially for women and the further E you go). It is recommended that women cover their shoulders and wear trousers

Seaside resort in the Ukraine

when arriving in port or going ashore. Shorts are not recommended attire for men when going ashore in Northern Turkey and Georgia.

#### Prescriptions and medical supplies

It is a good idea to have a well-stocked medical kit and to carry any prescription medications or medical supplies with you to the Black Sea. Pharmacies are abundant in cities and towns all around the Black Sea, and it is easy and inexpensive to obtain medicines in Turkey, Romania and Bulgaria that are commonly available only by prescription, and at much higher cost, in North America and western Europe. It is slightly more difficult to locate pharmacies in Georgia and Ukraine.

#### Provisions

Almost every provision can be found in the minimarkets and open-air markets around the Black Sea. Fruits, vegetables and cheeses abound, with an especially good selection from local markets in Turkey and Bulgaria. Fresh bread can be found everywhere, although the selection is quite limited in some places.

It can be almost impossible to find some speciality foods that are not part of the local diet, such as peanut butter or Marmite. Bring a good supply of such items if you cannot go without. If you have pets

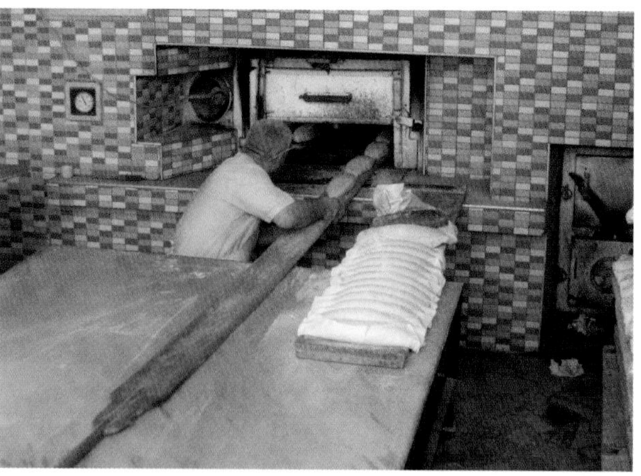

on board, dog and cat food is readily available, but cat litter may be harder to come by except in cities with large supermarkets.

#### Beer, wine and spirits

Depending on your drink preferences and where you plan to cruise, you may want to stock certain items. Good quality and reasonably priced beer can be found everywhere. If you like wine and are planning to cruise only in Turkey, you may want to top up your wine stores on the island of Bozcaada near the entrance to the Dardanelles, because the wine selection on the Turkish coast of the Black Sea is even more limited than what you find in tourist resorts on the Aegean coast. Georgia and Bulgaria have long traditions of wine making and offer interesting varieties of wine and brandy. In both places wine shops sell a diverse inventory of locally produced wine. Now that Romania and Bulgaria are part of the EU, European brands of beer, wine and spirits are more widely available. In Turkey, other than the locally favourite *raki*, alcohol is expensive, limited in selection and in short supply. The drinks of choice in the Ukraine are champagne and vodka and good quality labels of both can be purchased at reasonable prices. In Balaclava, for example, the local wine and champagne can be purchased from a distributor across the street from the marina entrance. Some of the local wines are sweet by European standards – taste before you buy! Fans of sparkling water may want to stock up on one of the famous Georgian brands, such as Borzhomi, which is much pricier in Europe. Speciality products such as these are described in the introductions for each country.

#### Gifts

Although foreign yachts are not the novelty they once were on the Black Sea, almost everywhere, but especially in Turkey and Georgia, you will experience tremendous hospitality and occasionally will be given presents of fresh fish, fruit, speciality foods and souvenirs. It is only courteous to reciprocate such gifts and to give small gifts as a gesture of thanks for kindnesses. Carrying a boat card or calling card is strongly recommended. Previous cruising guides have suggested picture postcard sets, flags and pins from your home country as appropriate. Other ideas include customised T-shirts, hats, mugs, pens or note cards with your yacht name, hailing port, national flag and/or an image of your yacht. The crew of *Gyatso* wanted to be able to give a more unique and personal gift and had T-shirts silkscreened for a reasonable price at Tee-shirt World in Marmaris (Turkey) with the boat name and 'Black Sea 2010' on front and a line drawing of the Tayana 37ft hull and sail plan on the back. They were much appreciated.

### Books

Books in English are hard to find, so bring plenty of your own (although Istanbul has several bookstores with English and other foreign language books). If you haven't purchased them already, buy travel guides, such as Lonely Planet, Rough Guides and DK Guides, for each country. These are especially helpful if you are planning to take inland excursions. Current travel guides to Georgia were out of print and hard to find in 2010, so you may want to keep an eye out for a used copy before you travel to the Black Sea if you plan to visit this former Soviet republic. Pocket-sized dictionaries and phrasebooks in Turkish and Russian (if visiting Russia or the Ukraine) are also helpful. The top dozen on the suggested reading list are:

*Black Sea* by Neal Ascherson (New York, 1995).

*The Black Sea: A History* by Charles King (OUP 2004).

*The Black Sea Coast of Turkey* by John Freely Istanbul (Redhouse Press, 1996).

*The Jason Voyage: The Quest for the Golden Fleece* by Tim Severin (New York, 1985).

*Keraban the Inflexible: Adventures in the Euxine* by Jules Verne (Amsterdam: Fredonia Books, 2001).

*Marine Biological Diversity in the Black Sea: A Study of Change and Decline* by Yu Zaitsev and V. Mamaev (United Nations Publications, 1997).

*Noah's Flood: The New Scientific Discoveries About the Event That Changed History* by William Ryan and Walter Pittman (New York, 1998).

*Odessa: Genius and Death in a City of Dreams* by Charles King (New York, 2011).

*Periplus Ponti Euxini* by Arrian. Edited with introduction, translation and commentary by Aidan Liddle (Bristol Classical Press, 2003).

*The Poems of Exile* by Ovid. Translated by Peter Green (Berkeley. U. California Press, 2005).

*State of the Environment of the Black Sea (2001–2006/7)* by Black Sea Commission. Edited by Temel Oguz. Istanbul: Commission on the Protection of the Black Sea Against Pollution, 2008.

*The Voyage of Argo* by Apollonius of Rhodes Translated by EV Rieu. (Penguin, 1971).

*Xenophon's Retreat: Greece, Persia, and the End of the Golden Age* by Robin Waterfield (Cambridge, Massachusetts, 2006).

## 2.5 Entrance, travel and exit formalities

### Ship's papers and ship's stamp

As is true in the Mediterranean, it is essential to show original vessel documentation at many harbours and at nearly every marina in the Black Sea. A copy of the certificate of insurance is also commonly requested. Some places require minimum liability coverage of €300,000.

Turkey, Georgia, Romania and Bulgaria make clear distinctions between yachts and commercial vessels. Russia and Ukraine do not consistently make this distinction and consequently yacht captains may find their 20-tonne vessel being treated like a 10,000 tonne vessel. In addition to the standard forms that apply to yachts, having on hand numerous copies of a *General Declaration on Arrival and Departure* and a *Crew List* will greatly speed up the process of checking in and out. There are no specific, rigorous formats for these forms. Examples are given in the Appendix. Numerous copies may be called for. Depending on your cruising itinerary, starting out with 30–50 copies of each document will meet the needs of lots of stops.

A ship's stamp is **essential** unless you only plan to visit Turkey. The stamp should contain: the name of the yacht, registration number, home port, country of registry, and owner or captain's name (see below). There is no standard shape, though oval and rectangular are most common. There is also no standard size, but about 12cm is typical. Self-inking stamps are the most convenient to carry aboard and ashore.

s/y YACHT NAME
Registration No.
Home Port
Country of Registry
OWNER'S or CAPTAIN'S NAME

### Certificate of Competence

Masters of commercial vessels are licensed and accustomed to producing evidence of their licences during entry formalities. Officials in Turkey, Georgia, Romania and Bulgaria distinguish between commercial ships and pleasure craft, but officials in Russia and Ukraine are not consistent in making such a distinction and may demand evidence of a yacht captain's proficiency. For citizens of EU countries, the most acceptable document is an International Certificate of Competence (ICC), a product stemming from the United Nations Economic Commission for Europe Inland Water Committee (UN ECE IWC) Resolution 40. The United States does not issue a comparable certificate, but a US coastguard master's licence will satisfy most Soviet-style officials' needs.

### National and courtesy flags

Upon arrival in a new country, the quarantine (Q) flag should be flown from a halyard to the starboard spreader until entry formalities have been completed.

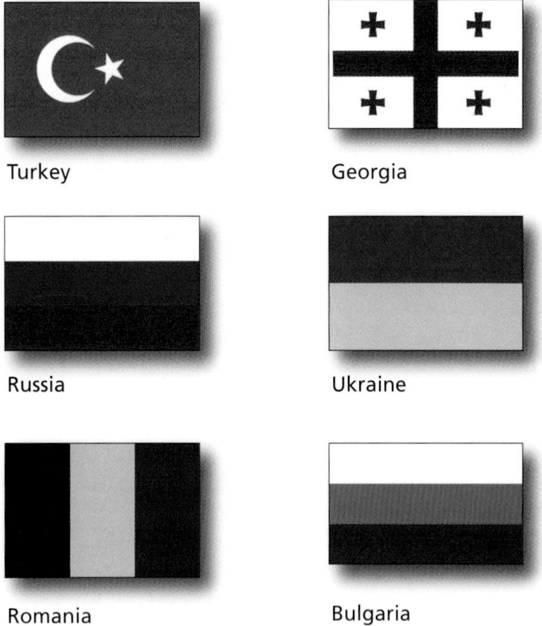


A courtesy flag, of good size and in good condition, is required and should be flown from a halyard to the starboard spreader. They are most readily available for sale on the internet or at chandleries in Istanbul. The flag of Georgia is the most difficult to locate outside of Georgia and potentially the most expensive, but it is relatively easy to find one in Batumi or Poti (ask authorities or local yachtsmen upon arrival). The Turks are the most sensitive about the courtesy flag being in good condition and may require that it be changed if it is not.

## 2.6 Navigation and charts

Electronic equipment needed for navigation or communication on the Black Sea is the same as on the Mediterranean, so it is not necessary to buy any last-minute gear. *Gyatso* was equipped with radar, a chartplotter, AIS, Navtex, and three GPS receivers, all of which were used constantly or regularly. The Navtex was particularly useful for notifying the timing and location of the military exercises which are conducted frequently by all of the shoreline countries. Weather warnings and forecasts may not be consistently transmitted, however

Taken as a whole, there is now abundant information for safe navigation as long as the prudent mariner takes the normal precautions. The key words are prudence and precautions, qualities that are closer to 'seamanship' than 'navigation'. *Gyatso* made a continuous effort to reach a secure mooring before nightfall, anchored in a harbour or tied to a pier. The dozens and dozens of small fishing harbours along the Turkish coast generally have quite narrow entrances, and some of the lights at the ends of breakwaters are not working, so it is safer to enter in daylight.

*Gyatso* was navigated using both electronic and paper charts at all times, supplemented by published cruising guides and by Google Earth and other satellite images to check the status of harbour changes and to locate new harbours.

*Gyatso's* Standard Horizon chartplotter used electronic charts from C-Map by Jeppesen. The entire Black Sea is covered on C-Map Max NT C-card EM-M917, Mediterranean and Black Sea. The cards are updated twice a year. Other electronic chart producers include Navionics (5P253XL, Black Sea) and Nobeltech (EM-P003, Eastern Mediterranean-Aegean-Black Sea). Unfortunately, *Gyatso* were not able to compare the Black Sea electronic charts of all three vendors, but were generally quite satisfied with C-Map. They experienced about two dozen instances in which the registration of the chart and the onboard GPS did not align correctly, mainly when zoomed in on a harbour detail. Sometimes the chartplotter showed the track to be crossing a breakwater as a harbour was entered or to be ashore when actually anchored near the centre. Such experience is common when sailing in areas charted long ago and not to WGS84 datum. Day after day *Gyatso* found the chartplotter to be a very useful tool that was accurate to within approximately 20m.

*Gyatso* carried paper charts published by the Hydrographic Institute of the Turkish Navy, the British Admiralty, and the US NIMA, and along the way acquired a smattering of other charts. They were not able to locate any local producer or seller of charts in Georgia, Romania, and Bulgaria. The charts found in Ukraine were actually from the former Soviet Union, and therefore quite seriously out of date (and in Russian).

**List of charts**

See Appendix I for suppliers of charts.

## 2.7 Communications

The primary voice and data communication devices carried aboard *Gyatso* were a standard VHF radio, a laptop with Wi-Fi modem, and a GSM cellphone with a 3G modem set up to provide local mobile phone service and wireless email and internet connections. For those with GSM mobile phone service in their home country, it should be possible to activate roaming service in all of the Black Sea countries. *Gyatso* did not use a single sideband (SSB) radio or a Globalstar satellite phone installed aboard. A modern SSB with a data modem might be

**Examples of pay-as-you-go mobile phone services**

| *Country* | *Company** | *Service Available* |
|---|---|---|
| Turkey | Turkcell, Vodafone | voice and data |
| Georgia | Beeline | voice and data |
| Ukraine | Beeline | voice and data |
| Romania | Cosmos, Vodafone | voice and data (special modem) |
| Bulgaria | M-tel | voice and data |

* Names of companies are provided as examples. Listing here is not an endorsement of the products and services they provide.

useful. *Gyatso's* satellite phone was equipped with a modem which allowed emails to be sent and received and weather reports to be downloaded while at sea. However, the service is expensive, so they relied on Wi-Fi and cellular data service when coastal cruising.

Public telephones are generally available as well as shops selling local and international calling cards. Because this technology is becoming a thing of the past, ask locally for the location of public phones and assistance with dialling instructions. Passenger terminals and bus and train stations are usually a good bet.

## 2.8 Weather forecasts

The Black Sea sailing season lasts from early May to late September, although it is reported that October can be good. Some yachtsmen recommend waiting until the beginning of June to enter the Black Sea and clearing out by the first week of September to avoid the first gale of the fall season. During winter months the cold northerly winds often bring violent storms.

There are settled weather conditions in the summer. Gales are rare, but there are a few days of F6 and the occasional wind event or thunderstorm lasting several hours. We found the internet to be a better source of weather forecasts than the radio. The www.windfinder.com forecasts were helpful, but must be consulted frequently when planning more than 24 hours out.

The Turkish official weather site www.dmi.gov.tr provides excellent weather information including satellite imagery and detailed wind information. Routine forecasts for Turkish waters are broadcast on Ch 16. www.windguru.cz may also be useful.

The main Navtex receiver codes for the Black Sea are:

| | |
|---|---|
| Mariupol | B |
| Odessa | C |
| Istanbul | O |
| Varna | J |

The Navtex reports of naval exercises alone justified having this equipment on board.

### Weather lore: hints from local yachtsmen

If the weather remains around 1015mb, the weather will be settled, good.

If seagulls sit on the water, the weather will be good, low flying, it will be stormy.

If a full moon rises red, yachtsmen should not sleep in bed. It will be a windy night.

A heavy dew in the morning brings settled weather and light winds.

In Batumi with W winds, alarming black clouds form on the mountains E of the entrance but do not indicate wind, rain or thunderstorm.

A strong wind may be experienced when crossing the Kerch Channel between Russia and Ukraine.

If Bear Point (Mis Ayu Dag) in Ukraine wears a hat of cloud, expect wind.

If the mountains NW of Yalta have cloud falling down on them, expect squalls from the NW of 35 knots lasting only about ½ hour.

Since ancient Egyptian times, the Coptic Wind Calendar has been used to predict significant weather events. Local sailors still refer to the calendar and believe it is fairly accurate within a day or two. *Gyatso* watched it closely after hearing a well-known yachtsman who is also a hunter confirm the local lore about the first gale of the autumn season during the first week of September. Turkish hunters refer to it as the 'quail gale', and they say it arrives in most years like clockwork.

While staying in Istanbul in May 2010, we experienced the predicted strong northerly winds and heard weather reports about the conditions on the Black Sea. Again at the beginning of September, we planned our route to find a safe harbour within 24 hours of the first hint of a gale in the forecast. On 8 September, with high wind warnings in the forecast, we made for the secure harbour of Sozopol, Bulgaria just as the wind and waves kicked up. We stayed until the gale blew itself out and the swell died down several days later. When we consider how quirky the weather has become in the age of global climate change, we found the Coptic Calendar to be fairly reliable. Sometimes we did not experience the 'strong wind' locally, but usually we could see it on the weather map or feel the swell it produced elsewhere.

### Coptic Wind Calendar

| | |
|---|---|
| 16 May | Strong wind, northerly |
| 20 May | Strong wind, northerly |
| 23 May | Strong wind, southerly |
| 2 June | Strong wind, northerly |
| 11–12 June | Strong wind, northerly |
| 22 June | Strong wind |
| 27 June | Strong wind |
| 11 July | Strong wind |
| 30 July | Strong wind |
| 5 August | Strong wind (3 days) |
| 31 August | Strong wind |
| 6 September | Gale |
| 21 September | Gale |
| 30 September | Strong wind |
| 5 October | Strong wind |

From *Cruise the Black Sea* by D. and A. Annan (2001)

Cloud forming over the Crimean coast

# 3. Natural history and human life

3.1 The name and the colour
3.2 Geography
3.3 Geology
3.4 Bathymetry
3.5 Hydrology
3.6 Currents
3.7 Chemistry
3.8 Marine life
3.9 Wetlands
3.10 Human history
3.11 Languages, cultures and religions
3.12 Contemporary international relations
3.13 National naval and coastguard operations
3.14 Commercial shipping
3.15 International organisations
3.16 Oil and gas
3.17 Fishing
3.18 Resorts

Doğanyurt

## 3.1 The name and the colour

Despite the great ethnic and linguistic diversity of the peoples and countries bordering the Black Sea, in modern times they all call it by their name for 'Black'. It is the *Karadeniz* in Turkish, black in comparison to the Akdeniz, the 'White' or Mediterranean Sea.

More than three millennia ago, the Greeks named it the *Euxine*, or Friendly Sea. Though it was challenging for mariners to sail and row in, the Black Sea was indeed friendly to the Greeks, who established colonies all around the shore.

In fact, the Black Sea is blue, many many shades of blue: dark steel blue-grey, cobalt, navy and turquoise. Close to river mouths the water is stained brown with eroded soil, creating plumes extending up to several miles. Algal blooms, particularly common in some isolated bays, such as behind Djarilgach Island off the Ukraine mainland, may stain the water bright green, charcoal green and purple. Neither rivers nor algae prevent the vast majority of the Black Sea's surface from appearing blue, and visible blooms are generally rare.

## 3.2 Geography

The catchment area (or 'drainage basin') of the Black Sea is more than two million km$^2$, covering part or all of 22 countries in Europe and Asia Minor. Among these, six states border the Sea: Turkey, Georgia, Russian Federation, Ukraine, Romania and Bulgaria.

Geographers identify five distinct segments of the catchment area. In the NW the Danube, Dnieper, Dniester, and Southern Bug rivers account for more than two-thirds of all the freshwater inflow to the Black Sea and nearly three-quarters of the total

Giresun, water feature in Kale park

Bridge over Rioni River, near Poti, Georgia

catchment area. The Don and Kuban rivers, which flow from Russia into the Sea of Azov, and then into the Black Sea through the Kerch Strait, account for more than one-tenth of the freshwater and nearly one-quarter of the Black Sea's total drainage basin. In contrast, the Caucasian coast (Russia and Georgia), the Anatolian Coast (Turkey), and the Bulgarian coast in total account for less than one-fifth of the discharge from rivers into the Black Sea. Here, on the eastern, southern and western sides, mountain ranges press much closer to the Sea so that the river basins are much smaller and discharge is lower, even though rainfall is generally heavier than in the N.

More than half of all the river discharge into the Black Sea is from the Danube, which is the sea's longest river (2,850km) and has the largest catchment area (817,000km²). The Danube flows through or forms the border of Germany, Austria, Slovakia, Hungary, Croatia, Serbia, Romania and the Ukraine. Its drainage basin includes parts of Bosnia-Herzegovina, the Czech Republic, Poland, Belarus, Slovenia, Switzerland, Italy, Macedonia, Albania and Moldova.

The surface area of the Black Sea is variously given as 423,000km² to 436,400km², not including the Sea of Azov.

Black Sea shoreline totals 4,338km in length:

| | |
|---|---|
| Bulgaria | 300 |
| Georgia | 310 |
| Romania | 225 |
| Russia | 475 |
| Turkey | 1,400 |
| Ukraine | 1,628 |

The longest E–W extent of the Sea is about 1,175km, equivalent to approximately 588M.

## 3.3 Geology

The geological history of the Black Sea is very unusual: it is one of both the oldest and youngest geological features on the Earth's surface. The Mediterranean, Black, Caspian and Aral Seas are all remnants of what was, 250 million years ago, the Tethys Sea, located more or less in the centre of the 'supercontinent' of Pangaea. Over time the huge sea became divided into smaller pieces by rising mountain ranges. Separated from the Mediterranean Sea, the Black Sea became the planet's largest brackish lake, with a salinity of perhaps 5%, only one-seventh that of the world's oceans. The surface of the lake was about 150m below the surface of the world ocean, separated by an uplifted sill in the narrow channel of what is now the Bosphorus.

In approximately 5600 BC, as the surface of the Mediterranean Sea rose from the melting glaciers that had covered much of Europe, the Bosphorus sill collapsed, catastrophically, creating a flume 85–145m deep. More than 40km³ of salt water a day spilled into the lake, at more than 80km an hour, raising the lake's surface by 15cm a day. After only two years the surface of the Black Sea had risen 100m, enough for it to reach through the Kerch Strait and turn the Azov plain into a sea, submerging more than 100,000km² of the exposed continental shelf.

Two Columbia University oceanographers, William Ryan and Walter Pittman, documented the scientific evidence for this story in their 1998 bestseller, *Noah's Flood*. The evidence began to accumulate during the height of the Cold War, when NATO mapped the bottom of the Black Sea as a measure to counter Soviet submarines. It gathered momentum in the mid-1980s, when boreholes for the pilings of the Galata Bridge, in Istanbul, revealed that the sediments in the Bosphorus were only 7,500 years old. But it only came together in a coherent picture after the end of the Cold War, when scientists could freely share their findings across borders. Ryan and Pittman argue that the flood was so traumatic for the people who lived on the shores of the freshwater lake that it became the myth recounted in the Bible as the flood survived only by Noah and the creatures on his ark.

Dating the latest connection between the Black Sea and the Mediterranean is still an ongoing challenge for marine scientists, and there are some who argue that the opening of the Bosphorus occurred as recently as 5,000 years ago. Regardless of the exact dates, the stupendous speed with which the geological and chemical changes took place have had a huge impact on the plants and animals living in the Black Sea.

## 3.4 Bathymetry

The total volume of Black Sea water is 534,000 to 547,000km³. The seafloor is commonly divided into the shelf, the continental slope, and the deep-sea depression.

Cide

The shelf is a continuation of dry land which has been covered by the sea. It represents about 30% of the total area of the sea. The largest portion of the shelf is in the NW, where it extends more than 200km, at a depth normally less than 100m but occasionally as much as 160m. In other parts of the Black Sea the shelf has a depth of less than 100m and a width of 2·2–15km.

Moving away from the shore, the shelf becomes a fairly steep continental slope, descending at an average angle of 5–8° in the NW and 1–3° near the Kerch Strait, but in some sections the gradient reaches 20–30°. The slope represents about 27% of the total area.

The centre of the Black Sea depression consists of a deepwater basin with a depth of 2,000–2,200m. The maximum depth is 2,212m. The basin apron and abyssal depths total about 43% of the total area of the sea.

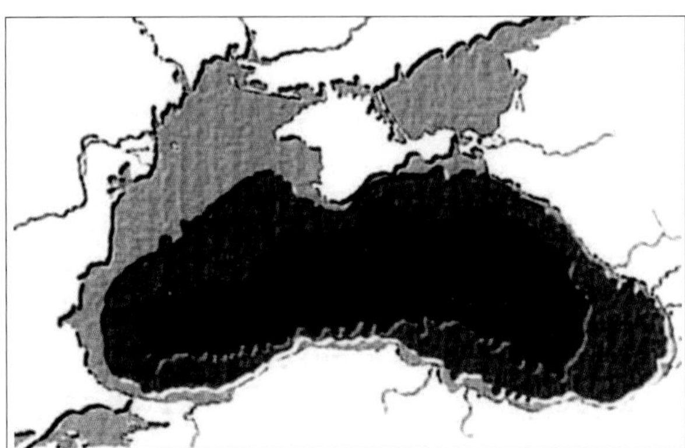

Image courtesy of the Black Sea Commission

Cide, stream emptying into Black Sea

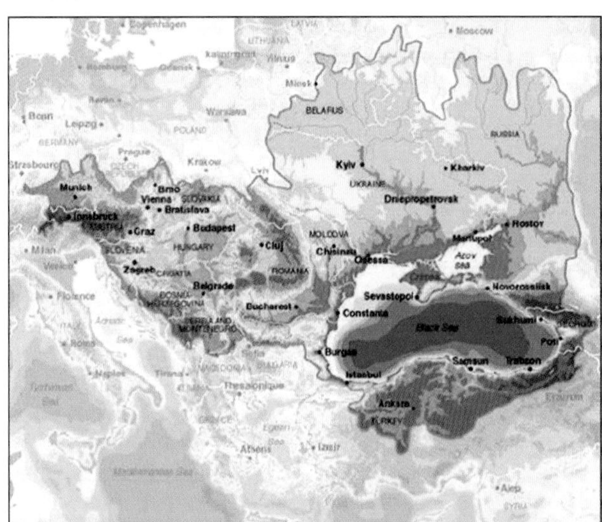


Image courtesy of the Black Sea Commission

## 3.5 Hydrology

In modern times, the Black Sea serves as a huge pool that collects fresh water from rivers and mixes with the world ocean. The mixing process occurs throughout the Turkish Straits, which extend 165M from the Aegean to the Black Sea, through the Dardanelles, the Sea of Marmara, and the Bosphorus. On the surface, the Turkish Straits seem to be a huge drain for the Black Sea, but this impression is severely mistaken. The surface current consists of relatively fresher and less dense water. Below the surface current, a counter-current of saltier water is flowing 'upstream' from the Aegean to the Black Sea.

Visual evidence for the 'upstream' sub-surface current was that golfball-sized markers on a lowered line started to bend into an S-shape as it reached the cold-water layer. But centuries before this, Byzantine mariners had discovered that they could use the counter-current to drag them upstream, by the simple expedient of lowering a vase or a rock into it.

Given the huge size of the Black Sea's catchment area, it is not surprising that there is a lot of variation from year to year in the quantity of runoff, direct precipitation, salinity, temperature, and sediment and pollution loads. It is this huge size that contributes to the two main threats to the Black Sea's health: nutrients from upstream and invasive species in ships' ballast water.

Down rivers, huge deltas separate the uplands from the Black Sea, and there is often a long distance to more populated areas. Eventually it reached the point that people forgot where the chemical and fertilisers that entered into the rivers upstream would end up. The rivers, and particularly the Danube, became a major source of nutrients – nitrogen (N) and phosphorus (P) that caused eutrophication, or over-nourishment, throughout the NW shelf, off the coast of Ukraine and Romania. The extent of this problem was described by teams funded by the Global Environment Facility (GEF) and led to a significant reduction in these unwanted chemicals, after some concerted effort by the Danube countries. Ongoing effort must continue reduction of chemicals from agricultural runoffs and industrial discharges.

The large size of the Black Sea also serves it poorly for ship owners. It is so large, and each ship seems so small. It is difficult to realise that the number and size of ships discharging ballast water creates a totally alien water source equivalent to a sizeable river. Bilge and ballast water has been a primary source of the invasive species that are now disrupting the marine life of the Black Sea. The joint United Nations GloBallast Programme is a flagship effort to address this.

## 3.6 Currents

The main currents of Black Sea circulate around the rim in an anticlockwise direction.

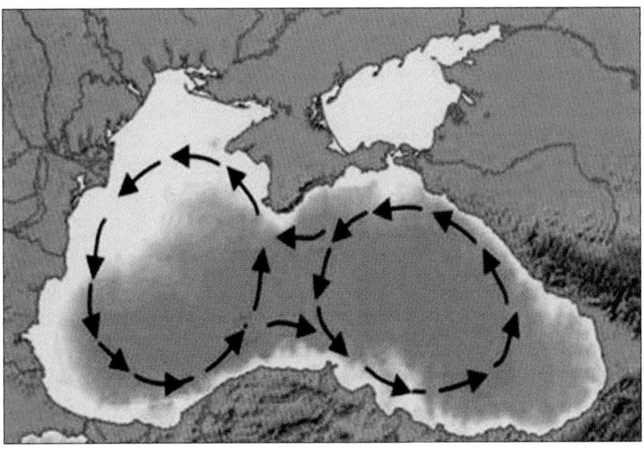

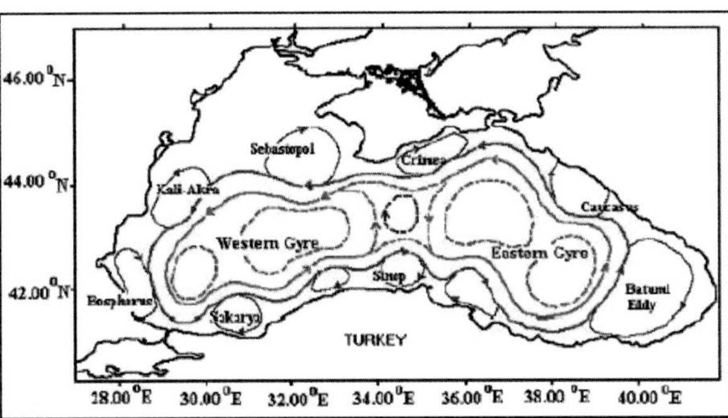


Images courtesy of the Black Sea Commission

## 3.7 Chemistry

The chemistry of the Black Sea is strongly stratified for temperature, density, salinity and oxygen.

The average salinity of the open Black Sea is 17–18% at the surface, or about half that of the world's oceans. Since salt water is heavier than fresh water, it sinks; the Black Sea's salinity is 22% below a depth of 2,000m.

The most interesting feature of the chemistry of the Black Sea is the enormous deep and (almost) lifeless pool of hydrogen sulphide that begins at a depth of 100–200m and extends to the abyssal depths.

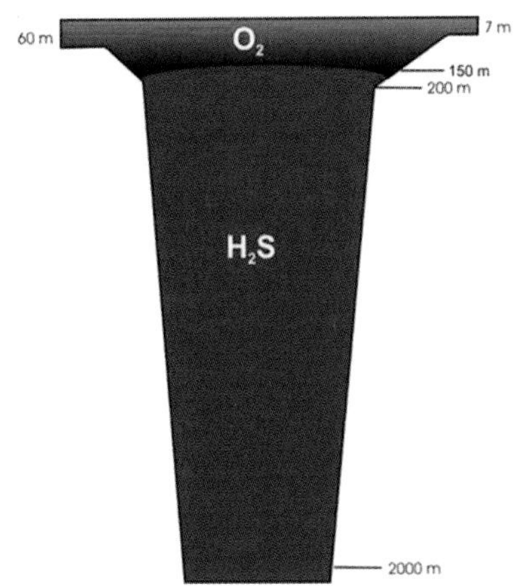


Image courtesy of the Black Sea Commission

## 3.8 Marine life

The plants and animals living in the Black Sea comprise several groups of species that share a common ecological origin. The most ancient of these groups is generally referred to as the 'Pontian relics', the species that existed in the brackish lake before the modern Black Sea formed. Today they can be found only in riverine areas, marked by waters with low salinity. The relic species include bivalves, crustaceans, gobies, sturgeon and herrings.

A second group, the 'cold-water relics', consists of thermophobic ('heat-hating') species that originated in cold seas. This group includes the spiny dogfish, sprat, flounder, whiting and Black Sea trout. It is difficult to know when or how these entered the Black Sea, but they definitely constitute the second-oldest group.

After the connection at the Bosphorus was re-established between the Black Sea and the Mediterranean, the salinity soon rose to the point that the Black Sea could support the third group of species, the Mediterranean settlers. Because they are adapted to warm salty water, the settlers are normally found in the upper layers of water less affected by rivers. This is by far the largest group, comprising 80% of the species of fauna in the Black Sea.

The extraordinarily rapid environmental changes placed enormous pressure on the Pontian relics, which either died off or took refuge in the estuaries, deltas and *limans*. The cold-water relics survived by spending the winter months below the thermocline in the pelagic zone, where the temperature does not exceed 10°C. Some fish species of the Mediterranean settlers adapted so well to the Black Sea that they formed local subspecies and even a distinct species, such as the turbot.

### Jellyfish

Gelatinous plankton organisms, commonly known as 'jellyfish', have bodies consisting of up to 99% water. They are a characteristic feature of marine zooplankton under eutrophic conditions and are probably the organisms that have brought the Black Sea its greatest notoriety. Based on news stories of impending Black Sea doom by jellyfish, we expected to see countless thousands every day and were surprised that often several days would pass with only isolated individuals coming into view, before coming upon a local bloom centred on a nutrient source such as a river or harbour. Although there are several species of jellyfish in the Black Sea, four of them are adequate to sketch the story and only the first two are likely to be seen in large numbers from a yacht.

*Rhizostoma pulmo* With an umbrella up to the size of a dinner plate and tentacles looking like something from a jet engine, *R. pulmo* is by far the most fearsome looking creature in the Black Sea.

*Aurelia aurita* Delicate, with a white four-leaf clover in the centre of its umbrella, *A. aurita* is probably the most common of the Black Sea's jellyfish.

*Mnemiopsis leidyi* The accidental introduction of this comb jelly is possibly the worst single environmental catastrophe among the many that the Black Sea has suffered in recent times. Native to the eastern United States, it was most likely accidentally introduced in the Black Sea in the early 1980s, in discharged ballast water of merchant ships. It is a textbook example of an invasive species, with no enemies and a voracious appetite for the zooplankton that many fish also eat, as well as for the eggs and larvae of those fish. There were three immediate outcomes. First, *M. leidyi* gained such a dominant spot in the Black Sea that by 1989 there were estimated to be a billion tonnes of it, making it the largest species on planet Earth, by weight. Second, by simultaneously attacking the food, the eggs and the young of fish, the anchovy and sprat fisheries nearly collapsed. And third, toxic algal blooms increased in both frequency and extent because the balance of nature had become so disrupted.

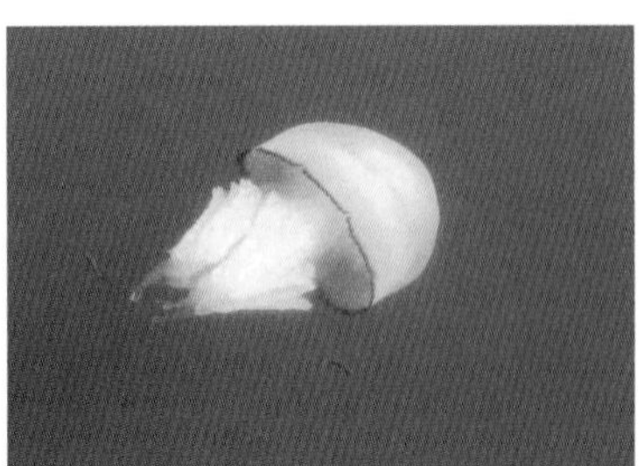

*Rhizostoma pulmo*

Common dolphin

*Beroe ovata* Biologists considered introducing one of *Mnemiopsis's* predators such as *Beroe ovata*, another comb jelly, to rebalance the food web. However, the idea seemed too risky because 'biocontrols' can go horribly wrong. Then, without any planned intervention by humans, in 1997, *B. ovata* established itself in the Black Sea of its own accord, either by migrating naturally from the Mediterranean or possibly in ship's ballast water again. Initial occupation of coastal areas spread rapidly and by 1999 there were *Beroe* populations in the entire NE region of the Black Sea. Since then, there has been a massive decline in the *Mnemiopsis* population while some species of plankton have begun to increase, but the long-term effects are still difficult to predict.

The Black Sea Commission and the Turkish Marine Research Foundation, TUDAV, (www.tudav.org) has set up an International Black Sea Jellyfish Programme to determine if the number of jellyfish is increasing as the Black Sea is warming. Observers are asked to report their observations by email to info@tudav.org.

### Marine Mammals

Until recently there were four mammalian species in the Black Sea: the monk seal (*Monachus monachus*), and three species of dolphins—the bottlenose dolphin (*Tursiops truncatus ponticus*), the common dolphin (*Delphinus delphis ponticus*) and the harbour porpoise (*Phocaena phocaena relicta*). Tragically, the monk seal seems to have become extinct in the Black Sea; the last recorded sighting was in 1995. But the dolphins are abundant, at least compared with their relative scarcity in the Mediterranean and Aegean Seas.

Harbour porpoises are easy to identify. Their active awareness extends at least 100m, and they only very seldom come closer than that to a yacht. In colour they appear to be black or charcoal grey. Group size is normally fewer than eight individuals, but groups of up to 100 harbour porpoises form during migration. When feeding, they appear to move only a short distance between breaths, and they rarely jump out of the water.

Bottlenose dolphins often respond positively to the wake created by a moving yacht, and they enjoy playing 'chicken' crossing the bow wake. Their colour is greyish. They normally live in groups of fewer than 20 individuals, but groups can grow to several hundred.

We usually spotted common dolphins farther offshore than the bottlenose dolphins. Closer, they are distinctive by the large white patch on their sides.

## 3.9 Wetlands

Black Sea coastal zone wetland ecosystems act as a buffer zone, or a relay mechanism, between the huge catchment area and the sea itself. They are highly productive ecosystems that are characterised as river flood-plains, inland lakes and lagoons, *limans*, deltas, sea lagoons and bays, and silt or sand shoals. Most wetlands also include dry land habitats such as sand dunes and barrier islands.

The largest Black Sea wetlands are situated in the coastal plain areas of Romania, Ukraine and the Russian Federation, in the deltas of the large rivers with huge catchment areas such as the Danube, the Dniester, the Dnieper, the Don, and the Kuban. The Crimean Peninsula extends into the Black Sea from a narrow isthmus that connects it to the Ukrainian mainland. Both E and W of the isthmus are huge wetland areas, particularly on the E, where they merge gradually into the very shallow Sea of Azov.

The coastal wetlands of Bulgaria, Turkey and Georgia are smaller, because mountainous terrain behind these coasts creates smaller river basins. The deltas of the KIzIlIrmak and the Yeşilirmak, in Turkey, and the Rioni, in Georgia are the largest of these wetlands.

The coastal wetlands provide homes and food sources for a huge variety of benthic communities, particularly fish. They are also a vital link in a vast network of wetlands that extends from the Arctic Ocean to South Africa and provides refuge for migrating waterfowl. They provide winter habitat for many bird species that nest in the Arctic, and nesting grounds for birds that spend the winter in Africa.

Many types of human activity have resulted in the degradation and loss of Black Sea coastal wetlands. They include:

- Reclamation of wetlands for agriculture, industry, forestry and home construction
- Deepening river beds for navigation and flood control
- Construction of dams
- Dumping of dredge spoils and solid waste
- Extraction of peat, sand, gravel and other materials.

In 1977 the international community created the Convention on Wetlands of International Importance, commonly known as the Ramsar Convention. All six of the Black Sea countries are parties to the convention, and all have designated major wetlands as 'Ramsar sites' to be managed through the convention's principles of 'wise use'. Three important and representative Ramsar sites are the KIzIlIrmak River delta, in Turkey; the Kolkheti National Park at the Rioni River delta in Georgia; and the Danube River delta, straddling the Ukraine-Romania border.

### Kızılırmak Delta

The KIzIlIrmak River, flowing N approximately 1,200km from central Anatolia, is the longest river in Turkey. In classical antiquity it was known as the Halys, or 'Red' river and was considered to be the boundary between Asia Minor and Asia. The delta, known as Bafra Burnu, is huge, 56,000ha of which 21,700ha are designated as the Ramsar area. It contains three major habitat types which are classified at threatened: Öksin saline swamps, South Black Sea permanent dunes, and SE European ash-oak forests. The delta is home to 29 species of fish, of which five are facing extinction, and more than 20,000 waterbirds throughout the year. More information is given in Chapter 4.

Purple heron in flight

Lake Paleostomi, Kolkheti wetlands, Georgia

### Kolkheti Wetlands

The Kolkheti wetlands occupy more than 33,000ha at the delta of the Rioni River, which flows westwards from the Caucasus Mountains into the Black Sea near Poti in Georgia. The wetlands are divided by nature into southern, northern and central segments, of which the central is the largest. The wetland habitats include bogs, marshes, swamps and salt marshes, as well as Lake Paleostomi. The lake, 18km² in area, is fed by seepage from the Rioni River, by groundwater, and occasionally by water blown upstream through the channel that connects the lake to the Black Sea.

There are three protected areas in Kolkheti: the Kolkheti National Park, Kobuleti Nature Reserve, and Kobuleti Managed Reserve, the first two of which have been designated as Ramsar Convention wetlands of international importance. More information is given in Chapter 5.

### Danube Delta

The delta of the River Danube is the third largest in Europe, after the Volga (on the Caspian Sea) and the Kuban (on the eastern side of the Sea of Azov). It covers an area of 4,178km² straddling Ukraine (18%) and Romania (82%). The delta is formed by three main distributaries of the Danube: Chilia, Sulina, and Sf. Gheorghe (Saint George). The Chilia branch makes a great arc for 120km to the N before entering the Black Sea through nine channels just N of the Ukraine-Romania border. The Sulina channel runs eastward for 64km and enters the Black Sea just beyond the Romanian port of Sulina. The Saint George channel runs SE for 70km before entering the Black Sea amidst scarcely populated sand dunes.

Wetlands along the Sulina Channel, Romania

Tulcea is the Romanian town located nearest to the upstream point where the delta begins, so it is the seat of the Danube Delta Biosphere Reserve Authority (DDBRA). The Authority is tasked with managing the Danube Delta Biosphere Reserve which covers an area of 5,800km² of habitat ranging from forests and dunes to vast reedbeds. More than 20% of the reserve is below sea level. More information is given in Chapter 8.

## 3.10 Human history

This cruising guide does not attempt to offer a proper history of human settlements along the Black Sea shores but, rather a quick reflection of personal interests.

The best traditional chronological history is Charles King's *The Black Sea: A History* (Oxford University Press, 2004).

If Ryan and Pittman's depiction of the Black Sea flood (Chapter 3.3) is correct, it must qualify as one of the most profound catastrophes in ancient history, right up there with the volcanic explosion of Thera. Tradition has it that Noah's Ark came to rest on the top of Mount Ararat, located in eastern Turkey, dominating the skyline of Yerevan, the capital of Armenia. No other mountain in the region commands the majesty of Ararat, which people have held to be sacred for thousands of years.

Nearly every harbour and port, every town and city on the Black Sea coast that a modern yachtsman might visit was initially identified and developed by the ancient Greeks. Their voyages of exploration of the Black Sea began in the Bronze Age, during the Mycenaean period, around the 13th century BC. The legend of Jason, the Argonauts and the Golden Fleece can be dated to this time, at least a generation before the Trojan War, but the *Argonautica*, the only written account that survives, is by Apollonius of Rhodes, from about 250 BC. If his account is to be believed, even Jason was not the first to row or sail on the Black Sea, because Phineus, the blind seer whom he met at the Bosphorus, was able to give him sailing directions all the way to Colchis, at the eastern end. It is a great story, with many dramatic moments, but it was generally considered to be only a legend until 1983, when Tim Severin built a replica of a Greek 20-oar scout galley and sailed and rowed it to Colchis, in modern Georgia. His experience closely paralleled the one described by Apollonius, down to the details of the Golden Fleece.

The greatest of the Greek epic poems, Homer's *Iliad*, includes 'catalogues' of the order of battle, the catalogue of the Greek ships and the catalogue of Troy's allies, among whom

> The Paphlagonians followed Pylaemenes, shaggy, great-hearted, from the wild mule country of the Eneti – men who held Cytorus and Sesamus and had their famous homes on the Parthenius riverbanks, at Cromna, Aegialus, and lofty Erythini. (II 851–856).

Ancient Cromna is modern Kurucaşile, Aegialus is Cide, and the Parthenius riverbanks are modern Bartin Liman. All of these can be visited by yacht. The mouth of the Dardenelles seemed awfully far away from Bartin, and it gave us a better appreciation of the geographic extent of the alliances.

It took the Greeks several centuries of exploration (and plundering) before they began to found colonies along the Black Sea shores, but by the 8th century BC a few Greek city-states were sending out colonists to establish permanent trading posts. Of course, the destruction of Troy removed an important obstacle to this. The main colonial impulse came from Ionia, the region of Greek city-states along the eastern coast of the Aegean, known subsequently as Asia Minor. The major colonial power there was the city of Miletus, now on the Aegean coast of Turkey, the southernmost and most important city in the region. During this same period, Miletus was also among the principal founders of colonies in the western Mediterranean, particularly southern Italy. The Dorians, from the Greek mainland, were much less active in colonising the Black Sea than the Ionians. The major Dorian Greek city-state with colonies on the Black Sea was Megara.

The Greeks sought places along the coast that met four basic criteria: (1) a promontory which offered a strong defensive position; (2) a beach on which ships could be pulled out of the water and which provided protection from the prevailing wind; two beaches, on opposite sides of the promontory were even better, and a natural harbour was best; (3) a good source of fresh water, preferably from springs, a large stream, or a river; and (4) access to the immediate interior, to facilitate trade with the local people.

Since the Black Sea shores had already been inhabited for thousands of years before the Greeks arrived, many of the ideal places they found had already been occupied for millennia, and nearly all of them remain important to this day. Sadly for archaeology fans, this has meant that the remains of Greek settlements are buried under Roman, Byzantine, Genoese, Ottoman, and modern roads and buildings. Scarcely a trace of the Greeks remains in most of the modern cities they founded more than 2,500 years ago. Despite a scarcity of physical artifacts, the Greek heritage lives to this day on the Black Sea in the names of many of the places they founded, especially in Turkey.

Among the interesting books to survive from antiquity is *Periplus Ponti Euxini*, an account of the rivers, headlands, and harbours along the Black Sea coast, written in about 135 AD by Arrian of Nicomedea, the governor of the Roman province of Cappadocia. The *Periplus* was written in Greek as an extended cover letter to an official report in Latin addressed to the Roman Emperor Hadrian. It has been well translated and edited by Aidan Liddle and makes a fascinating companion guide for a voyage around the Black Sea in a small boat.

Pontic Kingdom (pre-Roman) Fortress walls in Sinop, Turkey

Roman bath ruins in Amasra, Turkey

Model of Jason's ship, Kolkheti Wetland Centre, Poti, Georgia

Minaret in Amasra, Turkey

## 3.11 Languages, cultures and religions

Four languages dominate the Black Sea: Turkish, Slavonic languages, Romanian and Georgian. All originated in regions to the NE of their modern locations. Russian, Ukrainian and Bulgarian share many common Slavonic features. Romanian is derived from Latin; the root 'Rom' derives from 'Rome'.

The Roman Empire split into eastern and western pieces following the founding of the city of Constantinople by the Emperor Constantine, in 310 AD. During the more than 11 centuries that followed, the eastern Roman, or Byzantine Empire, carried Orthodox Christianity to the Georgians and the Slavs. Roman Catholics declared a schism from Orthodoxy in 1095 and sacked Constantinople in 1204 during a Crusade. Following the Ottoman conquest of Constantinople in 1453, Islam spread throughout the southern half of the Black Sea shores as well as the Balkans to the west, and to the northern Caucasus to the east.

Church in Sulina, Romania

In crude terms, it might be said that the Black Sea is surrounded by Turkish-speaking Muslims to the S and Russian-speaking Christians to the N, with other ethnic minorities and languages scattered about. The Black Sea minorities suffered terribly during the 20th century. Armenians still complain of Ottoman genocide. Greeks and Turks were forcibly relocated. Stalin exiled the Crimean Tatars. Hitler and his Romanian allies killed Odessa's Jews. For more information, Neal Ascherson's book, *Black Sea* is a meditation on ethnic turmoil.

## 3.12 Contemporary international relations

At least as far back in history as Roman times it was clear to emperors and their admirals that control of the Bosphorus offered an important degree of control over the entire Black Sea. Byzantium, which was successively renamed Constantinople in 312 AD and Istanbul in 1453 AD, is perfectly located to control the Bosphorus. Keeping foreigners out of the Black Sea was the top foreign policy priority of the Byzantine emperors right up to the sacking of Constantinople by the Venetians and Franks in 1204. This policy was continued unabated by the Ottomans from 1453 to 1918 and by the Republic of Turkey since its founding in 1923. The Treaty of Lausanne, ratified in 1924, recognised the sovereignty of Turkey and established the legal framework for Turkey to govern the straits connecting the Aegean and Black Seas.

In 1936, the Montreux Convention Regarding the Regime of the Straits gave Turkey full control over the straits, including the right to severely restrict the passage of non-Turkish warships, but it guaranteed the free passage of civilian vessels during peacetime. Both Turkey and the Soviet Union got what they most wanted; Turkey gained the control that it viewed as essential for its sovereignty, and the Soviet Union gained naval control over the Black Sea itself.

It is difficult to overestimate the importance of the Montreux Convention to Black Sea events during the Second World War, the Cold War and the modern era of globalisation. It prevented Nazi Germany from bringing its naval forces to bear at Stalingrad and the Crimea. It kept aircraft carriers and battleships out of the Black Sea during the Cold War and thus greatly moderated the intensity of the conflict there. And it has kept commodities, especially oil, flowing at an ever-increasing rate from Central Asia to Western Europe.

Beyond the Bosphorus there are two ongoing border disputes among the Black Sea countries. The first of these, between Ukraine and Romania, is being litigated through the international judicial process. The second dispute, between Russia and Georgia, led to war in 2008.

Romania has brought a case against Ukraine before the International Court of Justice (ICJ) in The Hague over the delimitation of the common border in the Black Sea and Snake Island, a tiny spot of land off the Danube Delta, just S of the border. It also opposes Ukraine's proposal to reopen the navigation canal from the Danube, which, it claims, will cause unacceptable environmental damage.

Russia invaded Georgia in an intense five-day war in August 2008, ostensibly in support of ethnic Russians and 'freedom fighters' in the province of South Ossetia. A number of independent observers have criticised the immensely popular Georgian President, Mikheil Saakashvili, for provoking the conflict, which caused significant damage in many parts of the country. Relations between the two countries remain strained in 2011, and Russia officially does not permit ships to land in Russian territory after visiting Georgia. Georgia officially does not permit ships to visit Sukhumi, the capital port city of the breakaway province of Abkhazia.

This international conflict is compounded geographically by the fact that Yalta, at the tip of the Crimean Peninsula, is the easternmost port of entry into the Ukraine. Consequently, the 350-mile line between Poti, Georgia, and Yalta, Ukraine, demarcates an interim 'Caution Zone' for yachts until relationships and co-operation improve (see 1.5 Caution Zone).

It would be a shame if scary-sounding sailing directions deterred yachts from visiting Georgia, because neither Georgia nor Russia is intentionally bent on interfering with private pleasure craft. The crew of *Gyatso* never saw a Russian warship in eastern Black Sea waters, and never feared for their safety between Poti and their next stop, on the Crimean Peninsula.

## 3.13 National naval and coastguard operations

After Turkey joined NATO in 1952 it received extensive support from other NATO countries to build a modern navy that could actively patrol the Turkish Straits and, if necessary, confront the Soviet Black Sea Fleet in time of war. No major naval confrontation occurred on the Black Sea during the following four decades, nor when the Soviet Union began to collapse. The Ukrainian navy was formally established in 1992, but not until 1997 did the division between the Ukraine and the Russian Federation begin. The division became particularly acrimonious because the territory of the Russian Federation on the Black Sea shore has no port with the capacity to base the fleet, so it has remained in the Ukrainian port of Sevastopol. The Yushchenko and Tymoshenko governments insisted that the Russian fleet must leave by 2017, but the Yanukovych government, voted into power in January 2010, agreed two months later to extend the lease for the Russian fleet at Sevastopol for 25 years,

Ukrainian coastguard vessel, Balaclava

Russian navy ships in Sevastopol

until 2042. The rusting remains of the formerly formidable Soviet Black Sea fleet are now mainly a tourist attraction for harbour trip boats in Sevastopol. Don't miss this somewhat farcical tour.

From the end of the Second World War until 1990, both Romania and Bulgaria received Soviet naval vessels as gifts of the Soviet Union, but after the Soviet collapse both countries became NATO members in 2004. Bulgaria has discontinued the use of submarines in its naval fleet, which in 2010 consisted of four frigates and three corvettes, based at Varna and Burgas. The Romanian navy, with three frigates and four corvettes, is based at Constanţa.

Georgia succeeded in obtaining only a few naval vessels following the breakup of the Soviet Union, and most of these were destroyed by the Russian navy in the August 2008 war. In 2009 the Georgia navy was merged with the coastguard, which is the maritime arm of the Border Police, in the Ministry of Internal Affairs. The main Georgia coastguard base is at Poti.

In 2010, the overwhelming naval security concern among the Black Sea countries fell upon the Turkish navy to maintain safe passage for commercial vessels travelling through the Turkish Straits, between the Aegean and Black Seas. The Turkish coastguard, known as Sahil Güvenlik, and the Ukrainian Sea Guard, known as 'Lebed', Ukrainian for 'Swan', maintain the largest fleets of coastal patrol boats, which are engaged primarily in search-and rescue and anti-smuggling operations.

All six coastguards maintain some degree of surveillance over yachts, but they are quite unlikely to board and inspect yachts, particularly in international waters. Along the Turkish coast, Sahil Güvenlik vessels have a substantial presence at many ports and actively patrol the coast. The Georgian coastguard has virtually no experience with foreign yachts. 'Lebed' is supported by good shore-based radar and VHF radio coverage but is very short on English-speaking radio operators and so almost never responds to calls.

## 3.14 Commercial shipping

In the 1930s, when the Montreux Convention was signed, 4,500 ships passed through the Turkish Straits annually. By the end of the 20th century this number had grown to more than 50,000 ships, of which more than 5,500 were oil tankers. Istanbul, with a population of more than 11 million people, is bisected by the Bosphorus and therefore vulnerable to catastrophic marine accidents. These have occurred with distressing frequency. As just one example, in March 1994 the tanker Nassia collided with another ship a few miles north of the city, killing 30 seamen and spilling into the straits 20,000 tonnes of oil which turned into an inferno that burned for five days.

Although international agreements grant Turkey the right to regulate civilian ship traffic in the Turkish straits for safety and environmental protection, the five other Black Sea countries have generally resisted tight traffic controls. By 2010 a number of important safety measures were in place, including the ending of two-way traffic in favour of two 12-hour one-way periods for passage through the Bosphorus. This has created an even bigger log jam of ships waiting for transit and has intensified the urgency of creating oil and gas pipeline routes to carry oil from the Caspian to the Mediterranean Seas, thereby reducing pressure on the Bosphorus.

Cross-sea ferries are growing in number and size in response to increased trade between Central Asia and Europe. Roll on Roll off (RoRo) ferries carrying lorries operate regularly from ports all around the Black Sea, including Istanbul (Derince), Zonguldak, Samsun and Trabzon in Turkey; Batumi and Poti in Georgia; Sochi and Novorossiysk in Russia; Kerch, Yevpatoria, Skadovsk and Ilyichevsk in Ukraine; Constanţa in Romania; and Varna and Burgas in Bulgaria.

Passenger-carrying hydrofoils served many cross-sea routes in the years before 1991, but their number has fallen considerably in the 21st century because of improvements in road and air transport. Probably the most popular international hydrofoil route is from Trabzon in Turkey to Sochi in Russia, bringing Russians for holidays and shopping.

## 3.15 International organisations

### Black Sea Commission

The Commission on the Protection of the Black Sea Against Pollution, known as the Black Sea Commission, is an intergovernmental body created by the six Black Sea countries through the Bucharest Convention, signed in April 1992. The Bucharest Convention created a Commission, comprising one representative from each of the six signatory countries. The work of the Commission is supported by a Permanent Secretariat, located in Istanbul with a small professional staff.

A series of protocols give specificity to the Bucharest Convention. They are:

- Protection of the marine environment against land-based sources of pollution
- Cooperation in combating pollution of the Black Sea by oil and other harmful substances in emergency situations
- Protection of the marine environment against pollution by dumping
- Biodiversity and landscape conservation.

In 2009 the Black Sea Commission adopted a Strategic Action Plan for the rehabilitation and protection of the sea, based on the four protocols. Advisory Groups to the Black Sea Commission are the main source of expertise, information and support to implementation of the plan. The main policy measures have been:

- Pollution reduction from rivers, priority pollution sources and vessels
- Conservation of biological diversity
- Introduction of integrated coastal zone management.

The intermediate target for all these efforts is to prevent the increase of pressures from human activities as the transitional economies of the Black Sea coastal states begin to recover. The strategic target is to achieve environmental conditions in the Black Sea similar to those observed in 1960s, when human-induced environmental degradation became obvious.

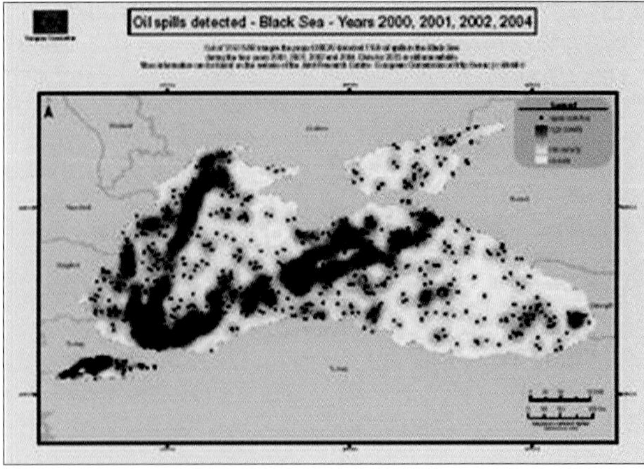


Oil spills detected 200-2004.
Image courtesy of Black Sea Commision

Debris such as this gets washed into the Black Sea after heavy rain

Plume of sediment and marine litter after heavy rain

Yachts are likely to encounter several different types of research vessels. Most are in the oil and gas exploration and production business. All the shoreline countries maintain active research involving vessels.

### The Black Sea Economic Cooperation (BSEC)

On 25 June 1992, the Heads of State and Government of 11 countries (Albania, Armenia, Azerbaijan, Bulgaria, Georgia, Greece, Moldova, Romania, Russia, Turkey and Ukraine) signed in Istanbul the Summit Declaration and the Bosphorus Statement giving birth to the Black Sea Economic Cooperation (BSEC). It came into existence as a model of multilateral political and economic initiative aimed at fostering interaction and harmony among the Member States, as well as to ensure peace, stability and prosperity encouraging friendly and good-neighbourly relations in the Black Sea region. The BSEC headquarters were established in March 1994 in Istanbul.

With the entry into force of its Charter on 1 May 1999, BSEC acquired international legal identity and was transformed into a full-fledged regional economic organisation. With the accession of Serbia and Montenegro in April 2004, the organisation's Member States increased to 12.

BSEC covers a geography encompassing the territories of the Black Sea littoral States, the Balkans and the Caucasus, with an area of nearly 20 million square kilometres. The BSEC region is located on two continents, with a population of some 350 million people. After the Persian Gulf region, it is the second-largest source of oil and natural gas.

### European Union

Bulgaria and Romania became full EU members on 1 January 2007. As the southeastern-most extent of the EU, the primary concern is to develop secure and environmentally friendly trade corridors to the Caucasus and Central Asia.

### NATO

Turkey joined NATO in 1954. Bulgaria and Romania joined in 2004. Georgia would very much like to join NATO but that is unlikely to happen until the disputes over Abkhazia and South Ossetia are settled.

## 3.16 Oil and gas

A vast amount of oil and gas is shipped across the Black Sea from its production sites in the Caspian Sea to its markets in Europe. A considerably smaller but growing amount of oil and gas is produced along the Black Sea shoreline, particularly on the NW shelf off Ukraine. Along the coast of Georgia Batumi, Supsa and Kulevi are major points to transfer oil by rail and pipeline from Azerbaijan to tanker ships headed out to feed an insatiable appetite in the west. It's a dirty and potentially dangerous business that keeps people awake at night in Istanbul, where Very Large Crude Carriers (VLCCs) can pass by as often as 12 times an hour.

All of the recent governments of Turkey have worked for regional cooperation to move Caspian Sea oil by pipeline to Cehan, Turkey's main Mediterranean oil port. There is a fairly widespread feeling that the Turkish Straits have reached their capacity to move oil in VLCCs safely, so there is some urgency to improve the pipelines.

Likewise, Bulgaria is using its strategic location on the west coast to service Russian oil shipments, particularly through the Lukoil terminal in Burgas Bay, on to pipelines westward.

An offshore oil buoy is at Supsa, Georgia, and is described in Chapter 5. Offshore production tripods are described in Turkey and Ukraine. Yachts should of course give these a wide berth. Whatever oil tanker ships a yacht encounters is likely to be moving internationally. Use of coastal tankers has dropped as more fuel is carried by road and rail.

## 3.17 Fishing

The abundance of fish in the Black Sea attracted the first Greek colonists in the 8th century BC and became a mainstay of local economies for the next two millennia. A total of 168 species of fish have been identified in the Black Sea, none of which are known to have become extinct in recent years. But in the decades since the end of the Second World War so many hundreds of thousands of tonnes of fish have been caught that the number of commercial fish species fell from 26 in the 1960s to only five in the 1980s. By 2010, just one species, the Black Sea anchovy, accounted for 90% of the entire commercial catch, and 80% of the total catch is taken by just one country, Turkey.

Three types of fishing vessel can be seen on the Black Sea. By far the most common are small open double-ended boats, typically built of wood and about 6m long, driven by oars or an inboard engine and drawing either a small net or hooked lines. There must be thousands and thousands of such boats, which usually carry one or two men and are normally drawn up onto the beach when not in use. The owners of these vessels typically belong to a local fisheries cooperative, and although the boats carry registration numbers and national flags, there is a very blurred distinction between their use for 'commercial' purposes compared to 'household subsistence'.

The next most common vessels are engine-driven, typically 12–15m long, locally built of wood and with a deckhouse that provides shelter for a crew of three or four men. These vessels draw nets, and the catch is sold through a local market. Some are used to harvest the large whelk *rapana*, an invasive species from Japan that has become a modest commercial success.

The largest fishing vessels are steel trawlers, 30–40m long, carrying advanced electronics and prominent net-handling gear, with a crew of up to 30 men. Nowadays these are usually found in the Black Sea only in Turkey. With the collapse of most fisheries, the large trawlers focus almost exclusively on anchovies, which the Turks call *hamsi* and devour breaded and fried whole.

Father and son fishermen in Akliman

A passion for fishing extends well beyond the use of boats, and virtually every pier and jetty has its share of anglers, some of whom use two or three separate rods. Although there is a 'recreational' component to this pastime, it also makes an important contribution to household nutrition.

## 3.18 Resorts

Every summer, the beaches of the Black Sea attract millions of people on holidays. The top vacation spots are along the SE coast, around Batumi in Georgia, the west coast, from Constanţa in Romania to Tsarevo in Bulgaria, and the north coast, along the Crimean peninsula of Ukraine. The Turkish Black Sea coast has relatively few sandy beaches, especially in the eastern half, where the new coastal highway has replaced the natural shoreline. The norms of dress and behaviour found in Turkey tend to be more conservative than the relaxed atmosphere of the big Ukrainian and Bulgarian resorts. Beach resort holidays became a treasured part of the annual cycle of work in the Soviet Union and Warsaw Pact countries, with a huge number of hotels and hostels constructed during the 1960s, 70s and 80s.

Local fishing boats in Turkey

Beach resort in Sveti Vlas, Bulgaria

# 4. Turkey east of the Bosphorus

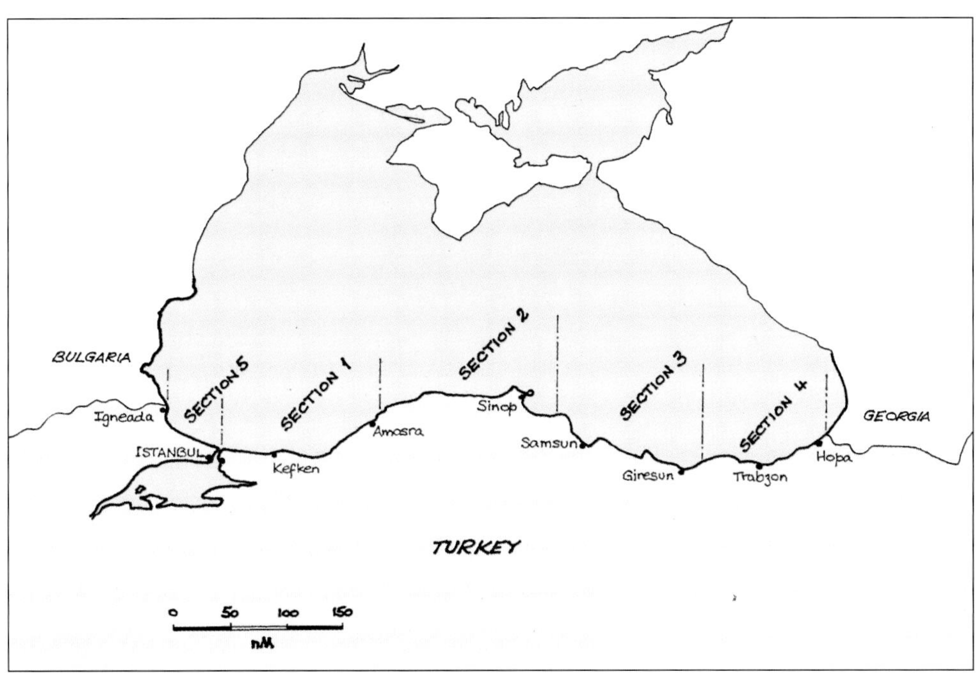


**Section 1 Bosphorus to Amasra**
**Section 2 Amasra to Bafra Burnu**
**Section 3 Bafra Burnu to Çam Burnu**
**Section 4 Çam Burnu to the Georgian border**

### The Black Sea coast of Turkey

Turkey is bordered by Georgia, Armenia, Iran, Iraq and Syria on the E and S and by Bulgaria on the NW. Its area is 783,500 km², making it 15% larger than France (for example) with a rising population of 76.8 million, again about 15% larger than France. Modern Turkey is a highly centralised country administered through 81 provinces. Each province is divided into several districts. Both districts and provinces have tourism development agencies which issue a great deal of material about local sights.

### History

Guided by one of the political geniuses of the 20th century, Turkey transformed itself from being the homeland of the great Ottoman Empire to become a secular democracy at the conjunction of Europe, Central Asia and the Middle East. Every community larger than a hamlet has a square with a tablet honoring Mustafa Kemal Atatürk, who put Turkey on the course which continues to bring growing appreciation for the country throughout the world.

The end for the Ottoman Empire began with the April 1915 assault on the Gallipoli Peninsula by British and French forces attempting to circumvent lower reaches of the Dardanelles, which the Ottomans had mined heavily. Col. Mustafa Kemal held them off at the outer defences of Istanbul, and Britain and France were forced to withdraw. But the Ottoman Empire eventually collapsed amid military failure, and the homeland of the Turks was nearly

The mountainous coastline east of Cide

Amasra

Tirebolu. The harbour festival takes place on 1 July in Turkey

Trabzon street scene near coastal highway

conquered by an army from Greece. The forced relocation of 1.25 million Greeks from Turkey and 750 thousand Turks from Greece made both countries more ethnically homogeneous and cemented ethnic tensions that continue to the present.

Modern Turkey was founded by Atatürk in 1923. From then until now the military has played a large role in running the country, and civilian vs military rivalries have swung back and forth. Turkey's membership in NATO has been very important for both sides. It put Turkey on the front lines of the Cold War from 1945–1991, but since then Turkey has created active cooperation with the Russian Federation and Ukraine, with the European Union, with the Arab nations, and with Israel, making it an essential stable democratic secular power in a really tough neighbourhood.

Of course, history did not start in 1915. Settlements in what is now Turkey go back to 9000 BC at Çatalhöyük. Later, the Hittites created in central Anatolia an empire that extended to the shores of the Black Sea. In the epic by Apollonius of Rhodes, Jason led a squadron of Greek knights on the rowing galley *Argo* to steal the most sacred relic of the people of Colchis, at the extremity of the earth on the eastern Black Sea. Within a generation the Greeks had defeated the city that guarded the entrance to the Dardanelles, Troy. They founded the city of Byzantium in the 8th century BC and established settlements all around the Black Sea, from where they imported cereals and dried fish.

*The Anabasis of Cyrus*, by the Greek historian Xenophon, became one of the most interesting guides carried aboard *Gyatso*. The *Anabasis* recounts the story of a large Greek mercenary army which joined the effort of Cyrus to overthrow his older brother, the Great King of Persia, in the year 401 BC. Three generations earlier, the Greeks had twice defeated attempted Persian invasions, but since then the Greek city-states had torn themselves apart during the recently-ended Peloponnesian War, so more than 10,000 battle-hardened Greek soldiers were happy to join Cyrus's cause. Unfortunately for them, though they performed well, Cyrus himself was killed in the winner-take-all battle against his brother on the outskirts of Baghdad, and the Greek mercenaries were forced to fight their way back home to Greece. They headed N until they reached The Sea above Trapezus, modern Trabzon. Xenophon, who initially joined only as an observer, gradually emerged as one of the key generals guiding the Greek army's desperate effort. His account of the exhausted mercenaries' sighting of The Sea! The Sea! is a jewel of literature. In Trabzon, Zenofon Tours can guide you to where this occurred, one of the most awesome spots on earth. Under Xenophon's leadership, the Ten Thousand marched and sailed to Giresun, Ordu, Akliman, Ereğli and Kerpe, all of which can be explored by yacht today.

Byzantium became Constantinople in 310 AD as the eastern capital of the Roman Empire. Though the government of the western Roman Empire collapsed a century later, the Bishops of Rome, as the heads of the Roman Catholic Church, sustained a growing rivalry with the Patriarch of the Orthodox Church, based in Constantinople, capital of the Byzantine Empire. The rivalry reached a peak in 1054 with the Great Schism, when the Romans declared the Orthodox to be schismatic. Military conquest came 150 years later, when in 1204, Constantinople was sacked by a Crusader army led by Venice. It was then only a matter of time before the city was captured by the Ottomans, in 1453, and immediately became the capital of their empire. The Ottomans lasted 465 years, to the beginning of this tale.

### Time

Turkey is in one time zone, UTC +2. Daylight Savings Time +1 hour from the last Sunday in March to the last Sunday in October.

### Communications

Telephone country code: +90.

### People

Ethnically, modern Turkey is based on shared national pride and identity as speakers of the most widely spoken of the Turkic languages. Azeri, the language of Azerbaijan, is very similar to Turkish, and the two countries consequently maintain close ties. The largest minority in Turkey are Kurds, who also live in Iraq and Iran. The Laz people inhabit the coast and mountains of the NE border with Georgia. The Armenians have nearly all departed since the turmoil brought on by the First World War.

Nearly every Turk practices Islam in a manner that leaves room for secularism and individualism. The formal ban on drinking alcohol is occasionally discreetly broken, and both beer and traditional spirits (*raki*) are available almost everywhere. Equally, the mosque is an important presence almost everywhere, and relaxation of the prohibition on alcohol does not translate into any diminished role of religion in the daily lives of Turks. The dress code for women becomes more restrictive as one travels east, and it blends seamlessly with standards across the border in Iran.

The Turks reinvented themselves during the immense reforms of the 1920s and 1930s under Kemal Atatürk's leadership. Social and political development among ordinary Turks has generally kept up with the rising rate of change in a fairly orderly manner, in sharp contrast to the experience of all of the countries on Turkey's eastern and southern borders. The great wave of Turkish 'guest workers' in Germany in the 1960s–80s brought back industrial skills and capital which contributed to the creation of a modern economy at the start of the 21st century.

Turks on the Aegean coast are accustomed to tourists, but along the Black Sea coast tourists are rare enough that they are likely to be greeted with far more generous hospitality than any would have reason to expect. People readily go out of their way to be helpful in ways that transcend the language barrier. *Gyatso*'s crew never once felt anxious in public social situations in Turkey, riding a bus, shopping in the market, eating in a restaurant, or wandering on a beach.

Friendly local people out for a boat ride, east of Trabzon

Yakakent, local fisherman and his wife

### Food and drink

Turks are justifiably proud of their cuisine, which varies quite a lot from one end of the country to the other. Public places serving food and drink range from coffee shops frequented only by men to cafés serving couples drinking beer or *raki*. Great fast food can be found at a sidewalk place selling *döner kebab*, meat or chicken sliced from a rotating spit by a grill. The next step up is a *Lokantasi*, serving stews and casseroles from hot trays. Most restaurants specialise in either *pide*, (local pizzas), *mezze* (small plates), grilled meats, or fish. Fish restaurants are very common along the Black Sea coast, where even little towns have great ones.

Although wines are made in Turkey, they are expensive compared to prices in the other Black Sea countries. Efes Pilsen beer is readily available from convenience stores in even the smallest hamlets. Popular brands of *raki*, such as Yeni Raki, are sold in towns and cities. *Raki* is normally drunk by adding cool water and ice, according to taste.

Manti, a meat dumpling with yogurt and walnuts

Typical Black Sea architecture in Giresun

Inebolu

Inebolu fishing boats

### Language

The Turkish language originates in Central Asia and is the most widely-spoken language of a family that includes Azeri, the language of the Azerbaijan Republic. Having virtually no similarity to any Indo-European language, Turkish is difficult for many Europeans to pick up casually; any degree of fluency requires a teacher and a focused course of study – some are available as audio tapes.

The good news is that Turkey uses Roman script with a few characters additional to the English alphabet. If words are said phonetically (and every letter is pronounced) the meaning of some everyday words and signs becomes readily apparent. There are some basic pronunciation rules:

c=j (*cami* = 'jami')
ç= ch (*Foça* = 'Focha')
ğ is silent and lengthens the vowel before:
(*Dağ* = 'Daa')
ş = sh
ö = er
ay as 'i' in 'hi'.
*Mi* ending is a question.

A smattering of words is not difficult to acquire and your efforts will be appreciated. For basics try:

| | |
|---|---|
| *merhaba* | hello |
| *günaydin* | good morning |
| *iyi* ('ee-ee') *akşamlar* | good evening |
| *lütfen* | please |
| *teşekkür ederim* | thank you |
| *hesap* | bill |
| *evet* | yes |
| *hayir* | no |
| *var* | there is (used to express availability, so: *ekmek var* = 'have you any bread?') |
| *yok* | there is not (the often-stated *problem yok* = 'no problem' – treat with caution!) |
| *benzin* | petrol |
| *motor yaği* | oil |
| *motorin/dizel* | diesel |
| *su* | water |
| *bir* = 1 | *beş* = 5 |
| *iki* =2 | *on* = 10 |
| *üç* = 3 | *yüz* = 100 |
| *dört* = 4 | *bin* = 1,000 |

Many Turkish charts include a glossary:

| | |
|---|---|
| Adası | an island |
| Boğaz | strait |
| Burun/Burnu | cape or promontory |
| Deniz | sea |
| Haraba | ruin |
| Kale | castle |
| Kaua-si | rocks |
| Köyü | bay or inlet |
| Körfezi | gulf |
| Limani | bay, harbour, port |
| Dağ | mountain |
| Tepe | hill, peak |
| Yarimadasi | a peninsula (*yarim* = 'half') |

Frequently seen colours of rocks and headlands are:

| | |
|---|---|
| Kara | black |
| Kızıl | red |

### Charts

Turkish charts are produced by the Turkish Navy's Office of Navigation, Hydrography and Oceanography, whose website www.shodb.gov.tr gives a current list of all charts and Sales Agents. This agency was founded by Piri Reis, the Ottoman Admiral who was among the greatest cartographers, and it retains great pride in its illustrious heritage. Chart *10* covers the entire Black Sea, charts *10a* and *10b* cover the western and eastern halves respectively. Charts *11, 12, 13, 14, 14a, 15, 16, 17* and *18* encircle the coast in an anticlockwise direction, starting and ending at the Bosphorus. Each of these is further subdivided.

### Ports of Entry

Istanbul is a Turkish port of entry on the Bosphorus. On the Black Sea there are ten Turkish ports of entry; from W to E, they are: Ereğli, Zonguldak, Inebolu, Sinop, Samsun, Ordu, Giresun, Trabzon, Rize and Hopa.

### Formalities

Every member of the crew must have a passport valid for the length of stay in Turkey, together with a visa stamp acquired (£10 for UK citizens) and dated at the port of entry. A visa generally lasts 90 days but this does vary for some countries. It is important to leave Turkey before a visa expires.

Turkey does not require a yacht captain to show a Certificate of Competence. He or she will be required to show original yacht registration documents as well as valid insurance papers. Copies of these and the captain's passport will be taken by all marinas and some harbour authorities.

### Certificate of Private Yacht Registration (Transit Log)

Yachts entering Turkey from international waters are required to obtain a transit log, which contains basic information about the yacht, the yacht's owners and crew, and the ports of destination. The transit log is managed by the harbourmaster and signed by him and officials from Customs Enforcement, Passport Police, and the Coastal Health Control Centre. The cost of the transit log is TL50 (2010). It is valid for one year. If the boat is left in Turkey it is wise to surrender the transit log into bond. It may be reactivated on return or a new log purchased. The transit log is likely to inspected at marinas, and may be checked by harbourmasters and occasionally by the coastguard.

Local fishermen stop by to welcome yachtsmen

Three bits of advice: First, it is not necessary to list every port that will be visited, just the farthest port on the shore you are sailing along. If you are planning to sail along the Turkish coast of the Black Sea, list Hopa, near the eastern border, as the port of destination. This will 'cover' you if you decide to depart from Turkey at one of the ports W of Hopa.

Second, the harbourmaster in Istanbul will not deal with you directly. *Gyatso*'s crew found that the only way to get anything signed in Istanbul was to find a yacht agent and pay an exorbitant 'fee'. Also, ask for help from 'Habeş Kaptan' to enter at or depart from Sinop.

Third, in most ports it is not necessary to hire an agent to acquire the blank transit log and get the four signatures. Harbourmasters were found to be generally friendly, accommodating and reasonably efficient.

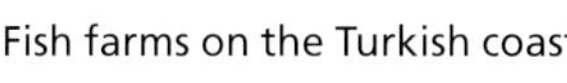

Fish farms on the Turkish coast

### Arrival and departure

Foreign-flagged vessels must fly the Q flag until formalities have been completed in a port of entry.

Yachts must depart from Turkey at an official port of entry, at which time the transit log will be signed out and a copy given to the yacht's captain.

### Travel ashore: taxi, train, plane, road

Everywhere in Turkey public minivans, called *dolmuş*, run very extensive local routes, stopping for passengers along the way. The fare is small and people are friendly. Taxis are found in the larger towns and all cities. Almost invariably they are in good condition, metered, with a courteous and reasonably cautious driver. (However, note that the word to slow down is *Havas*.) Buses are a common form of travel between towns. Like the public transportation system as a whole, buses are convenient, well-regulated and efficient. Good highways now crisscross the country, with an especially big impact along the NE coast, where the new Coastal Highway (the Yeni Yol) has contributed to a great increase in trucks carrying goods and passengers to the Caucasus and Russia, and to Iran and beyond. Airports handle domestic flights from all of the larger cities along the Turkish Black Sea coast.

### Medical

Good medical facilities exist in all the larger Turkish cities along the Black Sea coast, especially Istanbul and including Samsun and Trabzon. But elsewhere along the coast medical services are likely to be impeded by language barriers and a lack of specialists. Turkey is rapidly becoming a centre of excellence marketing medical services to a global market seeking treatment, but such sophistication does not yet reach every little fishing harbour.

### Pets

Dogs and cats need a recent health certificate from the country of origin and a rabies vaccination certificate that shows the animal received the vaccination between two weeks and six months before arrival in Turkey. Only one pet is allowed to be brought in.

### Further reading

Standard tour guides to Turkey give relatively little coverage to the Black Sea coast. An excellent regional guide is by John Freely, *The Black Sea Coast of Turkey*. Freely has gained a large following for his books on Turkey, and this is nice enough to have aboard to be worth spending a day searching for it among the bookstores off Istiklal Cadesi, in Istanbul.

Amasra, Turkey

# Section 1. Bosphorus to Amasra

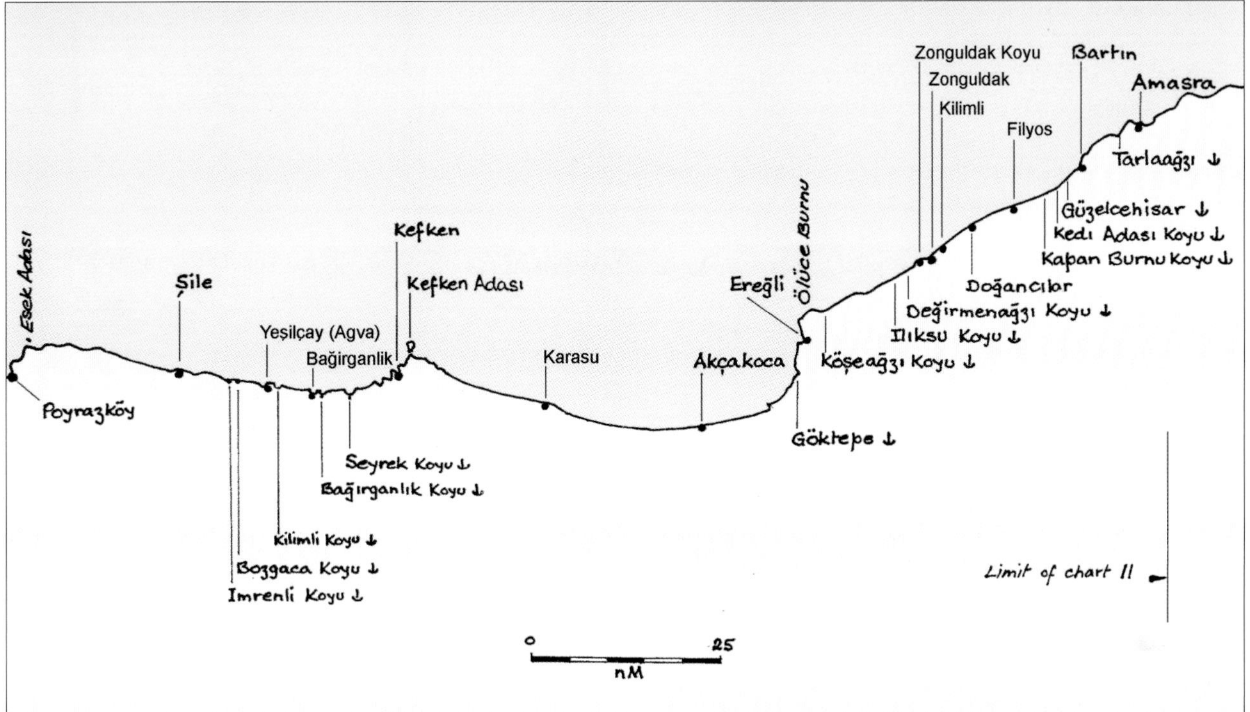


SECTION 1. BOSPHORUS TO AMASRA

Amasra is located about 165M E of the Bosphorus, with at least six harbours suitable for yachts along the way: Şile, Kefken, Akçakoca, Ereğli, Zonguldak and Filyos. The coast of the Bosphorus is cliff-lined for miles to the E, when it starts to become gentler hills. Kefken Adası should be passed well to seaward to avoid offlying rocks. E of Kefken Adası is a 55M long bay that extends to Ölüce Burnu, the prominent headland that protects the industrial port of Ereğli. Akçakoca is the only harbour on the bay. E of Ereğli are Turkey's main coal mines, centred on Zonguldak. Filyos is an off-beat fishing harbour where the only known Greek theatre on the Black Sea is being excavated. Amasra gets top marks from most visitors by yacht.

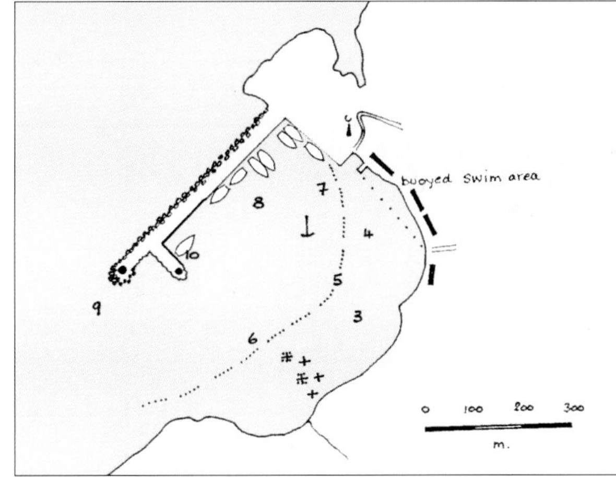


POYRAZKÖY

## POYRAZKÖY

41°12'·2N 29°07'·5E

A fishing harbour located at the N end of the Bosphorus on the Asian side and a good place to find shelter while waiting for suitable weather to enter the Black Sea. The large breakwater is conspicuous from the S. The quays are crowded with fishing boats, so anchoring out is recommended. Anchor in 5–6m inside the harbour keeping clear of the above and below water rocks extending from the S shore. In 2010, this reef was marked with a yellow buoy. Several fish restaurants line the shore. Short walks from the harbour lead to good views of the Bosphorus and the Black Sea. Basic provisions can be found ashore, or for additional shopping options, catch a *dolmuş* from the road along the beach to the nearby village of Anadolu Kavaği. On summer weekends the anchorage is a popular place for local boats from Istanbul.

### *Passage note: Garipçe and the Clashing Rocks*

41°12'·8N 29°06'·7E Garipçe
41°14'·0N 29°07'·0E Clashing Rocks (west side of Bosphorus at entrance to Black Sea)

Poyrazköy is the perfect place (and really the only place) to watch the goings-on at the Clashing Rocks, legendary guardians of the Black Sea. Tim Severin sorted the story out during his stop at Garipçe, just

Poyrazköy

Garipçe

opposite Poyrazköy. He identified Garipçe as the home of Phineas, the local king, endowed with precognition and blinded by Zeus for telling too much about the future. The Argonauts drove off the rapacious seabirds which tormented Phineas, so he repaid them with remarkable sailing directions taking them all the way to Colchis. Just getting into the Black Sea would be the most dangerous step – getting past the Clashing Rocks. Phineas said,

> 'When you leave me, the first thing you will see will be the two Cyanean Rocks at the end of the straits. To the best of my knowledge, no one has ever made his way between them, for not being fixed on the bottom of the sea they frequently collide, flinging up the water in a seething mass which falls on the rocky flanks of the straits with a resounding roar.'

After rowing through it, Tim Severin wrote, 'Much of Apollonius' description does ring true to anyone who navigates the straits in a rowed boat. His description of the swirled eddies between the rocks, the manner in which *Argo* lay helpless in the current – these are dramatised versions of very real difficulties.'

Phineas advised the Greeks to release a dove to fly ahead; if the dove made it through, they could follow, but if it came to grief they should turn back. He also said, 'Remember this, my friends. You have no better ally than that artful goddess, Aphrodite. Indeed, the happy issue of your venture hangs on her.'

At first glance, Phineas's sailing directions have no relevance to modern yachting. He tells them to 'sail on with the land of the Bithynians on your right' and on to the land of the Amazons, all the way to the River Phasis. But nearly all of the places he mentions have been identified and can be visited by yachts. The epic of Jason and the Argonauts still retains an emotional grip on a remarkably large number of people living around the Black Sea today, and many of the places associated with them have been sacred for a very long time.

There is some dispute about the exact location of the Clashing Rocks. Some say that the two are close together, with only a gash between them, as though they had closed together just off the west shore. Others insist that the two on the west shore are only one of the two Clashing Rocks, which froze in the open position, with the East Clashing Rock just off the E shore. The West Clashing Rock has become the backdrop for a restaurant, while the East Clashing Rock remains alone and scarcely noticed across the mouth of the Bosphorus.

Clashing Rocks

Bosphorus control tower

### *Passage note: Kara Burnu (Karaburun)*

41°13'·2N 29°23'·4E

The cape called Kara Burnu in Turkish means 'Black Cape' which was what it was known as in ancient times. (Sailors will come across a very large number of 'Kara Burnu' as they cruise the coast of Turkey – in areas with red rocks 'Kizil Burnu' becomes popular.)

## ŞILE

41°10'·7N 29°36'·0E

A large fishing harbour with room for yachts to tie alongside or raft to fishing boats on the quay inside the N breakwater. Note that children like to jump off the quay and swim in the harbour. Within easy driving distance of Istanbul, the pleasant coastal town of Şile is a popular weekend destination. Although the town is situated on the hillside, you will likely find busy foot traffic on the quay, especially in the evening, and loud music blaring from the all-night disco perched above the harbour. Alternatively, there is plenty of room and more privacy for yachts to anchor out.

### Approach

The approach is straightforward. The ruined castle tower on the offlying islets and rocks is conspicuous from all directions.

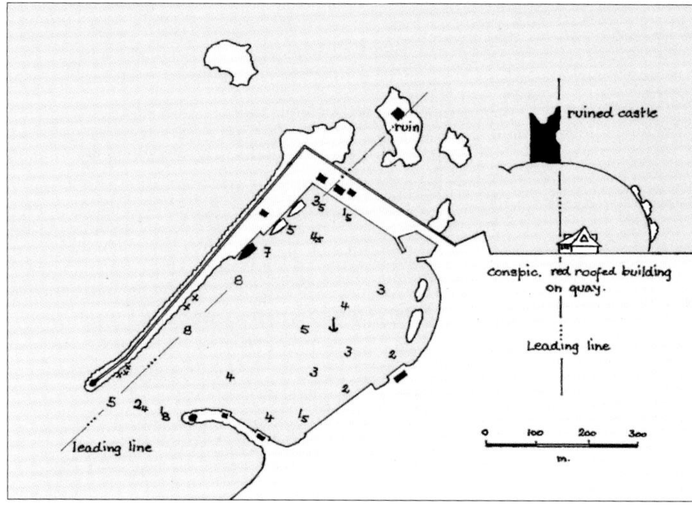


ŞILE

Dangers (1) The sandy bay to the W of the harbour is shallow. (2) A group of small islets and rocks lies to the N and E of the harbour and 0.5M N of the light on Nile Burnu. (3) Some shoaling on the S side of harbour entrance. Favour the N breakwater as you enter. (4) The wreck shown in previous harbour plans in the N portion of the harbour has been removed.

### Mooring

Go alongside or raft off a fishing boat on the outer portion of NW quay taking care to avoid the space reserved for the coastguard near the quayside restaurant boats. There is plenty of room to anchor out in 4–5m. The S quay and the small inner harbour are reserved for fishing boats. Future plans include the development of a small marina on the S side of the harbour; this has been quayed but pontoons have not been installed.

*Shelter* Good all-around shelter. In strong W winds, waves work in and the best shelter can be found by anchoring in S portion of harbour.
*Authorities* Harbourmaster.
*Charges* None.

Şile

### Facilities

*Services* Water from a tap on the NE quay.
*Fuel* Diesel and petrol available in town.
*Repairs* Minor repairs can be arranged through the harbourmaster.
*Provisions* Minimarket and stalls selling limited fresh fruits, vegetables and fish on quay in summer months. All provisions can be found in town. Market days are Thursday and Friday and a daily market is held at the square at the top of town.
*Eating out* Three fishing boats have been converted into floating fish restaurants and are tied alongside the NW quay. Several other restaurants are situated around the harbour. Additional restaurants and cafés can be found in town, some with panoramic seaside views.
*Other* Post office, ATM and Internet cafés in town. Bus station is located at the square in the upper part of town.

### General

Şile was founded by the Greeks in the 7th century BC. It has a Byzantine castle that was used by the Ottomans to protect them from attacks by sea. The black and white striped lighthouse was built by French architects in 1859. Sand dunes backed by pine forests stretch for miles along the coastline. The town is famous for the special cloth woven there: *Şile bezi*, an open weave cloth which is very cool to wear and used for making shirts and blouses. Some tourist guides describe Şile as the site of ancient Calpe, but this is an undocumented claim to fame intended to promote tourism. Ancient descriptions place Calpe closer to the modern-day harbours of Kerpe or Kefken.

## ANCHORAGES AND FISHING HARBOURS BETWEEN ŞILE AND KEFKEN

### ⚓ Imrenli Köyü

41°09'·6N 29°45'·6E

A sandy bay backed by white limestone cliffs, located 9M E of Şile, is reported to be a pleasant lunch stop in settled weather. The swell diminishes somewhat inside the bay.

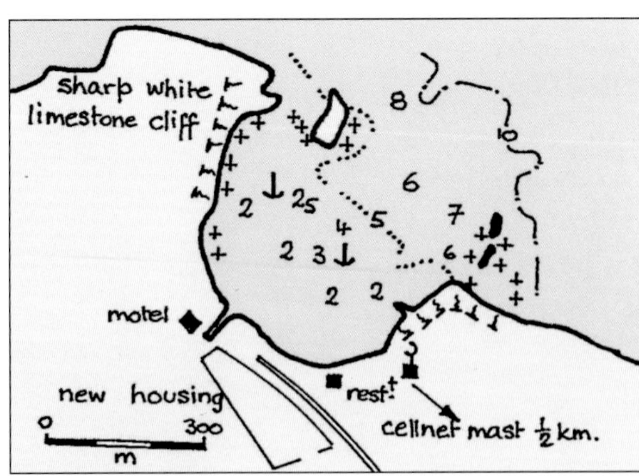


IMRENLI KÖYÜ

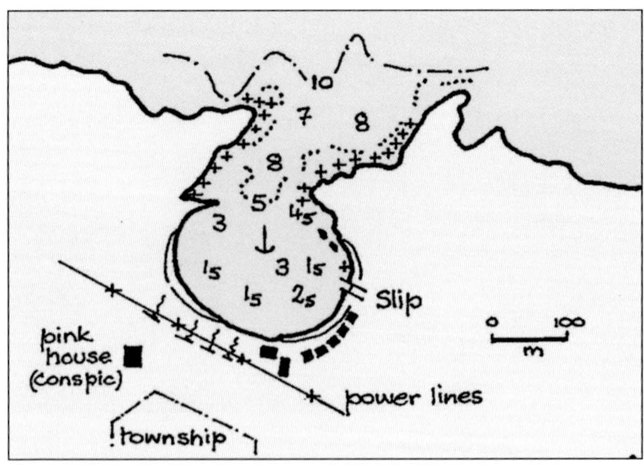


BOZGACA ISKLESI/KÖYÜ

### ⚓ Bozgaca Isklesi/Köyü

41°09'·5N 29°46'·7E

Just over 1M beyond Imrenli Köyü, this horseshoe-shaped bay is reported to have a gently sloping sandy bottom and an attractive beach. The narrow entrance of 60m provides some shelter from the swell. The bay is only suitable for a daytime stop in settled weather.

### ⚓ Yeşilçay (Ağva)

41°08'·5N 29°51'·1E

A river of the same name enters the Black Sea here. It is reported to provide a pleasant, daytime riverside

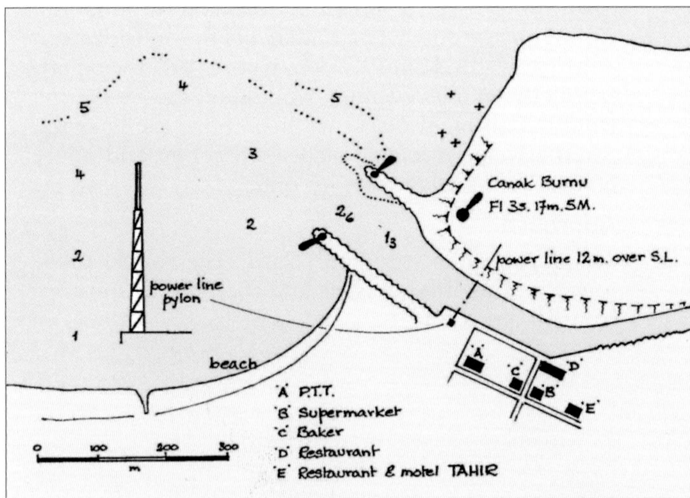


YEŞILÇAY (AĞVA)

Yeşilçay (Ağva)

stop, but shallow depths and a power line with 12m clearance prevent most yachts from entering or passing up the river. The depth of water over the bar at the entrance is dependent on the amount of water flowing in the river and whether the entrance has been dredged. This is not considered a suitable overnight stop for yachts.

## ⚓ Kilimli Köyü

41°08'·4N 29°52'·6E

Just E of Yeşilçay (Ağva), this tiny bay is barely detectable from ¼M off. Clear water for swimming and white shingle beaches are reported to make this a pleasant daytime stop in settled weather, but the bay is subject to the swell.

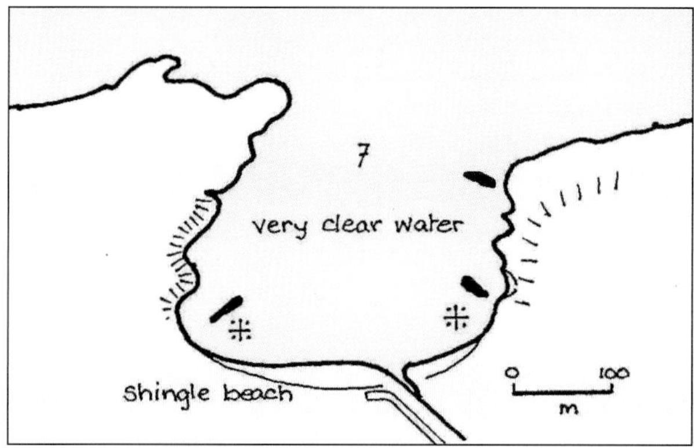


KILIMLI KÖYÜ

## ⚓ Bağirganlik

41°08'·3N 29°59'·9E

A newly completed fishing harbour 22.5M from Şile where a yacht can find shelter if needed. The harbour is now quayed and the extended breakwater should offer much better protection from the wind and swell. Local fishermen are said to be friendly and will make room for visiting yachts.

Bağirganlik

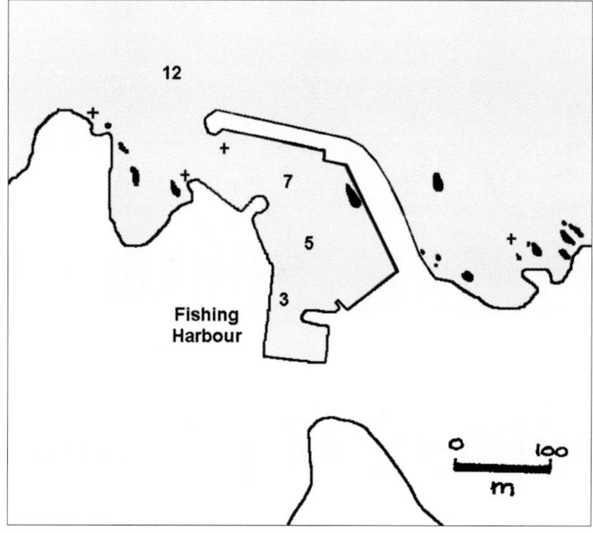


BAĞIRGANLIK

Note: harbour that was under construction in 2001 is now complete with breakwaters and quays. Depths uncertain

## ⚓ Bağirganlik Köyü

41°08'·3N 30°01'·2E

A sandy bay in attractive surroundings to the E of the fishing harbour which can be used for a daytime stop in settled weather. A shoal patch in the middle of the bay is easily seen and shows dark in calm weather.

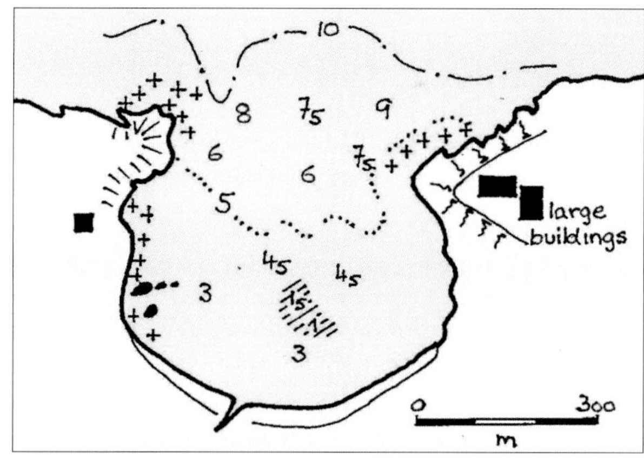


BAHIRGANLIK KÖYÜ

Bağirganlik Köyü

4. TURKEY EAST OF THE BOSPHORUS

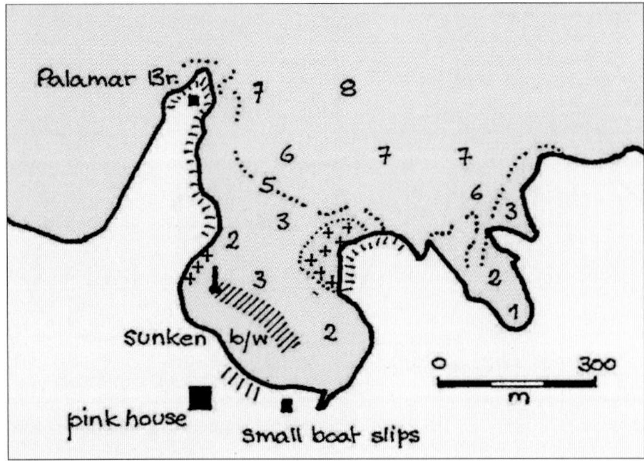


SEYREK KÖYÜ

## ⚓ Seyrek Köyü

41°08'·4'N 30°06'·1E

A small bay lying 28M E of Şile with a sunken breakwater behind which small boats are pulled up on the beach. The bay offers no shelter and is only suitable for a daytime stop in calm weather.

## ⚓ Kerpe

41°9'·5N 30°11'·1E

A bay open to the N and W which was used as an anchorage in ancient times before the modern fishing and military harbours at Kefken were constructed. Uncharted rocks are reported in the bay.

Kerpe is a W-facing cove on the Kefken Peninsula, S of Kefken harbour. The ancient Greeks called this Calpe, and it was apparently already established in some form before the Greek general Xenophon led an army of 10,000 Greek mercenaries here in 400 BC. He wrote:

> 'Calpe Harbour is in Thrace, in the part that is in Asia. Beginning from the mouth of the Pontus [the Bosphorus], this part of Thrace extends as far as Heracleia [modern Ereğli], on the right as one sails into the Pontus [Black Sea]. For a trireme using its oars it is a very long day's sail from Byzantium to Heracleia. In between there is no other city either friendly or Greek but only Bithynian Thracians, and these are said to treat with terrible insolence any Greek they take, whether they fall into their hand through shipwreck or in any other way. For those who are sailing between Heracleia and Byzantium, Calpe Harbour lies in the middle between both. There is a piece of land that juts out into the sea, with the part of it reaching down into the sea being sheer rock, no less than 20 fathoms [120 feet] in height at its lowest point, with the neck of the land that connects to the mainland being about four plethora [400 feet] in width. The land on the sea side of the neck is sufficient for ten thousand people to inhabit. The harbour is beneath the rock itself and has a beach facing toward the west. A spring of sweet water flows abundantly right beside the sea but is subject to control from the land above. There is also a great deal of wood of various sorts, but there is especially abundant and fine wood for shipbuilding right beside the sea. The mountain extends up into the interior as far as about twenty stadia [about 3.5 km] and it is loamy and free from stones, while the part beside the sea extends more than twenty stadia, thick with many tall trees of all sorts. The rest of the land is beautiful and vast, and there are many and well-inhabited villages in it. The land bears barley, wheat, all sorts of beans, millet, sesame, sufficient figs, many grapes, pleasant wines, and all other things except olives.'

Kerpe

## KEFKEN

41°10'·2N 30°13'·3E

### Approach

The approach is straightforward from the S or SW. Give the rocks off Burunuç Burnu a wide berth. The breakwater for the fishing harbour is difficult to see when approaching from the W, but light towers and tall radio antennas just S of the town are conspicuous. From the E, the breakwater and town are not visible until after rounding Kefken Adası and passing the military harbour just N of Kefken's fishing harbour. The military harbour, with a breakwater and guard tower in the bay to the N of

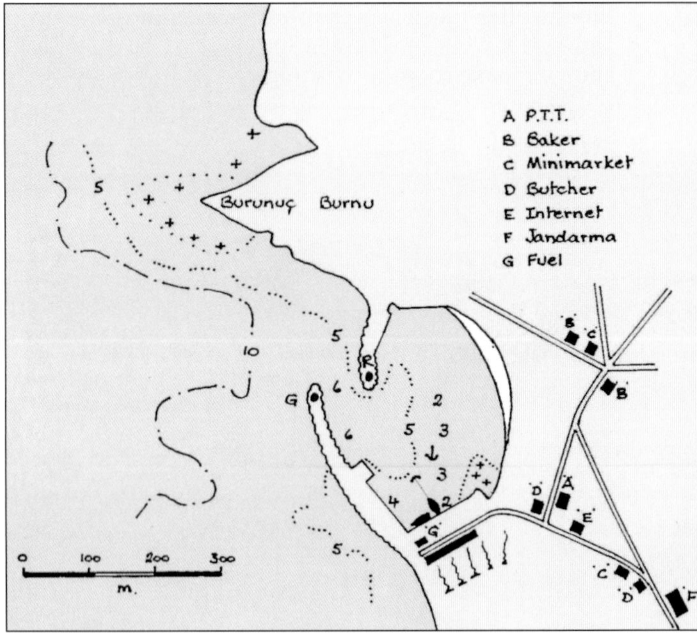


KEFKEN

Kefken's fishing harbour, is closed to yachts except in an emergency.

Dangers (1) Rocks off Burunuç Burnu, the point NW of the harbour entrance. (2) The lights on the end of the breakwaters were not working in 2010.

### Mooring

The harbour is busy with fishing boats in the summer. A few motor yachts lie on moorings in the harbour. Moor alongside or rafted off fishing boats in 2–3m on the concrete quay in the S portion of the harbour or anchor out in 3–4m. Keep clear of shoal water near beach on E side of harbour and rocks in the SE corner.

*Shelter* Good shelter from all but NW, when the best shelter is on the N side of the harbour, where you can raft off fishing boats with permission.

*Authorities* The harbourmaster's office is up a flight of steps opposite the quayside restaurant. The fishing cooperative office is on the quay. No requirement to check in, but if you moor alongside the quay, you may want to make a courtesy visit to the Cooperative office.

*Charges* None.

### Facilities

*Services* Water on S quay.

*Fuel* By jerry can and taxi.

*Repairs* Three marine railways on the N side of harbour. All technical services for fishing boats, including welding and carpentry, are available.

*Provisions* Small supermarkets, minimarkets, butchers, bakeries, and fish market in town.

*Eating out* Several simple restaurants and small cafés serving fish and Turkish specialities in town.

*Other* Turkish gas at shops near the harbour. ATM, Internet café and mobile phone top-up in town. *Dolmuş* to neighbouring towns.

### General

A small and somewhat crowded fishing harbour which is full of fishing boats. Like many of the fishing harbours along the Turkish coast, the largest boats raft up and conduct maintenance in the off-season from May–August. A number of smaller, private fishing boats go out every day to fish with nets or to dive for *rapana*, a whelk species which was accidentally introduced to the Black Sea through the ballast water of ships. Now commercially harvested, *rapana* are offloaded in red mesh bags onto a truck on the S quay. Yachts are welcomed but there are no facilities tailored to yachts. It is pleasant to stroll through the quiet fishing village or to walk up to the overlook on the hill at the S side of the harbour or along the long stretch of sandy beach beyond. Much of the growth in this small town in recent years is due to holiday home development along this beach.

Kefken

Kefken

## ⚓ KEFKEN ADASI

41°12'·6N 30°15'·3E

The anchorage at Kefken Adası is an alternative to the fishing harbour at Kefken and is protected by two long breakwaters extending S from the island. The fish farm which used to occupy the NE portion of the anchorage and reportedly looked like a giant octopus has been removed, but some gear may remain on the bottom in this area, where there have been reports of poor holding and snagging anchor. Both the location of this former fish farm and the rocky substrate in the NW portion of the anchorage should be avoided. Anchor in 5–6m to the E of the

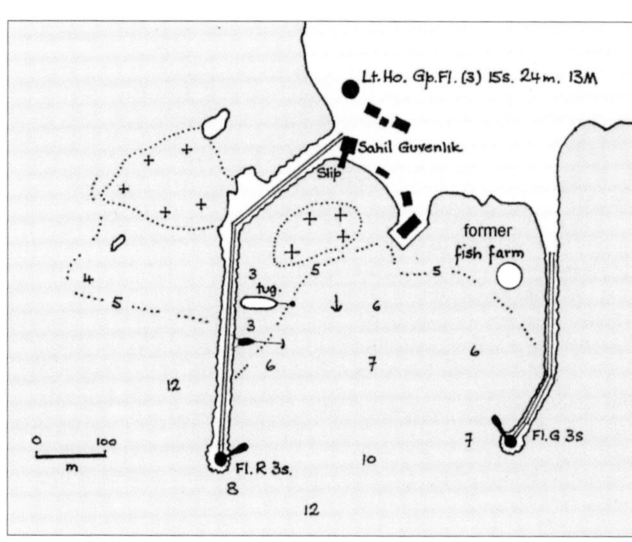


KEFKEN ADASI

### Apollonia

In his sailing directions to the Argonauts, Phineas mentioned the Isle of Thynias, a place where Bithynians lived. When they reached the island, the Argonauts experienced a vision of Apollo which led to the Greeks renaming the island Apollonia. Apollonius of Rhodes wrote:

> 'The crew of *Argo* all through the night ploughed the salt water with their oars. But at that time of day when heavenly light has not yet come, nor is there utter darkness, but the faint glimmer that we call twilight spreads over the night and wakes us, they ran into the harbour of the lonely isle of Thynias and went ashore exhausted by their labours.
>
> Here they had a vision of Apollo on his way from Lycia to visit the remote and teeming peoples of the North. The golden locks streamed down his cheeks in clusters as he moved; he had a silver bow in his left hand and a quiver slung on his back; the island quaked beneath his feet and the seas ran high on the shore. They were awe-struck at the sight and no one dared to face the god and meet his lovely eyes. They stood there with bowed heads while he, aloft, passed through the air on his way across the sea.
>
> Orpheus found his voice at last. 'Come now,' he said to the Argonauts, 'let us dedicate this island to Apollo of the Dawn and call it by that name, since it was here that we all saw him pass by in the dawn. We will build an altar on the shore and make such offerings as we have at our command. Now, let us propitiate him as best we can, with libations and the scent of burnt offerings. Lord of the Vision, look kindly upon us.'

After the Argonauts had built an altar with shingle, sacrificed a wild animal on it, and worshipped Apollo with dance and song, they swore an oath to stand by one another in unity forever. A millennium later, Apollonius of Rhodes claimed that the 'temple of Concord' that they built could still be seen 'to this very day', in 250 BC.

The Isle of Thynias became known as Apollonia, until acquiring its modern name, Kefken Adasi. We found no trace of the temple of Concord during our visit to the island. Regrettably, we know of no publication about archaeological surveys here. But one of us experienced a vision of Apollo at Dawn, an extraordinary celestial gift accessible to early risers on clear summer mornings.

Kefken Adası

Sahil Güvenlik (coastguard) vessel and SW of the concrete pier which extends into the middle of the harbour. The harbour is open to the SW and is not a pleasant place to be if an afternoon thunderstorm rolls off the mainland with gusty S winds. In settled weather, Kefken Adası is a remote and peaceful place to anchor out. The lighthouse facility serves as a Sahil Güvenlik station, and the staff are friendly to visitors who come ashore to explore the island.

Danger Do not pass between Kefken Adası and the mainland on passage E or W. It is recommended that yachts pass to the N of the island and give it a 1M berth. Since a major earthquake in 1999, depths are uncertain in this area as noted in the following Turkish coastguard Warning: 'substantial changes occurred in the sea bed and the charts of the area around the island are no longer accurate. The E passage between the island and the mainland is no longer recommended due to many rock pinnacles which have appeared.'

## SAKARYA RIVER

41°8'·1N 30°38'·9E (river mouth)

Sakarya River

Karasu

## ⚓ Karasu (Sakarya) Shipbuilding Harbour

41°07'·5N 30°40'·5E

A very large breakwater was completed in 2010 to protect the newly-constructed Gündoğdu Shipyard, which now occupies 65,000m² and is planned to be expanded to 95,000m² in coming years. What was described as a new harbour under construction in June 2001 is now a large, empty harbour where a yacht can find shelter from the prevailing wind and swell if needed. Since 2001, the earlier breakwaters have served as reinforced boundaries of a landfill upon which the new shipyard has been built, and the outer breakwater has been substantially lengthened. Depths of 6–8·5m can be found inside the breakwater. The harbour is open to the E.

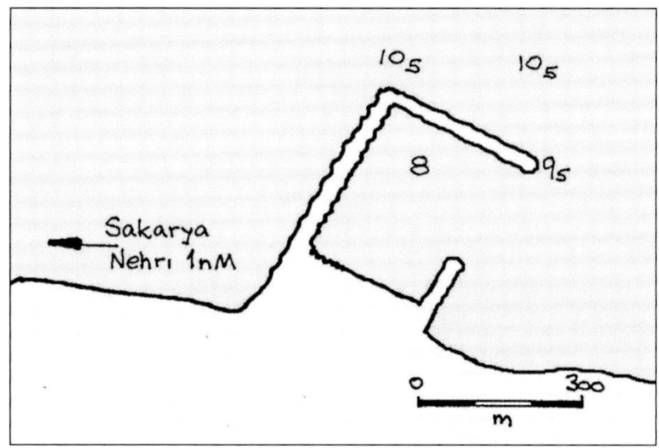

KARASU

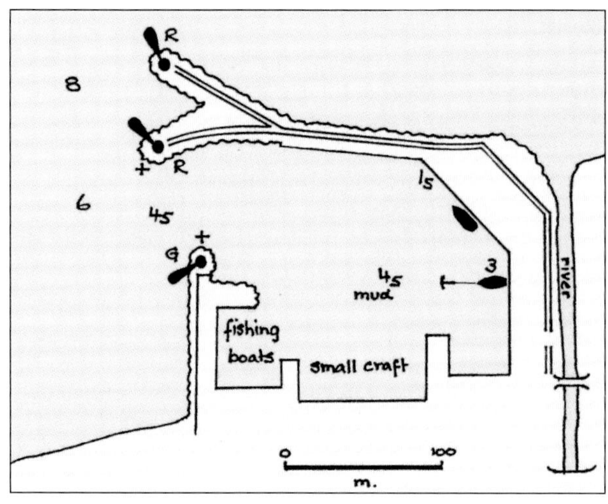

AKÇAKOCA

Akçakoca harbour entrance

## AKÇAKOCA

41°05'·5N 31°07'·1E

### Approach

The approach is straightforward. From the W, the breakwaters are easily seen, as are the high cliffs to the W of the harbour entrance. From all directions, two large minarets (looking like space-age rockets up close) and the town are conspicuous.

Danger In strong NW winds, the harbour entrance may be difficult and better shelter can be found in Karasu (to the W) or Ereğli (to the E).

Akçakoca

### Mooring

This is mainly a fishing harbour for small and medium-sized fishing boats, but visiting yachts are welcome. From the entrance, continue straight ahead toward the green-and-white striped awning of a small fish restaurant in the harbour, Balikçim. The owner, Fahrettin Karacan, will help you with your lines. Anchor in 4m of mud with very good holding and room for several yachts either stern- or bow-to the quay or fewer tied up alongside in 3m, as space allows.

*Shelter* Shelter is good from all directions except the W. It is reported that even in moderate W or NW winds, the swell sets in. Smaller yachts may be able to find shelter among the fishing boats in these conditions.

*Charges* None.

### Facilities

Limited facilities for visiting yachts, but all basic needs can be met.

*Services* Water on quay. Electricity by special arrangement with one of the restaurants.

*Fuel* By tanker delivery or jerry can and taxi from fuel station in town.

*Repairs* Basic mechanical and electrical repairs.

*Provisions* Several small supermarkets in town; one is conveniently located near the mosque. Look for the round loaves of rustic sourdough bread at this supermarket or at the small bakery near the mosque. Other bakers, butchers, greengrocers and fish markets within a few blocks of the harbour area. A weekly market is held on Tuesdays in a covered market 0·5km to the S of the harbour on the road that runs along the E side of the river.

*Eating out* Simple fish restaurants in the harbour area where you can watch the sunset and several other restaurants and cafés in town.

*Other* Post office, banks and ATMs near the harbour. Taxis and *dolmuş* service to neighbouring towns.

### General

The modern name of this place means 'White Beard'. In ancient times it was known as Lilaion, or Lillium. The Roman governor Arrian noted that there was an emporium here, a staging post for coastal merchant ships. This ancient tradition is still visible in the ornate pier which dominates the harbour and in the large local market which is still active today. The harbour is situated next to the traditional village centre, around which a larger, modern town has grown. Some of the many large modern buildings are entirely empty. There are parks and gardens along the waterfront. This is a pleasant town with friendly local people who are very welcoming to visiting foreign yachts. Attractive surroundings include steep cliffs along waterfront to the W of the harbour. Three kilometres from the harbour is a beautiful beach which has been designated as a Blue Flag for cleanliness.

### *Passage note: Akçakoca to Ereğli: Offshore gas tripods*

Production began in 2007 from three tripods offshore between Akçakoca and Ereğli. They are owned by the Turkish Oil and Gas Corp. (TPAO) with Toreador Resources (Dallas) and Stratic Energy (Calgary). Their names and locations are:

Ayazli 41°09'·8N 31°06'·2E
Dogu Ayazli 41°09'·7N 31°08'·5E
Akkaya 41°10'·2N 31°13'·0E

Offshore gas platform

## ALAPLI

41°11'·7N 31°23'·1E

This fishing harbour has reportedly silted to less than 1m depths and is not recommended for yachts.

### ⚓ Göktepe

41°13'·3N 31°24'·0E

A naturally sheltered bay where a yacht can anchor. The status of constructing a 300-berth marina associated with the holiday resort development is uncertain.

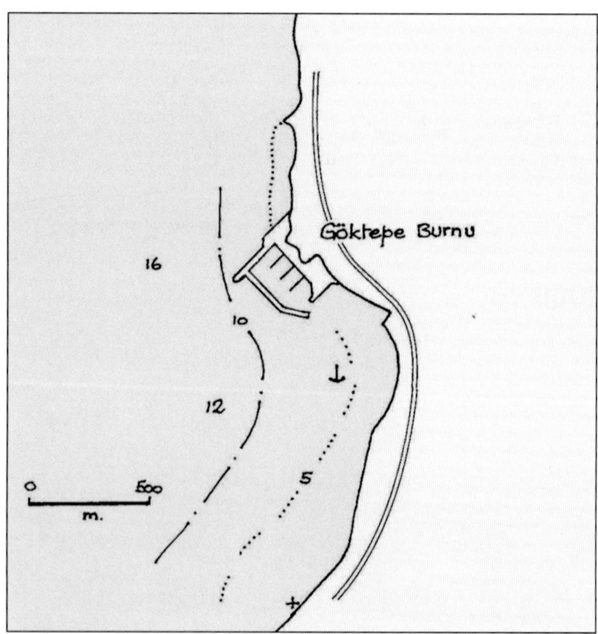


**GÖKTEPE**

Note: status of planned harbour construction is uncertain

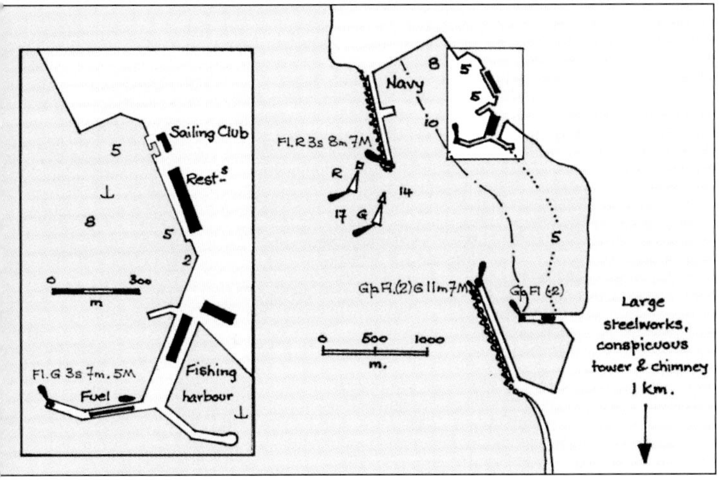


EREĞLI

Ereğli fishing harbour

## EREĞLİ

41°16'·8N 31°24'·1E

### Approach

From the W, the city and steelworks can be seen from a distance, but the harbour entrance is difficult to see until closer in. From the E, the harbour and entrance is not visible until rounding Ölüce Burnu (also known as Baba Burnu). A significant change in wind direction and strength is common around this cape when approaching or leaving Ereğli. There are no dangers in the approach, and the buoys in the approach can be ignored by yachts. From the S, a second commercial harbour, which is not suitable for yachts, can be found at: 41°14'·3N 31°23'·6E.

*Conspicuous* The city itself and smoke-stacks on steel works in the S portion of the harbour, and ships anchored off the harbour entrance, are conspicuous when approaching from the W.

*VHF* Ch 16 for harbourmaster. No requirement to call.

### Mooring

The large commercial harbour does not have a dedicated yacht harbour, but visiting yachts are welcome. There is a large fleet of small and medium-sized fishing boats which use the designated fishing harbour. This is not a place for yachts, except that space may be arranged when shelter is needed from strong SW winds. The sailing club has one yacht on a mooring in front of their clubhouse.

A yacht should make for the N harbour as the S part is for the steelworks and fishing boats. Anchor in 6m just N of the smaller inner harbour and to the W of the sailing club, distinguished by a small concrete apron for launching sailing dinghies and a building with large, round windows. From this position, you will also see a pink building on the shore at the base of the commercial quay. It is also possible to anchor to the S of the fishing harbour. Otherwise, it may be possible to moor stern-to or alongside the quay in the inner harbour next to the fuel dock if space is available. There are large tyres along this quay and some boat wash, so large fenders are necessary. If you tie up to this quay or take on fuel, the harbourmaster may ask to see your ship's papers. Anchoring near the naval facility in the N portion of the harbour is prohibited, and a yacht will be instructed to leave.

*Shelter* Good all-round shelter but the large size of the harbour and ship movements cause boat wash and surge.

*Authorities* Port of entry. Harbourmaster and health office at the fishing harbour. Police in pink building adjacent to fuel dock and anchorage.

*Charges* None.

*Contact information* If you stop by the local sailing club, you will find enthusiastic young sailors and coaches and a club president who will help with any needs, including free Wi-Fi, making appointments at the old *hamam* or giving you directions to the Hercules cave, described below.

### Facilities

*Services* Water at the fuel dock. Toilets and showers may be available at the Sailing Club.

*Fuel* Available at the fuel dock.

*Repairs* Most repairs are possible at the adjacent shipyards.

*Provisions* All provisions can be found ashore. The main shopping area is a 10-minute walk S along the harbour road. Market days are Monday and Friday.

*Eating out* Many restaurants, cafés and bars can be found along the waterfront and in town. Several good fish restaurants are located next to the fishing harbour on the broad quay which separates the two sides of the inner harbour.

*Other* Post office, Turkish gaz, banks and ATMs available in town. Internet at sailing club or at internet cafés in town. Long-distance buses at fuel station on the harbour road to the S of the river. *Dolmuş* and taxis available in town.

### General

The large, industrial city and commercial harbour is home to the largest steelworks in Turkey, located in the S portion of the harbour. The city itself is beautifully landscaped with gardens and a harbourside promenade lined with cafés and restaurants. There are nice views from the top of Kaletepe. An old *haman* is located across the road from the fishing harbour. A naval facility is located

Baba Burnu (Ölüce Burnu)

at the N end of the harbour. The Ereğli Iron and Steelworks Company is known as Erdemir. It produces three million tonnes of crude steel, 3·5 million tonnes of flat steel and also rolled steel and steel pipes. It is the largest steel mill in Turkey. The government owns a 46% share. The population of the town is 75,000. It seems to be a prosperous place.

***Passage note: Baba Burnu (Ölüce Burnu)***

The promontory is known as Ölüce Burnu or, more commonly, Baba Burnu, at position 41°19′·0N 31°24′·0E. It was known in ancient times as Promentorium Acherusias.

The Turkish name Ereğli sounds like Hereleia, which sounds a lot like its ancient name, Heracleia, a community dedicated to the greatest hero, Heracles. It was here that Heracles performed his 12th and final labour, to capture alive the three-headed dog Cerberus, guarding the entrance to Hades, the underworld. As Apollonius of Rhodes recounted it, a few days after their vision of Apollo at Dawn, the Argonauts

> 'with thankful hearts ... made harbour at dawn by the Cape of Acherusias. This lofty headland, with its sheer cliffs, looks out across the Bithynian Sea... On the landward side, it falls away into a hollow glen. Here is the Cavern of Hades with its overhanging trees and rocks, from the chill depths of which an icy breath comes up and each morning covers everything with sparkling rime that melts under the midday sun.'

For many years the promontory and its caves were under the control of the Turkish military, but they were recently released to civilian use as a tourist destination. To reach the caves today, follow the harbour road to the N end of the harbour and look for signs to the entrance on your right.

Farther E, even beyond Zonguldak, water in the near-shore areas is badly polluted by the coal mining along this coast.

Baba Burnu (Ölüce Burnu)

## ⚓ Köşeağzi Köyü

41°19′·8N 31°27′·8E

A double bay E of Ereğli, with steep cliffs and caves, which is suitable for a daytime stop in settled weather. The water is sometimes stained brown from coal washing operations along the coast.

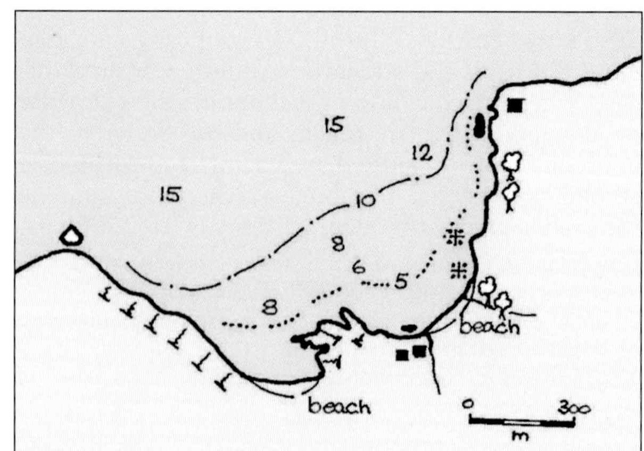


KÖŞEAĞZI KÖYÜ

## ⚓ Iliksu Köyü

41°24'·7N 31°40'·9E

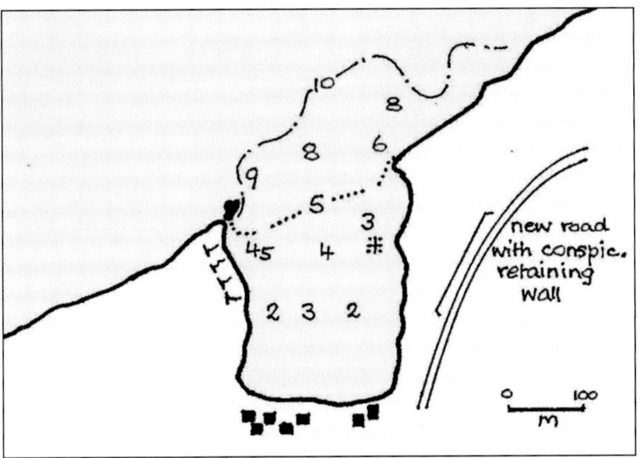


ILIKSU KÖYÜ

A bay backed by white cliffs which is suitable for a daytime stop in settled weather, but air photos indicate that sediment plumes from coal washing operations along the coast work into the harbour.

## ⚓ Değirmenağzi Köyü

41°25'·6N 31°43'·2E

This small bay is quite hidden on approach from the W. In 2001, this was described as a 'gem' providing good shelter from the W and with no swell. But since then, the 'gem' has been discovered and a new apartment building is being constructed near the beach, and the coastal road heading W from Zonguldak has been widened and is just behind the beach. The bay remains a popular spot for local people to swim, but air photos indicate that sediment plumes from coal washing operations along the coast work into the harbour.

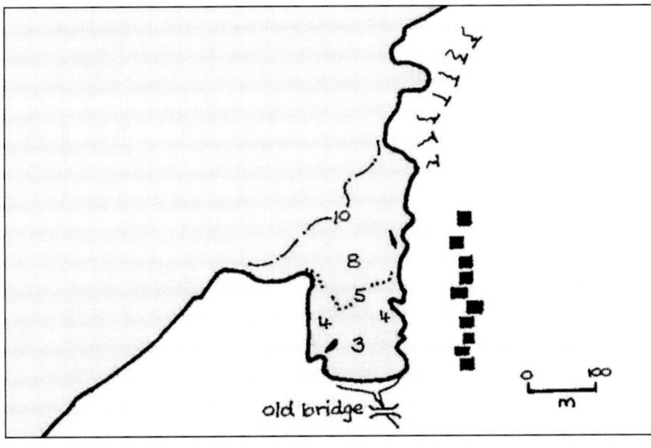


DEĞIRMENAĞZI KÖYÜ

Değirmenağzi Köyü

## KOZLU ZONGULDAK

41°26'·4N 31°44'·6E

A new fishing harbour, completed since 2001, is located 2M W of Zonguldak. It offers good all-around shelter and 9m depths at the entrance. Tie up alongside the pier or quay on the E side of the harbour. Alternatively anchor out in the harbour. A Total gas station is conveniently located next to the harbour. On the outskirts of Zonguldak, there is nothing of note ashore.

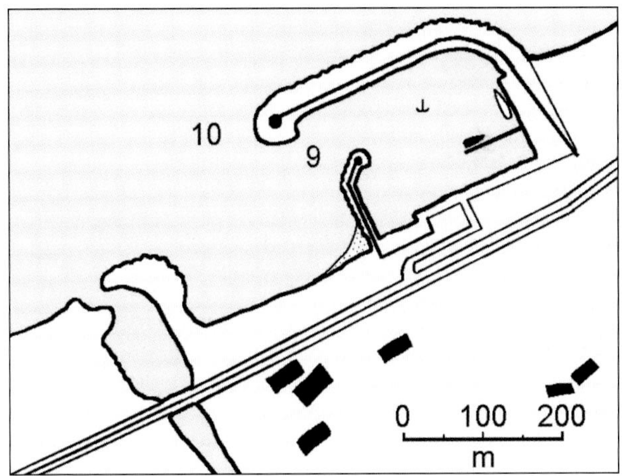


KOZLU ZONGULDAK

Kozlu Zonguldak

4. TURKEY EAST OF THE BOSPHORUS

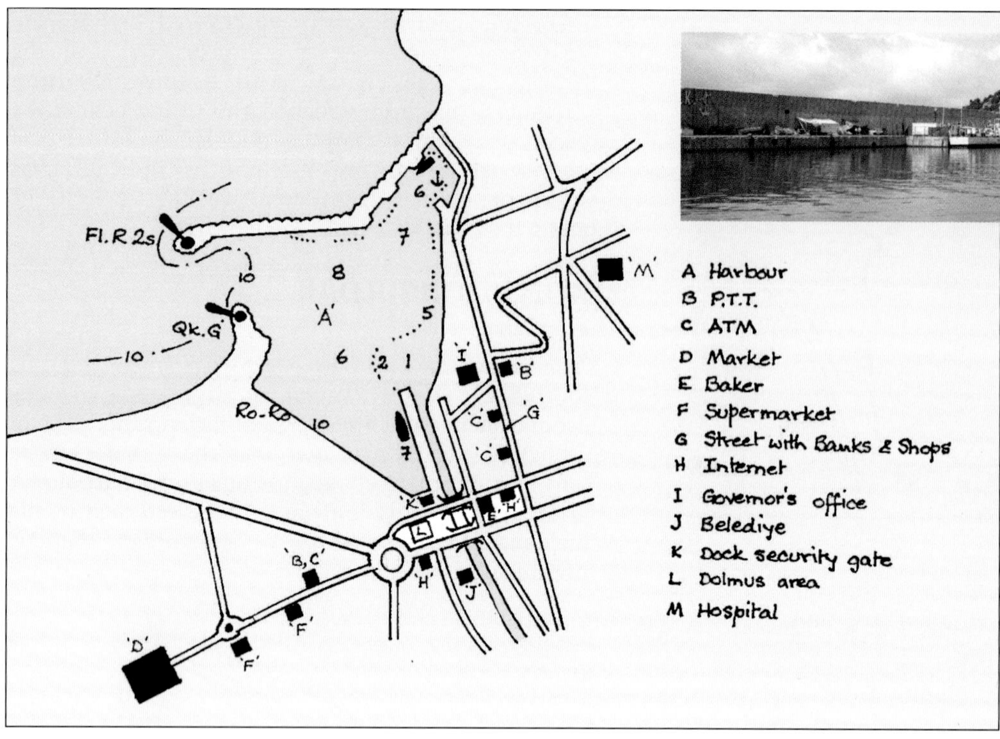


Zonguldak. Sahil Güvenlik (Coastguard)

## ZONGULDAK

41°27'·6N 31°46'·7E

A dirty commercial harbour in the heart of Turkey's coalmining area. Yachts are welcome but facilities are limited. The harbour is run-down and coal dust covers everything, including the quays. However, the city is pleasant once ashore. For a quieter and cleaner option along this coast, try the fishing harbour at Filyos, 14M to the NE.

### Approach

The approach is straightforward. The lights on the ends of the breakwater are visible on approach from the E or W. Large RoRo ferries inside this commercial and fishing harbour are also seen in the approaches.

### Mooring

Fishing boats occupy the N quay and are moored or pulled up along the E shore. Berth alongside a fishing boat on the N quay with permission or anchor out in the NE part of the harbour in 6m, although space is limited. There is a report of debris on the bottom in this area which scraped the bottom and caused damage to a yacht drawing 2m while at anchor in Zonguldak. Good all-around shelter. The harbourmaster may request to see ship's papers. No harbour charges reported.

### Facilities

Very limited.

*Fuel* Available by jerry can from fuel stations in the city.

*Repairs* Minor mechanical and electrical repairs can be arranged through the harbourmaster.

*Provisions* All provisions can be found in the city. A large open-air market operates on Wednesday and Saturday.

*Eating out* Many cafés and restaurants in the harbour area, especially around the small fishing harbour and in the city.

*Other* Post office, banks, ATMs and internet cafés throughout the city. *Dolmuş* service within the city. International airport with flights to London and domestic flights to Istanbul serving people who come to the city for medical treatments. RoRo ferry service to Yevpatoria and Skadovsk in the Ukraine.

### General

With a population of 106,000, Zonguldak offers little for the visiting yachtsman except a well protected harbour along this stretch of coast. Coal mining began in this area in 1829 and continues today, as you will no doubt notice in the change in water quality and visible dumping areas along the coast. Once ashore, the town is quite pleasant and bustles with activity. Nearby sights of interest include: the Seven Lakes natural area and spectacular caves now open to the public, including the Cumayani Cave which is famous for its length and the Gokgol and Sofular Caves which are known for their travartens. In ancient times, Zonguldak was known as Sandarake, or Sandrace, but not a trace of its Greek origin remains.

Zonguldak

Kilimli

Kilimli

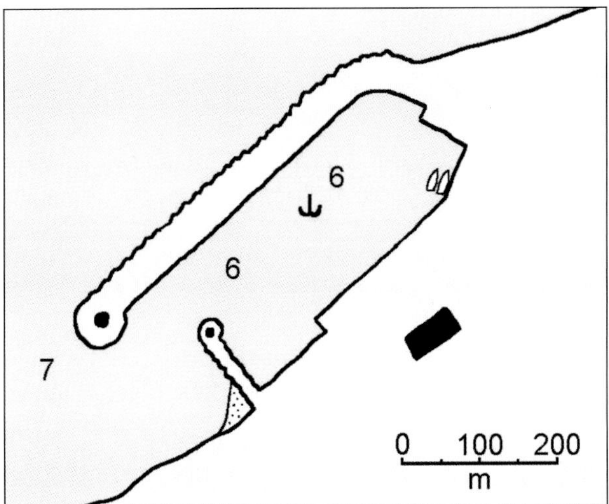


KILIMLI

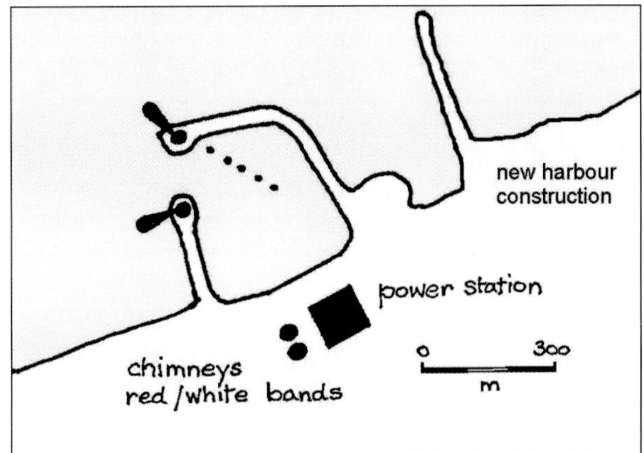


DOĞANCILAR

Doğancilar power plant

## KILIMLI

41°29′·8N 31°50′·4E

A newly constructed fishing harbour E of Zonguldak with 6–6·5m depths inside, which could be used by yachts, space permitting.

## ⚓ Doğancilar

41°31′·5N 31°53′·7E

This is a huge power station with a breakwater. The red and white banded smoke stacks and the breakwaters are conspicuous from all directions. The harbour is privately owned by the power company, provides excellent shelter and could be used in an emergency.

A large new port is being constructed immediately to the E of it, apparently for handling coal, in position: 41°31′·7N 31°54′·3E. This is not suitable for yachts.

## FILYOS (HISARÖNÜ)

41°33′·8N 32°01′·1E

A new harbour located 34M E of Ereğli, is marked 'Hisarönü' on C-Map and Admiralty charts, but it is known locally as Filyos. The fishing harbour was built on the site of an ancient one and offers a protected overnight anchorage for yachts in a small and somewhat scruffy town on the TCDD railway line from Ereğli. A substantial new breakwater has been constructed within the past few years, making it one of the most secure harbours along this coast.

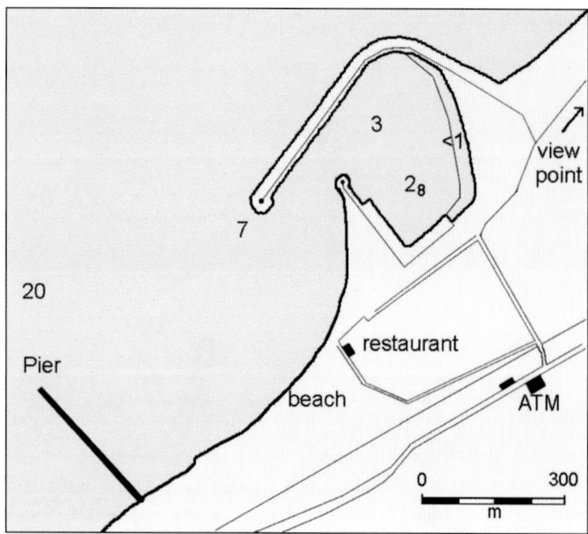


FILYOS (HISARÖNÜ)

Filyos (Hisarönü)

## Approach

From the W, an abandoned steel commercial pier extends several hundred metres into the sea, W of the harbour entrance. The town and the old fort on the headland to the E of the harbour are clearly visible.

Danger Rounding the headland of Hisar Burun from the E, give a wide berth to the Filyos River mouth because of silting. The small lighthouses on the breakwaters may not be lit at night.

## Mooring

The quays are reserved for local fishing boats. All of this area is taken up by small and medium-sized fishing boats and a vessel which is actively being used in offshore gas exploratory surveys. More small fishing boats are pulled up onto the beach. Anchor in 4m where convenient, taking care to avoid shallow water off the SE beach. Good holding in mud. The harbour provides excellent shelter from wind and swell. No harbour charges.

## Facilities

Very limited facilities for visiting yachts but a safe and comfortable place to spend the night. People in town are becoming more accustomed to visiting yachts as word gets out about the harbour. They are very friendly and accommodating. The children in town are especially curious, and some have apparently been given small amounts of money in exchange for services as a 'guide'. For provisions, you will find small supermarkets, minimarkets and bakeries in town as well as a hardware store, Aygaz store. The post office and ATM are located near the TCDD train station with service to Zonguldak. Options for eating out are limited to a few simple restaurants and cafés. A stroll on the promenade along the beach to the ruins of a fort on the headland offers good views of the town and the Filyos River beyond.

## General

Filyos is a new fishing harbour with ancient history. Arrian called it 'Tios, an Ionian Greek city, built on the sea, and a colony of the Milesians.' There are recent reports of important archeological finds on the headland, including the only remains of a Greek theatre on the entire Black Sea coast.

### *Passage note: Filyos to Amasra*

After passing the mouth of the Filyos River E of the harbour, you will pass several bays suitable for daytime stops in settled weather, including one which offers good shelter from NE winds if needed – the Bartin River and associated commercial/military harbour and the small harbour of Tarlaağzi Köyü – before reaching the large and picturesque harbour of Amasra.

Filyos (Hisarönü)

## ⚓ Kapan Burnu Köyü

41°35′·9N 32°07′·3E

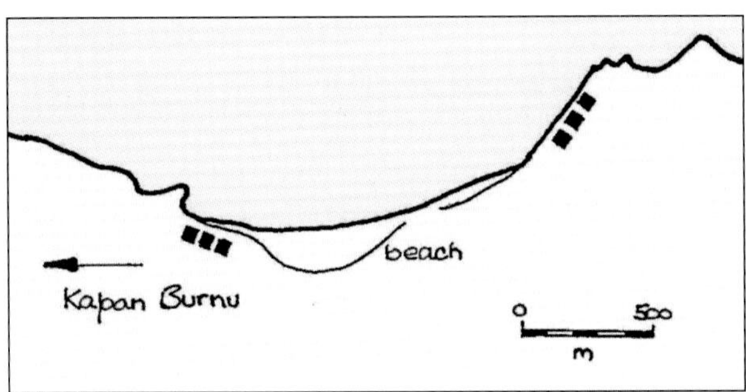


KAPAN BURNU KÖYÜ

An open bay with a beach which is reported to be suitable for a short stop in settled weather. Not suitable as an overnight anchorage.

## ⚓ Kedi Adası Köyü

41°36′·7N 32°09′·1E

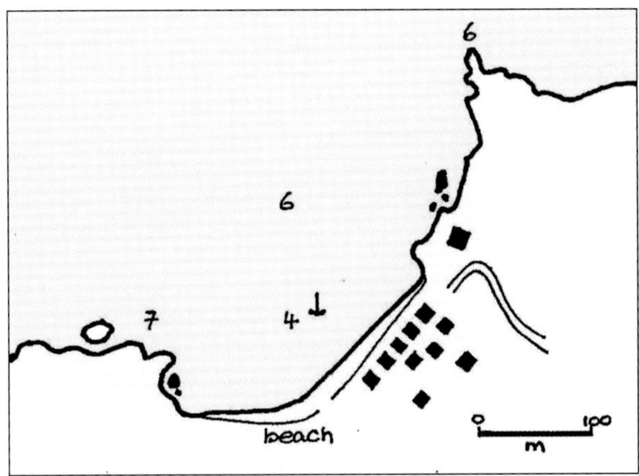


KEDI ADASI KÖYÜ

An open bay with sandy beach which is reported to be a pleasant daytime stop and popular with holidaymakers. Anchor in 4m where shown on the plan. Not a suitable overnight anchorage.

## ⚓ Güzelce Hisar Köyü

41°38′·1N 32°10′·6E

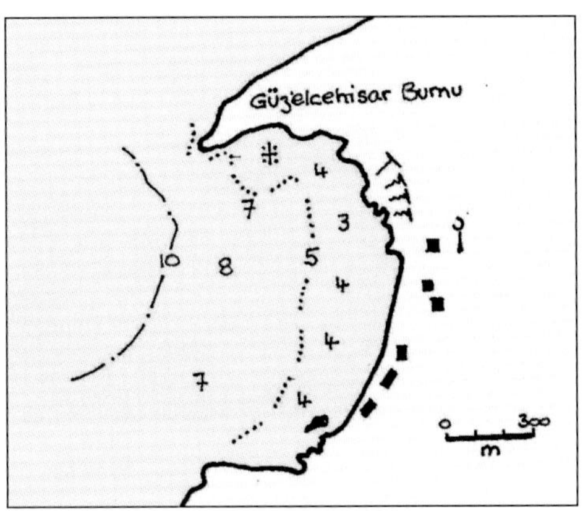


An open bay backed by cliffs and a small village which is reported to offer some protection from NE winds. Open to the W.

GÜZELCE HISAR KÖYÜ

## BARTIN RIVER (BARTIN ÇAYI) and BARTIN LIMANI

41°41′·1N 32°13′·4E

The S breakwater of the restricted Bartin Limani Commercial and Military Harbour serves as the entry point for the Bartin River. The town of Bartin, with a population of 35,000, is located 10km up the river. If a yacht is not restricted by the overhead cables which cross the river near the entrance, it is possible to travel upriver to the first bridge. The main wires are 26m above the water, but lower wires are estimated to be only 14m above the water. Yachts up to 14m in length and drawing 2m have reported passing under the wires near the river entrance and finding a berth alongside a quay at the first bridge. Others have made brief visits into the river and indicated that there is room to anchor once inside. From the first bridge, it is possible to make a dinghy excursion up the river to the town, which is famous for its women's market held on Tuesday and Friday. Bartin can also be visited from Amasra by *dolmuş* which passes through the town where you change buses to reach Safronbolu.

The Bartin River (Bartın) was known to the Greeks as Parthenius, referring to the virgin goddess of hunting, Artemis. Apollonius wrote that the Argonauts passed the spot 'where the Parthenius flows out to the sea; a gentle river this, in whose delectable waters Artemis refreshes herself before ascending to heaven after the chase.'

In former times, the river mouth was bounded on both sides by steep cliffs opening out at about 45° angles. In recent years the river mouth has become a wonder of civil engineering, with a huge breakwater extending N from the E bank of the river and another breakwater extending W from the E bank, forming a large and completely secure commercial and naval harbour.

Local yachtsmen warn against being on the river after heavy rains. Although the *Turkish Waters Pilot* reported the entire harbour to be 'completely closed to yachts, as of August 2005,' this is no longer the case. The heavens were about to descend on us as we neared the river and harbour mouths, chased by increasingly frightening lightning bolts, so with fervent prayers to Artemis, we ducked into the

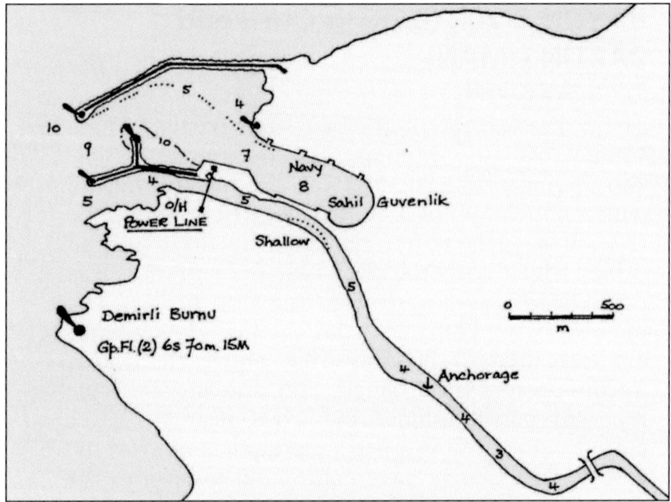


BARTIN ÇAYI AND BARTIN LIMANI

Bartin River

harbour and tied to the commercial wharf, by the police station. The policemen helped with our lines and assured us that there was no problem to stay until the storm had passed. Subsequently two separate officials, both polite and formal, visited to check our passports and transit log. Only one other ship was in the port – a coastal freighter unloading sand.

## ⚓ Tarlaağzi Köyü

41°43'·5N 32°20'·3E

A small harbour with good shelter which has been quayed since earlier reports in 2001 (we did not go in due to NE winds Force 6 and unsettled weather on the day we were on passage to Amasra). The islet and rock awash NE of the bay is clearly visible. Reports indicate that considerable NE swell works its way into the harbour in bad weather.

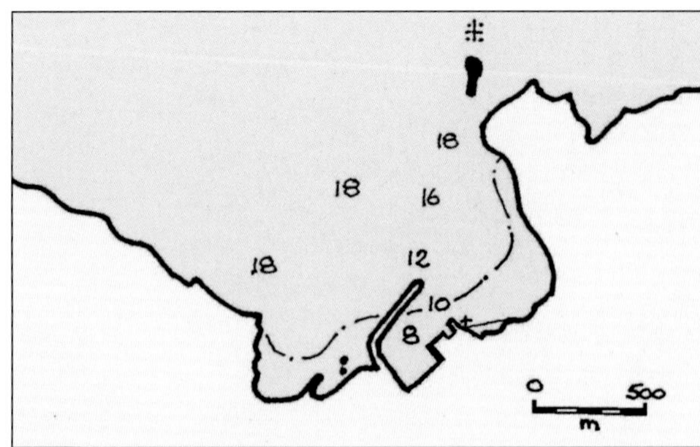


TARLAAĞZI KÖYÜ

## AMASRA

41°44'·8N 32°23'·8E (Outer breakwater)

The picturesque, multi-purpose harbour with historic town ashore offers good shelter and is a popular stop for yachtsmen along the Turkish coast between the Bosphorus and Sinop.

### Approach

The headland is easily seen from all directions. The ancient harbour, on the W side, is too exposed, and the large commercial and naval harbour on the E side should be used.

*VHF* Ch 16 for harbourmaster and sailing club (not necessary to call)

Danger When approaching from the W, give Ayibaligi Adası 200m offing to avoid offlying rocks and shoal water. From here it is a straightforward approach into the harbour.

### Mooring

A busy harbour, with fishing boats and harbour tour boats. Due to the size of the harbour and incoming swell, it is better to anchor off, as an unpleasant surge can build up along the quay. Room for several yachts at anchor where shown in 5–7m with good holding. For easier access ashore, tie alongside a fishing boat with permission, on the NW quay where it is more comfortable in the day. The harbour provides good all-round shelter, but heavy swell from the NE works its way in. Some wash from tour boats, especially on weekends. The harbourmaster's office is located behind the beach along harbour road in the commercial harbour. No harbour charges.

### Facilities

Water from taps on the quay. There is a convenient dinghy landing in the NW corner of the harbour. Fuel by tanker at the quay can be arranged. Wash/dry/fold laundry service is available at a dry cleaning shop in town. Basic provisions can be found in small supermarkets and minimarkets around town. A colourful local women's market operates in the small market area near the museum on Tuesdays and Fridays. Dursun Bölukgu, an excellent bakery selling cakes and sweets, is tucked away on a side

Amasra ancient harbour

## AMASRA

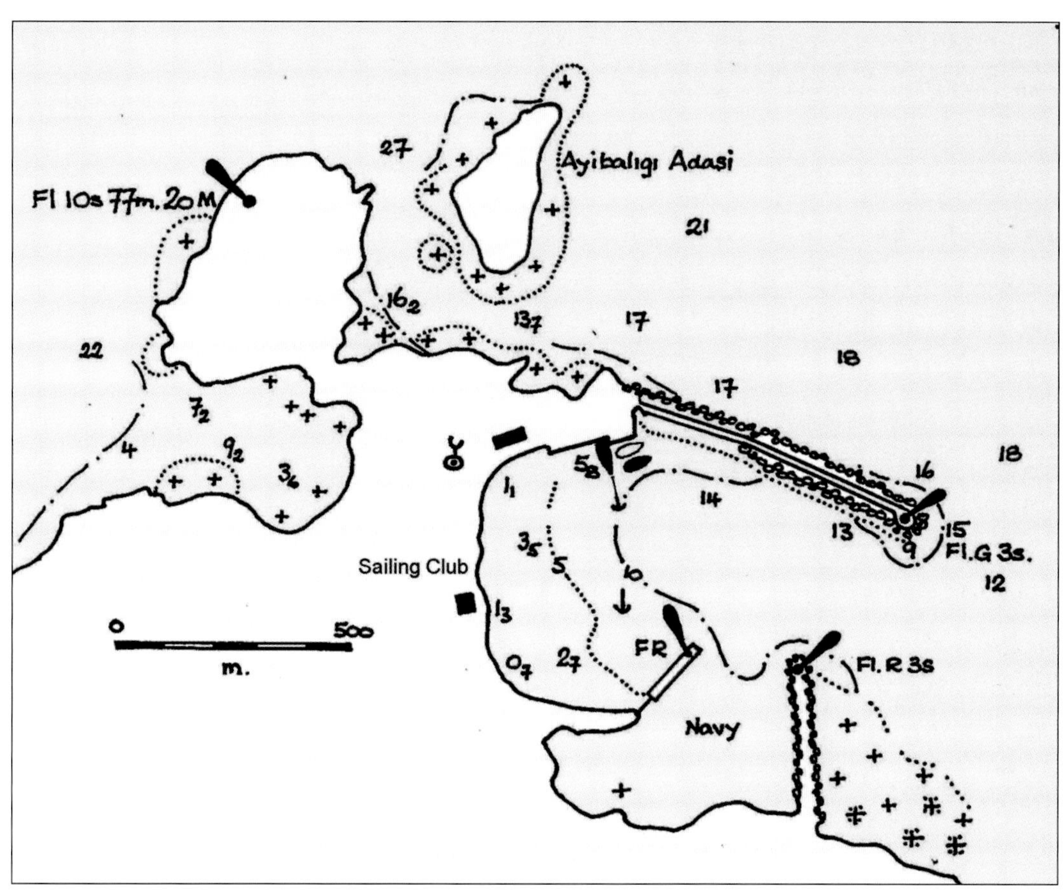


street just a few blocks from the beach. The street leading from the new harbour to the old harbour is lined with tourist souvenir shops selling the usual wares, including wooden bowls and utensils. Although mostly mass-produced today, the craft of wood carving in Amasra goes back to ancient times. Another street between the two harbours is lined with snack bars and ice cream shops. For eating out, there are many restaurants in town serving fish and traditional Turkish food, some with views over the new or old harbour. A post office, bank and ATMs can be found in town. Turkish gaz available at stores in town. *Dolmuş* service to Bartin and onward to Safronbolu. A taxi stand is located near the old harbour.

Amasra

### General

The modern town of Amasra derives its name from an ancient queen, Amastris. With a population of 6,000, it is now a popular beach holiday resort with fine beaches, although the beach inside the harbour is not particularly clean and the local sailing club is not as active as it once was. There are pleasant walks through town, across the bridge, and up into the old town. The archaeological museum is near the old harbour. The castle is Genoese. There are interesting old Ottoman-era houses inside the old walls. Castle, theatre and baths were built during Roman times. Amasra was an important military installation, an export centre for timber, fur and slaves, and at one time a small independent kingdom. Later it became a Genoese colony, and the Genoese cross and coat of arms can still be seen on many parts of the city walls.

An inland excursion to Safronbolu can be made from Amasra to see the well preserved examples of Ottoman architecture. Getting there and back involves a long, tiring day of travel. Catch a *dolmuş* from Amasra in the morning to Bartin and change buses to one going to Safronbolu (the one-way trip takes about 2½ hours). On the return, take the *dolmuş* from the main station if you want to be sure to get a seat before it fills up as it winds its way back through town.

# Section 2: Amasra to Bafra Burnu

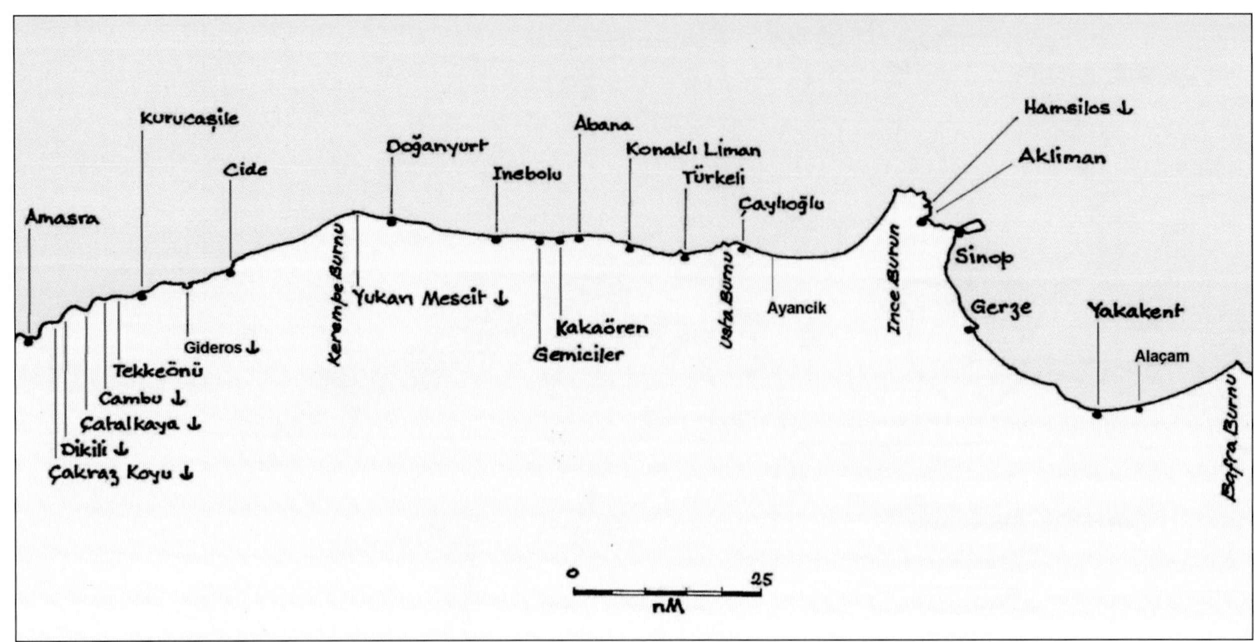


SECTION 2. AMASRA TO BAFRA BURNU

A passage from Amasra to Bafra Burnu passes over the central 'hump' of the Turkish coast, which is more or less opposite the Crimean Peninsula, the 'hump' on the Ukrainian coast. Sinop is by far the most important and interesting town in this stretch of coastline, and it is used by yachts as a jumping-off point from Turkey to make a passage to Yalta, as described in The Middle Circuit Cruising Route (Chapter 1.6). This stretch of coast also contains two of the tiny handful of natural harbours on the Black Sea: Gideros and Akliman. The DLH harbours provide for secure visits to interesting towns at Kurucaşile, Cide, Doğanyurt, Inebolu and Çaylioğlu. Bafra Burnu is the immense delta of the KIzIlIrmak River, a good portion of which has been declared a Wetland of International Importance. Bafra Burnu can be visited by hire car from Sinop or Samsun.

The coastline near Kurucaşile

***Passage note: Amasra to Kurucaşile***

Along the coast between Amasra and Kurucaşile there are several anchorages which could be used for daytime stops in settled weather and a small boat-building harbour with uncertain depths.

## ⚓ Çakraz Burun / Çakraz Köyü

41°47'·0N 32°28'·85E

Located 4M to the E of Amasra, this small bay is open to the N with a sandy beach and river running into it. In 2001, the Annans noted, 'Dangerous rocks shown on Turkish chart 121 are not as extensive or as far offshore.' Local tourist brochures feature this beach and the red rocks on the headland at the SW end of the cove, which is backed by apartment buildings.

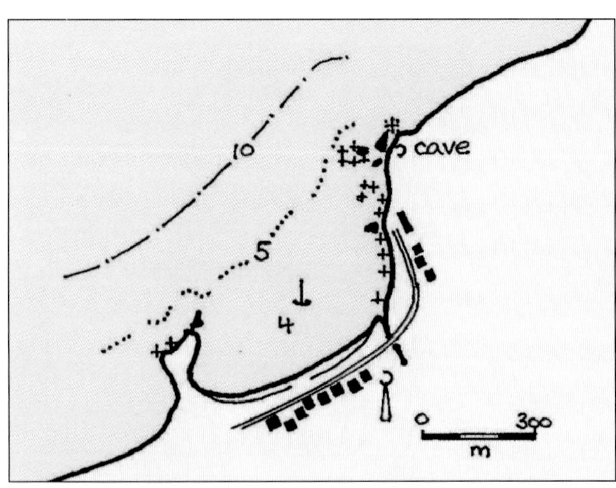


ÇAKRAZ BURUN / ÇAKRAZ KÖYÜ

This headland (and associated cove) was known to the ancient Greeks as Erythinoi. It was mentioned by Homer, with Kromna and Aigailoi and the river Parthenius (Bartin Çayı).

## ⚓ Dikili Köyü

41°48′·1N 32°30′·0E

A small inlet can be found after rounding Dikili Burnu from the W which is not apparent on Turkish chart *121* because of the scale. The spectacular rock arch at the entrance, clear water, isolated surroundings and a beach make this a pleasant daytime stop in settled weather. A house was under construction near the shore in 2010 which may change the remote feel of the place in the future. The ruins of a crane indicate past commercial operations here.

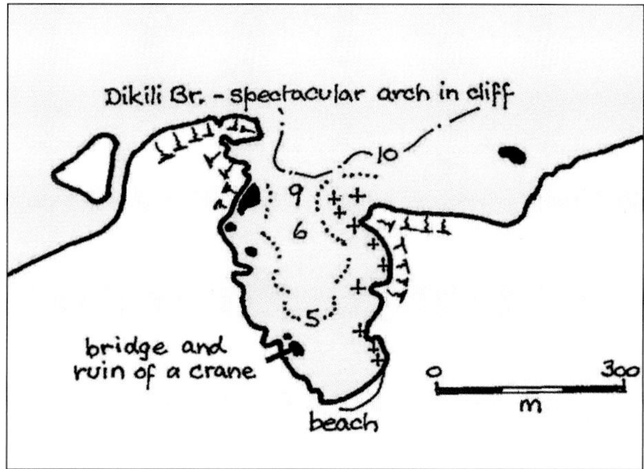


**DIKILI KÖYÜ**

## ⚓ Çatalkaya Köyü

41°48′·7N 32°32′·5E

The first of two similar bays open only to the N, Catalkaya, located 7·5M E of Amasra, has a sandy beach and offers a good daytime anchorage in settled weather. One large house and several smaller houses are near the beach.

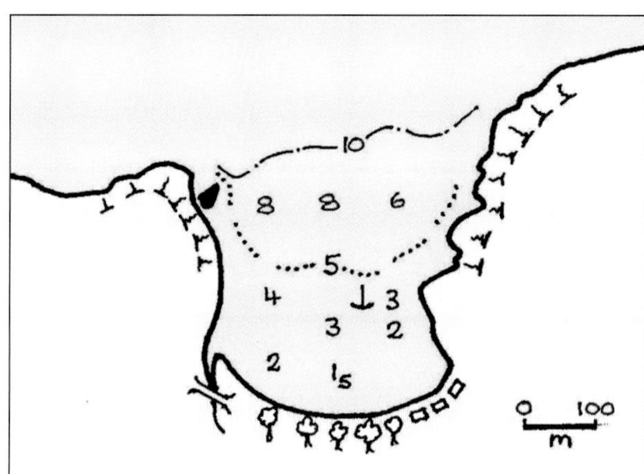


**ÇATALKAYA KÖYÜ**

Çatalkaya Köyü

Cambu Köyü

## ⚓ Cambu Köyü

41°49′·85N 32°37′·2E

The second of two similar bays open only to the N, Cambu, located 11M E of Amasra, also has a sandy beach and offers a good daytime anchorage in settled weather. Several houses are situated along the beach.

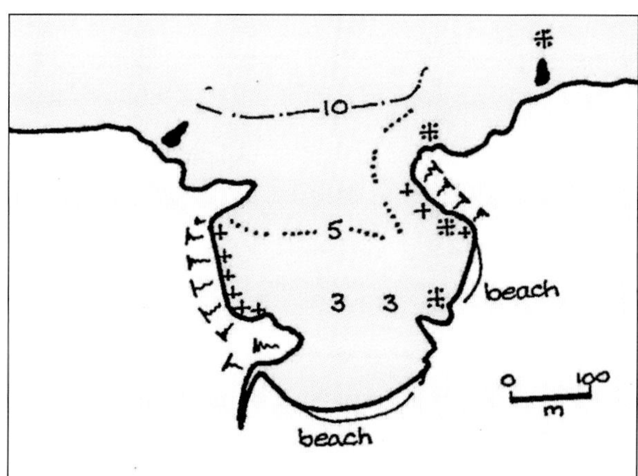


**CAMBU KÖYÜ**

4. TURKEY EAST OF THE BOSPHORUS

Tekkeönü (Ovaköy)

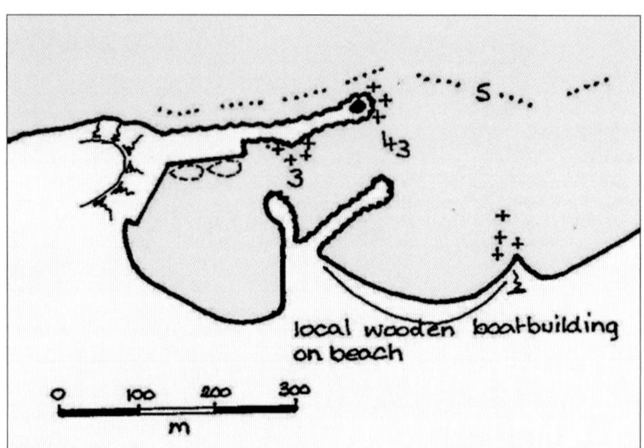


TEKKEÖNÜ (OVAKÖY)

Kurucaşile

Kurucaşile. Boatbuilding

## TEKKEÖNÜ (OVAKÖY)

41°49′·8N 32°40′·5E

The harbour is prone to silting with reported depths of less than 1m in 2001 but sufficient for a yacht drawing 1·5m in 2009. The town is known for wooden boat building, with many fine examples pulled up on the shore. Depending on the status of dredging operations here, the excellent harbour at Kurucaşile just 2·5 M farther E is a better option for finding a secure harbour to spend the night.

In ancient times this was known as Kromna, mentioned by Homer as being among the allies of Troy.

## KURUCAŞILE

41°50′·9N 32°43′·6E

Visiting yachtsmen are warmly welcomed in the boat building town of Kurucaşile with its large, clean fishing harbour located 16·5M NE of Amasra.

### Approach

The approach towards the harbour is straightforward from all directions. Kurucaşile Burun, with its light structure, is conspicuous as is the large shed at the W end of the harbour. After rounding the cape from the W, the harbour comes into view.

Danger Care should be taken with offlying rocks along the shore, to the S and E of the entrance. Make the final approach from a N direction when coming from the E.

### Mooring

There is space to anchor or to tie alongside the quay on the W side of the harbour, keeping clear of the sand loading area if it is active. About 25 small fishing boats use the harbour. The SE quay is

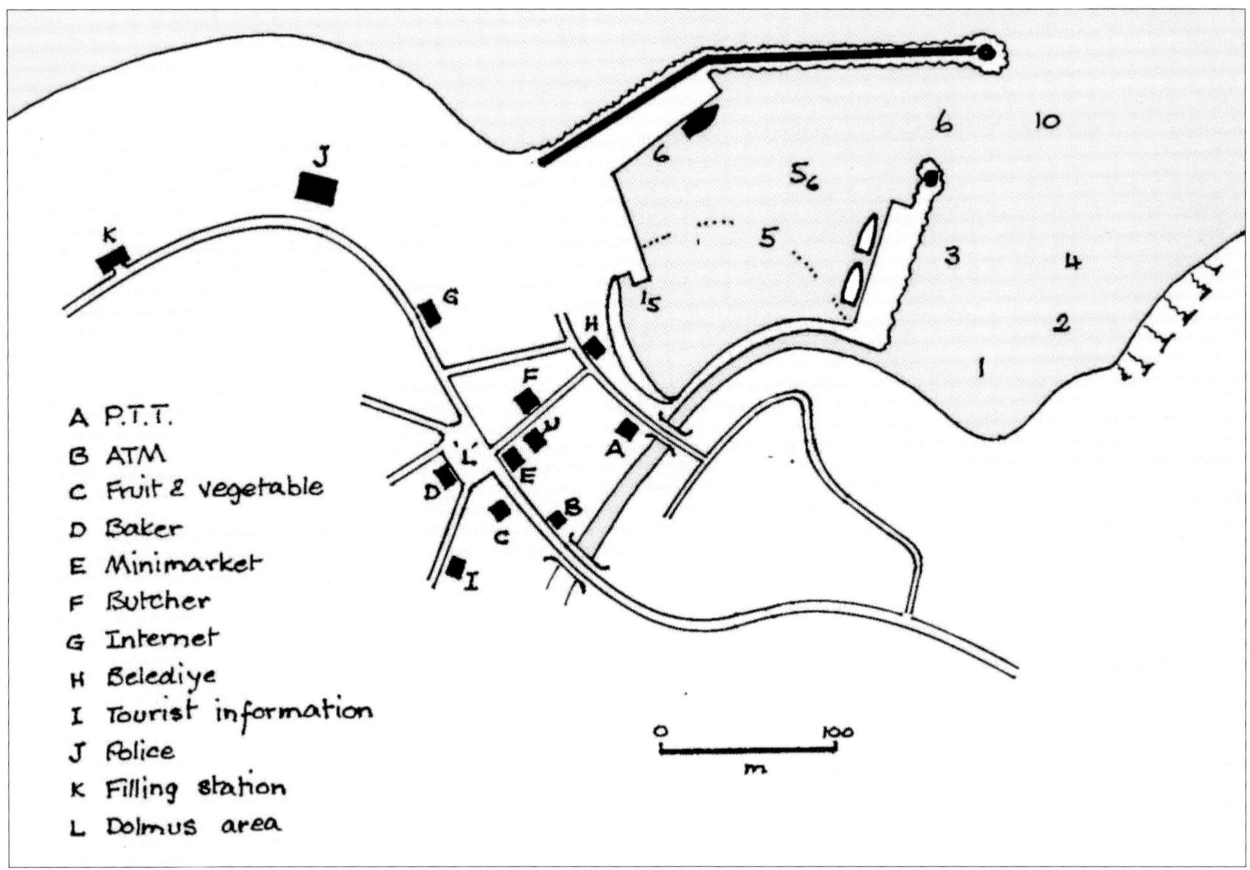


## KURUCAŞILE

Kurucaşile

reserved for the local fishermen's cooperative. Boatbuilders are located on the W quay and the large shed is a sand storage shed.

*Depths* Good depths of 5–6m throughout the harbour except near the small beach which shallows to 1·5m or less.

*Shelter* Excellent all-round shelter.

*Authorities* Friendly local police may stop by to see if you need anything.

*Charges* None.

### Facilities

*Services* Water and electricity on the W quay, by arrangement with the boat builders (long cable or hose may be required). No toilets, showers or laundry. No charge at the quay.

*Fuel* Diesel by tanker which can be arranged from the filling station on the road leading W from town, past the police station and lighthouse.

*Repairs* Basic mechanical, woodworking and electrical repairs are available in this boatbuilding town.

*Provisions* Several small supermarkets, minimarkets, butcher, and bakers in town.

*Eating out* A few simple restaurants and cafés in town. The Liman Restaurant is right at the harbour.

*Other* Internet café, post office, ATM, taxis and *dolmuş* service to neighbouring towns.

### General

Although a bit sleepy during the week, the town is filled with friendly local people. Many are involved in local wooden boat building operations. A walk to the lighthouse rewards you with good views of the Black Sea coast. The secure harbour and remote setting make this a nice overnight stop along this stretch of coast.

## ⚓ Gideros Limani

41°51′·6N 32°51′·3E

One of the few natural harbours on the Black Sea, Gideros is a suitable overnight anchorage in settled weather.

### Approach

The entrance to this natural bay is difficult to identify. It is located 1M W of Tosun Burnu. A 1m high white stone column is visible on the E side of the entrance. Favour this side to avoid rocks reported on the W side of the entrance.

Dangers (1) Rocks are reported with less than 2m depth on the W side of the entrance to the harbour. (2) Once inside, the harbour has many rocks which restrict the swinging room at anchor.

### Mooring

Anchor in 4–5m where shown. Due to the number of rocks in the harbour, you may want to take a line to shore or to one of the posts atop above-water rocks. The bottom is rocky; you may need to be persistent to find good holding. Dense algae growth in the bay can add to the challenge of finding a good place to anchor.

*Shelter* Good all-round shelter, though a N or W swell can work its way into the cove even in settled weather.

*Charges* None.

Gideros Limani entrance

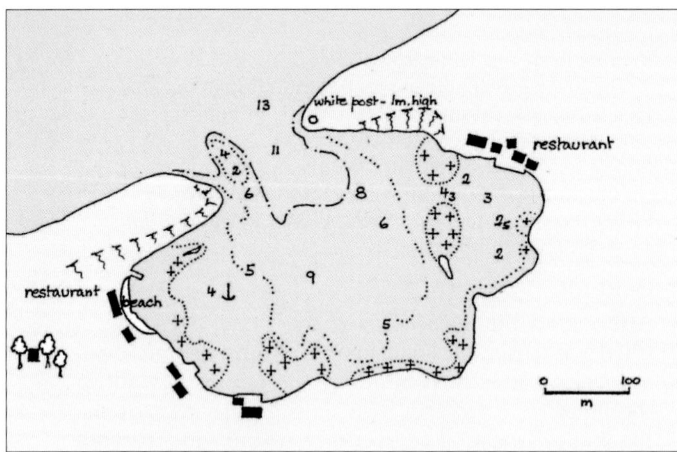


GIDEROS LIMANI

### Refuge at Gideros

This is a special place, a natural harbour. The landscape surrounding the cove is very scenic, with wooded hillsides, green fields and dramatic rocky cliffs. The ancient Greeks knew it as Kytoros. Homer's *Iliad* identifies this as ally of Troy. The Roman governor Arrian described it as 'a mooring for ships.' In 1983, Tim Severin and the 20 rowing crewmen of the modern Argo found refuge in this cove that had served as a god-send to mariners for millennia. As he recounted it,

> 'The wind freshened and turned more to the east. Now *Argo* was barely making a knot through the water, and ahead, over the crew's cheerful faces, I could see that the little galley was being driven towards the rocks. The prospect was distinctly uncomfortable. The water was much too deep to anchor off this grim iron-bound coast, and our only chance was to find a cove, marked on the Turkish charts, which cut a notch in the forbidding line of cliffs. ... I grew increasingly concerned. We were getting dangerously near the rocks. Then I saw a white mark at the foot of a cliff, a small dot which turned out to be a short stone pillar. It stood on a shelf of rock to one side of a narrow cut in the cliffs. Without the pillar to mark it, one would not have spotted the entrance of the cove until too late. The cove was a freak of geology. Some time in the distant past, the sea had weakened a fault in the line of cliffs, gnawing a hole about 30 yards wide. Breaking through this gap, water had rushed in and submerged the small glen behind the cliffs, to form a nearly land-locked basin. Its only entrance was the almost indistinguishable cleft in the cliff wall. The cove was a world apart. In 50 feet, Argo had passed from the outside waves and swell to a flat calm. All that remained of the angry sea outside was an arc of foam which fanned out into the cove from its entrance, and undulated gently.'

In 2010 an algae bloom and a high concentration of jellyfish were observed in the cove.

Gideros Limani

### Facilities

Very limited in remote location.

*Eating out* There are two restaurants on the shore, one on the W shore and one on the E shore. The owner of the restaurant on the W shore may row out to offer assistance and solicit your business. The restaurants are both popular roadside stops and specialise in fish.

*Other* The main road is up a steep hill from this cove. It is possible to find a *dolmuş* to Kurucaşile or Cide and onwards from there.

## CİDE

41°54'·1N 32°58'·8E

This large fishing harbour provides excellent shelter in scenic surroundings.

### Approach

From the W, the harbour and breakwater are clearly visible, but from the E they are hidden from view until after rounding Köpekkaya Burnu. The long bay to the W of Cide is only 8–10m deep, but there are no dangers in the approach and there are depths of 5–6m in the middle of the entrance. Favour the outer breakwater.

### Mooring

Anchor in the S portion of the harbour where shown or tie alongside the quay, which appears to have been originally built for commercial purposes but is no longer in active use during the summer. Depths at the quay are 5m, decreasing to 2m at the NE corner. About 50 small fishing boats use the harbour in the summer.

*Shelter* Excellent all-round shelter. However, in a SW wind it may be more comfortable to lie at anchor rather than tied to the quay, which is in line with the entrance.

*Charges* None.

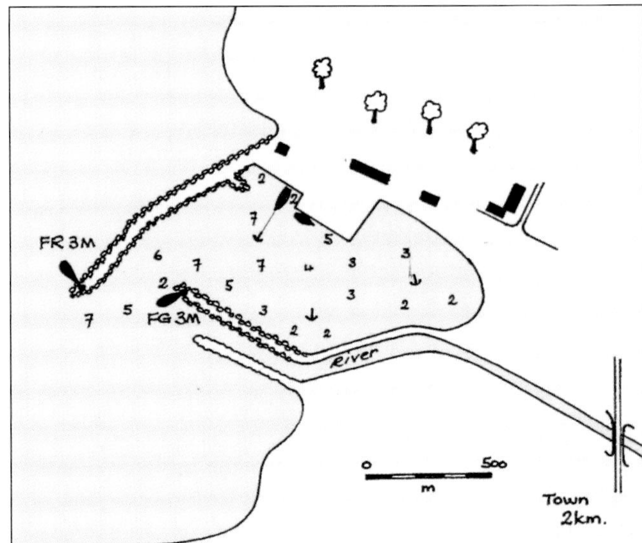


**CIDE**

### Facilities

*Services* Electricity (220V, 2-pin plug) is available by arrangement with one of the restaurants. A long cable may be necessary. Water is available at the quay. Ask for assistance at the floating fish restaurant at the SW corner of the quay (no charge). If you request services, you may want to show your appreciation by patronising their restaurant, but this is not a requirement.

Cide. View from harbour toward entrance

Cide quay

*Fuel* By jerry can and taxi from filling station in town.
*Provisions* The road toward town passes a sports complex and crosses a river on a large new bridge. Turn left on the main road to find a minimarket selling excellent cornbread and other basic provisions. All provisions can be found in town, which is located 2km S of the harbour. Market day is Friday.
*Eating out* Floating fish restaurant on boat tied to the quay. A kebab restaurant selling rotisserie chicken, and a café, are also found near the minimarket on the road leading into town.
*Other* An internet café with Wi-Fi is located on a jetty on the beach just W of the harbour, and other options in town. Taxis are available in town, or ask any restaurant to call one for you.

### General

A quiet, non-touristy town with lots of apartment blocks and a few old houses with well-tended gardens. The surrounding landscape is scenic, especially the mountain peak at the head of the river valley. The harbour area itself is not particularly attractive but the local people are friendly, and this makes for a pleasant overnight stop with a convenient water tap. The son of the family that owns one of the floating fish restaurants may come to help you with your lines.

A river empties into the sea W of the harbour, adjacent to the breakwater, and creates a brown plume off the entrance. There is a factory by the river. The town is at the end of a very long sandy beach. There might be a tendency for silting at the harbour entrance due to the proximity of the river. People seemed to enjoy strolling in the harbour area, but we did not see anyone fishing.

#### *Passage note: Kerempe Burnu*

From Cide, the coastal passage to Kerempe Burnu, proceeds generally ENE in waters clear of charted dangers. Kerempe Burnu is a high cape bordered by reddish cliffs with a lighthouse.

Keremp Burnu, lighthouse

## Yukarı Mescıt

42°01'·3N 33°21'·4E

Located 1·3M E of Kerempe Burnu, in 2010 this tiny harbour appeared to be abandoned.

## DOĞANYURT

42°00'·5N 33°27'·7E

A small but pleasant fishing harbour tucked under the high cliffs of Asar Burnu, which provide good shelter to the W.

### Approach

After rounding Asar Burnu, the headland to the W, the breakwater and small town are easily seen. Minarets and apartment buildings are conspicuous.

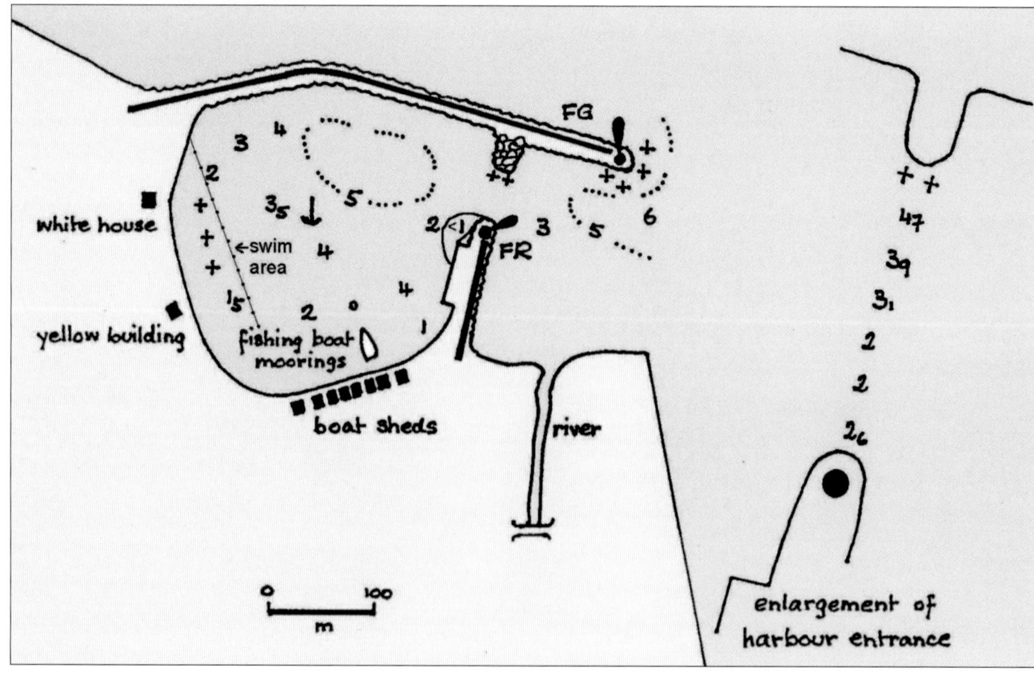


DOĞANYURT

Doğanyurt approach

Doğanyurt anchorage

In 2010, the green light on the outer breakwater was not working, the breakwater to seaward had been damaged, and the light tower was leaning slightly. The red light on the inner breakwater was dimly lit; steady, not flashing.

Depths at the entrance range from 2·5–3·5m, increasing to 4·5m once inside. A line of buoys mark the swimming area across the W side of the harbour. The coaster that used to occupy the quay is no longer present. Although N breakwater has suffered storm damage – in one section the upper two rows of concrete blocks have been knocked off onto the inner wall of the breakwater – this does not seem to compromise the overall protection that this harbour offers except perhaps in a severe winter storm.

Dangers (1) The N breakwater has suffered storm damage. Give the end of the breakwater at least 25m offing when entering the harbour. (2) Shoal water, less than 1m, extends about 10m W from the N end of the quay and on the inside of the S breakwater. This may be dredged periodically.

Doğanyurt damaged breakwater

### Mooring

Anchor in the centre of the harbour, outside the swim buoys in 4·5m leaving room to swing, or go alongside the quay as space allows, taking care to avoid shoal water on N half of quay and near inside of S breakwater.

*Shelter* Excellent. The harbour is well protected from N and E.

*Authorities* Fishermen's Cooperative in building on quay. Friendly local police and even the district governor may stop by to see if you need anything.

*Charges* None.

### Facilities

*Services* Water from tap on S end of quay. Toilets at municipal beach park on W side of harbour. Diesel and petrol at fuel station just across the bridge in town.

*Provisions* Several well stocked, small supermarkets, the biggest of which is on the left-hand corner just after the bridge. Market day is on Fridays, when the town is busy with activity. The bread from the bakery or the weekly market is especially good in this village.

*Eating out* Several *lokantasis* are located on the main shopping street, of which Kismet Lokantasi is the busiest. There is a small café on the right after crossing the bridge.

*Other* Post office, Aygaz and Ipragaz, bank and ATM just after the bridge. Internet café on main shopping street, the second left after bridge. *Dolmuş* service to Inebolu.

Doğanyurt market day

Doğanyurt bread vendor

### General

Doğanyurt is a village with a population of 1,500, located in the Inebolu District of Kastamonu Province. The town is a short walk from the harbour; cross the bridge over the Meset River. New apartment buildings have been built around a small traditional village centre. All basic provisions are available. Visiting yachts are a novelty here. The townspeople are very welcoming, helpful and curious. Chestnuts are the main crop here.

## GÜRGENLIK LIMAN (ZARBANA)

41°59'·3N 33°37'·2E

A tiny new fishing harbour located approximately 6M W of Inebolu with less than 3m depths in the approach and a visible sand bar extending from the inner breakwater across the harbour entrance. Although several large fishing trawlers use the harbour, it does not seem to be suitable for yachts.

Gürgenlik Liman (Zarbana)

## INEBOLU

41°58'·9N 33°46'·7E

A large, multi-purpose harbour serving large freighters, fishing boats, a coastguard station and the occasional visiting yacht.

### Approach

After rounding the headland from the W, the breakwaters are easily seen. A dry dock for large ships is now moored on a new quay constructed on the inside of the outer breakwater extension.

*VHF* Ch 16 for harbourmaster. No requirement to call.

### Mooring

Proceed into the commercial harbour and tie alongside the N quay at the W end in 4m but do not go too far into the corner due to ballasting. This provides the most convenient access to town but may be less comfortable in easterly winds. Alternatively, tie alongside the E quay if space is available or anchor out in sticky mud in 5·5m in the S half of the harbour, keeping clear of the Sahil Güvenlik (coastguard) quay. No mooring charges.

*Shelter* Very good shelter, but some swell works in with E winds and there is some wash from commercial traffic in the harbour.

*Authorities* Port of Entry with offices conveniently located in the S portion of the harbour.

*Charges* None.

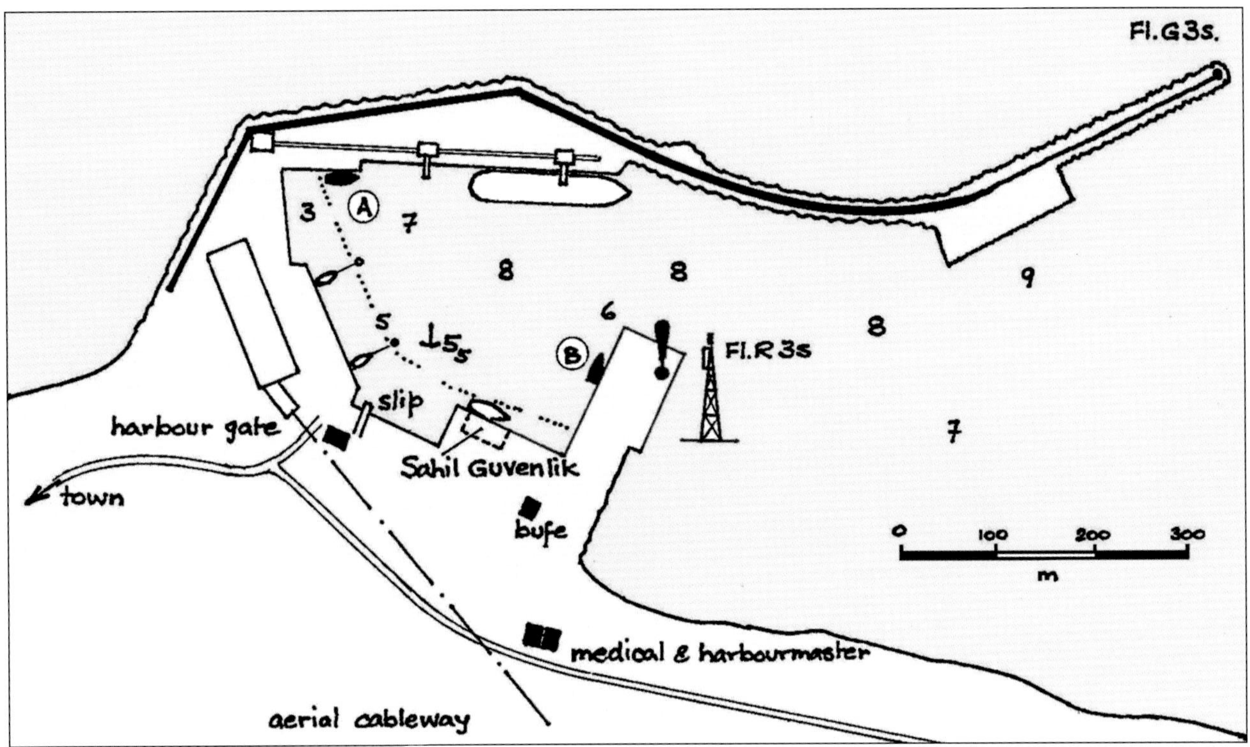


INEBOLU

Inebolu

## Facilities

*Services* Water is available at the Büfe, the boatyard or by tanker to the quay.

*Fuel* By tanker or by jerry can and taxi from the Petrol Ofis station on the shore road into town.

*Repairs* Mechanical and electrical repairs can be arranged through the boatyard.

*Provisions* Small supermarket and several minimarkets selling basic provisions in town. Large weekly market on Saturdays where people from the surrounding villages crowd into town for shopping. Daily market held along the same road on the E side of the river where speciality food shops can also be found.

*Eating out* Cafés, restaurants and ice cream shops line the waterfront in town. Several busy *lokantasi* and simple restaurants in town.

*Other* Post office, bank, ATM, internet cafés and cooking gas in town, as well as an old *hamam*. Taxis available for local transport as well as buses to major cities and *dolmuş* service to neighbouring towns.

## General

Just a short walk from the commercial harbour takes you to a waterfront promenade and the centre of the historic town. A scale model of a typical Ottoman-style house is on display. Many examples of the old houses can be seen in varying states of restoration and disrepair by walking through town and up the hillside. From the top of the hill, you will be rewarded with sweeping views of the Black Sea coast and gain a better understanding of the strategic location of this ancient trading port.

The west side of the commercial harbour is dominated by copper ore facilities of Eti Bakır AŞ, constructed with the north quay in the early 1950s but closed after being privatised in about 2004. Until then, a huge storage shed was fed by an aerial tram and served a large conveyer for loading the ore onto ships. Copper is still being mined in the area, but nowadays it is conveyed by truck; some is exported to Russia and Ukraine.

Inebolu is a safe place to leave your yacht for a scenic inland excursion by *dolmuş* to the provincial capital, Kastamonu. The *dolmuş* service runs regularly from the bus station near the river in town, and the trip up into the mountains takes about 1½ hours. Pack warm clothes for the cooler climate at 1,000m and book your return trip upon arrival at the bus station near the Kastamonu town centre.

## ⚓ Gemiciler

41°58'·5N 33°53'·6E

Known as the fishing harbour for Inebolu, Gemiciler's storm-damaged breakwater has been carefully repaired since 2001. The least depth was 3·5m at the inner breakwater with 5m once inside the harbour. With a small village ashore, the harbour offers little for the visiting yachtsman except a good overnight anchorage in settled weather.

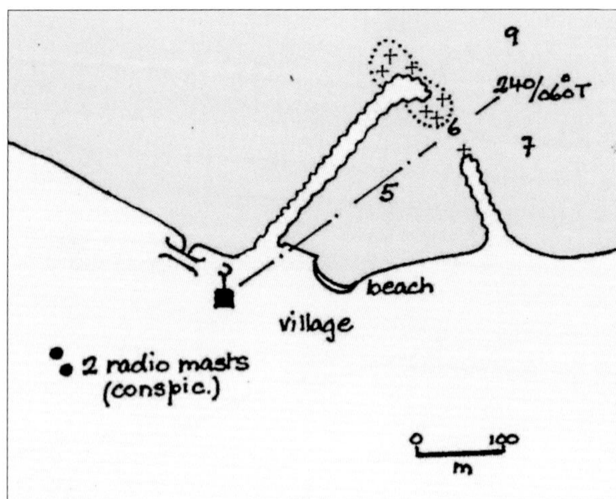


GEMICILER

Gemiciler

## KAKOREN / YAKAÖREN

41°58'·7N 33°57'·8E

Construction of this fishing harbour is now complete, but the entrance is prone to silting. In 2010, shoaling to less than 1m was visible on the right side of the entrance, extending from the inner breakwater. Favour the outer breakwater coming in, keeping clear of offlying rocks. Once inside, continue around the inner breakwater and tie to the cement quay on the right, along the inside breakwater, or anchor out in sand and weed. The water is clear, so it is possible to see the shoal area and to find a sandy patch. Keep clear of the shallow water near the small boats on the S shore and the roped-off swimming area on the E side of the harbour. The local fishermen in this remote harbour are very friendly and may offer to assist you with your lines or to give you a ride into the small village to the E where you can find basic provisions.

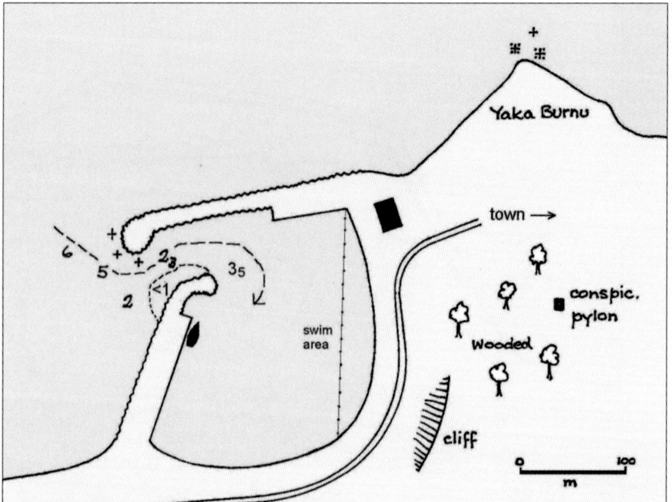


KAKOREN / YAKAÖREN

Kakoren / Yakaören

## ABANA

41°59'·1N 34°01'·4E

The breakwaters of this fishing harbour are easily seen to the E of the town and its associated shoreline development. Entering the harbour is not for the

Abana

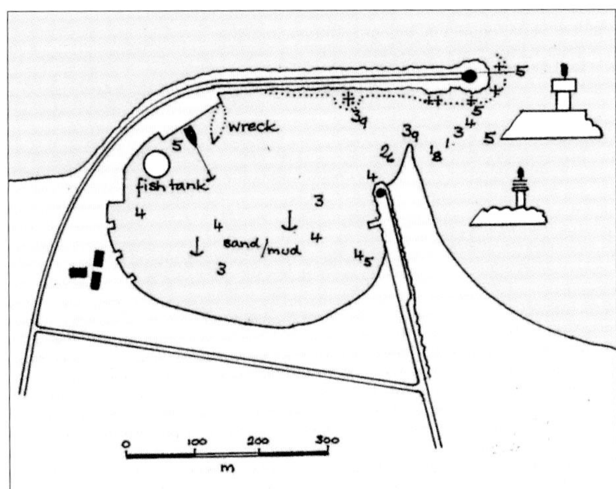


ABANA

Konakli Liman (Çatalzeytin)

Konakli Liman (Çatalzeytin)

faint of heart. An area of severe silting extends from the S breakwater across the harbour entrance, leaving only a narrow channel with sufficient depths for a yacht to enter. With bucket loaders and trucks on the bar, the sun in their eyes and the threat of afternoon thunderstorms, *Gyatso* did not enter, but other yachts drawing 2m reported entering with no problems in 2009 and 2010. In 2001, the Annans reported a village centre busy with holidaymakers where all provisions could be found and a local market in the village square on most days. The town is known for its yoghurt, brown bread and ice cream served like a kebab between wafer biscuits. No harbour charges.

## KONAKLİ LİMAN (ÇATALZEYTİN)

41°57'·85N 34°10'·3E

The large breakwaters with lights on the end of this fishing harbour are easily seen from a distance. The area inside the end of the outer breakwater has slight shoaling which makes the area popular with swimmers. Keep 20m off the end and stay in the middle of the entrance. There is plenty of depth once inside. Anchor in 6m or tie-up alongside the quay in 4·5m. The cliffs to the W and the large breakwater to the N provide excellent shelter but some movement is reported in the harbour in E winds. No harbour charges.

Situated in a beautiful coastal setting, Kaslica village is built on the hill above the harbour; the main town of Çatalzeytin is 4km to the E, where all provisions can be found.

## TÜRKELİ

41°56'·9N 34°20'·5E

Previous guides mentioned cautions about the shallow entrance of this fishing harbour E of Ayandon Burnu. The afternoon sun and discoloured water at the entrance prevented *Gyatso* from entering the harbour safely, but the harbour

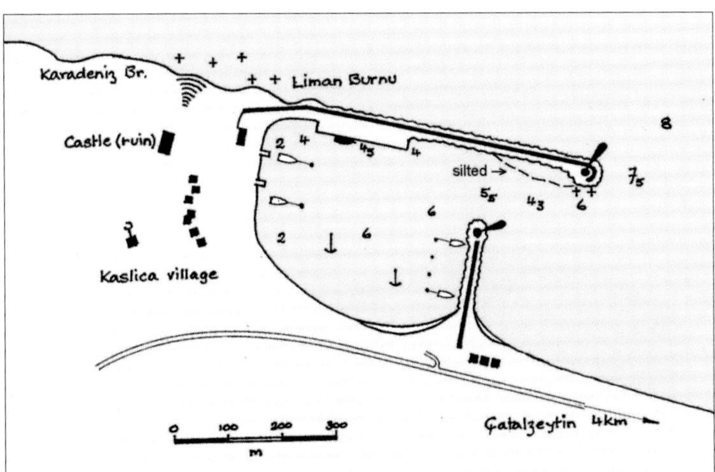


KONAKLI LIMAN (ÇATALZEYTIN)

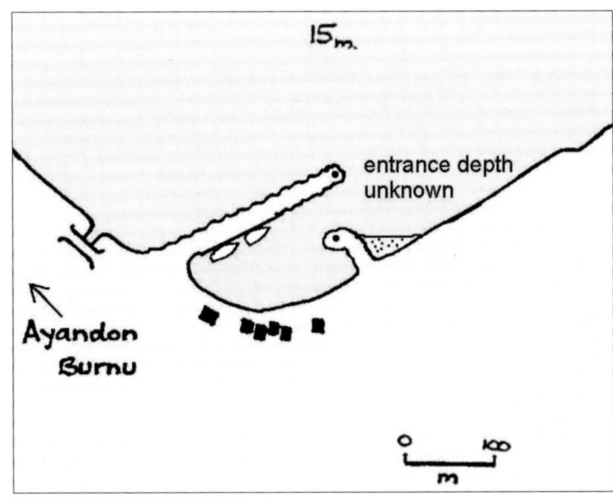


TÜRKELİ

4. TURKEY EAST OF THE BOSPHORUS

Türkeli

appeared to be much larger than what was described by the Annans in 2001, with light structures on both breakwaters and a sizeable town ashore.

## HELALDİ (New Harbour)

41°57'·6N 34°24'·6E

A new and very well built fishing harbour with 5–6·5m depths inside has been constructed W of Karac Burnu. Situated in a remote location with few boats inside, the nearest inland town is Helaldi. If needed, a yacht could tie-up alongside the empty quay. The harbour is entered from the W. The excellent harbour at Çaylioğlu, just 5M to the E and on the other side of Usta Burnu, offers better all-round shelter.

Helaldi

Helaldi

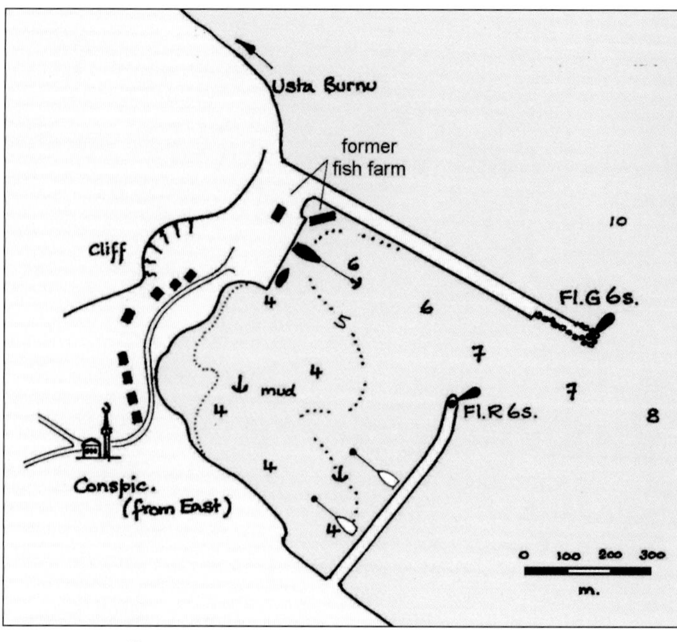


ÇAYLIOĞLU

## ÇAYLİOĞLU

41°58'·0N 34°30'·5E

The approach is straightforward. From the W, the harbour entrance can be seen after rounding Usta Burnu. From the E, the cliffs above the harbour as well as the breakwater and a minaret are easily seen.

Çaylioğlu is an excellent harbour with a tiny, quiet village in a remote setting. Moor alongside the large cement quay on the W side of the harbour or anchor out in 4–5m. Very good all-round shelter and a good place to wait for suitable weather for the passage around Ince Burnu to Akliman (32M) or Sinop (46M). Water from a tap just outside the harbour gate near fishermen's sheds on the road leading to the village. In 2010, the tap on the quay near the former fish farm buildings was no longer working and the fish farm was not in operation. About 20 small and medium-sized fishing boats moor along the shore just S of the quay or along the E breakwater. A short section of the outer breakwater near the light tower has suffered storm damage but has been reinforced and repaired. No harbour charges.

Çaylioğlu

Çaylioğlu

The small village is cut off from the main road, creating a quiet, country setting. Local people fish from the quay and donkeys stroll freely through town. This is a pleasant place to walk and to get a feel for what life was like on the Black Sea coast in days gone by. The larger town of Ayancik can be seen in the distance to the east.

## AYANCİK

41°56′·8N 34°36′·3E

A small fishing harbour with 4m depths at the entrance has been built to the E of town with room for one yacht to tie alongside the cement quay in settled weather. Friendly local fishermen will wave you in and offer assistance. No harbour charges.

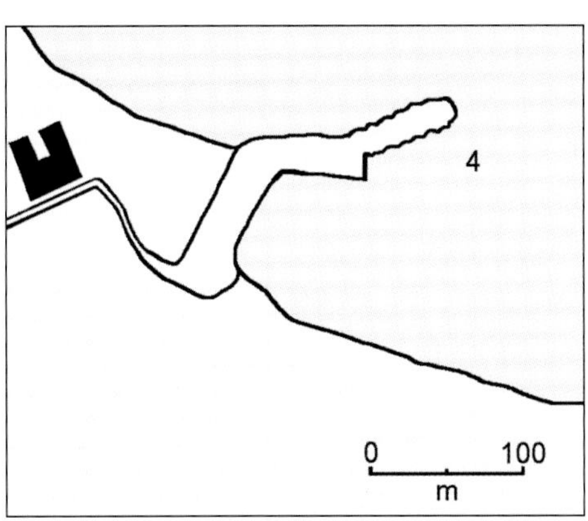


AYANCIK

Ayancik

Ince Burun

## 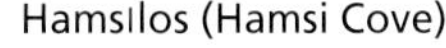 Hamsılos (Hamsi Cove)

42°03′·8N 35°02′·8E

The entrance to this scenic cove, 0·5M N of Hamsi Burnu, can be difficult to make out from the pine covered rocky shore which forms the backdrop of the coastline. Approaching from the N, a white building on the headland on the SE side of the entrance is easily seen. Leave this to port on your way into the narrow cut which provides a surprising

Hamsılos (Hamsi Cove)

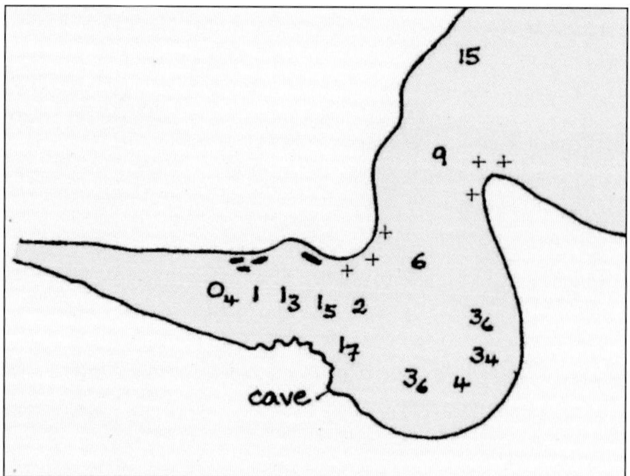


HAMSILOS (HAMSI COVE)

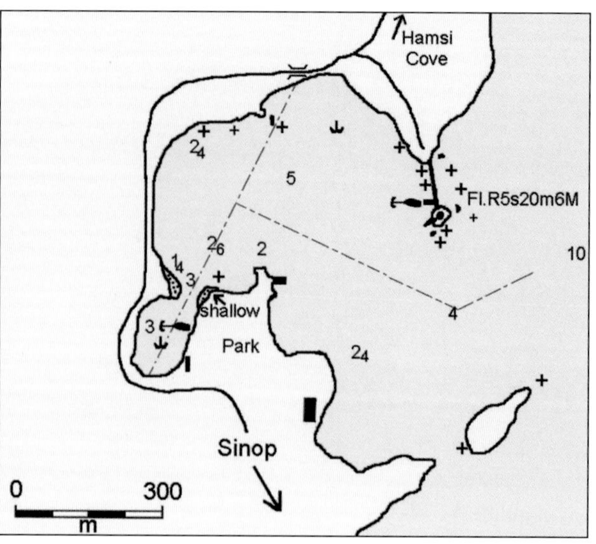


AKLIMAN

amount of shelter once inside. The headland is a popular stop for the occasional tourist buses which disgorge passengers for photo ops. There is room to anchor and take a line ashore, or you can visit the cove by dinghy or by land from adjacent Akliman. No harbour charges.

## ⚓ Akliman

42°03'·05N 35°02'·9E

One of the few natural harbours on the Black Sea, this offers good to excellent shelter in a peaceful setting, depending on where you decide to anchor.

### Approach

The entrance is 0·6M S of Hamsi Burnu. The N side is marked with a light structure on a small rock island which is connected to the shore by a cement breakwater and quay. Another narrow island marks the S side of the harbour entrance.

Danger Offlying rocks and rocky reefs to the S and E of the island with the light structure, and more rocks extending from the narrow island on the S side of the entrance.

### Mooring

Anchor in 3–4m in the N portion of outer harbour, taking care to avoid the above and below water rocks in the NW and NE shore on both sides of the sandy beach. When conditions permit, there is room for one yacht to moor bow or stern to the end of the cement pier near the island with the light structure. A chop builds up along this pier in W winds. As a better alternative, continue into the inner harbour where the fishing boats are moored, and anchor in 3m in the middle of this protected pool, or anchor

Akliman inner harbour

Akliman quay with chop

Akliman beach

and take a line ashore on the E side. Keep centred on entering the pool to avoid shallow areas off the two small points on both sides of the entrance. There is plenty of water right up to the shore once inside. Fishermen may offer to guide you in, show you where to moor, or invite you to tie alongside their boats. About 25 small and medium-sized fishing boats are moored in the inner harbour. Good all-round shelter in outer harbour and excellent all-round shelter in inner harbour. No harbour charges.

### Facilities

*Services* Water at tap in park with permission. Public telephone outside restaurant in park.

*Provisions* Minimarket with fresh bread, beverages and snacks 0·5km from fishing harbour along the road to Sinop. Slightly larger minimarkets are found 1km beyond the park entrance.

*Eating out* Reasonably-priced and good quality restaurant at Hamsilos Hotel 0·5km from fishing harbour along road to Sinop.

*Other* Regular *dolmuş* service every hour from road in fishing harbour to Sinop takes 30 minutes and passes the airport entrance (see Sinop for flight information). Less frequent service from Hamsi Cove.

### General

Akliman is an attractive natural harbour which has been used since ancient times and is now surrounded by a National Park. If you are looking for a change of pace from the commercial and fishing harbours along the Turkish coast of the Black Sea to the W, this is your best opportunity to spend time at anchor surrounded by rocky tree-lined shores, a sandy beach, and a small fishing harbour together with a park and picnic area. The entire park can be explored on foot or by dinghy, including the caves along the shore outside of the harbour. From the beach on the N side of the outer harbour, it is a pleasant walk along the road to Hamsi Cove. The park/picnic area on the S shore is used as a day and overnight camp for children, and it is recommended that you secure your dinghy with a lock if leaving it unattended. With the serene surroundings and the convenient *dolmuş* to Sinop, the inner harbour can be used as an alternative to the much busier harbour in Sinop. The hardworking fishermen are very friendly and accommodating and will do everything they can to make your stay pleasant.

## SINOP

41°01'·3N 35°08'·7E

This historic Black Sea port with a crowded fishing harbour will accommodate visiting yachts for short or long stays. Sinop is commonly used as the jumping-off point for yachts making passage to Yalta, on the Crimean Peninsula of Ukraine. It also forms an invisible threshold on the Turkish coast, beyond which few yachts venture further E.

### Approach

After rounding Boztepe Burnu and the small, offlying islet of Gazibey Kayasi, the approach to Sinop is straightforward. The town and peninsula are visible from all directions. The fishing harbour entrance is made from the W with a light structure on end of breakwater. The E harbour and ship terminal is not suitable for yachts.

*VHF* Ch 16. No requirement to call.

Sinop fishing harbour

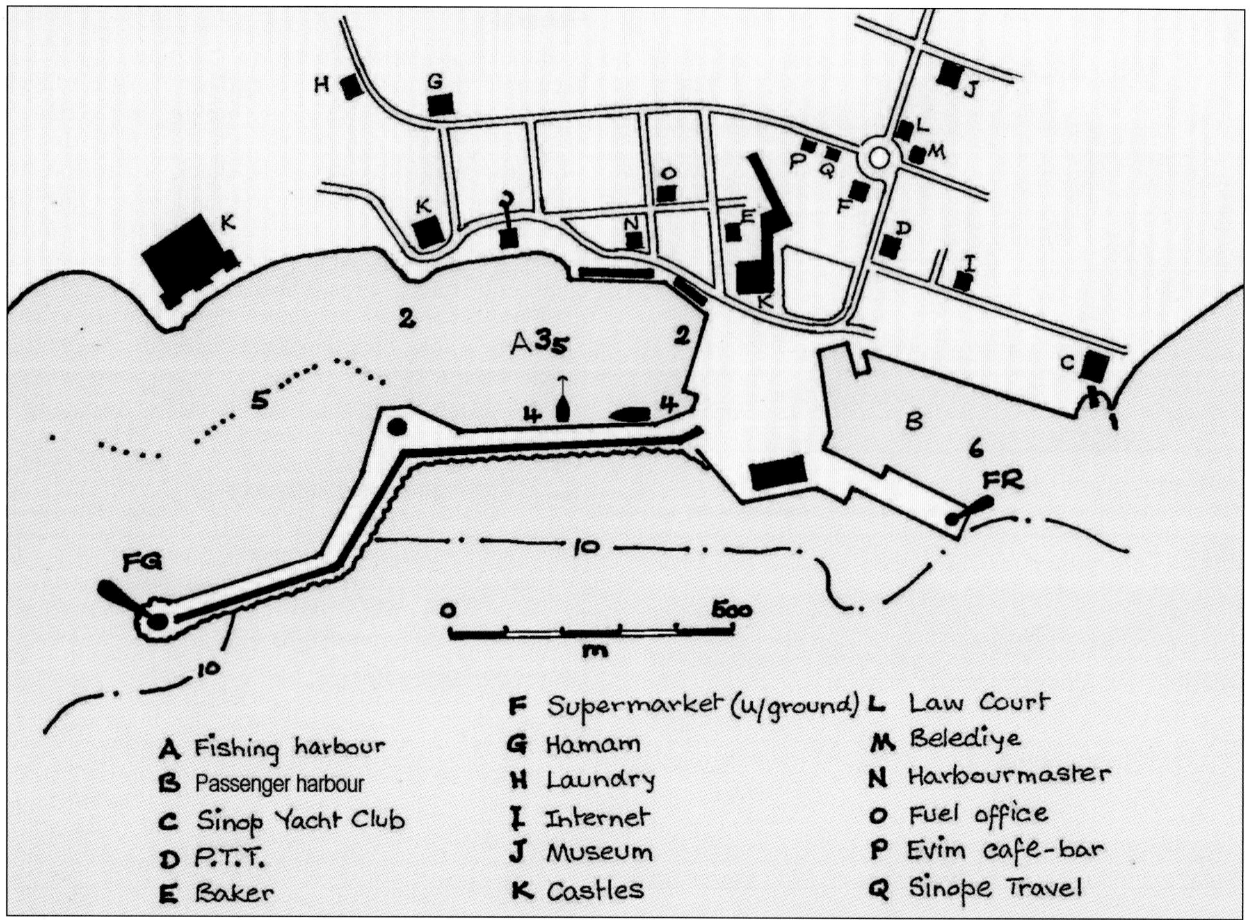


SINOP

Dangers (1) A small island lies off the SE side of Boztepe Burnu. (2) Some remains of the old fortress wall are located near the bend in the breakwater where depths decrease to 3·5m and then increase to 5–6m again inside the fishing harbour.

## Mooring

*Data* A fishing harbour with more than 200 boats and several large trawlers on the outer portion of the SW quay.

*Berth* In the W harbour alongside a fishing boat with permission or go bow or stern to the outer quay if space is available and instructed to do so. This is primarily a harbour for fishing boats and local tour boats but space will be made to accommodate yachts. The E harbour near the cruise ship pier is not suitable for yachts.

*Depths* 4m along S breakwater decreasing to 2m on the E side of the harbour.

*Shelter* Excellent all-round shelter.

*Authorities* Port of entry. Customs and Immigration found in building at the root of the cruise ship dock. Harbourmaster's office is located behind the harbourside restaurants. Fishermen's Cooperative office at the entrance to the outer quay. A ROTA shipping agent is likely to be among the first to greet you and solicit your business for clearance procedures in Sinop. However, all authorities are conveniently located and an agent is not a legal requirement. If arriving in Turkey here, it is helpful to bring a new transit log with you.

*Contact information* A local charter captain and former fisherman known as 'Habeş Kaptan' has served an informal role in assisting foreign yachts in Sinop. Now in his 80s, he keeps a tour boat tied to one of the harbourside restaurants, or just ask for him in the fishing harbour. For more than 20 years he has been welcoming and assisting crews on foreign yachts in Sinop. He can help arrange for fuel by tanker and all other repair needs. He enjoys meeting and helping foreign yacht people for no fee; however, if a service is arranged through him, the proper etiquette is to offer him a small, negotiable fee. Ask him about the appropriate amount in advance depending on the service arranged.

Habeş Kaptan *Mobile* 90 545 918 1092.

*Charges* None unless services such as water, fuel or repairs are requested.

## Facilities

*Services* Water available at tap in SE corner of outer quay. Another metered tap is located near the large fishing trawlers on the inside of the bend in the breakwater. The fisherman may request a fee of up to 60TL to fill your tanks. Agree on a price in advance.

*Fuel* Diesel available by tanker on the quay or by jerry can from the fuel station in town. Ask Habeş Kaptan to help arrange fuel delivery. Fishermen on large trawlers may ask for a fee to arrange fuel or water services for you.

*Repairs* Haul-out facilities and boatyard serves the fishing fleet. Most mechanical and electrical repairs can be arranged.

Sinop

*Provisions* A Carrefour Express supermarket is located underground at the rotary across the street from the provincial government buildings on Atatürk Cadesi. There are signs at the top of the steps leading down to the store. Near the harbour are a bank, ATM, minimarkets, butcher, bakeries, pastry shops, and fruit and vegetable stands. Other supermarkets, butchers and shops can also be found nearby. Market days are Monday and Thursday, with Thursday the larger.

*Eating out* Numerous restaurants, cafés and *lokantasi* in the harbour area and in town. Fish is the speciality along the waterfront, including several floating restaurants popular with tourists and a few informal places selling raw or fried mussels (*midya dolma* or *tava*). To sample local specialities, try *börek*, or *manti* (meat dumplings topped with nuts and yogurt) at Örnek Manti Börek Nokul Salonu. For Turkish-style kebabs, theAntep Sofrasi on Atatürk Cadesi is a local favourite. Join the college crowd and locals for tea, drinks or backgammon at one of the busy harbourfront bars.

*Other* PO, banks, ATM and internet cafés with Wi-Fi in town. Turkish gaz and camping gaz available from shop in area of Atatürk Cadesi (ask in harbour area for directions). Telephones available at Türk Telecom office next to post office at base of Atatürk Cadesi. Tourist information office at E end of waterfront promenade. Old *hamam* near the fishing harbour. Two laundry services are available near the *hamam*. Follow the road along the fishing harbour past the cafés and bars and turn right on the road leading to the *hamam*. The first laundry is on the left before you get to the *hamam* and the second can be found if you continue to the left around the *hamam*. The latter is recommended for wash/dry/fold service. They will also iron the laundry for an additional fee. *Dolmuş* service to neighbouring towns and buses to major cities. The *otogar* (bus station) is located just outside the fortress walls on the W side of the city. Airport with Turkish Airlines flights to Istanbul six times a week. Several travel agencies and hire cars available in town, and a tourist information office is located on the waterfront.

## General

Sinop is rapidly emerging from a rather sinister reputation for its prison to becoming a university city supporting the arts. It's a great example of a port town being sited where it could be defended. Nessebar, in Bulgaria, is geographically similar, on a smaller scale. In the 1960s, the Americans built a huge surveillance facility on the crest of the peninsula, aimed at the Soviet Union to the N. Since 1991, the Turkish military operates it as a communications centre. Sinop is a good base for exploring inland, including the KIzIlIrmak River delta, Bafra Burnu.

### *Passage note: Sinop to Samsun*

Yachtsmen have many choices in planning the passage from Sinop to Samsun. Roughly halfway between them is Bafra Burnu, the tip of the huge delta of the KIzIlIrmak River. Nonstop, the trip is 75M, a long summer-day's journey. But there are three good harbours between Sinop and Bafra Burnu: Gerze, Yakakent and Alaçam. There is one good harbour between Bafra Burnu and Samsun: Dereköy, which starts the descriptions in Section 4.3, Bafra Burnu to Çam Burnu.

Sinop Museum mosaic

Construction of the Coastal Highway (Yeni Yol) begins between Gerze and Yakakent. From this point onward, the highway is a dominant feature of the coastline and has affected many harbours, filling some in and resulting in the construction of numerous others which are suitable for yachts. While it has greatly improved transportation along the coast and benefited the economy, it has also changed the nature of the coastline. With a few exceptions where the highway has either bypassed an area or has not been extended along the coast (e.g. Gerze to Dereköy and bypass of small peninsula Jasun Burnu), the multiple lanes of traffic, rock groynes and retaining walls, newly constructed (sometimes huge and sometimes tiny) harbours exemplify modern Turkish engineering at the expense of nature.

## GERZE

41°47'·8'N 35°12'·15E

A fishing harbour with excellent shelter and plenty of room for yachts to anchor with a quiet resort town ashore.

Gerze

### Approach

Located 15M S of Sinop, the lighthouse and town are easily seen when approaching from the N. The breakwater comes into view after rounding Kosk Burun. From the E, the town and breakwater are clearly visible from a distance.

Danger A shoal with less than 10m depth extends out from the lighthouse. It does not pose a hazard for sailing yachts.

### Mooring

The harbour is home to 75 small and medium-sized fishing boats which are moored along the shore and quays to the E and W of the main pier. In 2010, there were no signs of the large trawlers seen in a historic photo of the harbour from the 1930s, before the breakwaters were constructed. Anchor out in 4m on either side of the central pier, according to wind conditions. The best shelter from prevailing winds and swell can be found to the E of the pier, and the best place to land a dinghy is at the base of the pier on the E side. There is space for yachts which draw 2m or less to tie alongside the quay in the NE portion of the harbour, but there is underwater ballasting extending out in places. The quay on the SW breakwater is reserved for a coastguard vessel.

*Shelter* Excellent.

*Authorities* Harbourmaster's office is located in the white building on the left-hand side of the road which runs along the top of the bluff to the E of the main pier. No need to check in.

*Charges* None.

### Facilities

*Services* Water from a tap in the park near the sailing club by special arrangement with harbourmaster.

*Fuel* Available by jerry can from town.

*Provisions* BIM supermarket: follow the road leading away from harbour to the main rotary with a large statue of a chicken in the middle of it. Turn left. Minimarkets, as well as butchers, bakers and greengrocers in town. Market day is on Monday in the covered market near the green mosque. A small daily market operates here, except on Sundays.

*Eating out* Restaurants, cafés and tea gardens in the harbour area. *Lokantasi, kebab salonu, pide* shops and other cafés in town.

*Other* Post office, bank and ATM near main rotary. Internet café near the base of the main pier on the road leading away from the harbour. *Dolmuş* to Sinop.

### General

With the construction of breakwaters in the 1990s, this former anchorage was transformed into a harbour that provides excellent shelter for visiting yachts. In 2010, additional works were in progress to improve landscaping along the quays in the harbour and to create a park which includes a building for the local sailing club. The history of the harbour, which has been used as an anchorage since ancient times, can be seen in a display of old photos on a path leading E on the N side of the harbour.

The small town of Gerze is a local resort with several hotels and pensions for summer visitors. Although the town lacks much character from an architectural standpoint, there are a few old-style

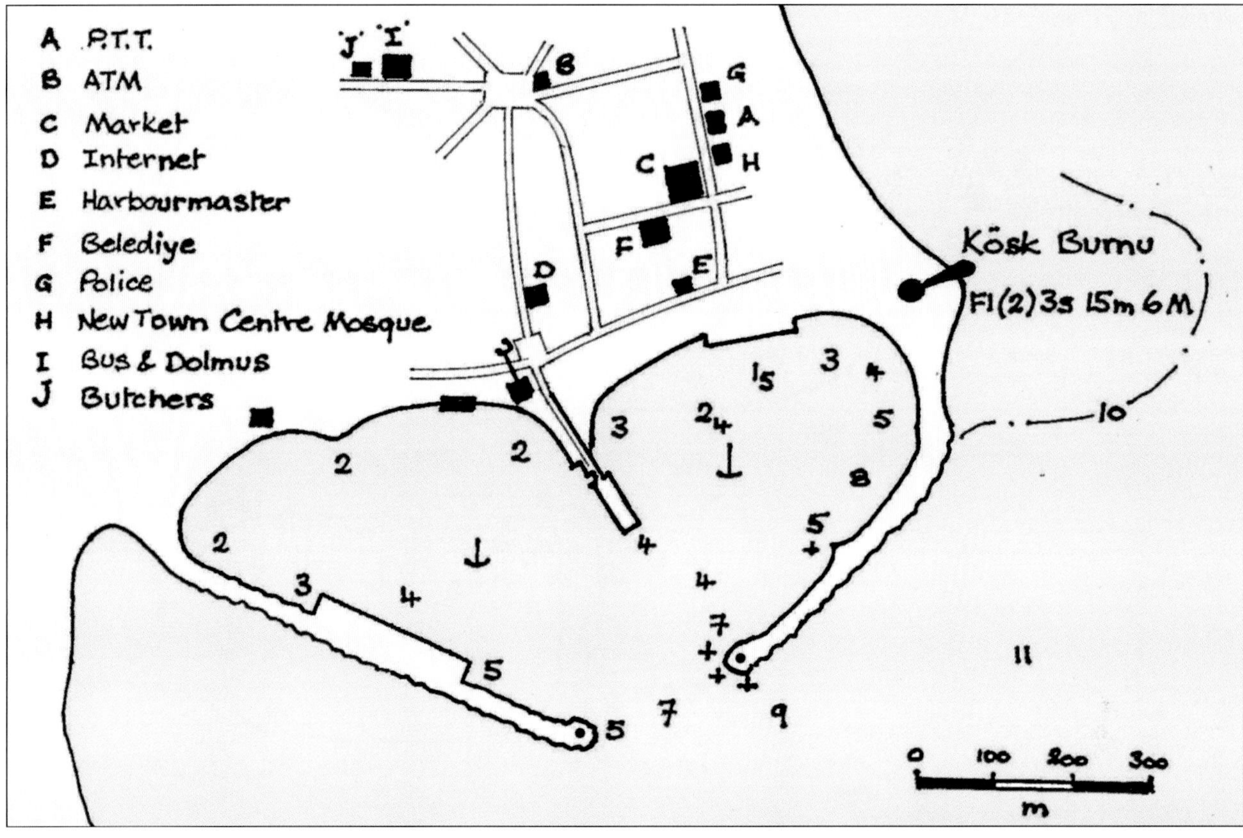


GERZE

houses sprinkled in among the more modern concrete houses and apartment buildings. Walking around town, you will notice many tidy, well-kept gardens and water fountains. The quiet town comes alive on weekends when people are strolling along the harbour, fishing from the pier and sipping tea in the cafés. Children enjoy jumping off the high pier and swimming across the harbour. The fishermen and local people are friendly and helpful.

Gerze was ancient Karousa, but no indications of this ancient past can be found in the town today. Arrian called it 'an anchorage for ships' which is exactly how it remained, with the exception of building the central pier, until the modern breakwaters were constructed in the late 1990s.

Cockerel, symbol of Gerze

Raft of fishing boats, Yakakent

## YAKAKENT

41°38'·5N 35°30'·7E

A fishing harbour with very good shelter which makes for a suitable overnight stop or a secure place to leave your yacht for inland travel. From here, it is 42M to Dereköy or 55M to Samsun, on the other side of Bafra Burnu.

### Approach

Three large blue tanks on the shore and the breakwater with a light structure on the end are easily seen to the W of the town. The approach is straightforward.

Danger Approaching from the E, take care to avoid three fixed fish pens off the coast between Gerze and Yakakent in position: 41°41'·5N 35°27'·0E, 41°40'·8N 35°28'·0E and 41°40'·0N 35°29'·2E respectively.

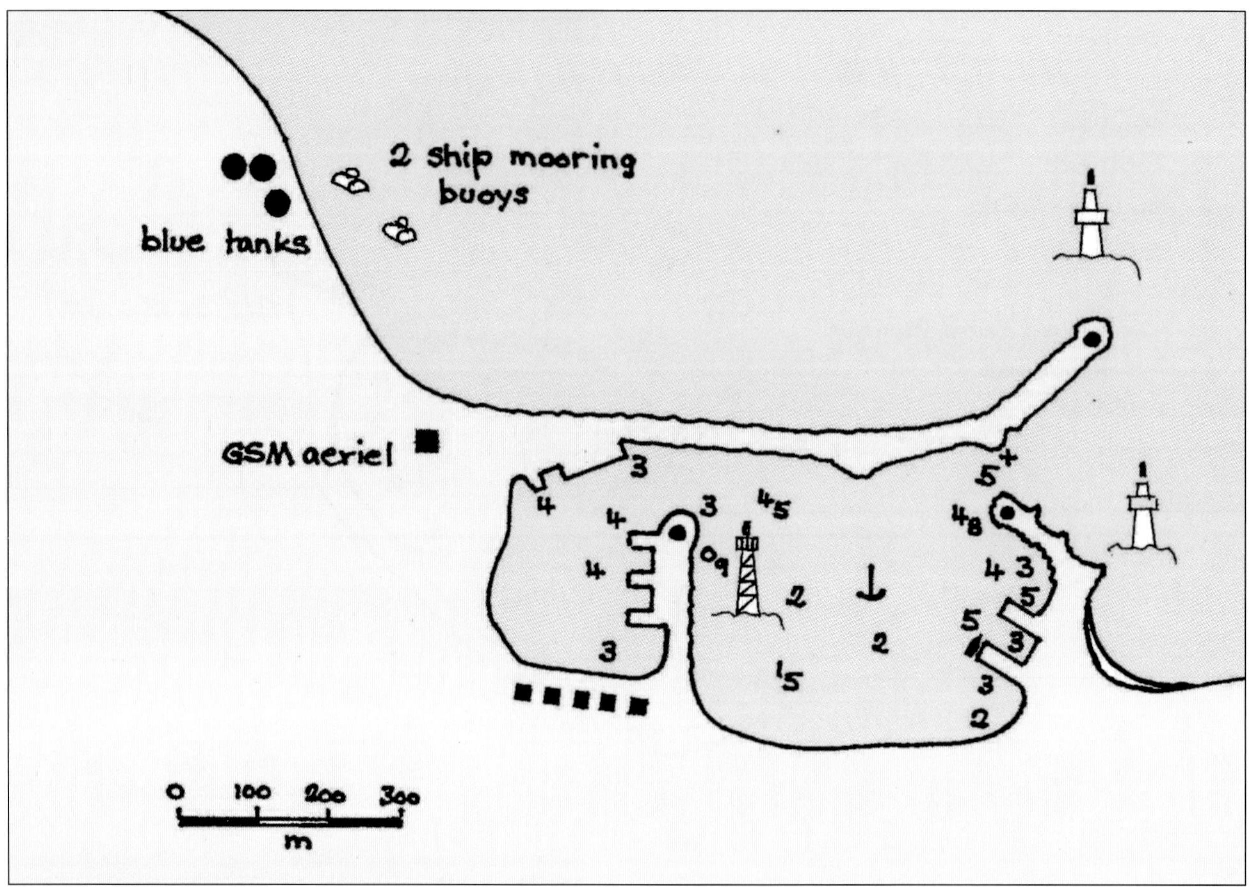


## YAKAKENT

### Mooring

With permission, tie to a fishing boat off the end of the second jetty in 5m, go alongside the cement jetty inside the pen in 3m if space is available, or anchor in 4·5m in the outer harbour. Avoid the shallow area in the SW corner. The first jetty is reserved for the Sahil Güvenlik (Coastguard), and the inner harbour is reserved for fishing vessels. Ask for permission to leave yacht in the harbour if you plan to make inland excursions. The Sahil Güvenlik and fishermen may agree to keep an eye on it while you are away.

*Shelter* Very good all-round shelter and excellent inside the pens.

*Authorities* Fishermen's Cooperative located in the inner harbour (no charges and need to check in).

*Charges* None.

### Facilities

*Services* No electricity. Water on the quay at the base of the jetty.

*Fuel* Diesel by tanker from the fuel station S of the harbour on the road leading into town.

*Repairs* Hardstanding: marine railway for fishing boats, on the S shore of the outer harbour.

*Provisions* Minimarkets in the fishing village adjoining the inner harbour. A 2km walk E, on a brick paved promenade, brings you to the town, where there are small supermarkets, butchers, bakeries, greengrocers, hardware stores, bank and ATM, internet café and mobile phone top-up.

*Eating out* A few restaurants specialising in fish in the small village around the fishing harbour. Cafés, tea houses, ice cream shops and several simple restaurants can be found along the promenade leading into town.

*Other* Post office, bank, ATM, hardware stores and cooking gas (Turkish gaz) available in town. In one of the shops along the promenade, you can watch people at work making hammocks. *Dolmuş* service is found along the main coastal road and a bus station is located in the town square overlooking the sea with long distance service to Sinop, Samsun and beyond.

### General

This friendly small town stretches 2km E from the harbour, reached by a promenade along the shore or by the road. It is a local summer resort, and on summer evenings people stroll along the seafront or gather on their porches overlooking the sea. There are simple houses with well-tended vegetable and flower gardens.

The tobacco growing region of Turkey begins in Yakakent and stretches E along the Black Sea coast. In the summer, you will see tobacco drying on rails and people threading leaves on a string for drying. You will also notice tea factories scattered along the coast.

Coastline off Yakakent

Alaçam harbour entrance

Alaçam harbour

## ⚓ Alaçam

41°39'·0N 35°40'·2E

A small fishing harbour has been constructed 7M E of Yakakent to serve the inland town of Alaçam. The breakwaters have been completed, but there are no quays. There are a few houses along the beachfront, and fishing boats are pulled up on the beach and moored along the inner breakwater. Entrance is made from a NE direction. Depths range from 4·5–6m at the entrance and 3·5m inside. A yacht could anchor with good shelter within the harbour if needed. The setting is rural and remote on the Bafra Peninsula.

### *Passage note: Rounding Bafra Burnu*

Bafra Burnu Light is a white round metal framework on a hut, 25m in height, located just W of the Kızılırmak river mouth.

The Admiralty sailing directions caution that the coastline around the deltas of the Kızılırmak and Yeşilirmak may differ from that charted due to shoaling and recommends giving these headlands a wide berth. However, shoaling seems to be a thing of the past. Up to 1960, the Kızılırmak River annually carried 23 million tonnes of sediment to the Black Sea, but since the construction of the Derbent Dam and the Altinkaya Dam (1987), the sediment load has fallen to only 0·5 million tonnes. The growth of the delta has come to a halt, coastal currents, waves, and wind have caused erosion of up to 1km, and large groynes are now being constructed to protect

Bafra Burnu, lighthouse

the estuary. In June 2010, *Gyatso* found water depth of 8m approximately 100m from the river mouth and a canyon, approximately 100m deep, extending directly out from the river. Current, from the W, reached 1·2 knot.

### Kızılırmak Delta

The Kızılırmak Delta, with a total surface area of 56,000ha, is considerably more important than its low flat appearance suggests. A 21,700ha portion of the delta was among the first places in Turkey to be declared a Ramsar site, a wetland of international importance. It is a good example of Black Sea coastal wetland, composed of habitats including the sea, river, saltwater lakes, freshwater lakes, wet meadow lands, reed lands, bogs, salty marsh, pasture, mixed broad leaf forests and coastal sand dunes. It hosts a great number of endangered flora and fauna species, including more than 20,000 water birds throughout the year and a much greater number during the winter. Until the dams were built, several species of sturgeon inhabited the river, but these have nearly been eliminated by the change in water regime.

A visit to the Kızılırmak Delta is easily undertaken by rental car from either Sinop or Samsun, via the large town of Bafra, which is on the river and gives the great cape its name. The town of Bafra is known in Turkey as a centre for processing tobacco. An excellent map and description of the Ramsar site is at www.ramsar.org.

In ancient times the Kızılırmak was known as the Halys. Arrian reported, 'This river was of old the boundary between the kingdoms of Croesus and of the Persians, and now flows under Roman rule – not from the S, as Herodotus says, but from the direction of the rising sun. And there, where it flows into the Euxine, it separates the territories of the Sinopeans and Amisenians.' Croesus (595–547 BC) was the king of Lydia and the richest man in the world, a bastion against the Persians for the Ionian Greeks. Preparing to wage war against the Persian king Cyrus, Croesus asked the oracle of Delphi what would happen if he crossed the Halys River and was told, 'A great empire will be destroyed.' Convinced that this foretold his success, he crossed the river but was defeated by the Persians, who took over his empire. The empire that was destroyed was his own.

Bafra Burnu, beach

Water buffalo at Kızılırmak Delta

# Section 3: Bafra Burnu to Çam Burnu

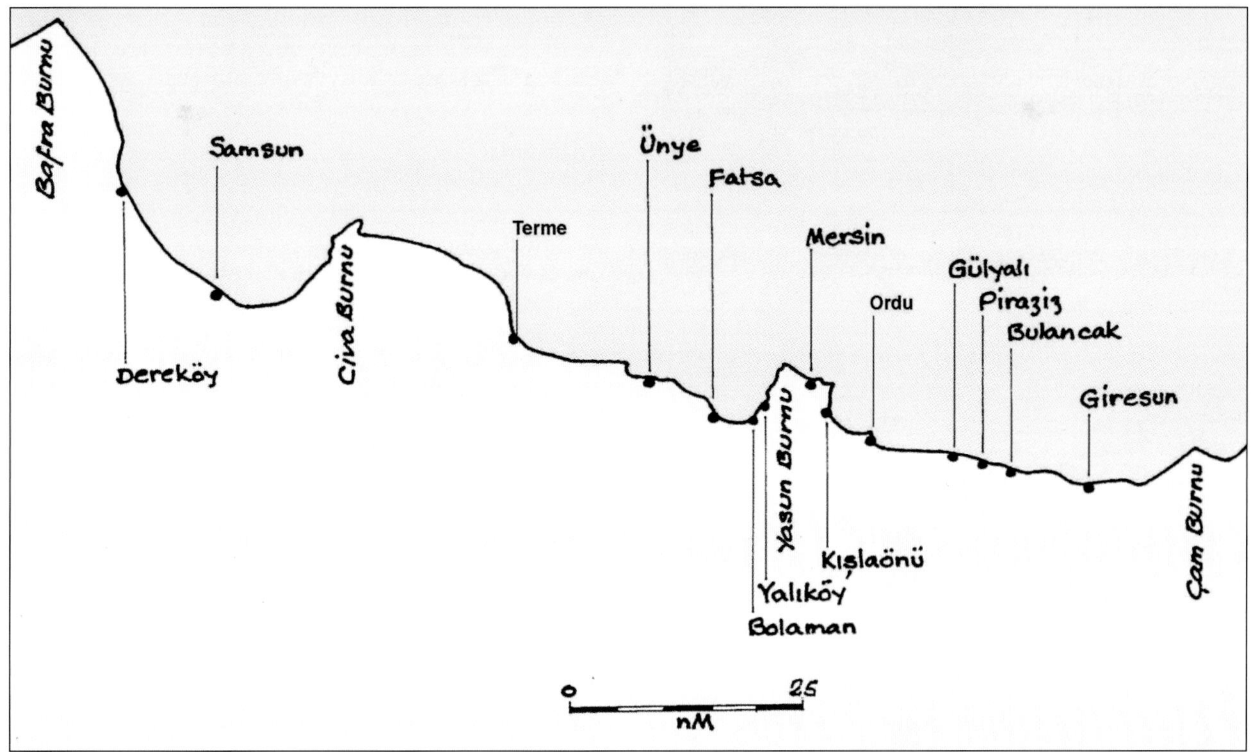


## BAFRA BURNU TO ÇAM BURNU

It's about 125M in a generally ESE direction between Cape Bafra and Cape Çam. Two capes jut out from the shore in between: Civa and Yasun. Cape Civa is the delta of the Yeşilirmak River. Yasun Burnu is special because the coastal highway goes straight across the base of the peninsula, leaving the coast untouched as a nostalgic reminder of how much the coastal highway has rearranged things. And there are two interesting port cities along this coast: Samsun and Giresun.

## DEREKÖY

41°28'·0N 36°08'·2E

A fishing harbour located on the E side of Bafra Burnu, 13M NW of Samsun and a suitable overnight stop for yachts. If sailing between Yakakent and Samsun, this intermediate stop gives you the option of reducing the distance of rounding Bafra Peninsula to 42M from 55M.

### Approach

Approach is straightforward and the breakwater is easily seen. There are relatively shallow depths (minimum 4·5m) but no dangers in the approaches. The least depth at the entrance is 4m with some rocks off the end of breakwater. A suspicious area identified in 2001 was not found, but brownish water flows along the outer breakwater from a river, creating the appearance of silting.

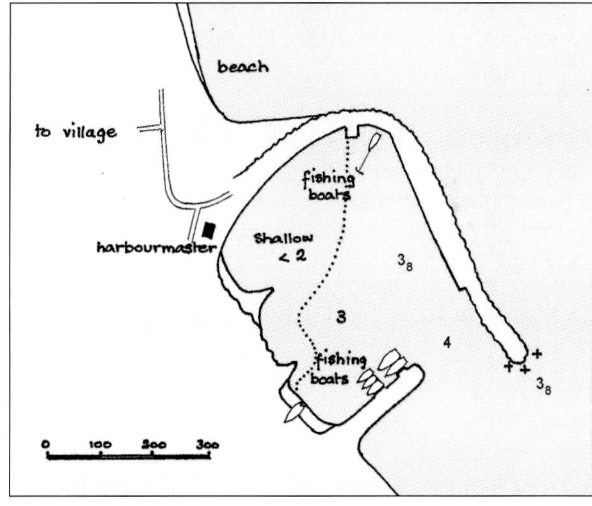


DEREKÖY

### Mooring

The quay on the inside of the outer breakwater has been extended. A coaster no longer occupies this quay, which is now used by fishing boats to offload their catch. Yachts should tie alongside this quay where convenient, leaving space for fishing boats or anchor out in 3·5m. A local fisherman advised us not to go into the W half of the harbour, which has less than 2m depths.

*Shelter* Good but some movement in strong winds when it is better to anchor out.
*Authorities* Harbourmaster (no need to check in)
*Charges* None.

Dereköy fishing fleet

Dereköy. Unloading the large whelk *Rapana*

### Facilities

Very limited. A small village with shops and a café is close to the harbour. The main coastal highway is 1·5km inland from the harbour with *dolmuş* service to Bafra and bus service to Samsun. The Samsun Yacht Club is a better place to leave a yacht than Dereköy.

Samsun Yacht Harbour

## SAMSUN

41°19'·0N 36°20'·5E (Yacht Harbour)
41°18'·6N 36°21'·4E (Commercial Harbour)

A large commercial harbour and adjacent yacht harbour with a marina operated by the Samsun Sailing Club in a busy port city with an ancient history.

### Approach

The approach is straightforward. The breakwater for the commercial harbour can be seen from a distance, but it is difficult to distinguish the breakwater for the new yacht harbour until you are much closer in because it blends with the extensive riprap for filled parklands associated with the new coastal highway. As of 2010 there was no light structure on the breakwater of the yacht harbour, which is located immediately W of the commercial harbour. There are two choices for mooring in Samsun: in the marina operated by the Samsun Sailing Club in the yacht harbour or anchored off of their former location in the commercial harbour.

*VHF* Ch 16 for harbourmaster and for marina (not necessary to call ahead)

Danger Busy shipping traffic near the commercial harbour and ships at anchor outside the harbour.

### Samsun Yacht Harbour

The Samsun Yelkin Külübu (SYK), the Samsun Sailing Club, was formerly located in the SE corner of the commercial harbour but moved to its own new yacht harbour in 2005. The club was founded in 1961. The harbour has been quayed on the W side, where visiting yachts can find a berth alongside in 4·5m, or bow or stern-to in 5–6m with laid moorings tailed to the quay. The marina has space for 30 yachts and 50 small powerboats. Small fishing boats moor along the inner breakwater. Space will be made for visiting yachts.

**SAMSUN YACHT HARBOUR**

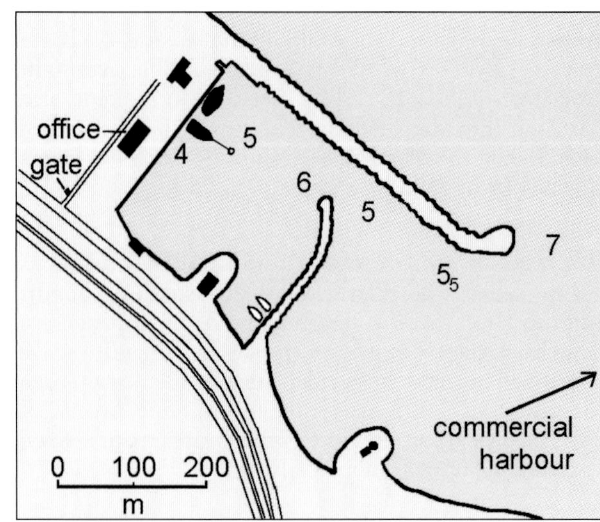

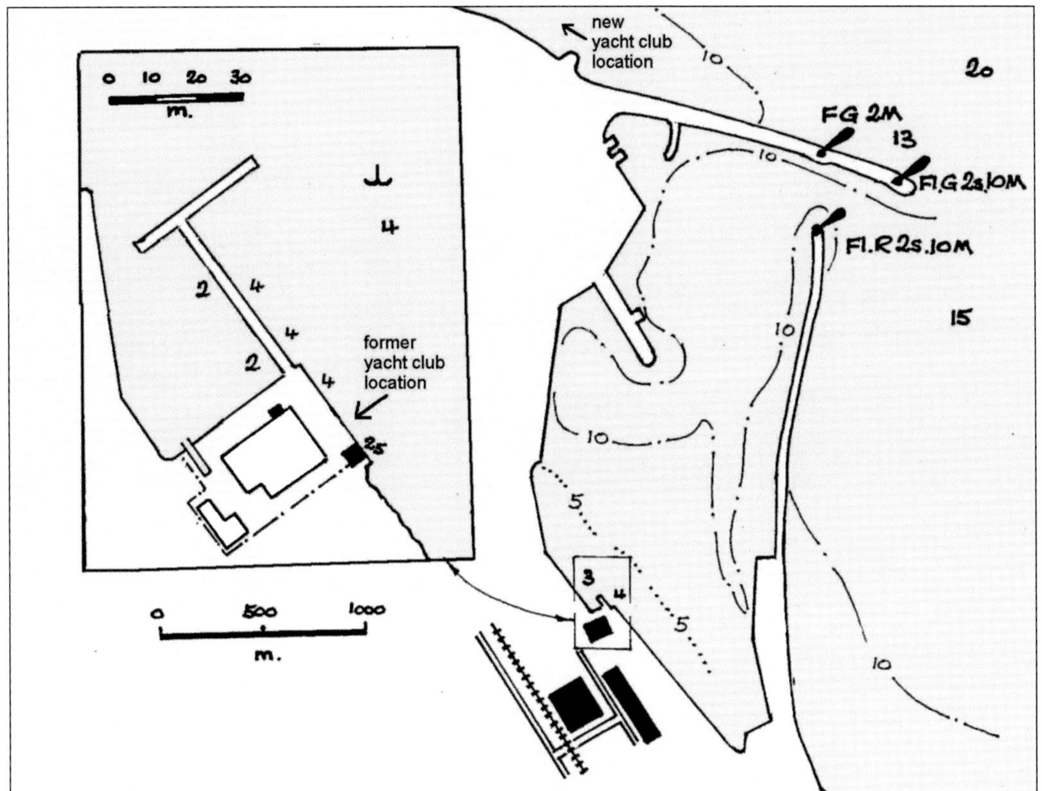


## SAMSUN COMMERCIAL HARBOUR

*Shelter* Very good all-round shelter.
*Authorities* Samsun is a Port of Entry. All authorities are located near the ferry dock in the commercial harbour. Samsun Sailing Club marina staff, in the office located upstairs from marina restaurant, will assist with any formalities, if required.
*Charges* A charge of US$50 per day was quoted, payable in equivalent Turkish Lira at the current exchange rate. Apparently the rate is irrespective of yacht size. The charges are as high as commercial marinas operating in Turkish harbours on the Aegean coast due to the cost of leasing the harbour from the government, which they say is the same rate for the Black Sea. Alternatively, you can anchor out in the commercial harbour for free if port authorities do not object (see below).
*Contact information* Samsun Sailing Club Baruthane Mevkii- Batipark/ SAMSUN
✆ 362 445 2295, 362 4452675 *Fax* 362 445 3244
www.samsunyelkin.org.tr

### Facilities

*Services* Water and 220V two-pin electricity is available at each berth. An adaptor is needed to connect with the normal 3-pin (3-phase) plugs found in marinas in the Mediterranean and Aegean. 24-hour security with guard and gate. Free Wi-Fi in the marina. Toilets and showers in the building near the quay. Wash/dry/fold laundry service can be arranged through the office with pick-up and drop-off service.
*Repairs* There is hardstanding adjoining the yacht quay. Haul-out by crane. The largest yacht observed on the hardstanding was approximately 10m. All repairs are possible.
*Fuel* By tanker or jerry can and taxi to nearby filling station.
*Provisions* Nothing convenient to the yacht harbour, but a large shopping centre with Migros supermarket is a short taxi ride to the W. A smaller Carrefour Express supermarket is found along the main coastal road in the same direction but closer to the marina. Other supermarkets in the city centre.
*Eating out* Good quality restaurant located on-site at the Samsun Sailing Club marina. Many other options for eating out in the city centre, including French food in the French Quarter, and along the beach at the outskirts of Samsun, W of the yacht harbour. Several nightclubs are also found along this stretch of beach.
*Other* Post office, banks, ATMs and internet cafés in the city centre. The marina office can arrange a hire car for you with pick-up and drop-off service available. *Dolmuş* and local bus service can be found along the coastal highway and in the city centre. Long-distance buses to Amasya and major cities depart from the *otogar* (bus) station. Daily direct flights to Istanbul with Turkish Airlines and Onur Air with minibus service to the airport from their offices in the city centre.

### Samsun Commercial Harbour

There are only very limited facilities for yachts in the commercial harbour now that the Samsun Sailing Club has moved to the yacht harbour. Yachts can anchor off in 4m and get ashore at their former location in the commercial harbour, but port authorities may ask you to move to the yacht harbour. Once ashore, it is a short walk through the covered market to the museums and city centre.

Samsun Commercial Harbour

## General

With a population of 364,000, the city of Samsun is the capital of Samsun Province. If sailing east from the Bosphorus, you will find the first purpose-built yacht harbour with a marina operated by the local sailing club. Although expensive by Black Sea standards, it is a secure place to leave your yacht for inland excursions and offers marina-type amenities and services which are otherwise rare in these parts. With direct flight connections to Istanbul, Samsun is a convenient port for crew changes.

Samsun has been an important trading centre since Neolithic times because it is located on the Black Sea coast roughly equidistant between the deltas of the large KIzIlIrmak and Yeşilirmak Rivers, at a place which offers quite easy access to the hinterland of Anatolia.

Ancient Samsun, called Amisos, was founded c.564 BC by Ionian Greeks, probably from Miletus and Phocaea. The harbour was not as good as that of Sinope (at Akliman), but it had much better access to the Pontic interior. The Greeks settled on a 44ha promontory, Baruthane Hill, which projects NNW into the sea about 3km W of modern Samsun. The modern harbour of the Samsun Sailing Club is probably quite close to the ancient port. Arrian wrote, 'Amisos, a Greek city and colony of the Athenians, is built on the sea.' Amisos reached its peak during the reign of the Pontic kings, during the Hellenistic period (330–30 BC) but in 71 BC the Romans burned the city to the ground. It eventually recovered, and for the next 15 centuries Amisos/Samsun was the most important port on the Black Sea. In 1954–56, the Americans levelled the top of the hill to build a radar facility, and much of the ancient Greek city was obliterated. Some of the hill remains under military control, but in 2004–6 the municipal government commissioned archaeological studies of two *tumuli* on the hill which revealed two burial chambers dug into the conglomerate bedrock. Cable cars now carry visitors up from the seafront park, just W of the yacht harbour, to Amisos Tepesi, a small visitor centre and café, and a walkway has been constructed around the tumuli. The Archaeology and Ethnography Museum is located near the commercial harbour W of the Valiliği building.

Samsun retains a prominent place in modern Turkish history because it was here that Kemal Atatürk landed, on 19 May 1919, to begin organising the movement that led to Turkish independence four years later. In 2003, the municipal government built a small harbour and a full-size replica of his ship, the *Bandirma*, with an exhibition hall of photos and memorabilia. The Atatürk Museum is located next to the archaeology museum.

Possible excursions from Samsun include the historic Anatolian city of Amasya, which lies in gorge of the Yeşilirmak River about 2½ hours inland by bus or hire car; the vast Hittite city of Hattusas with its sphinx gate guarding one entrance through the massive ramparts and still dominating the countryside after 4,400 years; and the wetlands of the KIzIlIrmak River delta which forms the Bafra peninsula. Each of these makes a good day trip, most conveniently made in a hire car. The roads are good and a guide is not essential.

## BELEDIYE KÖYÜ

41°16'·3N 36°23'·1E

Two harbours are located just E of the Samsun commercial harbour. One is a tiny fishing harbour with reported depths of 1·8m or less which is not suitable for yachts. The other is a newly constructed harbour with no further information regarding its suitability for yachts.

### *Passage note: Samsun To Terme*

The passage from Samsun to Terme rounds Civa Burnu, the delta of the Yeşilirmak River. The delta is not nearly as large as Bafra Burnu, and the light is almost 2M inland.

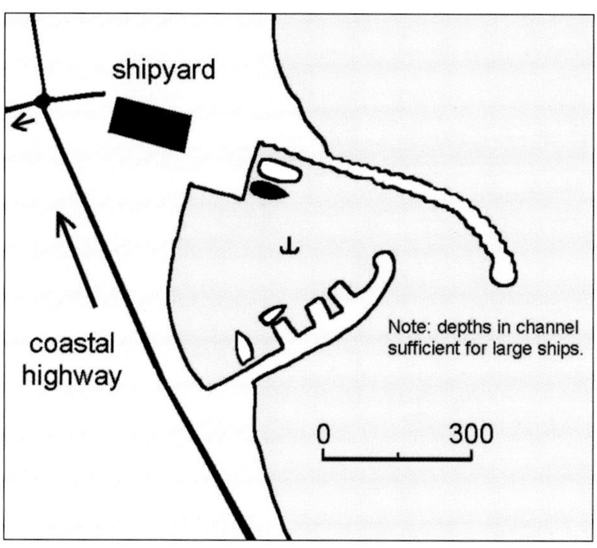


TERME

## TERME

41°11'·8N 37°2'·1E

A new fishing harbour and shipyard has been constructed on the E side of Civa Burnu which is a suitable harbour for yachts, if needed, on passage between Samsun and Ünye. The breakwater and shipyard are easily seen about 15M W of Ünye. Entrance is made from the E and the harbour is reported to have sufficient depths for yachts. *Gyatso* did not enter this previously unknown harbour, but we returned by land and met the manager of the shipyard who said he would welcome yachts. If space is available, the shipyard will allow yachts to tie alongside one of their tugs or alongside the cement quay. Alternatively, anchor in the middle of the harbour or tie up among the fishing boats off one of the jetties on the S breakwater. Shelter is good but there is some movement in the harbour. The coastal highway is a 10-minute walk inland with *dolmuş* service into the town of Terme, where all provisions and simple restaurants serving Turkish specialities can be found.

*Contact information* Ali Ihsan Dumlu, Manager, Terme Tersanesi AŞ Shipyard
*Email* alihsandumlu@gmail.com

### The Amazons

The ancient Greeks considered themselves to be the greatest people on earth and to rank other societies according to how similar they were to the Greeks. To men, for whom ideal females were stay-at-home wives and mothers with limited legal rights, nothing could be more barbaric than a tribe of warrior women, such as the Amazons.

The blind seer Phineas's sailing directions to the Argonauts stated, 'Then comes the mouth of the River Thermodon, which after wandering across the continent, flows into a quiet bay by the cape of Themiscyra. Here is the plain of Doeas, and the three towns of the Amazons near by.'

As Apollonius of Rhodes continued the story, 'In the bay beyond the cape, as the sea was getting rough, the Argonauts ran ashore at the mouth of the Thermodon... The headwater is a single stream which flows down to the lowlands from mountains called the Amazonian Heights.'

> 'Had the Argonauts stayed here as they intended and come to grips with the Amazons, the fight would have been a bloody one. For the Amazons of the Doeantian plain were by no means gentle, well-conducted folk; they were brutal and aggressive, and their main concern in life was war. War, indeed, was in their blood, daughters of Ares as they were and of the Nymph Harmonia, who lay with the god in the depths of the Acmonian Wood and bore him girls who fell in love with fighting.
>
> But Zeus once more sent forth the North-West Wind, and with its help the Argonauts stood out from the curving shore where the Amazons were arming for battle.'

The Amazons are long gone, and the Thermodon is now called the Terme Süyu, but it still flows into the bay where the Argonauts ran ashore.

View of the Amazonian Heights

Terme

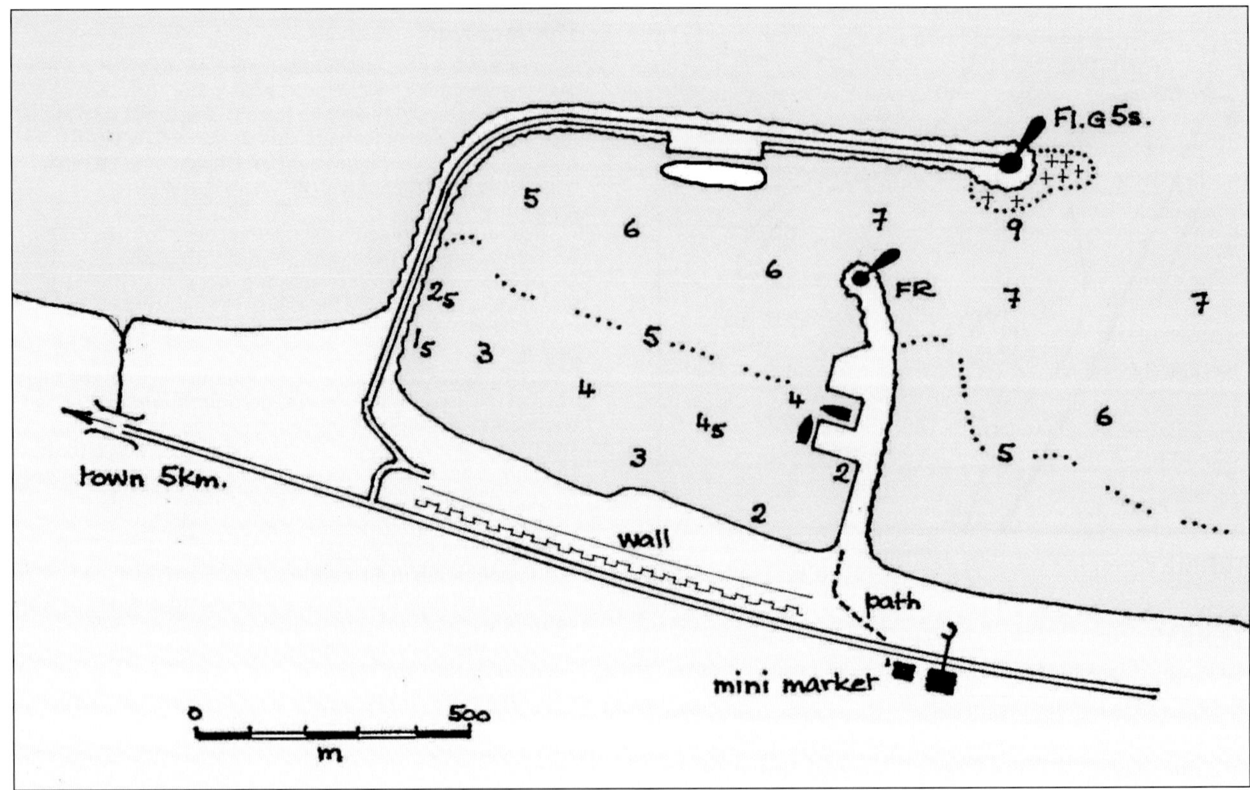


ÜNYE

Ünye looking north

## ÜNYE

41°07'·0N 37°21'·0E

The large and well-sheltered, multi-purpose commercial and fishing harbour is conveniently located near the coastal highway with easy access by *dolmuş* to the town centre 5km away.

### Approach

When approaching from the W, take care when rounding Tuskana Burnu. Otherwise, the approach is straightforward. The large cement works to the W of the harbour are conspicuous from all directions and the breakwaters with light structures on the end are easily seen.

Dangers (1) Tuskana Burnu, Fl(2)15s19m10M, located 4M W of the harbour, should be given a reasonable offing when approaching from the W. (2) Storm damage to the N breakwater has resulted in rocks lying off its E end. (3) In fresh NE winds, waves build up near the entrance but are not dangerous.

### Mooring

Go alongside the inside or ends of the pen on the inner breakwater in 4–5m, or there is plenty of room to anchor out. Fishing boats tend to use the W and S side of the southern jetty, but the walls on the inside of the pen are usually free for visiting yachts. Small freighters use the quay on the N breakwater to offload sand for the cement works. Very good shelter, especially inside the pens. No harbour charges.

### Facilities

Limited facilities for visiting yachts but a relatively secure harbour. A path at the base of the inner breakwater leads up stairs to the coastal highway, which is separated from the harbour by a high retaining wall. Just across the road near the small mosque are two minimarkets, and a roadside café selling freshly baked bread and the famous *köfte* (lamb patties) which can be grilled to order for eating in or takeaway meals. The friendly shopkeepers are eager to help visiting yachtsman and will offer tea and warm hospitality during your stay. From the coastal highway, you can catch one of the regular *dolmuş* minibuses headed toward town. In the city centre, you will find one of the best daily markets on the Black Sea coast. A weekly market takes place on Wednesday. Small supermarkets, banks, ATMs, internet cafés and the usual selection of restaurants in town. Nicer restaurants can be found along the waterfront.

### General

Set amidst hazelnut groves, the small city of 52,000 shows obvious signs of prosperity from the large cement works nearby. Many people gather in the square with a modern mosque and the 18th century town hall nearby. An old *hamam* can be found E of the main square which is open to men in the morning and to women in the afternoon. Nearby sites of interest include Ünye Castle, a ruined fortress founded by the Pontic Greeks and rebuilt by the Byzantines, located about 7km inland and reached by *dolmuş* and a short hike or by taxi.

## FATSA

41°02'·8N 37°29'·5E

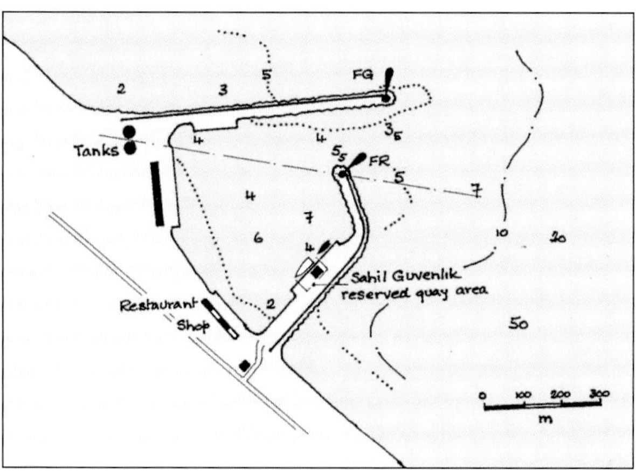


A nearly empty fishing harbour which provides very good shelter and offers little for the visiting yachtsman except a pleasant place to rest-up for a day or two.

### Approach

The breakwaters with green and red light structures on the end are visible to the N of town, as is the light structure on Fatsa Bank in the approaches. Two large circular tanks on the shore are now obscured by trees and apartment buildings, but the NW corner of the harbour can be used as a sightline in the final approaches.

Dangers (1) Fatsa Bank is located 1M NE of the harbour and marked by a lighthouse Fl.3s10M. (2) The N breakwater is prone to silting. On final approach, keep 100m off the end of the breakwater and head S until the end of the inner breakwater is in line between the two tanks. Then head in, staying in the S half of the entrance.

### Mooring

If space is available, go alongside the S quay in 4m but not in the space reserved for the Sahil Güvenlik vessel. Several local power boats tie stern-to the quay on the inside of this space. The quays on the W side of the harbour are reported to have less than 2m depths alongside. There is plenty of room to anchor out in 4–6m.

Fatsa Bank

Fatsa harbour

*Shelter* Very good.
*Authorities* None. The Sahil Güvenlik may ask to see your transit log and ship's papers if you tie alongside the S quay.
*Charges* None.

### Facilities

Limited.
*Services* Water at S quay.
*Fuel* By jerry can and taxi.
*Provisions* A minimarket is located on the road leading away from the harbour. A bakery which produces the large, rustic loaves is just across the main road. Town is within walking distance (1·5km), where more options for provisioning are available.
*Eating out* Many cafés and restaurants serve good food in town. One of the specialties here is *lahmacun*, a Turkish-style pizza made with a thin, pitta-like dough topped with cheese or minced meat and baked in the oven. They take an elongated shape in Fatsa.
*Other* ATM and internet cafés in town. *Dolmuş* service runs along the coastal highway to neighbouring towns and to the hot springs at Ilica which is reported to be worth it for the inland scenery alone.

### General

It seems that the coastal highway and construction of hotels, modern sporting facilities and a 4km-long beach promenade E of town have had some effect on attracting tourists to the area, judging by the number of new apartment blocks and amount of development stretching along the coast in either direction. With a population of 54,000, Fatsa attracts mostly local tourists.

Bolaman (not suitable for yachts)

## BOLAMAN

41°02'·5N 37°36'·0E

This small, shallow fishing harbour is prone to silting at the entrance and is not suitable for yachts. The larger fishing trawlers seen inside are able to power themselves through the mud, but the swell which builds up at the entrance and brown-stained water from the adjacent river make it difficult for a sailing yacht to safely check whether entrance depths are adequate. The harbour of Yaliköy is a much safer bet. From there, it is just 3km by *dolmuş* or taxi to see Bolaman Castle and the many examples of wooden houses in various stages of restoration and disrepair.

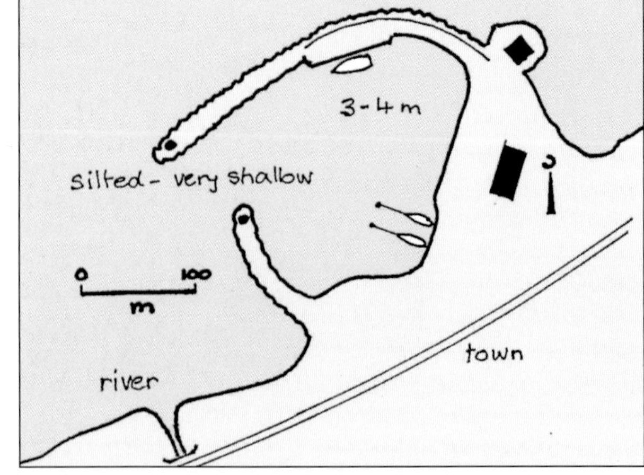

**BOLAMAN**

## YALIKÖY

41°03'·1N 37°36'·6E

A yacht-friendly fishing harbour in lovely, forested surroundings set apart from the main coastal highway which bypasses the peninsula several kilometres to the S.

### Approach

Yaliköy is located 5M E of Fatsa, on the E side of Fatsa Bay. The approach is straightforward, but the breakwater is built of dark stone which is difficult to see against the dark shore.

Dangers (1) No dangers in the immediate approach, but the adjacent headlands have offlying rocks and a good offing is advised. (2) The N breakwater has suffered storm damage and should be given 50m offing to avoid offlying rocks which are obvious and sometimes marked with a small buoy.

### Mooring

With permission, raft-up alongside one of the large fishing trawlers in 4m on the N breakwater. The fishermen are usually hard at work tying nets or maintaining their boats but will assist with mooring lines. There is also space to anchor in the harbour with limited swing room.

*Shelter* Very good.
*Authorities* Fishermen's cooperative on the quay.
*Charges* None.

### Facilities

*Services* Water at quay.
*Fuel* By jerry can and taxi.
*Provisions* Minimarkets, a bakery and a butcher in the village for basic provisions.

Yaliköy

*Eating out* Waterfront cafés serve simple food. Yaliköy is famous for its *köfte* which is served at roadside cafés throughout the area.
*Other Dolmuş* service can be found on the main coastal road leading to Fatsa or Jason's Cape.

### General

The village surrounds the harbour and is spread along the main road on both sides of the river, which has an outlet at the E end of the outer breakwater. Yaliköy is not mentioned in the typical tourist guides, and now that the coastal highway bypasses this peninsula, it is a pleasant place to experience what this stretch of coast was like before construction of the Yeni Yol. Lush forests interspersed with hazelnut groves cover the hillsides, and the volcanic rock formations along the shore are interspersed with small, picturesque coves and beaches. The friendly local people go out of their way to make you feel welcome.

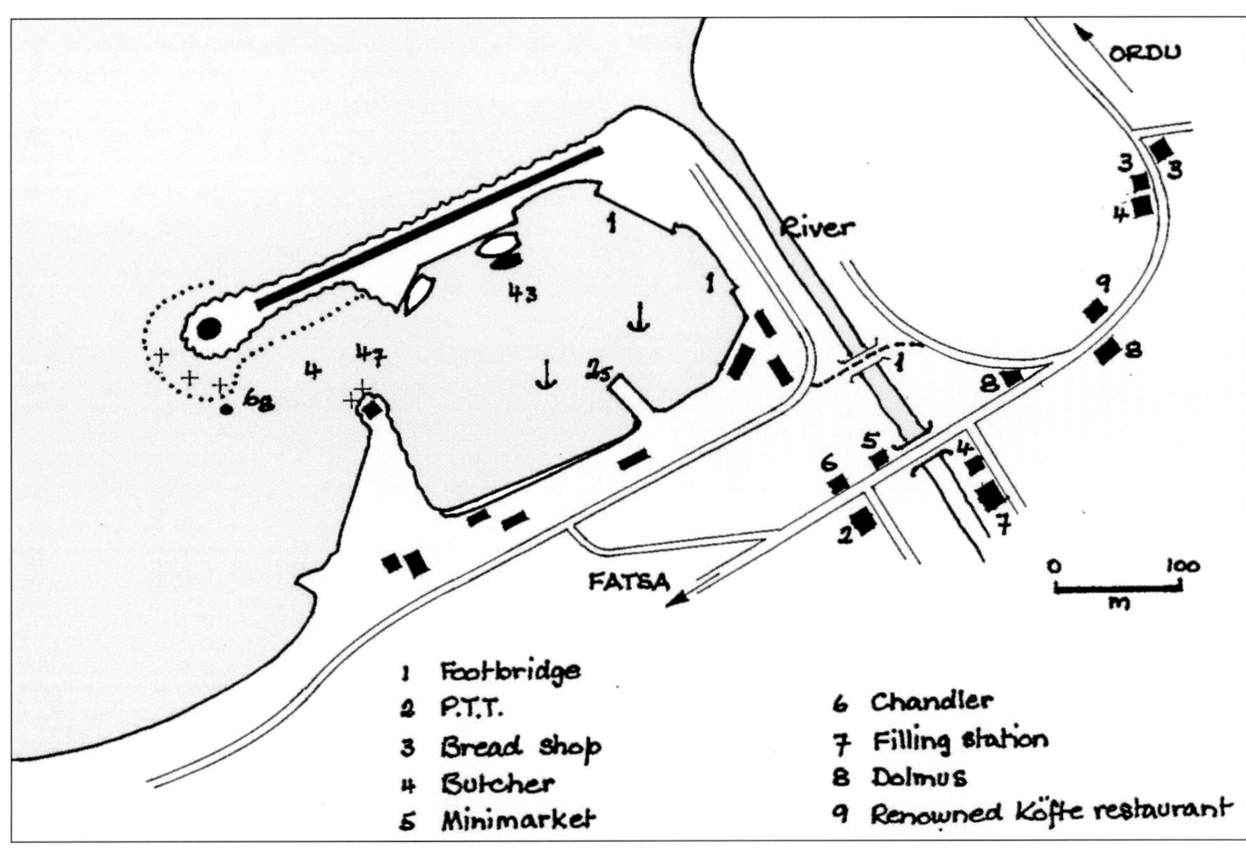


YALIKÖY

### Jason's Cape (Yasun Burnu)

From Yaliköy, you can flag down an eastbound *dolmuş* to Jason's Cape (Yasun Burnu) which will drop you at the entrance road leading to the park-like setting on the headland. On weekends, a small café sells refreshments and snacks near the site of Jason's Church.

The legend of Jason and the Argonauts became so enshrined in the lore of the Black Sea that many places became associated with Jason's voyage even though they were not mentioned in the account by Apollonius of Rhodes. Yasun Burnu, Jason's Cape, is one such place. Local lore has it that Jason and the Argonauts stopped here during their flight from Colchis, carrying with them the king's daughter, who was also the High Priestess, and a sacred relic of the Colchian people, the golden fleece. The point at the end of the cape has been sacred to Jason for a very long time, certainly well before Christianity came on the scene. Some time long ago, the Greek Orthodox Church built a small church dedicated to Jason. The church operated until the expulsion of ethnic Greeks from Turkey, in 1923. Recently it reopened to the public as a museum to itself.

On sunny summer Sundays, families flock to the end of the cape to picnic, stroll, fly kites, watch performances and relax.

Yasun Burnu festival

Yasun Burnu. Police chief dancing

## MEDRESEONÜ (CAVUSOĞLU)

41°04′·9N 37°37′·5E

A newly-constructed very small fishing harbour located 2M N of Yaliköy. It is not suitable for yachts.

## MERSIN (PERŞEMBE)

41°07′·0N 37°46′·0E

Mersin (Perşembe)

After rounding Yasun Burnu (Jason's Cape) from the W, the next fishing harbour is Mersin Perşembe. The outer breakwater and a mosque at the end of the quay are conspicuous in the approaches. There are no dangers in the immediate approach, but above and below-water rocks lie 200–300m E of the harbour entrance. The storm-damaged breakwater is evidence of the severe storms that batter this coastline in winter. The end has been reinforced and a light structure added to it. The friendly fishermen will wave you into the harbour and make you feel welcome. They will also warn you to avoid the rock

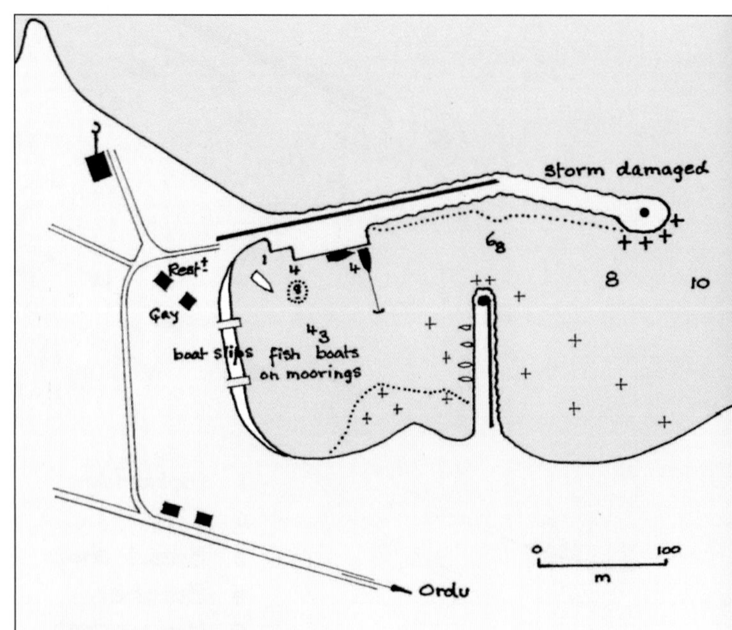


MERSIN (PERŞEMBE)

with less than 1m depths over it near the W end of the quay on the N breakwater. Go alongside this quay on the E end in 4m. There is no room to anchor among the numerous moorings for fishing boats in this harbour. Now that the breakwater has been reinforced, the shelter is considered good in normal summer conditions, but if bad weather is expected you may want to seek better shelter in Ordu Fishing Harbour to the E or Yaliköy, Fatsa or Ünye to the W. A minimarket, bakery and restaurant can be found near the picturesque harbour.

## KIŞLAÖNÜ (PERŞEMBE)

41°04'·8N 37°46'·7E

A crowded fishing harbour on the E side of the peninsula. After rounding Çam Burnu from the N the breakwaters are not immediately apparent, but there are numerous fish farms along this stretch of coast to the N and E of the harbour. It is amongst the most densely packed fishing harbours to be found on the Turkish Black Sea coast, perhaps due to the excellent shelter found inside and the proximity to fish farms. With permission, a yacht could tie alongside one of the fishing boats in 2·5–4m, but given the busy traffic and work being done on the large trawlers in the off-season, you will find more space at Ordu Fishing Harbour (also called Eferli), 5M to the SE. A small shopping area is located in the harbour area with tea houses, fish restaurants and a minimarket. Fresh fish from the fish farms are sold from a stall near the mosque. The town of Perşembe is 2km E of the harbour and has the usual shops, cafés, bakeries and an ATM.

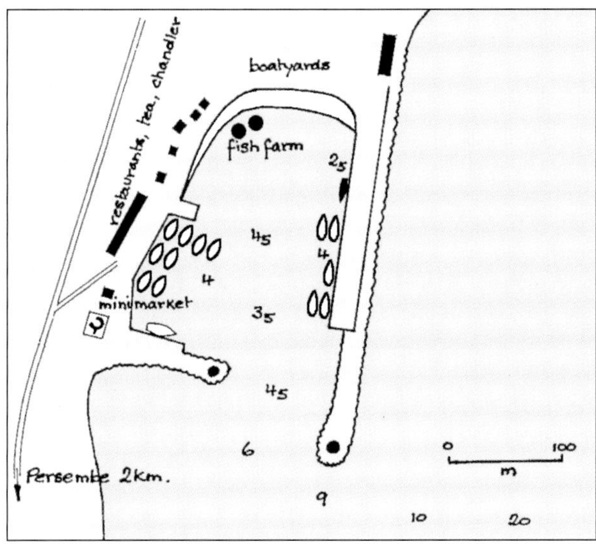


KIŞLAÖNÜ (PERŞEMBE)

## ORDU

41°01'·2N 37°51'·5E

Construction of Ordu's fishing harbour, also called Eferli and Kumbaşi in previous guides, was completed in the past 10 years and provides a convenient harbour with excellent shelter and easy access to the city by *dolmuş*.

### Approach

The approach is straightforward and the breakwater is easily seen from all directions.

### Mooring

One local motor yacht is kept alongside the E quay on the inner breakwater, and the owner frequently moves his yacht to make room for visiting yachts or

Ordu fishing harbour

Kişlaönü (Perşembe) approach

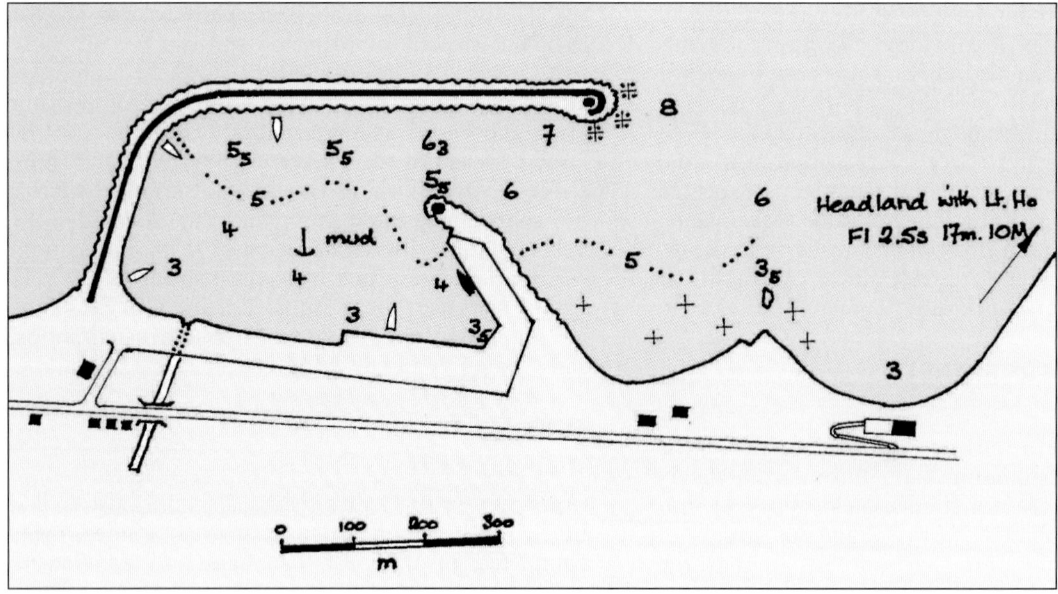


**ORDU, ALSO KNOWN AS EFERLI AND KUMBAŞI**

will give permission to raft-up. Alternatively, there is plenty of room to anchor out in the harbour in 4m of mud with good holding. This may be the more comfortable position with prevailing winds from the NW.

*Shelter* Excellent.

*Authorities* Harbourmaster and Fishermen's Cooperative in the building at the end of the quay (not necessary to check in).

*Charges* None.

## Facilities

*Services* Water and electricity on the E quay, with permission. The friendly yacht owner will lend you a water hose connected to a tap covered by a wooden box at the N end of the quay. He may also share his electrical connection in the same location.

*Fuel* By mini-tanker or jerry can and taxi.

*Provisions* For basic provisions, a minimarket is located E of the harbour on the coastal highway, about a 10-minute walk away. The village of Kumbaşi is a 10-minute walk to the W. All provisions can be found in Ordu, where a local market operates daily in the town centre with a good selection of fresh fruits and vegetables. Vendors also wheel carts along the main pedestrian shopping street selling seasonal products such as mushrooms and cherries. Several good bakeries sell fresh bread, including the well-known large, rustic loaves and a delicious, dense cornbread.

*Eating out* Numerous restaurants and cafés on the streetside and waterfront in Ordu.

*Other* Post office, banks, ATMs and an internet café in the city centre. At the base of the quay in the fishing harbour, a flight of stairs leads up to the coastal highway. From here, you can flag down a *dolmuş* heading E to reach the bustling seaside resort city of Ordu. Stay on the *dolmuş* until it reaches a stop near the main pedestrian street in the city centre, or continue a few stops to reach the market area and bus station. Ask locally for instructions on where to pick-up a return *dolmuş* to 'Ordu Liman'.

## General

The coastal highway now dominates this stretch of coastline, which used to be surrounded by beautiful countryside with hazelnut groves. The city of Ordu has a population of 117,000 and a busy city centre with tasteful shops selling jewellery and other high-end goods. It feels much like other Turkish cities of its size, but its location on the Black Sea coast gives it added appeal. The coastal highway becomes a seaside boulevard which separates the commercial area from a more park-like setting on the water. But the busy road is never far from being seen or heard. A large, metal jetty is still used by ships. Many of the old homes are being repaired. One is used as a hotel, another as a restaurant and one as a museum.

The Pasha's Palace and Ethnography Museum was closed for renovations in 2010 but when it reopens, it may be a good place to learn about the Ottoman lifestyle in the 19th century. To get there, follow signs to the Müze or Museum from the city centre. There are nice views of the city and coast from Boztepe headland reached by *dolmuş* (6km).

### *Passage note: Ordu To Giresun*

Three small harbours are found along the 24M passage between the Ordu fishing harbour and Giresun. The harbours tend to be shallow and prone to silting along this coast, and only one (Gülyali) is suitable for visiting yachts. An earnest student of outdated cruising guides might detect that they disagree on the names and locations of a few tiny harbours along this stretch of coast. It is considered that the information that follows is accurate but, of course, subject to improvement.

## GÜLYALI (CATALKAYA)

40°58′·4N 38°03′·15E

A small fishing harbour located 9M E of Ordu fishing harbour. The coastal highway passes along the S shore of the harbour and a small development of holiday homes sits on the hillside across the road. The breakwater is easily seen along with a dredger or two which appear to be permanently moored at the quay on the inside of the N breakwater. The water in the final approaches and in the harbour is somewhat shallow but sufficient, with care, for most yachts. From a safe point at 40°58′·5N 38°03′·2E, head for the inner end of the E breakwater at approximately 225° until the entrance opens, then enter on 090°. The quay areas were crowded with local boats, but there was room to anchor and tie stern-to the NW quay in 2–3m. The shelter is reported to be good. Water can be obtained at the restaurant which serves fish to passing motorists from the corner of the harbour. Like much of this part of the coast, the coastal highway dominates the otherwise remote setting.

Gülyali

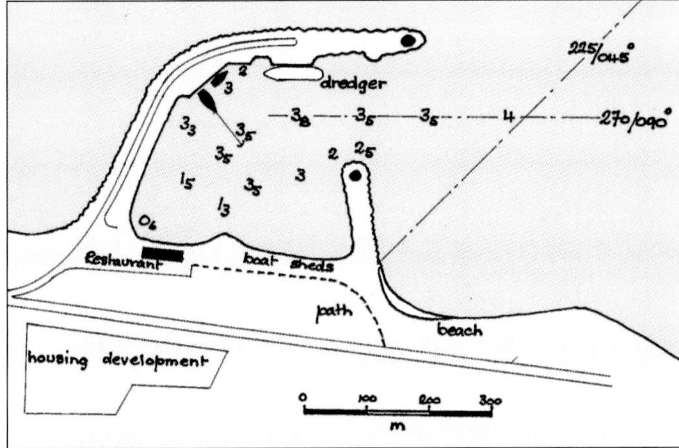

GÜLYALI (CATALKAYA)

The village of Gülyali is 1km E of the harbour near the salt pans where you can find several shops, bakeries, several cafés, a post office, a filling station and a market area used on Tuesdays and Thursdays.

A large breakwater extends N from the shore 0·8M E of the harbour entrance, but plans seem to have been abandoned for filling the area between this and another breakwater and turning it into an airport runway.

## PIRAZIZ

40°57′·4N 38°07′·45E

A quarried hillside and two radio towers are conspicuous in the approach, which should be made in a S direction due shallow water about 100m E of

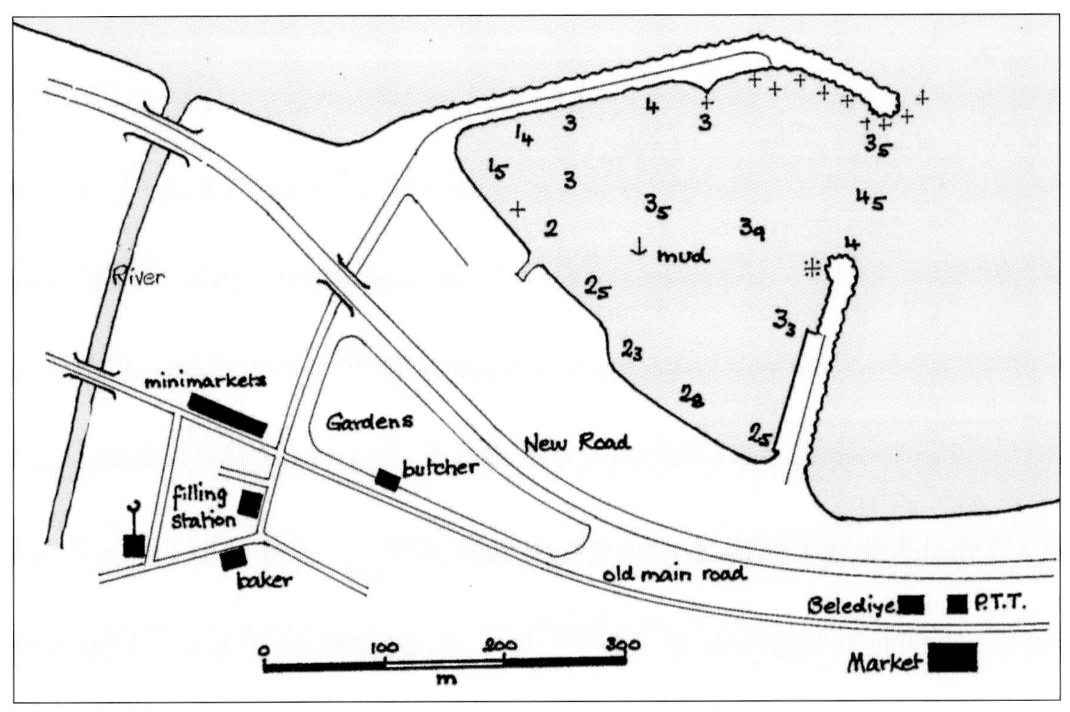

PIRAZIZ

Piraziz

the harbour entrance. DLH appears to have spent a lot of money to develop this small fishing harbour, but it is prone to silting at the entrance and the coastal highway separates the harbour from the town of Piraziz, which is a district capital in Giresun Province. With a swell running, *Gyatso*'s keel touched the bottom entering the harbour, and there is not much there, so it is at best only marginally suitable for yachts. Discolouration of the water at the river mouth just W of the harbour makes it very difficult to judge depths.

## BULANCAK

40°56′·65N 38°11′·3E

A crowded, shallow fishing harbour which is prone to silting at the entrance and not really suitable for visiting yachts even though Bulancak is a district capital in Giresun Province. Giresun, situated 9M to the E, is a much better option.

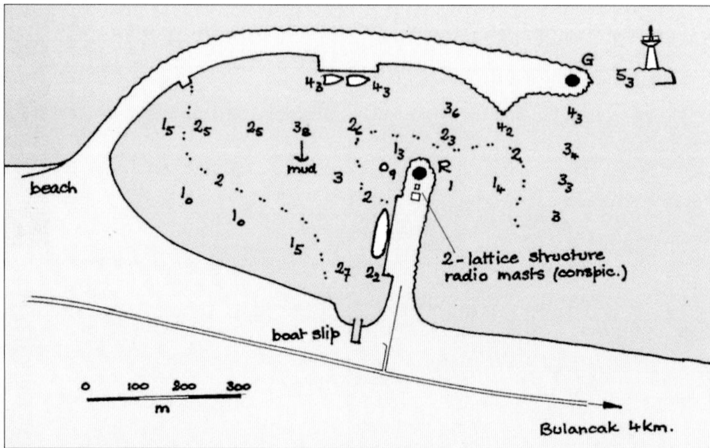


BULANCAK

Bulancak

## GIRESUN

40°55′·1N 38°22′·4E

A commercial harbour with a separate fishing harbour and a small 'yacht club' that welcomes visiting yachts.

### Approach

From the E, pass well outside Palamut Rock (Palamut Kayasi) before making for the harbour entrance. The large breakwaters, the city and prominent headland are easily seen from the W, but from the E the harbour is not visible until rounding Palamut Rock and the headland. From the W, the breakwaters and town are clearly visible. From the E, the breakwater is not visible until after rounding Palamut Rock and the headland. The large N breakwater which was damaged during a storm in 1998 has been repaired and extended in a southerly direction since 2001.

*VHF* Ch 16 for harbourmaster (no need to call).

Dangers (1) From the E, take great care to pass N of Palamut Rock (Palamut Kayasi) marked with an unlit cardinal buoy to avoid it and the below-water rocks to the S. On a direct course from Giresun Adası to the harbour entrance, the rocks are difficult to see because they barely break the surface of the water and underwater rocks extend to the S.

### Mooring

Proceed into the commercial harbour and anchor with a line ashore near the end of the inner breakwater where the Giresun Yacht Club maintains a small pontoon for two local yachts. Visiting yachts are warmly welcomed and the club has plans to develop this area further but permission has not yet been granted. Another option is to moor alongside or stern-to the cement quay near the SE corner of the harbour in 7m, but there is no security or gate in this area. The adjacent fishing harbour is crowded with large and medium-sized trawlers where yachts are allowed, but they will be in the way of the summer maintenance activities: sanding, painting, tying nets, etc.

*Shelter* Excellent, but some wash from minimal commercial traffic in the harbour.

*Charges* None at the yacht club; however, they can arrange for someone to keep an eye on your yacht, and in this case, a negotiable fee or a gratuity of around 20TL per day would be appropriate for the person who provides this service. Reported harbour charges of 30TL if you use the commercial quay.

Giresun. Coastal highway E of city centre

Giresun commercial harbour

Contact information:

M Volkan Türkilmaz, Owner, Hotel Çarikçi, Osmanağa Cadesi No. 6, Giresun
➀ +90 (454) 216 1026 *Email* volkturk@yahoo.com.
Volkan is an excellent host and avid world traveller. The hotel is a short walk from the yacht club's pontoon.

Özer Akbasli, President, Giresun Hazelnut Organic Union *Email* ozerakbasli@gmail.com
www.organikfindik.org.tr
Özer is also President of the Giresun Yacht Club and an excellent host.

## Facilities

*Services* Water and electricity at the yacht club pontoon. Fence and gate to prevent foot traffic (members of the yacht club will also help keep an eye on your yacht).

*Fuel* By jerry can and taxi.

*Provisions* Speciality food shops catering to the every day needs of locals are located across from the commercial harbour and one block in from the coastal highway. Here you will find a butcher with high quality meats from animals raised in the high pastures. They sell *köfte* which are especially good. Further inland is a local bazaar spreads out onto the streets on Thursdays. A new Migros supermarket is on the main commercial street in town, on the left-hand side of Gazi Cadesi as you climb up the hill leading away from the harbour from Atapark. Keep an eye out for excellent bakeries selling locally famous, dense cornbread and pastry shops serving sweet treats. Another locally-owned supermarket and a bakery are located across the coastal highway from the fishing harbour.

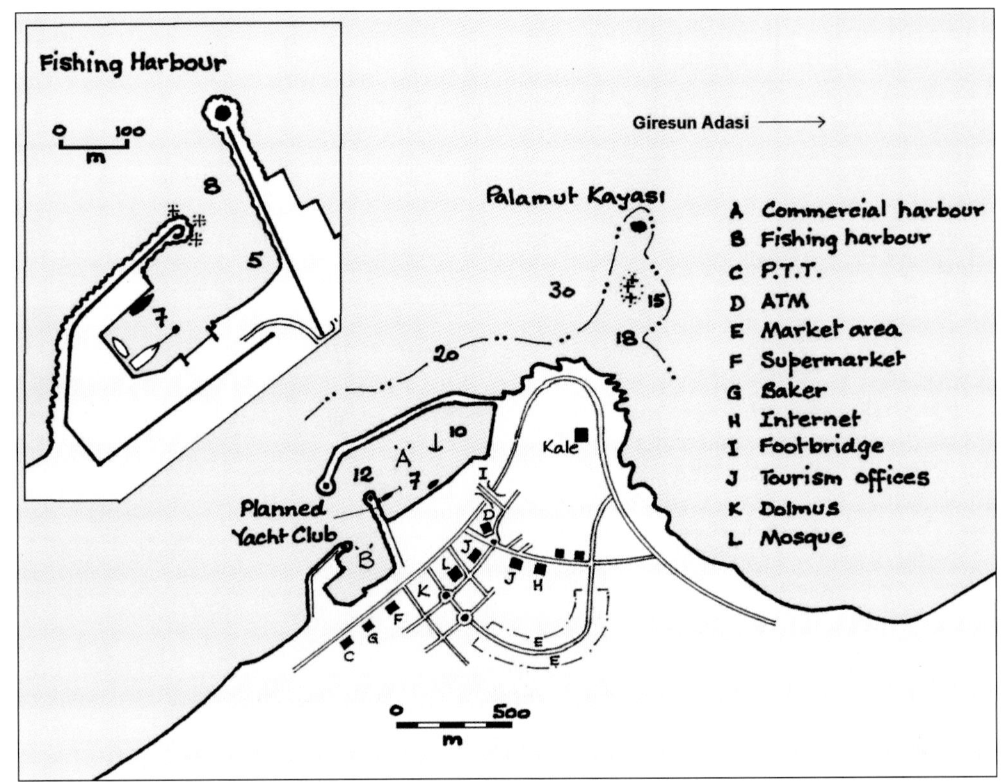

GIRESUN

Giresun Yacht Club

*Eating out* For a special meal, try Eskina, a waterfront restaurant S of the fishing harbour where the view and food are equally exceptional. Many other restaurants, *lokantasi* and cafés in town serve very good local specialities on Gazi Caddesi and adjacent pedestrian lanes.

*Other* Post office, bank, internet café and an ATM in the city centre. Bus and *dolmuş* service in the city and to neighbouring towns. With improvements to the coastal highway, the regular ferry service to Istanbul was discontinued.

### General

The coastal highway dominates the waterfront area, cutting between the harbour and the historic city centre. Pedestrian bridges make the crossing safer and easier. Once inside the bustling provincial capital city, the coastal highway fades away. For suggestions on what to see and do in Giresun, stop by the yacht-friendly Hotel Çarikçi and ask for the owner, Volkan, who speaks English. For a pleasant outing and great views of the city and Black Sea coast, he might suggest that you walk or take a taxi to the park-like setting at the castle (*Kale*) perched atop the hill. From here, wind your way back down the hill to the waterfront, stopping off in the historic neighbourhoods on the S side of the hill, the Archaeology Museum which is housed in an 18th-century Greek church with views over Giresun Adası and other local sites of interest (guidebooks and maps of the town are available).

The name for Giresun is derived from the Greek word for cherry. It is believed that that the first cherries were taken from here to Rome in ancient times. Today, the delicious, plump cherries you find in the markets are grown elsewhere in Turkey – the ones of Giresun's fame are the wild cherry variety. Turkey produces 85% of the world's supply of hazelnuts (think Nutella, etc.), and today Giresun is the main centre of hazelnut production in Turkey. A million Turkish farm families make their living from hazelnuts, which are sprinkled liberally on many local dishes or ground into a paste and used in baking and sweet desserts.

The city was founded by the Greeks, and as with so many places they found appealling, a steep promontory extends toward the sea, offering shelter to ships and a defensible position upon which to build an acropolis. Although subsequent fortification by the Romans, Byzantines, Genoese and Ottomans have obliterated nearly all traces of the original Greek settlement, the setting is completely consistent with all of the other important Greek ports in Mediterranean and Black Seas.

From Giresun, it may be possible to join a local tour into the high summer pastures, known as *yaylas*. Ask Volkan for assistance or stop by the local tourist board office to see if any tours are scheduled.

## GIRESUN ADASI (ISLAND)

40°55'·9N 38°26'·2E

This is one of only two islands off the S coast, the other being Kefken Adası, sacred to Apollo at Dawn. This was known in ancient times as Aretias Island, and Apollonius of Rhodes features it as the Island of Ares, where the Argonauts spent a night after driving off the warbirds who inhabited it. But it's a tiny place 2M east of Palamut Rock. There is a small dock, but with the constant swell it is not a suitable place for a yacht to tie up or anchor off the island. It is better to visit the island with a good dinghy from Giresun, or stop by the small boat harbour on the E side of the promontory and ask a fisherman to bring you out (negotiate a price in advance). The festival on 20th May each year includes a pilgrimage to the ruined Greek monastery on the island. A sacred black boulder is on the shore.

#### *Passage note: Giresun Adası To Tirebolu*

From Giresun Adası to Tirebolu, rounding Çam Burnu, you will see several tiny fishing harbours which are not suitable for yachts, as well as numerous groynes, breakwaters and retaining walls designed to protect the coastal highway.

View of Giresun Adasl from Kale in Giresun

# Section 4: Çam Burnu to the Georgian border

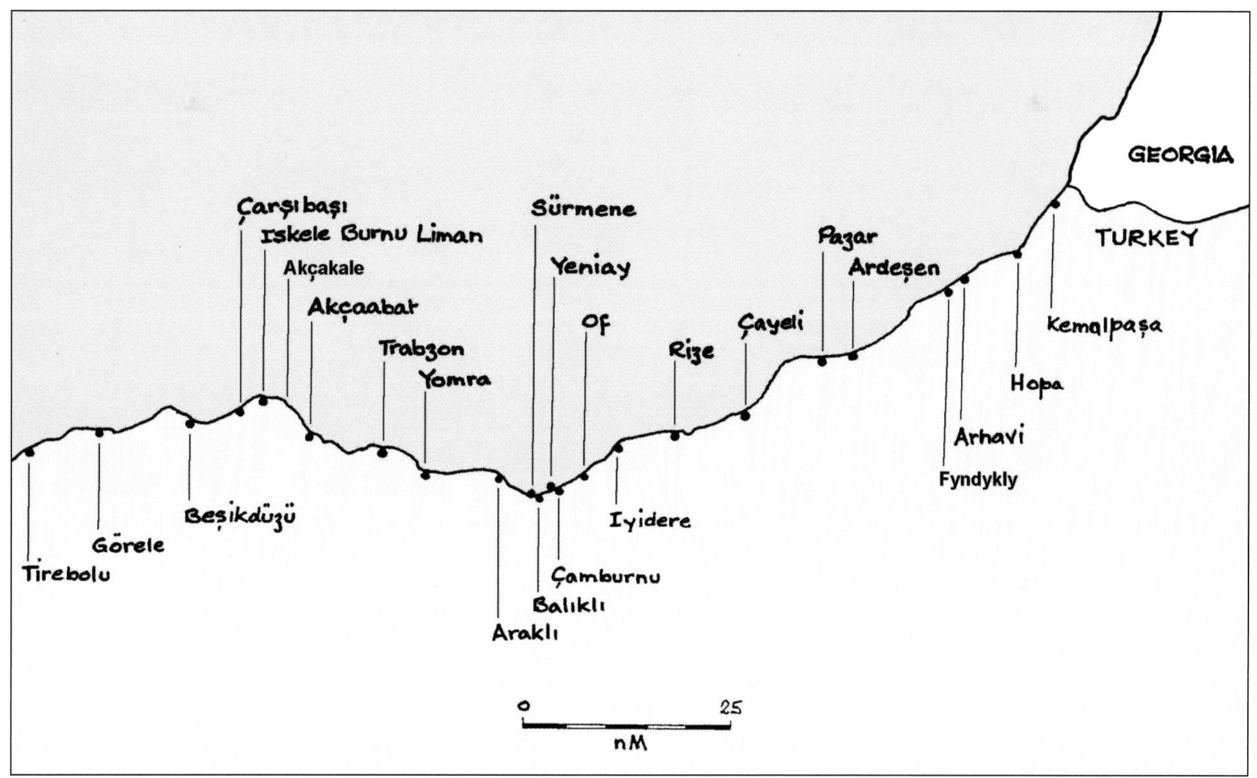


ÇAM BURNU TO THE GEORGIAN BORDER

### *Passage note: Çam Burnu to the Georgian border*

It is approximately 125M of coastal sailing between the town of Tirebolu, in the west, to Hopa, the Turkish port of entry in the east. In the middle lies Trabzon, about 45M east of Tirebolu. For most of its very long life, Trabzon has been the most important city on the Black Sea. Less than 40M east of Trabzon is Rize, the jewel of the far eastern Black Sea coast of Turkey. In Rize one begins to see Laz people. By Çayeli, the next town along the coast, Laz is the predominant language. This is tea growing country, the source of the black tea so important for Turkish socialising. Near the Georgian border, the village of Kemalpaşa is an 'orphan' in the sense that it should not be visited after having checked out of Turkey.

## TIREBOLU

41°00'·65N 38°49'·2E

### Approach

From the west the approach is straightforward. From the east the final approach to the harbour should be made from the N to avoid shallow water associated with the river mouth 1M to the E.

*Conspicuous* The town is built on three promontories. The old part of town is built on the middle promontory. The E promontory is crowned by a Byzantine fortress, conspicuous behind the N breakwater. The N breakwater has been extended considerably since 2001, as well as new quays which have been constructed on the inside of the N breakwater and the W side of the harbour. A buoy reported in 2001 in the bay W of the harbour is no longer seen and presumably marked the location of the end of the breakwater when it was under construction.

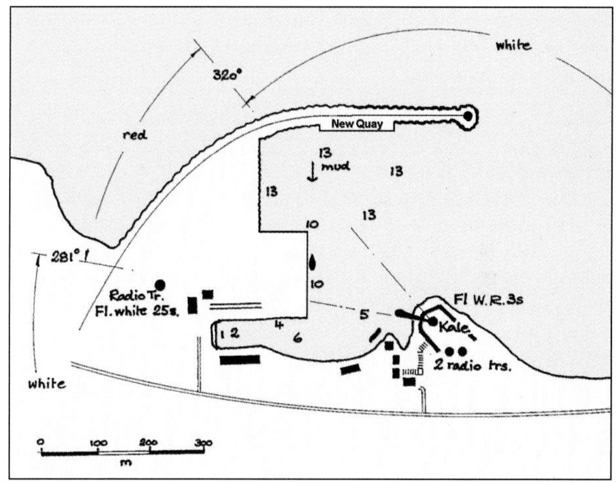


TIREBOLU

Dangers (1) The coastline to the W has numerous above- and below-water rocks, generally near the shore but extending out as far as 0·5M. Give an offing of at least this much along this coast. (2) Shallow water associated with a river mouth 1M to the E of the harbour entrance.

Tirebolu

## Mooring

Go alongside the new W quay in 10m where convenient. There is plenty of room to anchor out with 9–13m in mud with good holding. The area in the S is reserved for small fishing boats. The harbour is a secure place to leave a yacht while exploring the surrounding area.

*Shelter* Very good, but the harbour is somewhat open to the E.

*Authorities* The harbourmaster's office is located in the blue building on the road leading from the W side of the harbour. The harbourmaster is very welcoming to yachts and appreciates a courtesy visit. The Fishermen's Coop is in the building next to the harbourmaster. They operate a small fish market on the ground level, facing the small boat harbour.

*Charges* None.

Tirebolu castle

## Facilities

*Services* Electricity is on the quay, by special arrangement, but it requires an extra-long cable. A water tap is near the small boat harbour.

*Fuel* Diesel by tanker, arranged by harbourmaster.

*Repairs* Minor repairs can be arranged through the harbourmaster.

*Provisions* A large weekly market is held on Fridays on the road next to the harbour. There are several minimarkets and a shop selling fresh produce nearby the harbour, in town. A small supermarket is located across the coastal highway from the harbour.

*Eating out* Many cafés, ice cream shops and stalls selling snacks along the waterfront promenade on the S shore of the harbour. Look for the locally made ice cream. There are two or three restaurants at the base of the fortress, one of which specialises in *lahmacun*, the Turkish-style pizza.

*Other* Banks and ATMs in the waterfront area.

## General

Tirebolu is the capital of a district in Giresun Province. Residents particularly welcome foreign yachts, which are still something of a novelty. Situated on a peninsula which is connected to the modern town, the old town is built around a square surrounded by old buildings. This is the western edge of Turkey's famous Eastern Black Sea tea growing area. On the eastern side of the harbour is the Çaykur tea processing plant.

In ancient times, Tirebolu was known as Tripolis, 'three cities', because it was built on three promontories. The old part of town is atop the central promontory, while the east and west promontories are fortified. The eastern fortress, known as Kurucakale, is among the best preserved and most impressive fortresses on the Turkish Black Sea coast and is built on the acropolis of the ancient city. Nowadays it is a local attraction and well-lit at night, with cafés. The lighthouse in the castle serves as a mark for the south breakwater of the modern harbour, which is a case study in port development. Arrian mentioned Tripolis but said nothing about it having even an anchorage. In 1842 the British explorer William Hamilton noted that in the bays between the promontories 'there is very deep water; but as they also contain many sunken rocks, the anchorage is not safe.' In 1993 the Nelsons found only the beginnings of a breakwater. The anchorage was safe 'only in calm and settled weather.' In 2001 the Annans found construction work underway. There was 'no suitable place to tie up but anchorage is possible.' By 2010 the harbour was suitable for coastal freighters to tie alongside an impressive quay. The local government's website is www.yenitirebolu.com.

## GÖRELE

41°02'·2N 39°00'·5E

### Approach

The approach is straightforward and the outer breakwater is easily seen. The N breakwater has been extended somewhat to incorporate offlying rocks that were reported in 2001. An inner breakwater has been constructed in place of the former town pier, and in 2010 preparations were underway to build a quay for large fishing boats along this breakwater. There are light structures, painted white, on both breakwaters.

A sand bank extends to the S of the N breakwater, near the entrance and into the harbour. Stay close to the S breakwater and follow it around to the left on entrance, where there are depths of at least 3m. The harbourmaster or a local fisherman may show you the way in, but this is not essential for safe navigation.

### Mooring

Proceed to the small inner harbour and tie alongside a fishing boat or anchor in sand in 3m, S of the entrance. A quay has been added to the N breakwater, which is used by large trawlers. Boat sheds line the SW shore of the harbour.

*Shelter* Good all-round shelter in the outer harbour and excellent shelter in the small inner harbour.
*Authorities* Harbourmaster's office on the W side of the outer harbour. He welcomes visiting yachts and appreciates a courtesy visit.
*Charges* None.

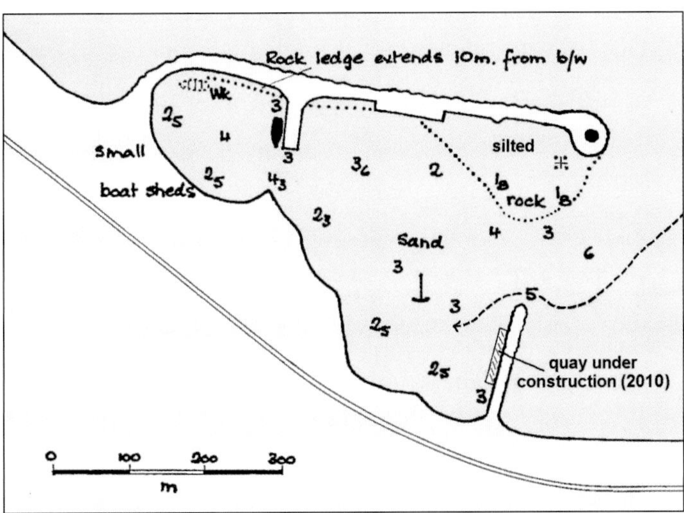


GÖRELE

Görele. Boat sheds along shore of harbour

### Facilities

Water at the boat sheds in the inner harbour. Fuel is by jerry can. The new coastal highway running through the town has created opportunities to open new tourism-oriented facilities including a bus station, cafés and *pide* shops. The town is known for its large round loaves of bread and *pide* shaped like submarines topped with cheese or sausage and an egg. An ATM, internet café and provisions of all kinds can be found at small shops in town.

### General

Görele is a district capital in Giresun Province and is a pleasant stop.

## BEŞİKDÜZÜ

41°03'·9N 39°13'·5E

A small fishing harbour with a convenient filling station next to the harbour, very good shelter and plenty of room for a yacht to anchor or tie alongside a fishing boat.

### Approach

The breakwater is easily seen in the approach. An Otogaz filling station on the coastal highway, at the SW corner of the harbour is conspicuous. Now there is a light structure, painted white, on the outer

Beşikdüzü

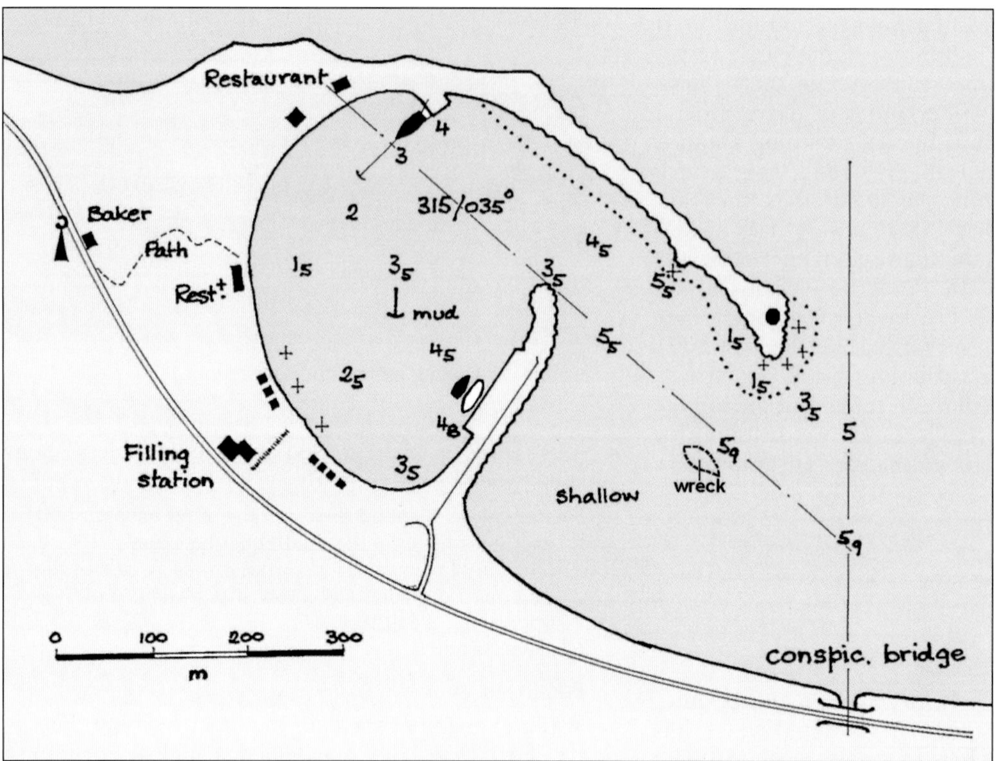


BEŞIKDÜZÜ

breakwater, which has been extended to incorporate some of the offlying rocks noted in 2001. A white-painted light structure and flagpole has also been installed on the inner breakwater. The final approach should be made in a southerly direction, at least 50m off the E end of the breakwater. Pass between this and the masts of a sunken fishing boat, and then close to the inner breakwater.

Danger The sunken wreck of a fishing boat with only the masts sitting above water is located immediately to the S of the end of the outer breakwater. Shallow water is reported S of the wreck, so pass between it and the end of the breakwater when entering the harbour.

### Mooring

Raft-up alongside a fishing boat on the quay on the inner breakwater or anchor in 3·5–4·5m where convenient. Despite appearances, with the wreck in the entrance, the shelter is very good. No harbour charges reported.

### Facilities

*Services* Water from restaurant on the W shore of the harbour.

*Fuel* By jerry can from the Otogaz filling station which can be seen across the road from the harbour.

*Provisions* Basic provisions can be found in the nearby town. A bakery is a short walk W on the coastal highway where they sell the large, round loaves baked in a wood oven. A rough path through the woods leads back to the harbour.

*Eating out* There are two restaurants at the harbour itself.

### General

The harbour is surrounded by a small fishing village in a rural setting. Beşikdüzü town centre is about 1·5km to the SE along the coastal highway.

***Passage note: Beşikdüzü to Carşibaşi***

Between these two harbours, there are numerous groynes, breakwaters and retaining walls associated with the coastal highway and several small fishing harbours which are not suitable for yachts.

## CARŞİBAŞI

41°05'·0N 39°22'·2E

This is a busy fishing port with good shelter if needed, but since other good harbours, such as Görele and Akçakale, are nearby, this is not the best choice for yachts.

### Approach

The breakwater is easily seen. Some electrical pylons and a microwave mast on the hills behind the harbour help to identify the approach to the harbour, which should be made at a bearing of 190°. The sandbank shown on some charts in the middle of the harbour has been removed. The shallow water at the entrance would make entrance difficult in fresh NE winds.

### Mooring

If space is available, raft-up with a fishing boat with permission or anchor in 4m of mud with good holding. The harbour is well protected. No harbour charges.

### Facilities

Water is available on the quay. There is a harbourmaster, a fuel station, and everything that can be expected in a good-size town. A minimarket across from the harbour supplies basic provisions. The large village nearby has a rose-filled square and tea gardens. Many shops, an internet café, ATM and

## CARŞIBAŞI

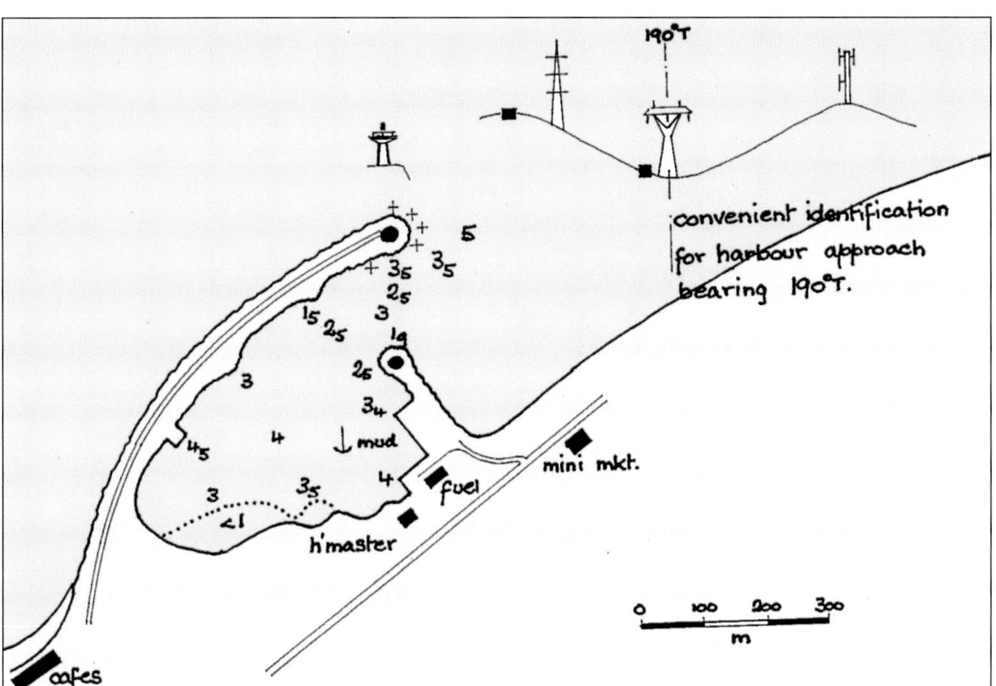

Carşibaşi

several larger supermarkets can be found here. Saturday is market day when local produce is on sale.

### General

A black sand beach, popular with locals, is located west of the harbour. Tracks through tea gardens and vegetable gardens are said to lead away from the harbour and up into the surrounding hillside with good views over the harbour.

## IŞIKLI BURNU LİMAN

41°06'·25N 39°25'·85E

This harbour, which is immediately alongside the coastal highway, seems to have been built to facilitate offloading of the anchovy catch onto trucks. It is situated in a scenic area of the peninsula.

### Approach

The outer breakwater with a light structure on the end is easily seen after passing the lighthouse on Iskele Burnu. The old harbour has disappeared with the construction of the coastal highway. Give both breakwaters 20m offing to avoid offlying rocks.

### Mooring

A DLH dredger is berthed on the quay at the SE corner of the inner breakwater, and dredging was actively underway in 2010. There is shallow water near the quay on the N breakwater, where medium-sized fishing boats are rafted. We observed a man standing chest-deep in the water outside of these boats. Raft-up with permission alongside fishing boats on the S jetty in 3·5–4m. Good shelter in this part of the harbour. No harbour charges.

Işıkli Burnu Liman

IŞIKLI BURNU LIMAN

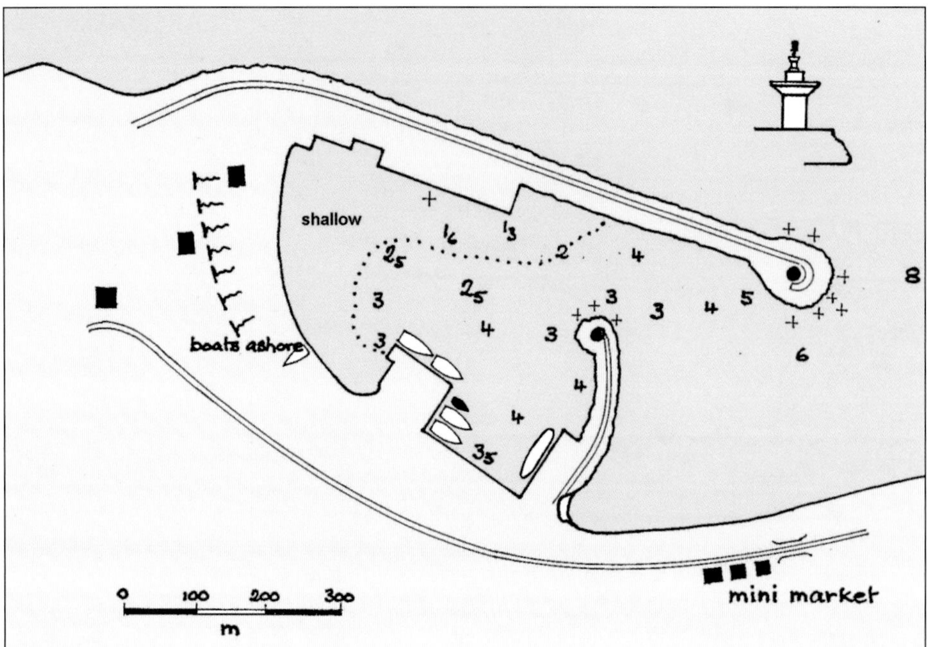


### Facilities

*Services* Water at main quay where boats are on the shore.
*Fuel* By arrangement with the fishing boat supply.
*Provisions* Basic provisions available from a minimarket near the bridge on the coastal highway.

### General

There is nice scenery and good walking country here.

## AKÇAKALE

41°04'·6N 39°30'·6E

A new fishing harbour tucked in behind a small peninsula 5M NW of Akçaabat which provides a suitable overnight stop for yachts.

### Approach

The breakwater extends E from a conspicuous promontory with the ruins of a 13th-century Byzantine castle on it. After rounding this small peninsula, the approach is straightforward with more than adequate water depths at the entrance and inside.

### Mooring

Fishing boats occupy a quay on the N breakwater. They are happy to have yachts tie alongside them. Small fishing boats occupy the southern shoreline, but there is room to anchor out in 7–9m. The shelter is very good. No harbour charges.

### Facilities

*Services* Water and electricity by arrangement with the fishing boats on the N quay.
*Provisions* Minimarkets in town.
*Eating out* There are simple restaurants close to the harbour
*Other* Buses to Trabzon.

### General

There are ruins of a 13th-century Byzantine castle on the peninsula.

AKÇAKALE

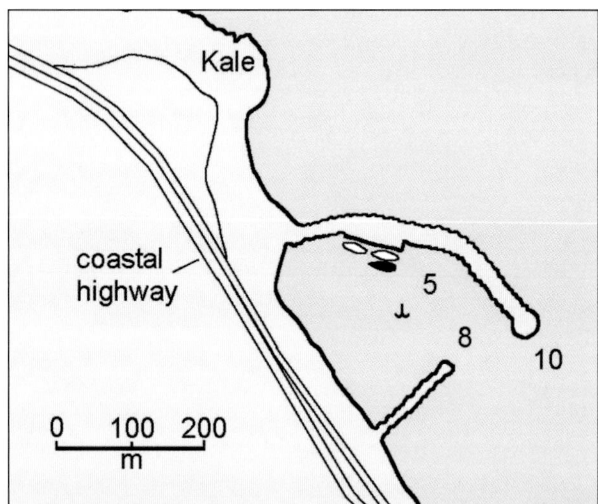

Akçakale

### *Passage note: Harbour near Hotel Saray*

A small new harbour near the Hotel Saray in position 41°03'·1N 39°32'·5E does not appear to be suitable for yachts. No further information is available.

## AKÇAABAT

41°01'·6N 39°34'·1E

A small but pleasant fishing harbour located 8M W of Trabzon Commercial Harbour.

### Approach

The breakwaters lie at the W end of the town, which has expanded along the coastal highway. The outer breakwater has a white-painted light structure and a large Turkish flag flying from a flag pole at the end of the breakwater. A second inner breakwater has been added outside the old one, and both have light structures (the newer one is painted white). The harbour is backed by large apartment buildings and a conspicuous modern building with a dome-shaped roof immediately SE of the harbour. Once inside the harbour, you will find tea houses built on the N breakwater and boatsheds lining the shore. A large steel pier at the E end of town is for ships and offers no shelter for yachts.

Danger A line of six unlit orange pyramid buoys lies W of the harbour extending to the shore in position: 41°02'·2N 39°34'·3E. They are not interconnected and mark the line of a sewage treatment plant outfall pipe. Divers work in this area, which could pose a hazard at night.

### Mooring

Tie alongside fishing boats on the quay inside the outer breakwater or anchor in 3·5m. This is a secure place to leave your yacht for excursions into Trabzon and the surrounding area.

*Shelter* Very good.
*Authorities* Fishermen's Cooperative on the quay.
*Charges* None.

### Facilities

*Services* Water on the main quay.
*Fuel* By arrangement from the fishing boat supply.

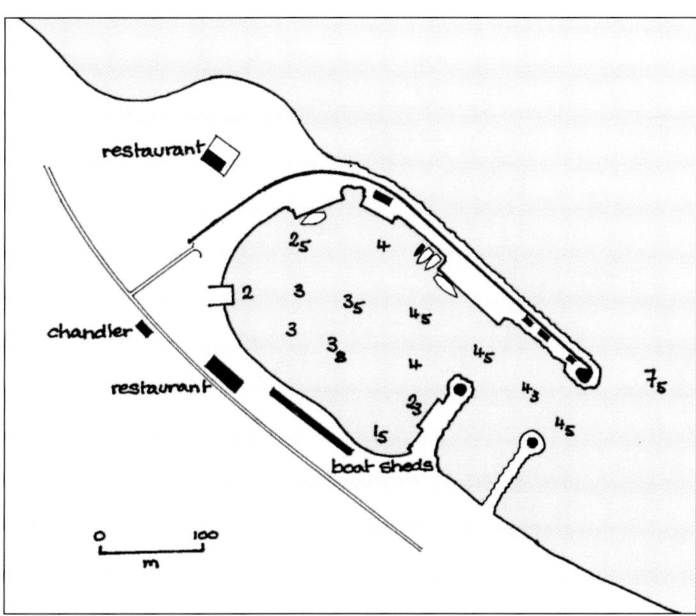


AKÇAABAT

Akçaabat

Akçaabat. Köfte restaurant

*Provisions* A large shopping centre has been developed across the road from the harbour where all provisions can be purchased. A yacht chandler here is said to have a good selection of stainless steel bolts, pumps and pump spares.
*Eating out* Restaurants in the area serve the famous Akçaabat *köfte* to busloads of tourists from Trabzon. Several are in the immediate harbour area.
*Other* ATMs and internet cafés can be found in the town centre behind the police station. Tour buses and *dolmuş* service to Trabzon.

### General

This is a holiday resort town spread along the coastal highway W of Trabzon. It is built on three ridges, the harbour being at the foot of the W-most of these. The main town is on the E ridge. The town's population is 36,000. In ancient times this was called Platana, and nowadays it is sometimes known as Pulathane.

## TRABZON

41°00'·45N 39°45'·05E (Commercial Harbour)
41°00'·05N 39°47'·9E (Trabzonspor Yacht Harbour)

The largest city on Turkey's Eastern Black Sea coast has four harbours, three of which are suitable for yachts.

### Yalimahalle

41°00'·7N 39°42'·6E

Trabzon's fishing harbour which is home to several large fishing trawlers and is said to be a suitable place for yachts. The approach is straightforward, and the harbour is conveniently located across the coastal highway from the city. A small boat harbour is located between here and Güzelhisar Burnu.

### Trabzon Commercial Harbour

41°00'·45N 39°45'·05E

The large commercial harbour is located just E of Güzelhisar Burnu.

### Approach

The approach is straightforward. The cranes, silos and ships in the commercial harbour are easily seen in the approaches. The green buoy marking the extent of storm damage must be passed on its E side. Yachts should proceed into Kuçuk Liman, the inner harbour in the SE corner.

*VHF* Ch 16 for port control (not necessary to call).

Yalimahalle

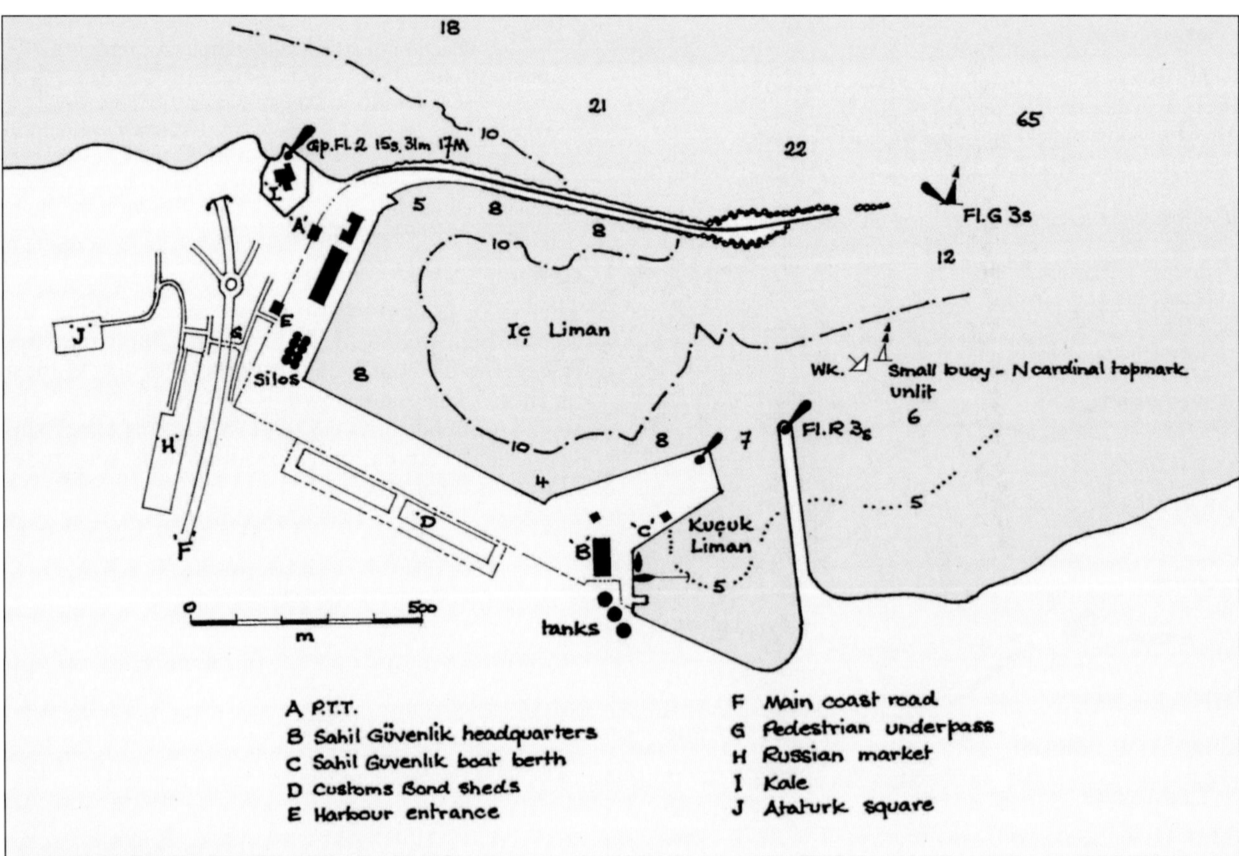


TRABZON COMMERCIAL HARBOUR

Trabzon Commercial Harbour

Dangers (1) A small, unlit N cardinal buoy on the S side of the entrance channel marks a wreck. (2) Just E of the harbour, a line of five unlit orange pyramid buoys extend from the shore to the position: 40°59'·7N 39°49'·0E. They mark the line of a sewage treatment plant outfall pipe. Divers work in this area which could be a hazard at night.

### Mooring

Go alongside the quay to the S of the Sahil Güvenlik berth in 4m or where directed by port authorities. The Sahil Güvenlik may give permission to lie at their quay.

*Depths* 4–5m in Kuçuk Liman.
*Shelter* Very good.
*Authorities* Port of Entry. Port authorities are located on the W side of the commercial harbour near the passenger terminals.
*Charges* None.

### Facilities

*Services* No electricity. Water by courtesy of Sahil Güvenlik or by mini-tanker arranged through the harbourmaster's office.

*Fuel* Jerry can and taxi. Ask port authorities for permission to have fuel delivered by mini-tanker. See fuel contact information for yacht harbour below.

*Provisions* The large port city is an excellent place to provision a yacht. In addition to the usual supermarkets and minimarkets near the harbour and the underpass to the harbour gate, speciality food shops are found in the heart of the commercial district near Medan square, including one block with a butcher's shop, bakery, greengrocer, deli and gourmet food shop featuring local specialities. A daily market operates near the waterfront along the coastal highway W of the commercial harbour with a larger weekly market on Saturdays. The modern Forum shopping mall, with many well-known European chains, including a Migros supermarket, is located E of the city centre and can be reached by *dolmuş* or taxi.

*Eating out* Many good restaurants serving local specialities are situated around Medan square and the pedestrian streets around the square. Take your pick from the Balik Lokantasi which serves tasty grilled and fried fish at very reasonable prices or one of the more traditional *lokantasis* with outside seating on a pedestrian alley. Try one of the shops selling *pide* cooked in a wood oven, a *lokantasi* serving the famous Akçaabat *köfte* (grilled lamb patties) or a simple restaurant serving *manti* (meat dumplings in a yoghurt sauce). Join the locals at one of the tea gardens in the square or taste the sweet treats at one of the cafés to experience for yourself why Trabzon is known for producing the best bakers and pastry chefs in Turkey. Several tea gardens are tucked in under the *Kale* (castle) walls in a quiet setting with views over the small boat harbour and the Black Sea.

*Other* Post office, banks, ATMs and internet cafés in the city centre. Turkish gaz from shops near the *sanayi* (light industrial park) along the coastal highway to the E of the commercial harbour. Pak Çiti Laundry with wash/dry/fold service is located on Cumhuriyet Mah. Zeytinlik Cd. 18/8. *Hamams* (Turkish baths) near Medan Square and W of Çarşi Camii. Bus and *dolmuş* service in the city and to surrounding towns. International airport with daily flights to and from Istanbul and charter flights to UK, Azerbaijan and elsewhere. Overnight ferries to Sochi, Russia.

## Trabzon Fishing Harbour

41°00'·2N 39°45'·8E

A small fishing harbour surrounded by private boathouses is located between the commercial harbour and the Trabzonspor Yacht Harbour and near the modern Forum shopping centre. This is reserved for local boats and at present is not suitable for visiting yachts.

## Trabzonspor Yacht Harbour

41°00'·05N 39°47'·9E

Just 2M E of the commercial harbour is a purpose-built yacht harbour which has never officially opened as a marina. Visiting yachts can use the harbour with permission, but no services are provided except 24-hour security. This is a good place to leave your yacht for inland travel.

### Approach

Situated 2M E of Trabzon Commercial Harbour, the breakwaters are easily seen from all directions and the approach is straightforward. The harbour is adjacent to the airport and the control tower is conspicuous.

### Mooring

With permission (see note below), go alongside one of the pontoons where space is available or where directed by security. For security reasons, the club asks that you not use the cement quays along the shore. The pontoons are constructed of cement with fender boards mounted on the sides. Due to the lack of maintenance since the marina was constructed, some of the boards are loose or missing. Several fishing boats and a handful of local yachts are moored on the pontoons.

*Depths* 6m at the entrance and 3–4m alongside the pontoons.
*Shelter* Excellent.
*Authorities* Trabzonspor (see below).
*Charges* None.

*Note* This yacht harbour was built by DLH specifically for yachts in 2000, perhaps the first on the Black Sea coast of Turkey. Its management was subsequently acquired by Trabzonspor, the owner of a competitive Turkish football team with players from around the globe. The club knows everything about managing a football team but nothing about managing a yacht marina, which has become an orphaned asset. Water is plentiful to sprinklers for young trees but not available on the piers. Electricity is nowhere to be found – the club has

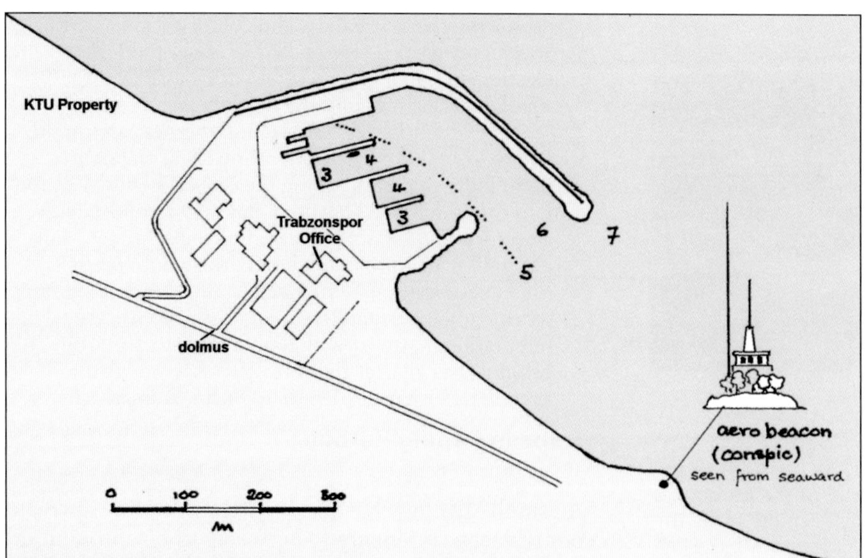


## TRABZONSPOR YACHT HARBOUR

Trabzonspor Yacht Harbour

shut off power to the marina. This is not a manifestation of ill will but simply of a lack of know-how in a highly competitive sports environment. There are no plans to open a marina.

If you arrive without prior communication, your yacht will be treated as a potentially serious security threat, which is a manifestation of the attitude that a top club has toward protecting its players. It is preferable to arrive after communicating your wishes to the club; without this, you may be asked by a security guard to leave immediately. We received this treatment in 2010 and can pass along this advice: secure your yacht and ask the guard to take you to the club offices ashore in order to make arrangements to stay in the harbour. Permission is usually granted for yachts to remain in the harbour as long as they wish with the understanding that no services will be provided. The best contact is Merve Yazicioğlu who speaks English and French and serves as the liaison to the club management.

*Contact information* Trabzonspor Kulübü, Mehmet Ali Yilmaz Tesisleri, Havalimanı Yazicioğlu, 61000 Trabzon. *Mobile* +90 533 540 48 93 (Merve Yazicioğlu)

### Facilities

*Services* Although service infrastructure has been installed in the Yacht Harbour, Trabzonspor has turned off water and electricity in the marina. Water can be delivered by mini-tanker. Ask one of the local yacht owners to arrange water delivery for you. The club does provide a security gate which is staffed during the day and remotely monitored 24 hours a day with security cameras. For this reason alone, the Yacht Harbour is the best place to leave your yacht for inland travel from Trabzon.

*Fuel* For delivery of diesel by mini-tanker, phone the Petrol Ofisi tanker truck dispatch from Örnek Petrol, ✆ (0462) 325 2084. The service is quick but fuel must be paid in cash (local currency only). In 2010, the cost was 2.94TL/litre.

*Provisions* The closest place for provisions is the large Migros supermarket in the Forum shopping mall. Other options for provisioning in the city centre 5km to the W (see above information for commercial harbour).

*Eating out* Karadeniz Technical University (KTU) operates a hotel, restaurant, terrace café and sports club (swimming pool, tennis courts and beach) for students and faculty at a waterfront property next door to the Yacht Harbour. The facility is used to train students at KTU's Culinary Institute and in the Hotel and Restaurant Management Program. KTU welcomes visiting yachtsman to their facility, which can be reached from the road leading to the yacht harbour or by walking along the waterfront on a path in front of the Youth Sports Training Complex (Natatorium and other facilities for the 2011 Junior Olympics were under construction in 2010). The food and service are very good in a pleasant setting overlooking the Black Sea. Students are anxious to practise English and other foreign languages. The facility is closed on Mondays.

*Other* The best way to reach the Forum shopping mall or the city centre is by *dolmuş* which stops every 30 minutes at the entrance road to the Trabzonspor club's complex, just beyond the security gate for the harbour, or by taxi (ask the club office to arrange one for you or get the card of a reliable taxi service you can call yourself from the taxi stands in Medan square or at the Forum). A Youth Sports Training Complex next to the Trabzonspor club offices will host the Junior Olympics in 2011. New facilities were under construction in 2010.

### General

Trabzon is a masterpiece of geography, located at a site that combined both an excellent harbour and massive defenses with a compelling position on the silk route, the loose network of trading centres that linked China to Western Asia. In Trabzon, inter-regional and intensely local factors combined to create the city that has had the longest and most significant history of any place on the Black Sea shores. But Trabzon is a big challenge for a tourist to comprehend. The main problem is that it has nearly buried itself in urban development; mighty walls that stood from the Middle Ages to the beginning of the 20th century have been nearly overwhelmed by run-of-the-mill concrete apartment houses in 'modern' Trabzon. It almost requires the imagination of an archeologist to visualise the city as it once was, or as it should be today.

To start with, the ancient waterfront has been obliterated with modern landfill which has extended the shoreline outward at least 100m. The two 'castles' which formerly dominated the harbour are now merely modest outcrops. The 'Byzantine' castle, from which the Greek general Xenophon looked down on the harbour in 400 BC and the Roman Emperor Hadrian looked down in about 130 AD, is now a Turkish military post dominated by a large flag and tea shops. A kilometre or more to the east, the 'Genoese' castle overlooks the coastal highway, an amusement park and a gas station. The proud harbour of Hadrian now lies beneath six lanes of asphalt.

There is some controversy about the meaning of Trapezous, the ancient name of the city. Some authorities translate it to mean 'trapezoid' to describe the shape of the promontory enclosed by walls. Others translate it to mean 'table' to describe the elevated land that received centuries of fortification. Either way, it's clear that the old city was built on a promontory extending right up to the shore, between Kuzgun Creek on the W and the Iskleboz River on the E. The promontory between these watercourses rose in three levels: the lower, middle and upper cities. In the normal way of things, the lower city was where trade was conducted, at the port; the middle city was where the bourgeoisie lived, and the upper city was limited to the royalty and aristocracy.

Modern Trabzon (population 182,000) thrives on the heritage of this past. With an international airport, an active international ferry port and the largest indoor shopping mall in eastern Turkey, today's Trabzon welcomes throngs of Russians, Iranians and Saudis to enjoy a tolerant and prosperous democracy in which sports, culture and shopping have replaced mighty stone walls as the impregnable defense.

The excellent Tourist Information Office near Medan Square can provide you with information about Trabzon and the surrounding area, including hire cars, sightseeing tours, tourist sites and other travel logistics. Contact information: Yahya Saka, Information Officer, GSM +90 0532 426 3525, *Email* yahasaka61@hotmail.com.

Sumela monastery

The Sumela Monastery is among the most amazing tourist sites in eastern Turkey. Founded during the 4th century, it was dedicated to the Virgin Mary and occupied for nearly 1,500 years, until it was abandoned in 1923 following the expulsion of Greeks from Turkey. It can be visited conveniently from Trabzon, and it is on the way to the high pastures (*yayla*) from which the 'Ten Thousand' Greek mercenaries first saw the Black Sea during their retreat from Baghdad, in 400 BC. This spot, which was discovered only in 1996, is at an altitude of more than 2,550m in one of the most breathtakingly beautiful places on earth. Taner Demirbulut, the manager of Zenofon Tours, in Trabzon (GSM +90 532 646 5127, *Email* taner@zenofontours.com) can lead you to both places.

One option for visiting the Russian Federation coast of the Black Sea is to take the overnight ferry from Trabzon to Sochi, Russia. Russian visas are most easily arranged from your home country, but depending on your nationality, you may be able to obtain a visa from the Russian consulate in Trabzon. You should expect to pay more to expedite the visa application or for an agent to handle the paperwork for you.

High pasture (*yayla*)

## YOMRA

40°57′·65N 39°51′·5E

A large harbour 4M SE of Trabzonspor Yacht Harbour which is used for fish farms and offloading sand for cement manufacturing. A yacht can find excellent shelter at anchor or alongside a cement quay.

### Approach

The harbour breakwater is easily seen to the E of the large Petrol Ofisi storage tanks.

Danger Five fish farms with marker buoys and unlit ship mooring buoys for the oil terminal to the NW of the harbour. The fish farms are privately owned with an annual capacity of raising 5,000 tonnes of trout and sea bass.

### Mooring

Go alongside the quay in the NW corner of the harbour or anchor clear of the fish farms and sand dredgers moored to the outer breakwater. With expansion of the coastal highway near the harbour, security might be a concern if leaving your yacht unattended. The harbour is used by small fishing boats at moorings on the E breakwater and several sand dredgers moored to the N quay, the latter making the quays dirty.

*Depths* 2–4m alongside the quay and 3–5m at anchor.
*Shelter* Excellent.
*Charges* None.

### Facilities

*Services* Water at boatsheds with permission.
*Fuel* Jerry can from the convenient filling station. Ask here whether fuel can be delivered by minitanker instead.
*Provisions* Small shops selling basic provisions near the mosques in town.
*Other* Post office, ATM and internet café near the mosques in town. It is easy to travel by *dolmuş* or taxi to Trabzon airport (8km) or Trabzon city centre (12km).

### General

With almost continuous development stretching along the coastal highway, the town is essentially a suburb of Trabzon. A *sanayi* was built on the hillside above town where brick making is the main employment. The jetty in town was previously used for commercial shipping.

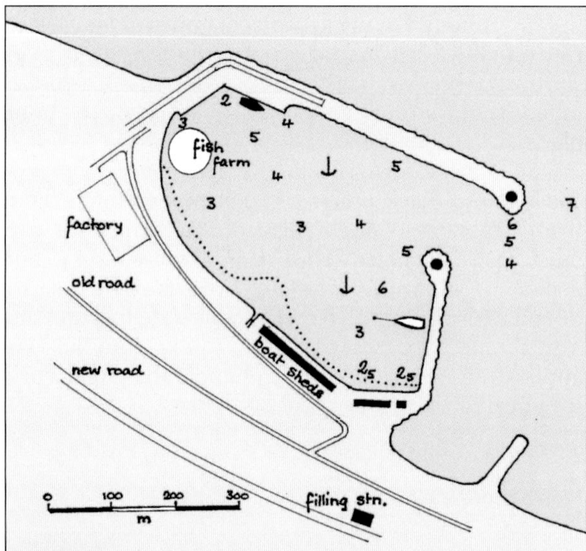


YOMRA

Yomra

## ARAKLI

40°56′·7N 40°03′·4E

A busy fishing harbour which sits in the shadow of two coastal highway overpasses emerging from a tunnel behind the harbour. As with other harbours near the coastal highway, the 'delightful' setting reported in past years has been completely transformed by the highway construction. The

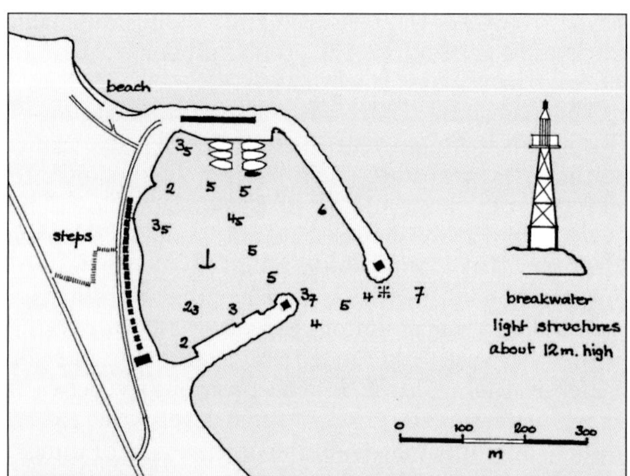


ARAKLI

Arakli

breakwaters with large light structures are easily seen in the approach from all directions. Take care to avoid the rock awash off the end of the outer breakwater. There is plenty of room for a yacht to anchor in 3–5m with excellent shelter, or with permission, to raft-up alongside one of the large fishing trawlers. The town of Arakli is 0·5km from the harbour and is said to have an excellent selection of shops, a small covered market with an internet café, ATM and post office. A small supermarket is situated near the beach NE of the harbour. This is a convenient place to leave your yacht to visit Sürmene, but security will be a concern.

## SÜRMENE

40°54′·9N 40°08′·2E

Construction of a small harbour 4M E of Arakli Harbour is now complete with a quay on the inside of the N breakwater. The previous harbour has been partially filled with construction of the coastal highway. Depths in the harbour are unknown, and with other excellent harbours nearby, Sürmene harbour is not recommended for yachts.

Tuesday is market day in Sürmene. Women dressed in colourful scarves come down from the nearby *yaylas* (high summer pastures) to buy and sell fresh produce at the market which stretches along the main road and side streets. Homemade cheeses are sold together with dense cornbread, a local speciality. With a population of 17,000, Sürmene has shops selling all basic provisions and can be visited by *dolmuş* from any of the nearby ports.

## BALIKLI

40°54′·9N 40°09′·4E

A small fishing harbour is located 1M E of Sürmene. With shallow depths, Balikli is not recommended for yachts. The large new harbour at Yeniay, 1·5M to the E, has much more room and excellent shelter.

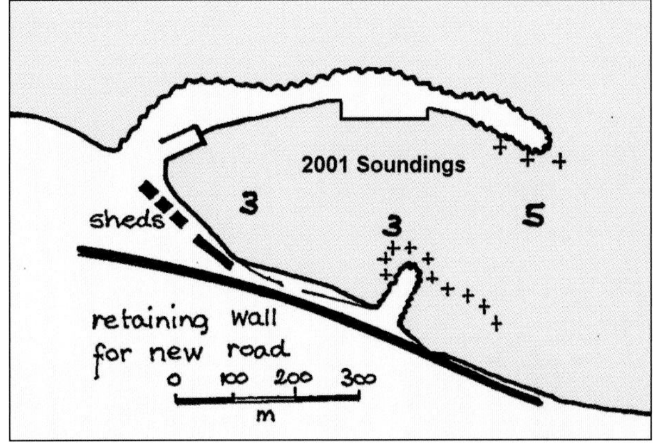


BALIKLI

## YENIAY

40°55′·6N 40°12′·0E

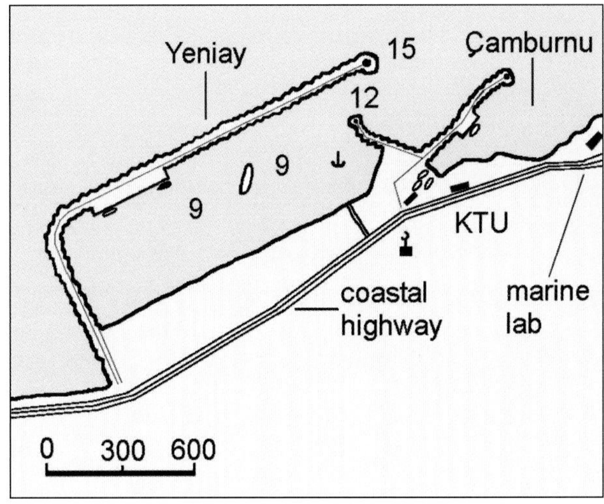


YENIAY

Construction of a large new commercial harbour was completed in January 2010. There is plenty of room for yachts to anchor out in the excellent harbour or to tie alongside the cement quay inside the N breakwater.

### Approach

The approach is straightforward, and the large outer breakwater with a light structure painted white, just W of the storm-damaged breakwater of Çamburnu, is easily seen from all directions. Like the old harbour, entrance to the new one is made in a SW direction.

### Mooring

Go alongside near the E end of the commercial quay on the N side of the harbour, if space is available, or anchor out near the inner breakwater for easier access to the town of Çamburnu. From the quay, you must walk about 1km to reach the shore. Several large fishing boats and the KTU research vessel use the commercial quay. One or more ships may be anchored in the harbour. Future plans include moving the shipbuilding yard from the adjacent harbour of Çamburnu to this harbour.

*Depths* 11·5m quayside and 8–12m in the harbour.
*Shelter* Excellent.
*Charges* None.

### Facilities

*Services* Water and electricity has been installed on the commercial quay for ships and may be available to yachts in the future.
*Fuel* By jerry can from fuel station on the road (ask locally for a ride or to have it delivered by car).
*Repairs* All repairs can be arranged at shipyards in Çamburnu.
*Provisions* A minimarket and bakery are on the main road across from the harbour.
*Eating out* See Çamburnu.
*Other Dolmuş* service to neighbouring towns.

Yeniay

## General

The harbour described by the Annans in 2001 as 'one of Okura's favourites on the whole of the Black Sea,' has been completely filled in. With the construction of the large new commercial harbour and a greatly expanded highway along the shore, the beautiful sandy beach and former charm of the place have been completely lost. The coastal highway is on elevated lanes which completely dominate the coastline alongside the harbour until it disappears into a tunnel at Çamburnu.

Catch a W *dolmuş* to visit Sürmene Castle, a recently restored example of Black Sea architecture. Originally built in the 19th century, it remained in the original family until recently and makes it worth a visit. The local government manages the site as a tourist attraction which is a popular stop for bus tours from Trabzon. The area inland of the castle is said to be good for hiking with paths leading past a small village with beautiful, old wooden houses, attractive woodlands and local people going about their daily chores.

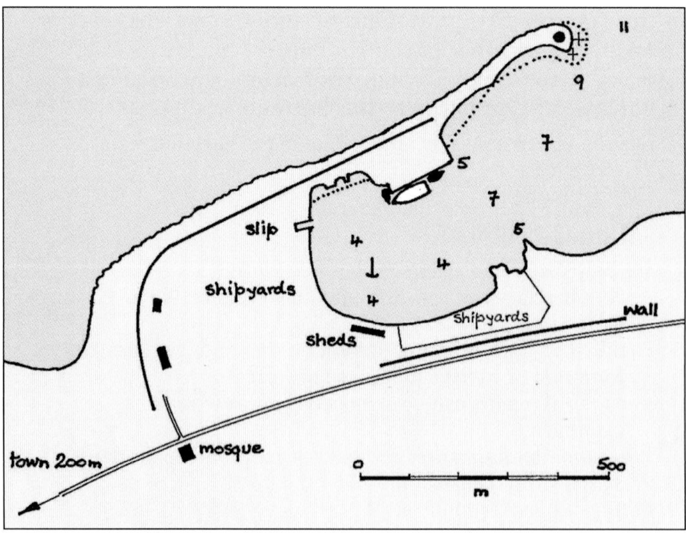


ÇAMBURNU

# ÇAMBURNU

40°55'·5N 40°12'·25E

This is a very crowded fishing harbour and ship repair harbour, and therefore not as suitable for yachts as the adjacent new harbour at Yeniay, which has been built to accommodate the ships waiting for repairs at Çamburnu.

## Approach

The breakwater is adjacent to the breakwaters for Yeniay harbour and has suffered storm damage. The light structure is askew, distinguishing it from the freshly painted white light structures of Yeniay's breakwaters. A large mosque is located on the inland side of the harbour and a modern building housing the KTÜ marine college is conspicuous.

## Mooring

The harbour is filled with fishing boats and shipbuilding activities leaving little room for yachts. Some swell works its way into the harbour. The adjacent harbour of Yeniay is much more suitable for yachts. If the shipbuilding works move to Yeniay Harbour, it may open up more space for yachts to go alongside or raft-up with fishing boats on the N quay or to anchor out in 4m.

## Facilities

*Services* Water and electricity on the quay.
*Repairs* All repairs can be handled at the shipyard.
*Provisions* The small town has a few shops for basic provisions.
*Eating out* Several restaurants along the main road; one is locally recommended for serving very good fish.
*Other* Post office in town and *dolmuş* service to neighbouring towns and sites of interest.

## General

The marine science faculty of Karadeniz Technical University (KTÜ) operates a marine sciences laboratory on the shores of the Black Sea adjacent to the shipbuilding harbour in Çamburnu. If you are interested in learning more about marine science research being conducted on the Black Sea, the faculty and students welcome visiting yachtsmen to their research facility, which is the large white

Çamburnu. Storm-damaged breakwater

building on the shore E of the harbour. The students are interested in practising English and other languages. They also have a lovely beach area which is immediately south of the harbour entrance.

*Contact information* KTÜ Faculty of Marine Science, 61530 Çamburnu / Trabzon, ✆ +90 462 752 2419 *Email* sdb@ktu.edu.tr www.deniz.ktu.edu.tr

## OF

40°57'·5N 40°16'·85E

Construction of the multi-purpose fishing and commercial harbour 4M E of Çamburnu is now complete, and with excellent shelter it is a suitable overnight stop for yachts. The boat sheds along the S shore serve as a buffer from the noise of traffic on the coastal highway.

### Approach

The chimney of a tea factory behind the harbour is conspicuous. There are no hazards in the approach, but both breakwaters have offlying rocks. Least depths of 5·5m in the entrance.

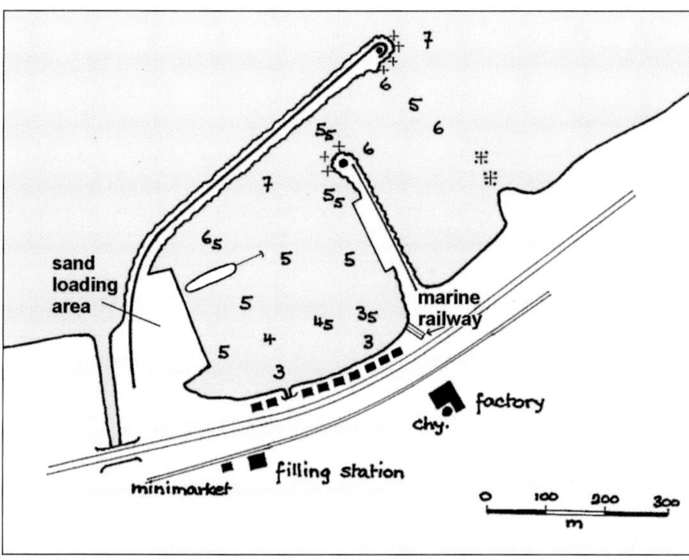


OF

Of

### Mooring

Cement quays have been constructed on the W and E sides of the harbour. There is plenty of room to anchor in the harbour in 5m or to go alongside the quay on the inner (E) breakwater. The W quay is used for offloading sand from dredgers moored stern-to the quay. Boat sheds line the S shore.

*Authorities* Officials from the local Jandarma post may visit the yacht and ask to see ship's papers.
*Shelter* Excellent.
*Charges* None.

### Facilities

Very limited.

*Fuel* By jerry can from the Shell fuel station 1·5km NE of the harbour.
*Provisions* Two supermarkets near the mosque. One of the local specialities here is butter made from the milk of cows that feed in the *yaylas*.
*Other* ATM and internet café are located near the post office.

### General

The town of Of, with a population of 22,000 is a 10-minute walk from the harbour. A large mosque has been built in the town which is said to rival the interior design of the Blue Mosque in Istanbul. The view of the mosque from the water is now obscured by large apartment buildings which have been built around it. From Of, ride a *dolmuş* to the scenic Uzungöl lake situated 1,100m above the Black Sea. A popular weekend destination for tours departing from Trabzon, it is best to visit the lake during the week.

## IYIDERE (DEREPAZAR)

40°00'·9N 40°21'·6E

The breakwaters of the harbour are easily seen. Because of the numerous groynes and retaining walls associated with the coastal highway, the harbour should be approached from a W direction. Half of the harbour has been lost to the coastal highway, and the remaining harbour is too deep (12·5m or more) to swing at anchor comfortably. With permission, it might be possible to anchor and take a line ashore to one of the boat houses. A coaster uses the quay at the inner breakwater for loading sand, and the coastal highway is immediately adjacent to the harbour. Unlike Of, the boat sheds along the

Iyidere (Derepazar)

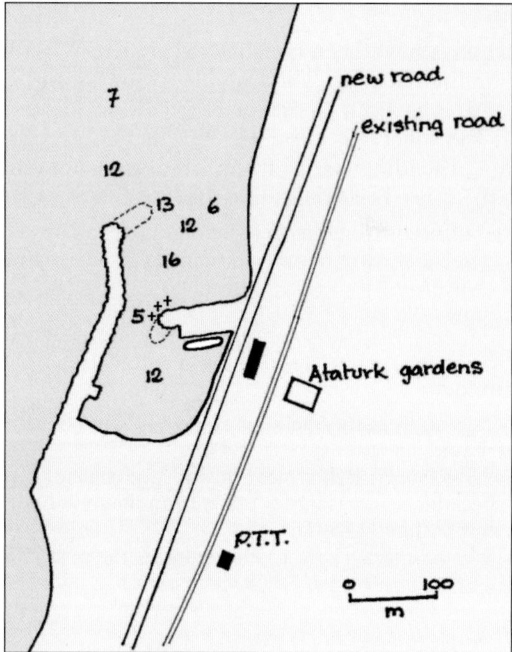


IYIDERE (DEREPAZAR)

shore do not provide as much of a buffer separating the harbour from the highway. Because of these detractions, and the fact that there is no obvious space for a yacht, Rize is a better bet 8M to the E. However, the local fishermen and residents of the small town are very friendly and welcome visitors arriving by yacht.

## RIZE

41°02'·3N 40°31'·1E

Rize lies 16M E of Yeniay and Çamburnu, where yachts can find a suitable mooring in the commercial harbour, or even better, in the adjacent newly constructed fishing harbour.

### Rize Commercial Harbour

41°02'·0N 40°30'·0E (Mooring position)

### Approach

The approach is straightforward. Leave the E cardinal buoy to starboard when entering the harbour. The highrise city buildings and outer breakwater are easily seen from a distance.

*VHF* Ch 16 for harbourmaster. Not necessary to call.

Dangers (1) The outer section of the breakwater has by damaged by storms. The outer end of the breakwater is marked by an E cardinal buoy in position 41°02'·34N 40°31'·14E. (2) Abandoned fish farms are located in the bay to the E of the harbour in the approximate position: 41°02'·1N 40°32'·2E.

### Mooring

Anchor and lie stern-to the small stone jetty in the S corner of the harbour adjacent to the Sahil Güvenlik (note that there is ballasting on the jetty) in 3m with your anchor in 6m, or go where directed by the Sahil Güvenlik or harbourmaster. The adjacent fishing harbour provides a more secure and comfortable mooring for yachts.

*Shelter* Good.

*Charges* A watchman may be asked to care for your yacht, and in this case, charges are possible.

*Contact information* See fishing harbour contact below.

Rize. Coastline view toward unfinished yacht harbour in the distance

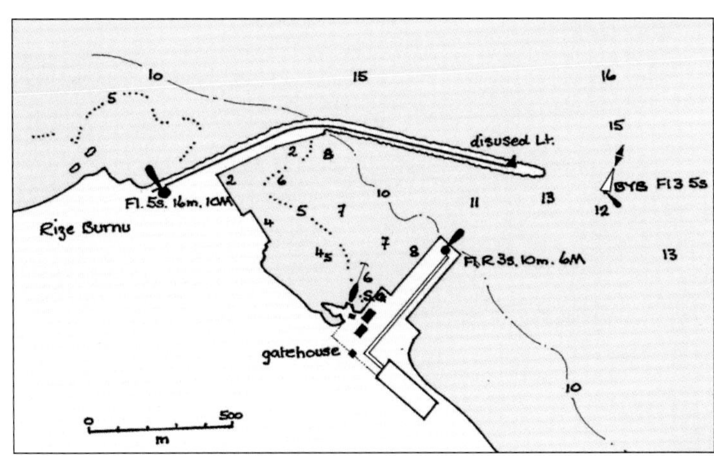


RIZE COMMERCIAL HARBOUR

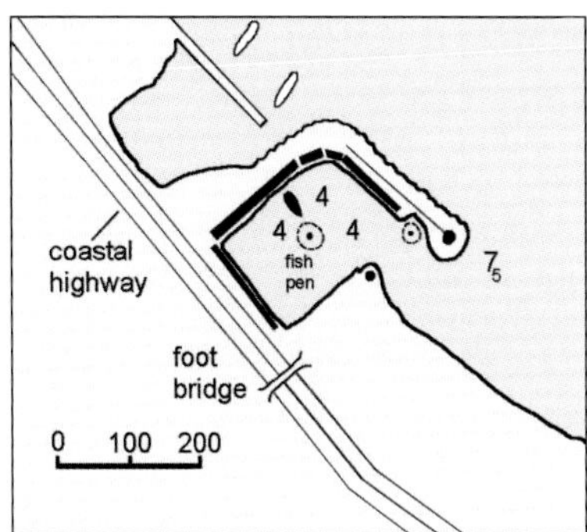


RIZE FISHING HARBOUR

### Facilities

*Services* Water and electricity on the jetty.
*Fuel* By jerry can and taxi.
*Repairs* Contact RIPORT office, adjacent to the mooring position near the jetty.
*Provisions* All provisions available from supermarkets and speciality shops in the city centre. A large market operates daily near the fishing harbour.
*Eating out* Numerous restaurants to choose from in the city centre and in the garden area to the E of the foot bridge over the coastal highway.
*Other* Post office, Turkish gaz, banks, ATMs, hire cars and all the usual services available in a provincial capital city. Bus and *dolmuş* service in the city and to surrounding towns. The ferry service to Istanbul was discontinued with the construction of the coastal highway.

### Rize Fishing Harbour

41°01'·9N 40°31'·1E

A new harbour for small and a few medium-sized fishing boats has been built since 2001. The new breakwaters and large Turkish flag on a tall pole at the end of the outer breakwater are easily seen to the S of the entrance to the commercial harbour, with entrance depths ranging from 6–7·5m. Fish pens are situated inside the entrance near the outer breakwater and in the middle of the harbour. The harbour is surrounded by boatsheds, one of which, on the NW side, is owned by a fisherman's family who welcomes visiting yachtsman (see contact information below). With permission, anchor or pick-up an unused mooring and tie back to the shore at one of the sheds in depths of 4·5m.

The small harbour provides excellent shelter. Security is also excellent: the local fishermen will keep an eye on your yacht. Water and electricity is being installed in the harbour but, in 2010, service had not been activated due to a dispute between the local government and the Fishermen's Cooperative. The harbour is conveniently located near the city centre, which is on the other side of the coastal highway.

Rize Fishing Harbour

*Contact information* Hasan Tecimer is a local businessman who speaks English well and owns one of the sheds at the fishing harbour. His GSM is +90 532 324 7213.

### Rize Yacht Harbour

40°02'·0N 40°33'·0E

The yacht harbour, which was described as being under construction in 2001, was never completed. The yacht harbour is 2km from the town centre, making it an inconvenient location. In 2010 a partially completed breakwater was observed, but it was in a dilapidated condition. Local yachtsmen report that there are no immediate plans to complete the harbour.

### General

Rize, with a population of 74,000, is the capital of Rize Province. The town was built alongside the Rhizios river. It is said that the acropolis of the Greco-Roman town was built atop a steep promontory that reached the seashore. Today, the promontory is crowned by a fortress, originally built by the Byzantine Emperor Justinian in the 6th century AD. The local government operates a tea garden at the fortress, a very pleasant place to relax with a spectacular view. The Çaykur company operates a tea research centre there, but it is not open to the public. A huge new hospital is nearing completion near the shore.

***Passage note: Rize to Çayeli***

A handful of small fishing harbours and one small commercial harbour have been constructed along the coast in the 10M between Rize and Çayeli. Most are tiny and not suitable for yachts, but one new fishing harbour is recently completed and may be suitable for yachts in position: 41°03'·4'N 40°36'·7E. A yacht may also be able to find some shelter in the new commercial harbour which has a coaster moored inside and appears to be recently dredged at position: 41°04'·8N 40°41'·1E. Because they are so close to Rize and adjacent to the coastal highway, *Gyatso* did not visit these harbours, and no further information is known.

*Warning* After heavy rains, a large plume of brown, sediment-laden water filled with plastic debris, large logs and branches washes into the Black Sea from the rivers along this section of coast. Depending on the wind direction and near shore currents, the plumes can extend a considerable distance from the shore. Use extreme caution to avoid unseen objects, including half-sunken logs just below the surface when crossing this and other river plumes after heavy rain along this coast.

## ÇAYELI

41°05'·5N 40°43'·4E

Another fishing harbour which has been overwhelmed by the coastal highway. The conspicuous breakwaters and small harbour backed by modern buildings are easily seen from a distance. The basic harbour configuration has not changed since 2001, but quays have been added along the shore where one fishing boat was tied alongside, and boat sheds have been constructed under the highway, which is elevated at this point. A river enters the Black Sea SW of the harbour, and care should be taken when entering the harbour after heavy rains. There is room to anchor in 6–7m or to tie alongside the quay in 5m, but the quay is immediately adjacent to the retaining wall for the coastal highway. The harbour is open to the N and the swell works its way in. A quayside restaurant caters to passing motorists. Unlike most harbours on this section of the coast, no one waved us in or invited us to tie up in the harbour.

With a population of 19,000, Çayeli can supply all basic provisioning needs. This is said to be the last town along the coast where Turkish is the native language. From here to the Georgian border, Laz is the local language.

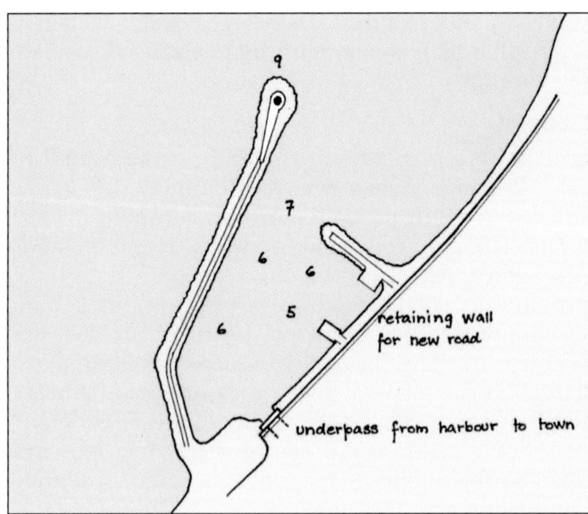


ÇAYELI

Çayeli

## PAZAR

40°11'·95N 40°54'·8E

### Approach

Situated 11M NE of Çayeli, Pazar's main fishing harbour is hidden from view until rounding Kizkalesi, GpFl(3)5s. The light structure at the end of the breakwater is easily seen 2M E of the town.

Dangers (1) W of the harbour, there are offlying rocks from Kizkalesi and another patch between here and the harbour. (2) The end of the breakwater is foul and should be given an offing of not less than 50m.

### Mooring

Proceed to the S or W side of the cement quay and go alongside where space is available. Large fishing trawlers use this quay, and the E side is reserved for coasters and Sahil Güvenlik. There is room to anchor in the SE corner of the harbour in 3–5m.

*Shelter* Excellent.

*Authorities* Harbourmaster is located near the base of the outer breakwater and appreciates it if visiting yachtsmen check with him on arrival and departure. The Sahil Güvenlik may request ship's papers if they visit the harbour.

*Charges* None.

### Facilities

*Services* Water and electricity on the quay by arrangement (very long cable required).

*Fuel* Arrange for mini-tanker delivery with the harbourmaster.

*Provisions* All provisions can be found in town 3km to the W. The local market day is Thursday.

*Eating out* The restaurant facing the beach near the base of the outer breakwater serves simple but delicious fried fish dinners.

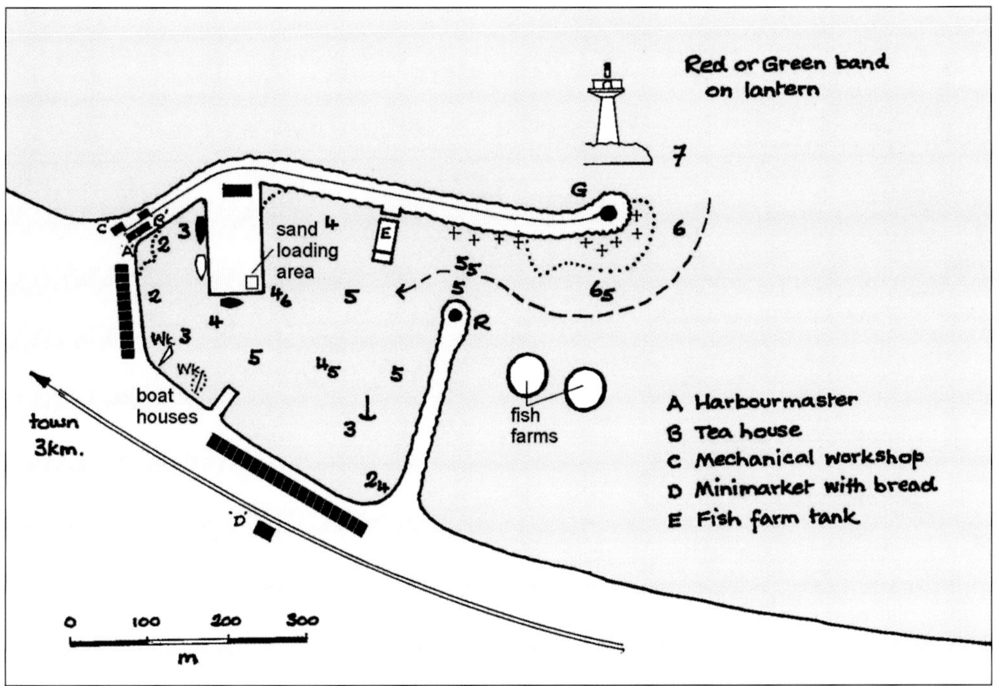


## PAZAR

Pazar

*Other* Pazar serves as a *dolmuş* hub in the area with each district having its own starting point. Although somewhat confusing for visitors, the friendly local people and drivers are said to be helpful in making sure you find the right bus. Combined with a secure harbour, this makes Pazar a good place to leave your yacht for inland excursions (see suggestions below).

### General

We spent a night here tied to a quay, and friendly fishermen brought us bottled water. Other locals stopped by to chat and see if we needed anything. Another man took us to dinner.

An inland excursion suggested by the Annans is to take the *dolmuş* from Pazar to the village of Hemşin (not to be confused with Çamlıhemşin in the valley leading from Ardeşen) where there is good hiking, but the area is very wet. Along the way, the road passes many humped-back bridges and wooden suspension bridges which cross the river to small settlements on the other side. Walking along the river in Hemşin, you may see beekeepers who live on platforms which hang precariously from the side of the cliff where they hang their hives from branches to protect them from bears. Another excursion is to Ayder and some of the castles inland, including Zilkale, built on a crag above the cascading Firtina River. The hot springs and natural charm of Ayder have been discovered as a tourist attraction. The local speciality is a cheese fondue (made from the stringy cheese you see in the local markets) which is served with the dense cornbread. In addition to enjoying the hot springs, guided treks for up to six days in the Kaçkar Mountains can be organised from Ayder and Çamlıhemşin.

### *Passage note: View of Mount Kaçkar*

Sailing between Pazar and Ardeşen on a clear day, it is possible to see Mount Kaçkar, the highest peak of the Black Sea mountains at 3,972m and one of the highest points on earth visible from sea level.

## ARDEŞEN

41°11'·9N 40°59'·6E

Ardeşen lies just 3·5M E of Pazar. The breakwaters with green and red light structures and tall buildings in town are easily seen. The large, clean harbour offers excellent shelter with plenty room to anchor in 8–10m of mud. In 2010, boatsheds were under construction on the S side of harbour and a dredger was active outside of the harbour. Works were also underway to fill sand behind the highway underpass but none of this affected the relatively empty harbour. The quay on the E (inner) breakwater is reserved for the dredger and used for loading sand. There is a small, shallow patch along the S shore where a stream empties into the harbour. The elevated lanes of the coastal highway run along the S shore of the harbour.

Ardeşen

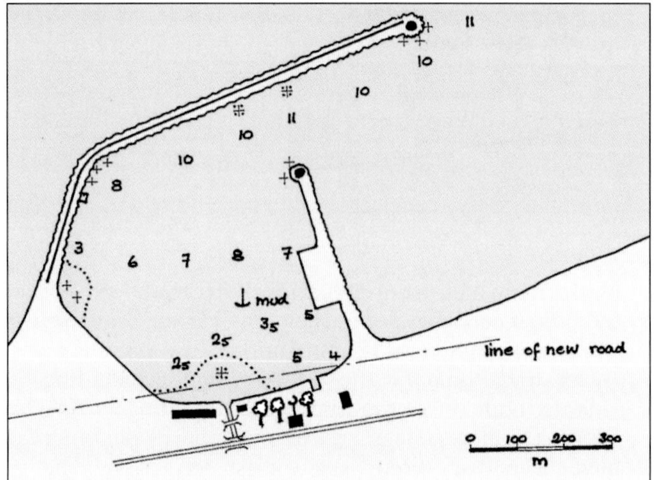


ARDEŞEN

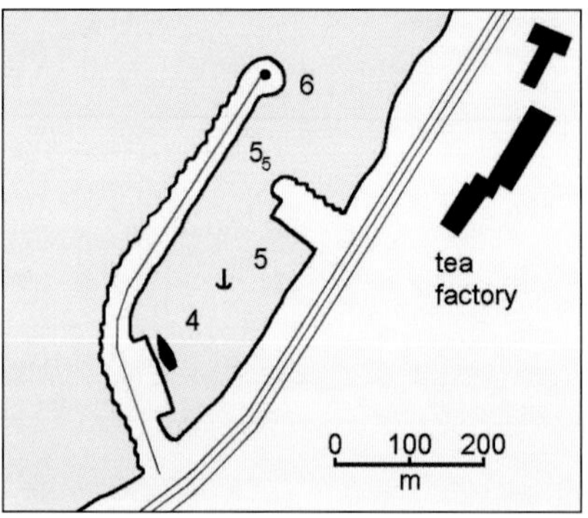


FYNDYKLY

The harbour is conveniently located in the middle of town, making this a good place to stock up on provisions; the markets in Hopa are not as conveniently located. Unfortunately, there is no convenient place to obtain fuel in Ardeşen. In this case, Hopa is a better unless you are continuing on to Georgia, where fuel can be purchased at much lower cost. With a population of 33,000, the tidy and well kept town has friendly local people and the usual assortment of banks, ATMs, internet cafés, tea houses and restaurants, including attractive fish restaurants.

## FYNDYKLY

41°15'·7N 41°07'·6E

A new harbour at Fyndykly was nearing completion in 2010. There is plenty of room to anchor with depths of 5·5m in the centre of the harbour, and there are concrete quays on the inner breakwater and in the SW corner of the outer breakwater, with depths of 4m alongside. New boathouses were under construction which appeared to be more like summer cottages than typical fishermen's sheds. A tea factory is located on the N side of the harbour, across the coastal highway. Friendly local anglers and children on quay waved us in, and others in boats waved as they passed by.

Between Fyndykly and Arhavi there are several tiny harbours, none of them really suitable for yachts.

Fyndykly. Local people enjoy an afternoon boat ride

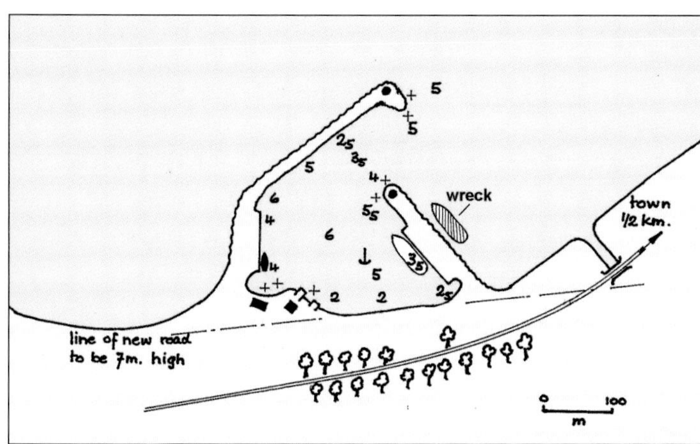


ARHAVI

Arhavi

## ARHAVI

41°21'·15N 41°17'·6E

The harbour is situated about 1km W of the town. There is a wrecked freighter just outside the entrance, along the inner (E) breakwater. The coastal highway has filled in a substantial portion of the harbour, and the entrance appeared shallow and prone to silting. Overall, this place is probably no longer suitable for yachts.

There are several tiny new harbours between Arhavi and Hopa.

Hopa

## HOPA

41°25'·3N 41°25'·85E

Hopa is the easternmost port of entry in Turkey, the place to check out if voyaging to Georgia or elsewhere.

### Approach

The small town spread along the shore has large breakwaters for the commercial harbour, with conspicuous silos and large cranes. Steel jetties along the beach are not suitable for yachts.

*VHF* Ch 16 for Port Control (no requirement to call).

Danger There is a wreck in the corner of the fishing harbour, S of the commercial harbour.

### Mooring

Proceed toward the inner harbour and moor where directed, probably alongside the cement quay in the location shown in the plan, with a depth of 8m. Alternatively, anchor in the NE section of the harbour in 6–10m. Plans to develop marina facilities in the harbour have not materialised, but free winter storage is said to be available. The harbour managers are friendly and helpful and will make yachts feel welcome.

*Shelter* Very good, but the harbour is subject to some movement from swell and the wash of boats in the harbour.

*Authorities* Port of Entry. Port authority will visit yacht and provide instructions for checking in. Sahil Güvenlik may visit yacht and request ship's papers. They will also brief you regarding border crossing to Georgia (see passage notes in the following chapter). All authorities are conveniently located, but they have almost no experience dealing with yachts and are only marginally helpful. We departed from Hopa on a Sunday, and although the Customs and Immigration office was open, it took a lot of cajoling to process our paperwork; they wanted to wait until the banks were open, the following day, rather than take the 7TL fee in cash. In contrast, the security staff at the harbour gate were very helpful, and one man drove us into town in his own car. An agent will visit the yacht, but an agent is not necessary to clear in or out of Turkey.

*Charges* None.

### Facilities

*Services* Water by arrangement with the harbour management. Connection to electricity may be difficult to find.

*Fuel* By jerry can and taxi or may be able to arrange for mini-tanker quayside.

*Repairs* Minor repairs can be arranged through the harbour office.

*Provisions* All basic provisions can be obtained from minimarkets near the gate of the commercial harbour and small supermarkets in town.

*Eating out* Very good *lokantasis* in town catering to the truckers and travellers passing through the town, one with especially good *lahmacun* baked in a wood oven and topped with cheese and egg.

*Other* Post office, Turkish gaz, bank and ATM in town. Taxi stand in town and *dolmuş* service to surrounding towns.

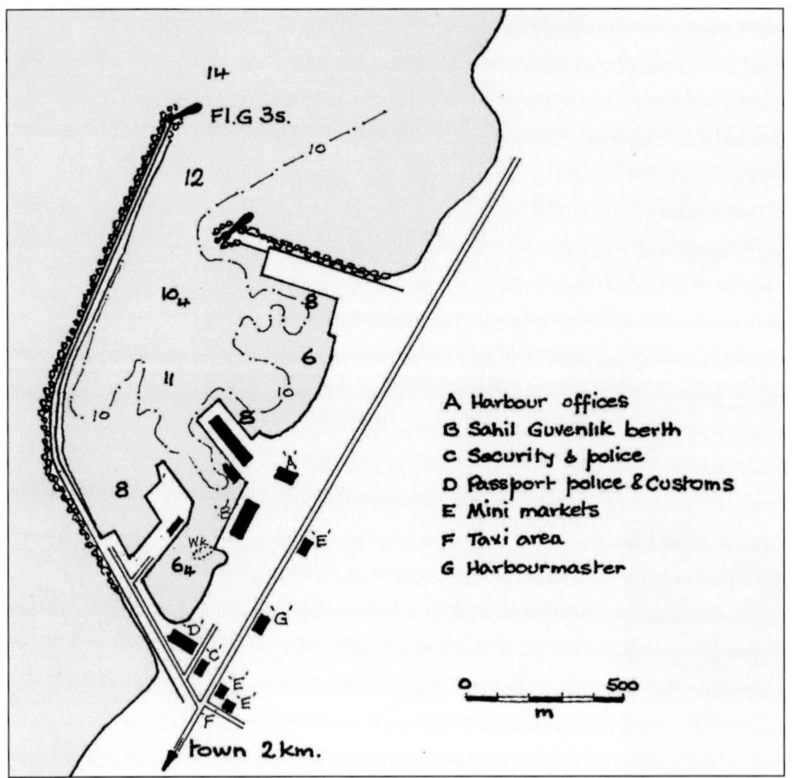


HOPA

## HOPA

### General

The massive investment in the coastal highway has virtually killed the coastal shipping business. The Port of Hopa seemed almost abandoned, but a very long line of heavily-loaded lorries were waiting to cross the Turkish-Georgian border. The town has a population of about 14,000, spread quite thinly along several kilometres of waterfront.

## KEMALPAŞA

41°29′·0N 41°31′·0E

Kemalpaşa is about 5M NE of Hopa. It is technically illegal to visit this small town after checking out of Turkey, and it is probably not advisable to stay here before checking in.

We met only one foreign yachtsman who had ever visited Kemalpaşa. He had spent four seasons on the Black Sea coast of Turkey. His yacht, about 13m long, had encountered no problems visiting Kemalpaşa, and he said that he had enjoyed the place.

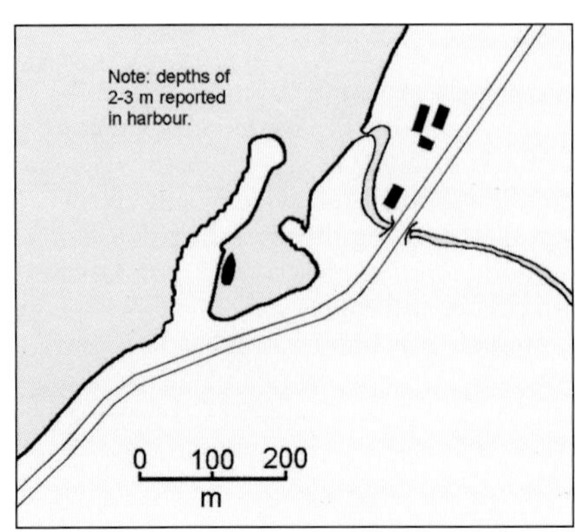


KEMALPAŞA

### *Passage note: Hopa to Batumi, Georgia*

Heading toward Georgia, Hopa is normally the port of departure from Turkey, approximately 7M W of the international border. The Turkish coastguard advises yachts to cross the border in international waters, that is, at least 12M from the coast. They say that this is a Georgian regulation and that as far as they are concerned, yachts can leave Turkish waters anywhere. The Commander of the Batumi sector of the Georgian coastguard stated that the 12-mile 'prohibited zone' shown on Admiralty charts applies only to commercial vessels and that yachts can cross the border wherever they want. However, *Gyatso* was told that in the past at least one foreign-flagged yacht was confiscated for crossing the border closer to shore and sold to raise money for coastguard operations. It is certainly better to be safe than sorry in this crossing: keep at least 12 miles out when crossing the border.

At the Turkish-Georgian border, yachts should call the Georgian coastguard on Ch 16 to report the yacht name and flag and crew names and nationality. Keep calling until there is a definite reply! At six miles from Batumi, call Batumi Port Control on Ch 16 with this information, the ETA and a request to enter the port. The Port Captain will provide instructions or send a pilot boat to escort the yacht into the small basin where yachts are moored. The Sheraton Hotel is very conspicuous.

# 5. Georgia

## The Black Sea Coast of Georgia

Georgia is one of the four countries with territory in the Caucasus region, the mountainous stretch between the Caspian and the Black Seas. The other three countries are the Russian Federation, Azerbaijan and Armenia. Although the area has been conquered by outsiders many times, the people who identify themselves as Georgians today trace their ethnic identity, with immense pride, back to the Bronze Age. It is a small country of 69,700km$^2$. Adjoining countries are Russia to the north, Azerbaijan to the east, and Armenia and Turkey to the south. Georgia's ethnic population of 4·6 million is declining, slightly, due to out-migration.

Georgia is administered through nine regions and two autonomous republics – Adjara and Abkhazia. Adjara is fully incorporated into Georgia, but Abkhazia remains bitterly disputed between Georgia and Russia.

## History

Russia conquered Georgia through a series of military campaigns from the 18th to the 20th centuries. It was a Soviet Socialist Republic until 9 April 1991, when it declared its independence. Eduard Shevardnadze was President from 1995–2003.

In August 2008 Georgia undertook military operations in the South Ossetia region, which provoked an invasion by Russia. The war between Georgia and Russia lasted five days and caused widespread damage in Georgia.

Georgia holds a key location in the movement of crude oil from Azerbaijan to Turkey and the West. An important pipeline runs from the Azerbaijani capital of Baku through Tbilisi and then to the Black Sea coast, from where some continues by pipeline to the Turkish Mediterranean port of Ceyhan; some is refined at Batumi for domestic consumption and export, and some crude oil is put on ships at Supsa and Kulevi.

## Time

Georgian time is GMT +3 hours.

## Communications

Telephone code +995

## Climate and Weather

The climate of the Black Sea coast of Georgia is totally unexpected – it is sub-tropical.

A tour boat moored in Batumi yacht harbour

### People: customs, religion, holidays

Georgia has a population of approximately 5·4 million people of whom Georgians make up about 70%. The largest minorities are Armenians (8%), Russians (6%) and Azeris (6%). They are proud, passionate, fiercely independent and among the most hospitable people on earth. Georgians believe that a guest is a gift from God, and they act accordingly.

Christianity spread to Georgia during the 4th century AD, and it was primarily a Christian country before it came under the rule of the Ottoman Turks, in the late 15th century. Christianity was suppressed throughout the period of Soviet rule, 1921–91, and many churches were destroyed or converted to secular public uses.

Most authentic folk holidays are tied to the calendar of the Georgian Orthodox Church and celebrated in villages or within one or more provinces. National holidays include:

| | |
|---|---|
| 1 January | New Year's Day |
| 3 March | Mother's Day |
| 9 April | Memorial Day |
| 26 May | Georgian Independence Day |

### Food and drink

Georgians are immensely proud of both their food and their drink, and both are plentiful. Classic dishes use lamb, chicken, or fish, hazelnuts and walnuts, aubergines, plums, corn, pomegranates, kidney beans, coriander, spring onions, peppers, mint and basil. Meat dumplings (*khinkali*) and a sort of cheese pie (*khachapuri*) are also common Georgian foods.

*Khachapuri* (cheese pie)

Georgians assert that the art of winemaking began in Georgia. More than 500 varieties of wine grapes are cultivated throughout the country, and at least 60 wines are produced commercially. For typical European tastes, Georgian red and white wines tend to be rather sweet, though dry wines are also available. Both Batumi and Poti have speciality shops selling wine.

### Language

Georgian is the native language of about four million people in Georgia and is the official language of the country. It is not an Indo-European language; rather, it is the most widespread of the Kartvelian languages of the southern Caucasus. The script has

Traditional Georgian serving tray

33 letters which correspond to the sounds of the language, but the individual letters look nothing like those of any other Western language. (It looks vaguely like Thai script.) English is not widely spoken, but we never experienced any problems from language barriers.

### The Black Sea coast

The Black Sea coast of Georgia extends for 310km, including Abkhazia. Because the status of Abkhazia is hotly disputed by Russia and Georgia, their maritime boundary is unresolved.

As an efficiency measure, the Georgian navy and coastguard were joined together in 2010.

### Charts

The Admiralty and Turkish charts offer adequate coverage, as does C-Map.

### Formalities

Georgian entry and exit formalities involve four separate agencies: Border Police, Customs, Health, and the Port Captain. A representative from each of these will visit the yacht as a team and will conduct their work in a speedy and very professional manner. They expect to be given the original ship's registration papers, the passport of each person aboard, and four or more copies of the General Declaration and Crew List. They will conduct a quick inspection of the yacht, scan the passports, and issue visas on the spot. If you are prepared with the necessary documents and the ship's stamp, the whole procedure takes about 15–30 minutes.

Perhaps because yachts are so unusual in Georgia, there is no 'transit log' such as is issued by Turkey, Ukraine, Romania and Bulgaria. Any yacht departing from either Batumi or Poti must check out of the country even if the destination is the other port of entry in Georgia. Call Port Control on VHF Channel 16 to set up the checkout.

### Ports of Entry

Batumi and Poti are Georgia's ports of entry.

*Gyatso* was told by Russian diplomats that Russian port authorities will not permit entry into Russia by a yacht that has visited Georgia. But it seems that Georgian authorities do not refuse entry to a yacht that has visited Russia. The exception is

Sukhumi, the capital of the 'breakaway' province of Abkhazia; the Georgian coastguard does not permit foreign vessels to enter Georgian waters after visiting Abkhazia.

### Travel ashore: taxi, train, plane, road

Taxis are abundant and inexpensive in both Batumi and Poti, but they are likely to be in very poor condition and to be driven by a maniac on roads that are poorly maintained and lack any speed limits. For all but local trips, trains may be a better way to travel. Trains link both Batumi and Poti to Tbilisi, the capital. However, the overnight train to Tbilisi, the capital, is reported to be uncomfortable and not meeting earlier guides' recommendations.

During Soviet times, the only way to fly to Tbilisi was from Moscow, but in the past 20 years Georgia has made a huge effort to attract flights to Tbilisi, with the result that 15 foreign airlines served the capital in 2010. The Batumi airport has also been greatly expanded to serve 600,000 international passengers annually. A new airport is being built in Poti by the Ras Al Khaimah Emirate, which has also purchased the Poti Seaport.

### Provisions

Provisions are readily available in both Batumi and Poti.

### Medical

Private medical options have expanded since Soviet times, but visitors to Georgia should have medical evacuation insurance. In case of serious medical problems, contact your embassy in Tbilisi.

### Money / currency

The currency is the Lari, abbreviated GEL. 1 GEL = €0.41

One of several international chain hotels in Batumi

### THE GEORGIAN COASTLINE

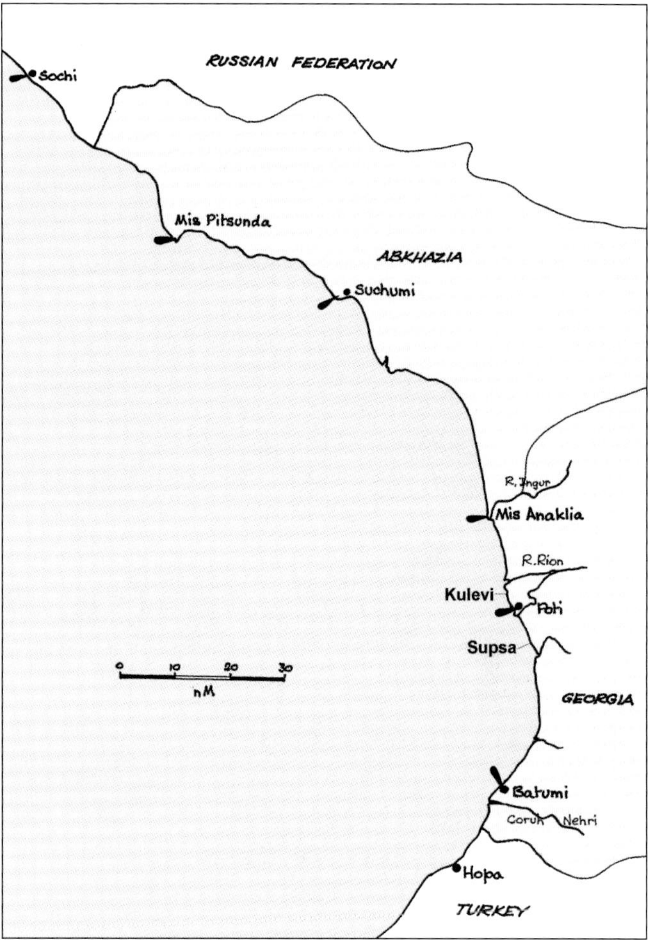


### *Passage note: Hopa (Turkey) to Batumi (Georgia)*

From Turkey the mountainous coastline continues to sweep up to the N and NE. Heading toward Georgia, Hopa is normally the port of departure from Turkey, approximately 7M west of the international border. Yachts leaving Turkey from Hopa are not allowed to visit Kemalpaşa, the final Turkish port before reaching the Georgian border. The Turkish coastguard advises yachts to cross the border in international waters, that is, at least 12M from the coast.

At the Turkish-Georgian border, yachts should call the Georgian coastguard on VHF Ch 16 to report the yacht name and flag and crew names and nationalities. Keep calling if you do not receive a reply. At 6M from Batumi, call *Batumi Port Control* on Ch 16 with this information, the ETA, and a request to enter the port. Repeat this call upon arrival in the port. The Port Captain will provide instructions or send a pilot boat to escort the yacht into the small basin where yachts are moored.

In 2010 *Gyatso* was boarded by the Georgian Coastguard but this action is thought to be unusual and due to a local security concern at the time.

# HARBOURS AND ANCHORAGES

## BATUMI

41°39'·0N 41°38'·7E

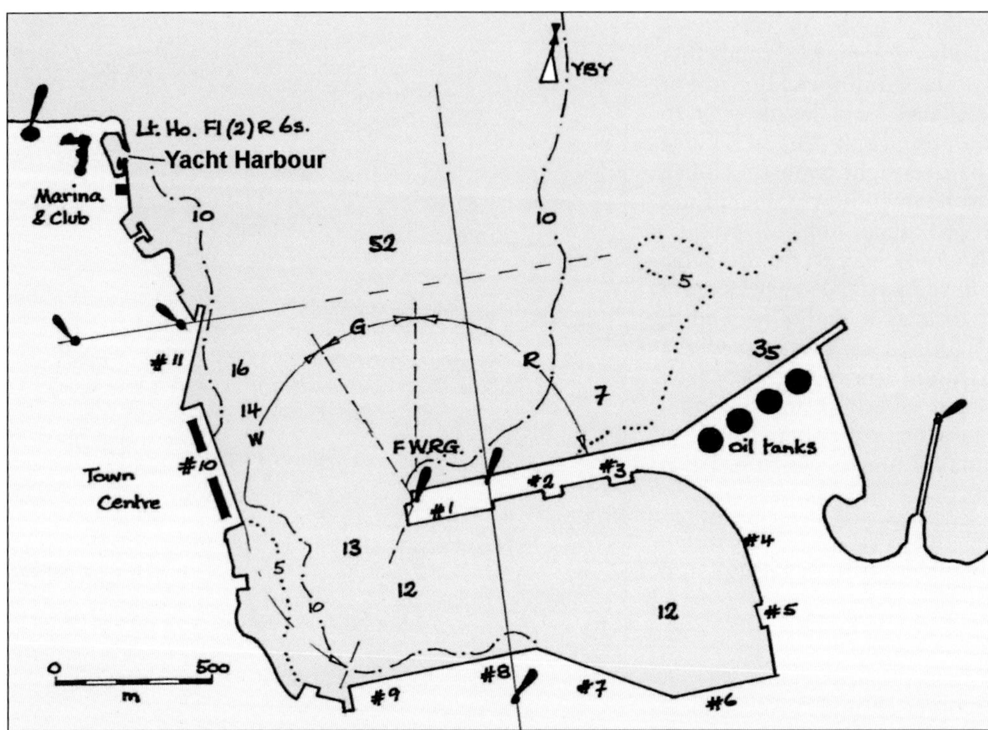


BATUMI

### Approach

The approach is straightforward. Approaching from the SW (see instructions regarding restricted zone along the Turkish-Georgian border), the view of the harbour is obscured by beachfront development. The harbour is situated in a bay behind. The yacht harbour is in a small basin on the right, immediately after passing the lighthouse. Yachts should not enter the commercial harbour.

*Conspicuous* The lighthouse, white Sheraton Hotel and other high-rise buildings.

*VHF* Ch 16 for Batumi Port Control. Begin contacting at five miles and again upon arrival in the outer harbour to request permission to enter the yacht harbour.

Dangers None.

### Mooring

The yacht harbour is used by several day-trip and dinner boats, a small day charter sailboat as well as tugs and local recreational boats. Space will be found for a visiting yacht.

Batumi beach as seen in the approach

*Berth* Yachts are usually directed to berth inside the small yacht basin, alongside the cement quay on the left as you enter.

*Depths* 4m in the yacht basin.

*Shelter* Excellent all-round shelter.

*Authorities* Port of entry. Port officials (customs, immigration police, health and harbourmaster) will arrive immediately and conduct clearance formalities onboard. Do not leave your yacht until clearance formalities are complete (see chapter introduction for detailed information about clearance procedures). Likewise, do not depart Batumi without clearing out, even if you are only traveling to Poti. Contact the Port Officer on VHF Ch 16 to arrange departure formalities.

*Charges* None at present.

*Contact information* Although there is no yacht club or marina in Batumi, two helpful contacts who speak English include:
David Pirtskhalaishvili, local yacht owner,
*Mobile* +995 599 14177 *Email* davidpirts@yahoo.com
Dimitri 'Smart One' Ship Chandlery (can arrange private security, car and driver, inland tours, etc.)
84, Sulabendze, Batumi, ✆ +995 222 47 293
*Mobile* +995 879 97 6060

## Facilities

*Services* Water is available with a long hose. Electricity is available at some berths but not where yachts are usually moored. Arrange with the harbourmaster for security for your yacht (private security is not necessary on the outer quay because it can be blockaded from foot traffic and the port police keep an eye on the yacht harbour). Private security can be arranged for a negotiable fee through Dimitri at 'Smart One' Ship Chandlery. No toilet or shower facilities at present.

*Repairs* Most repairs can be arranged (see contacts listed above).

*Provisions* A well-stocked Populi supermarket is located several blocks from the yacht harbour near the Circus Casino. Other small shops sell basic provisions, baked goods, local food specialities and fresh produce. Georgian wine can be purchased from a number of wine shops in town. A large, daily market operates in the city centre near the commercial harbour.

*Eating out* Ialkani is a good restaurant and bar serving Georgian cuisine and seafood; it is located in the passenger terminal next to the yacht harbour. There are many other restaurants and bars on the boulevard near the harbour. The Sheraton Hotel has a bar and restaurant with an all-you-can eat breakfast buffet which can be used with permission by visitors who are not hotel guests. For traditional Georgian cuisine further afield, the restaurant Megrul-Lazuri, near the Botanical Gardens, (Maxinjauri Tbilisis-gzatkecili No. 16, ✆ 8 97 67 37 60. Nukri, Director) is worth the trip. Batumi is known for making the best coffee in Georgia, and several places are recommended: an outdoor café on Gogebashvili Street, near the fishing port and the Second World War monument; a café at 14 Gogebashvili Street, S of the yacht harbour; and at the Oriental Sweet Shop at on the corner of Rustaveli and the former Lenin streets.

*Other* Banks and ATMs near harbour and in beach hotels. No post office (private couriers are used). Inner- and inter-city buses and trains to Tblisi, the capital city. Hire cars are only recommended with driver; be sure to arrange for a reputable car and driver with one of the local contacts. Most types of cooking gas bottles (e.g. camping gaz, propone) can be filled on the outskirts of Batumi.

Batumi

Batumi yacht harbour

## General

Batumi, a port of entry, is the capital of the Adjara Autonomous Region of Georgia, a territory which had a prickly relationship with the central government in Tbilisi in the early days of Georgian independence, in April 1991. Although Batumi was identified as a port of entry, yachts in the Kayra Rallies visited Batumi only in 2001. Uncertainty about clearance formalities, its location on the distant eastern shore of the Black Sea and a brief war between Russia and Georgia as recently as 2008 are some of the many reasons that few yachts visit Georgia. It remains a virtually 'undiscovered' spot for cruising yachts on the Black Sea shore, which is a shame because Batumi is a most unusual city, and the Georgian people are most welcoming.

Some of Batumi's unusual qualities are obvious. Having a sub-tropical climate is certainly one factor. Summers tend to be very hot and humid, but breeze from the Black Sea cools the air somewhat. The people of Batumi are certainly another factor. The Adjara region has been a frontier among highly diverse people for millennia, and the Adjarans have learned how to get along with others. And recent history is probably a factor, beginning with the Russian Tsars' efforts to develop Batumi as a railhead and port for the export of Caspian oil. But none of this quite explains the 'Batumi Miracle' which was in full swing in 2010, beginning in the old historic centre.

The old town resembled a war zone, with mile after mile of streets torn open to install new water and sewer pipes and fibre-optic cables for telephone, TV and internet. The technology to do this wasn't sophisticated – picks and shovels vastly outnumbered backhoes – but the rebuilding of the old city was being carried out with great vigour and considerable care to maintain an atmosphere of bygone elegance. People weren't joking when they insisted that it would all be finished in one year.

It is the newer parts of the city that are almost unbelievable. The 203-room Sheraton Hotel opened in 2009 and is running smoothly. The Hyatt, with 344 rooms, the Radisson, with 166 rooms, and the Hotel Batumi, with 250 rooms, were on track to open in 2012. The new seafront boulevard, with its 'dancing fountains', the dolphinarium, the F3 racing circuit with its massive sculpture, and the grand opera house all opened in 2009 and 2010.

Batumi is the Dubai of the Black Sea, but with a big difference. Dubai confronts visitors with the power of oil money. Batumi aims to entice visitors to relax, enjoy the beaches, and, if they are so inclined, to gamble. The Caucasus region being what it is, even the origin of tourists is controversial. The mayor of Batumi has made a considerable effort to attract visitors from Armenia; it's only 300km as the crow flies to Yerevan, the capital of land-locked Armenia. But the President of Azerbaijan warns that Armenia would like to use tourism as a way to take over Adjara as it did with the Nagorno-Karabakh region of Azerbaijan. Political theatrics notwithstanding, Batumi is a safe and welcoming place to visit.

Statue of Medea in Batumi

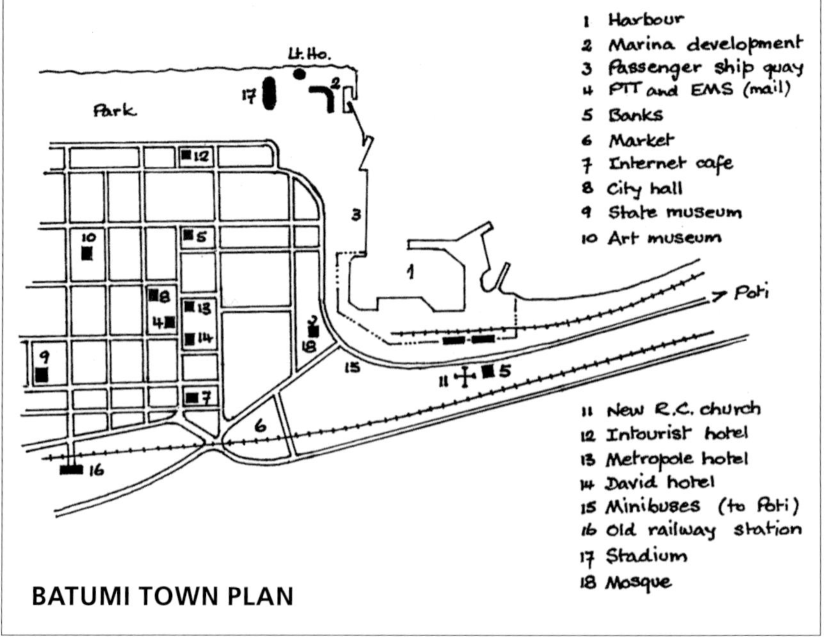


BATUMI TOWN PLAN

The world of yachting has not yet become a significant consideration amidst the orgy of construction in Batumi, but in the summer of 2010 it was widely rumored that 'Donald Trump's people' had visited Batumi to discuss construction of a marina-and-gambling complex. Meanwhile, the reality is that a small marina usable by yachts actually exists, just to the right of the entrance to the commercial harbour.

One nearby site of interest includes the Botanical Gardens, 9km N of Batumi on the 'green cape'. Take a bus or train from Batumi to a stop near the lower entrance (ask locally for detailed instructions). It is a short taxi ride to the lower or upper park entrance from here. Ask the taxi to take you to the upper entrance if you prefer to walk downhill through the park.

### *Passage note: Batumi to Poti*

(SUPSA Oil Terminal 42°00'43.7N 41°44'35.9E at the shore)

Supsa, a Georgian coastal town S of Poti, is the Black Sea terminus of the Western Route Export Pipeline, an 830km refurbished Soviet-era pipeline that is owned by Azerbaijan International Oil Consortium and operated by British Petroleum (BP). The terminal has four reservoirs with a capacity of 120,000 tonnes. From the shore a pipeline runs offshore to a Catenary Anchor Leg Mooring (CALM) buoy. Hoses of up to 50cm are used to transfer crude oil to tankers with a deadweight of up to 150,000 tonnes. The Russian military bombed the pipeline on 10 and 12 August 2008, and it remained closed until November 2008.

Yachts are advised to stay at least 3M from the Supsa terminal and the oil transfer buoy, which is guarded by a small patrol boat.

## POTI

42°09'·6N 41°38'·8E

Located 33M N of Batumi, the large commercial port of Poti contains a small yacht club. Construction of the Poti Sea Port (www.potiseaport.com) began at the end of the 19th century, at the same time, and for the same reasons, as the port of Batumi: the trans-shipment of crude oil from the Caspian Sea to Europe. The port is located at the delta of the Rioni River, known to the ancient Greeks as the Phasis. The delta is a large wetland, known as Kolkheti and designated as a 'wetland of international importance' under the Ramsar Convention.

The Poti Sea Port Yacht Club was founded within the port in 1971 and soon began training sailors who attained championships by the mid-1970s. The most famous Poti sailor is Jumber Tsomaia, known to all as Juki, who built the 25m Whitbread Round the World sloop *Fazisi* (named after the local river, Phasis) and served as a crewmember on all six stages in 1989–90.

In 2008 the Government of Georgia privatised the port of Poti, selling 100% shareholding interest to the Ras Al Khaimah Investment Authority (RAKIA). Ras Al Khaimah is one of the seven emirates federated in the United Arab Emirates. RAKIA is one of the largest investors in Georgia. A new harbour is under construction immediately N of the harbour entrance.

The Russo-Georgian war of 2008 lasted for five days, from 8–12 August. It followed increasingly threatening military exercises on both sides, mostly focused on the South Ossetia region, which both sides claimed. It began as a Russian response to a Georgian effort to reestablish its control in the enclave. Russian military forces bombed several



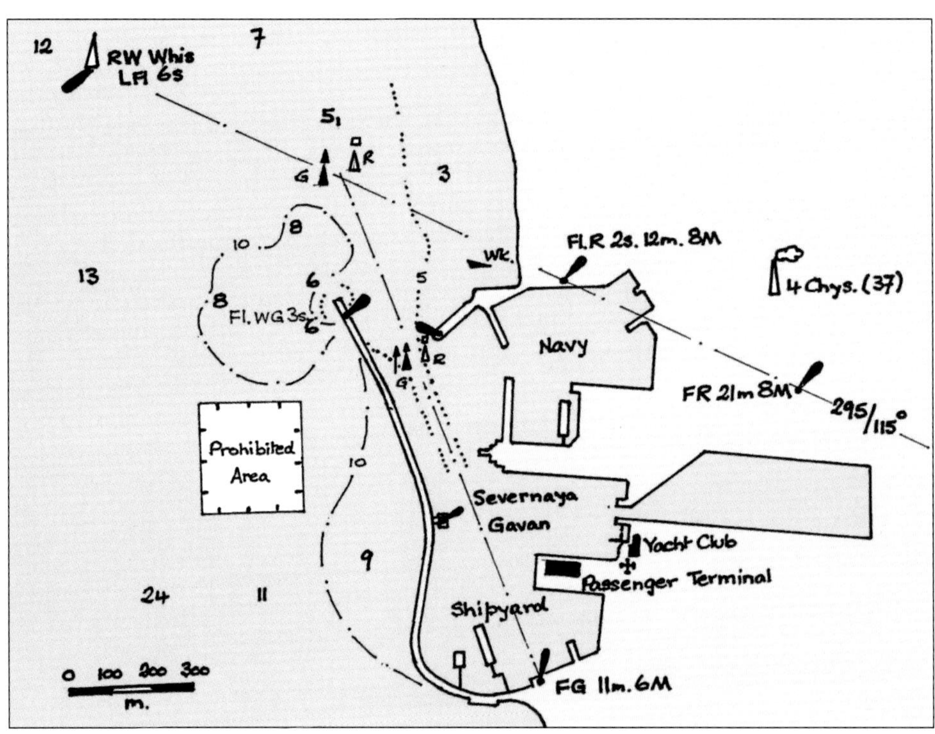


POTI SEA PORT

Poti yacht club

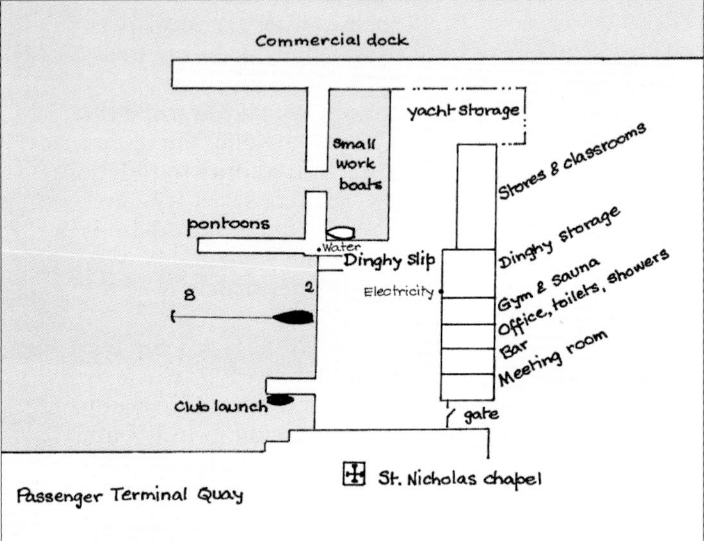


**POTI YACHT CLUB**

places throughout Georgia and attempted to blow up the Baku–Tbilisi–Ceyhan oil pipeline. Among the places that came under aerial attack was container terminal N7 of Poti Sea Port, where three port workers were killed amidst extensive damage to the terminal.

Formerly there were as many as 75,000 residents in Poti. As of summer 2010 there were about 60,000, including 10,000 Georgians displaced from Abkhazia who are now living in Poti. About 15,000 Russians were living in Poti before 2008. Almost all left for Abkhazia or Russia during and immediately after the August 2008 war.

Today Poti is a sprawling but pleasant town with few architectural or historical attractions, in various stages of repair or decline. There are friendly people, beautiful surroundings and an excellent food market. It is a safe place to leave a yacht to visit nearby sites of interest, including the overnight train to Tbilisi, the ruins and museum of the ancient city of Vani and the monastery of Gelati.

## Approach

Yachts should enter the commercial harbour, not the river, and follow the shipping channel into the harbour from the fairway buoy. Once inside the harbour, continue past the naval harbour toward the passenger terminal (leaving it to starboard) to the Yacht Club.

*Conspicuous* A red and white striped lighthouse S of harbour entrance; the breakwaters and cranes in the commercial harbour are easily seen. One or more ships are usually anchored outside the harbour awaiting approval to enter.

*VHF* Ch 16 for Batumi Traffic Control at five miles out. Contact *Batumi Traffic Control* for permission to enter the harbour upon arrival and indicate that you are going to the Yacht Club. VHF Ch 16 also for the Yacht Club.

Dangers (1) Beware of the large ships entering and leaving the harbour. (2) Avoid shallow water E of harbour entrance. (3) The shoreline and shoal areas associated with the delta of the Rioni River are no longer building out and the shoreline is eroding due to the diversion of the main flow of the river to a branch N of the harbour entrance. This area is now actively accreting sediments seaward and should be given a wide berth.

## Mooring

The Poti Yacht Club is located at the centre of the port, in the inner harbour between the N and the S basins. The club has two fixed pontoons for visiting yachts, with connections for electricity and water. A long cable and a household 2-pin adapter are required. There is an active youth racing programme using small fleets of Optimist dinghies and Lasers. The air conditioned clubhouse has a good restaurant offering the best waterfront dining in Poti, complete with wireless internet connection. Everyone – staff, club members, and visitors – is very friendly and security is generally excellent.

A cultural quirk in Georgia and other former Soviet Republics including Russia and the Ukraine, creates a minor security challenge: people love to

Approach to commercial harbour

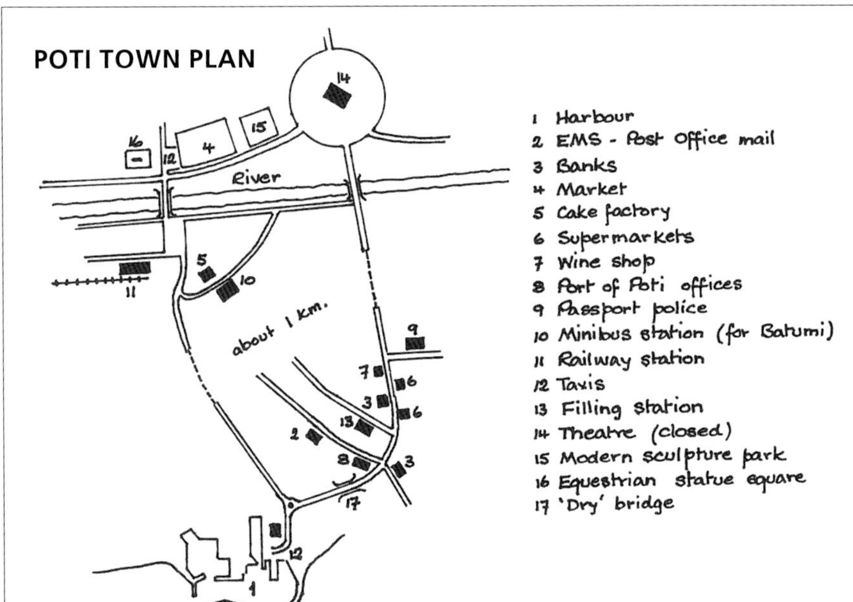

Orthodox Church, Poti

pose for snapshots in exotic locales. Foreign yachts are so seldom seen in Poti that *Gyatso* was like a huge magnet drawing a steady stream of brides and grooms, partygoers, and local tourists and dignitaries to be photographed with this novel backdrop. Mostly out of different conceptions of privacy, occasionally photographers may push the boundaries and try to board a yacht. A polite, 'Photos are OK, but no boarding' should stem the tide. The security guards did keep an eye on the yacht and discouraged overly intrusive behaviour.

The Poti Yacht Club operates a youth sailing program (Lasers and Optimists), and although no local yachts are currently moored there, the club can accommodate visiting yachts of all sizes. Planned additions to the Yacht Club, including additional pontoons and a dry storage area, have not materialised and are not likely under the new management of the Poti Sea Port.

*Services* Water and electricity with long hose and cable. Toilets, showers and self-service laundry in the clubhouse. Fitness room. Pay phones available outside the Poti Seaport security gates. 24-hour security at Yacht Club gate but busy with foot traffic for restaurant and bar.

*Fuel* By jerry can and taxi. One inconvenience at the yacht club is that the Customs authorities prohibit fuel tanker trucks to enter the port, so it is necessary to hire a taxi to shuttle cans between the club and one of the several petrol stations.

*Repairs* Most repairs and haul-out by crane up to 15 tonnes can be arranged through the Yacht Club staff. No hardstanding area for storage of yachts at present but this can probably be arranged in the port area.

*Provisions* Small supermarkets near the Yacht Club. A large daily market and shopping area for all provisions, including fresh produce, baked goods and local food specialities, is located about 2km from the Yacht Club in the centre of town and is easily reached by local taxi.

*Berth* Where directed alongside one of two finger piers or bow- or stern-to the sea wall with your own anchor (no tailed moorings). A yacht club RIB will meet you as you enter the harbour and help to tie up.

*Depths* 8m at end of Yacht Club pontoon, decreasing to 2m quayside.

*Shelter* Excellent all-round shelter, some wash from commercial traffic in the harbour.

*Authorities* Port of entry. Yacht Club staff will contact port officials who will come to the club to conduct formalities including customs, immigration and health inspection, either on board your yacht or at one of the Yacht Club's tables depending on availability. Officials

Poti yacht club

## Kolkheti National Park

Well worth a visit is Kolkheti National Park, located on nearly 29,000ha essentially surrounding Poti. The park, which opened in 2000, is managed from a modern headquarters where guided boat tours can be arranged. A centrepiece of the national park is Lake Paleostomi ('Old Mouth'). Long ago it was a lagoon on the shore of the Black Sea, but over time a barrier beach built up, eventually creating a freshwater lake that was 3m deep. At the beginning of the 20th century, a canal was cut through the barrier beach. Although this improved drainage and helped to protect Poti from flooding, it also allowed salty water to enter the lake under storm conditions. The lake is filling with sediment and is has far too high nutrient levels. There used to be 44 species of fish, but now there are only 15, of which only two species can be fished. With the disruption of natural flushing, in the next couple of decades the lake is expected to become less than 2m deep.

Despite its present-day environmental problems, Lake Paleostomi offers a glimpse of one of the most famous places in ancient literature, the spot where Jason and his squadron of nobles aboard the row galley Argo came ashore in the land of Colchis. As Apollonius of Rhodes recounted it:

> Night fell, and presently, under the guidance of Argus, they reached the broad estuary of Phasis, where the Black Sea ends. They quickly lowered sail and yard and stowed them in the mast-cage; next they let down the mast itself to lie beside them; and then rowed straight up the mighty river, which rolled in foam to either bank as it made way for Argo's prow. On their left hand they had the lofty Caucasus and the city of Aea, on their right the plain of Ares and the god's sacred grove, where the snake kept watch and ward over the fleece, spread on the leafy branches of an oak… Jason… told his men to row into the reedy marshes and moor the ship with anchor-stones in a spot where she could ride.

National Park headquarters

The goddesses Hera and Athena noticed what was happening and prevailed on Aphrodite to have her son Cupid shoot an arrow into Medea, daughter of Aeetes, King of Colchis. Medea promptly fell in love with Jason and used her position and skills as High Priestess to help him accomplish his magical tasks and steal the most sacred object of the Colchian kingdom, a golden fleece.

In his 1983 Jason Voyage, Tim Severin convincingly placed the mountainous Georgian region of Svanetia, as the Colchian's source of gold, and he showed that the Svan people were taking gold out of their streams by weighing down the fleece of sheep; the gold became fixed by the natural lanolin.

Lake Paleostomi in Kolkheti National Park

are professional and efficient if you are prepared with ship's stamp, general declaration and crew list. Yacht Club staff will also assist with formalities and translation, as necessary.

### Facilities

*Eating out* The Yacht Club has a good restaurant. The Anchor Hotel in town is reported to serve excellent fried fish. Many other restaurants serve Georgian cuisine. Bars and small cafés with snack menus near seaport gate.

*Other* Banks and ATMs in town. Local taxi can be arranged through the Yacht Club office or can be found outside the port entrance gate. Buses and train to Batumi and Tbilisi.

### *Passage note: Poti (Georgia) to Feodosia (Ukraine)*

Three items of note in the 330M passage between Poti (Georgia) and Feodosia (Ukraine) include: Kulevi Black Sea Terminal, a 2010 recommendation regarding a Yachting Caution Zone, and information about Abkhazia.

### Kulevi Black Sea Terminal

The oil terminal at Kulevi, less than 10M N of Poti, possibly illustrates better than anywhere else on the Black Sea coast the trade-offs between economic development and environmental protection. Located well inside the borders of the site designated as a Ramsar wetland of international importance, it has become something of a rally point for environmentalists who argue that an oil terminal is incompatible with 'wise use' of wetland habitats, as defined by the Convention to which Georgia is a contracting party.

The Kulevi Black Sea Terminal, opened in 2008, is owned by the State Oil Company of Azerbaijan Republic (SOCAR). The terminal incorporates three piers, a canal for tankers, a tank park with overall storage capacity of 320,000m³, and two berths for receiving tankers with tonnage up to 100,000 tonnes. Railway trestles make it possible to discharge 168 oil tank trucks simultaneously. The terminal has annual processing capacity of 10 million tonnes of crude oil and refined products.

Train along Rioni River

### YACHTING CAUTION ZONE (Recommendation 2010)

Based on *Gyatso's* assessment of acceptable risks, they recommend that yachts stay out of a 'Yachting Caution Zone' delimited approximately by the line between Poti, Georgia and Feodosia, Ukraine. The ongoing tensions between Russia and its neighbours are summarised in Chapter 3.12, and Map 1 shows the Caution Zone. The zone includes parts of three countries in the NE corner of the Black Sea: Abkhazia, the Russian Federation, the Kerch Straits and Ukraine E of Feodosia.

Departing from Poti, yachts are advised to head WNW to a point S and W of 42°27'·N 40°26'E. This is the SW corner of 'Area 740', marked 'Occasionally Dangerous to Navigation' on Admiralty Chart *2236*, Tirebolu to Tuapse. This point is more than 30 miles from the coast and outside the Abkhazian coastal area patrolled by Russian naval vessels. From this waypoint, a course of 296° leads to Yalta, 300M distant.

It would be a shame if the caution zone deterred yachts from visiting either Georgia or the eastern Crimea; neither Georgia nor Russia is intentionally bent on interfering with private pleasure craft. The crew of *Gyatso* never saw a Russian warship in eastern Black Sea waters, and we never feared for our safety between Poti and our next stop, on the Crimean Peninsula. It is to be hoped that political change will allow this area to be explored by yachts in the future.

### ABKHAZIA

Abkhazia is a territory of about 8,700km² located in the NW corner of Georgia. Depending on your point of view, it is either an Autonomous Republic in sovereign Georgian territory or an independent nation recognised only by the Russian Federation and Nicaragua. Abkhazia seceded from Georgia soon after Georgia itself became independent from the Soviet Union, in April 1991, and it was the scene of a bitter ethnic war for the next 2½years, until the Georgian army was forced to withdraw. For the past 20 years, the waters off the coast of Abkhazia, and particularly its capital, the port of Sukhumi, have been a chronic area of dispute between Russia and Georgia.

Officially, Georgia forbids all foreign vessels from visiting Sukhumi, and in 2009 it impounded five merchant vessels which had traded in Sukhumi. Among them was the Turkish cargo ship *Buket*, whose captain was sentenced to 24 years in prison but was quickly released at the behest of the Turkish Foreign Minister. Rumours continued into 2010 of confrontations off the coast of Abkhazia between Georgian coastguard and Russian naval vessels.

The coastline of the Russian Federation cannot be seen from a distance of 30M or more offshore.

# 6. Russian Federation

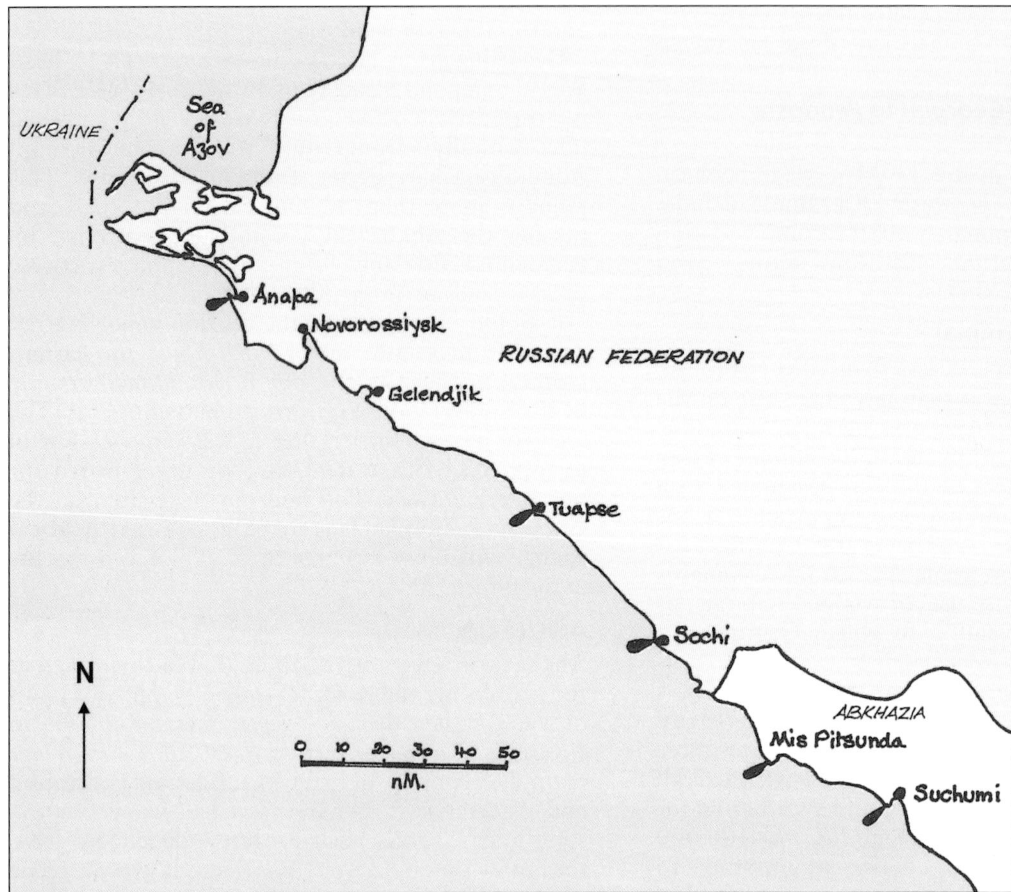


Although visiting Russia by yacht is not banned outright, yachtsmen wishing to visit all six countries on the Black Sea are likely to face major obstacles with Russia. In planning their voyage around the Black Sea, *Gyatso* found no accounts of a foreign yacht being allowed to visit Russia in the previous five years. Those who had tried faced many hassles. Despite these reports, *Gyatso* proceeded with plans to visit Sochi in Russia in hopes that their successful bid for the Winter Olympic Games in 2014 would help smooth the way for foreign visitors. But on the eve of obtaining their Russian visas, *Gyatso* cancelled plans to visit Russia for several reasons.

First, they could not get assurances from Russian officials that they would be allowed to visit Russia by yacht. Although the officials in Istanbul were optimistic that they could visit Russia, the officials at the Russian Consulate in Trabzon informed them that foreign yachts are not allowed to visit Russia if they have been to Georgia first. This presented a second problem for *Gyatso* since they chose to sail around the Black Sea in a counterclockwise direction to follow the prevailing wind and current patterns, a path which has been used by sailing and rowing vessels since ancient times. The modern bureaucratic requirement of visiting Russia before Georgia required a several hundred mile detour in an already ambitious itinerary with no assurances that they would be allowed to bring their yacht into a Russian port once they arrived. Further complicating matters, Russia briefly waged war in Georgia in 2008, and the two countries have an ongoing dispute over the Abkhazia region in Georgia. Finally, *Gyatso* learned that a European-flagged yacht was denied entry to three separate Black Sea ports in Russia in early July 2010, despite having all paperwork in order and a fluent Russian speaker onboard.

*Gyatso* briefly considered visiting Russia by ferry from Trabzon, but in the end decided to stay focused on gathering updated cruising information rather than visiting a country that did not welcome foreign yachts. Although disappointed to drop one country from their itinerary, they were not sad about avoiding the expense and hassles to do so. Until the situation changes in Russia, ***Gyatso* advise yachts to avoid Russian ports and territorial waters.** For this reason, only a brief outline of the most essential information for cruising yachts is provided here.

### Time

The Russian Federation is GMT +3 hours in the summer months.

### Communications

Telephone country code: +7.

### Weather

Summer can be very hot along the Russian Black Sea coast and water temperatures can rise to 30°C.

### People

The Russian people are reported to be friendly and helpful to visiting foreign yachtsmen, but the Soviet-style officials are unwelcoming and bureaucratic.

### Language

Russian is the language most commonly spoken. English is not widely spoken, and a translator would be required. The Cyrillic alphabet is used on signs and in written documents.

### Travel ashore

There is extensive rail service in Russia and an international airport in Sochi. Transportation infrastructure and tourist services are expected to improve with developments related to the Winter Olympic Games in 2014.

### Provisions

Goods of all kinds are available in the major ports and costs are comparable to European countries.

### Money/currency

The Russian currency is the Rouble with an exchange rate of 1Rub equivalent to €0.025. ATMs are available and currency is dispensed in either roubles or US dollars.

### The Black Sea Coast of Russia

The Black Sea cost of Russia, known as the Russian Riviera, stretches 200M from the Georgian border to the Kerch Strait. At present, the few ports of interest to the crews of visiting foreign yachts are off-limits for all practical purposes (see formalities below). The Border Police prohibit foreign yachts from anchoring in bays.

### Charts

Soviet-era charts of the Russian coast are available in the Ukraine (see Sevastapol harbour detail), but it is best to arrive with Turkish or British Admiralty paper charts, as well as electronic charts.

### Formalities

Russia has not developed formalities for visiting foreign yachts and this presents a challenge for yachtsmen wishing to visit all six countries on the Black Sea. In fact, the barriers to visiting Russia by yacht are more bureaucratic and financial rather than an outright ban. Foreign yachts are likely to be treated as if they are a commercial vessel fully loaded with valuable cargo. Upon arrival in a Russian port of entry, the owners of foreign yachts have reported facing hostile officials looking for bribes, threats of arrest and impoundment of their yachts, enormous harbour charges and requirements to pay large fees for agents to enter each Russian port on the Black Sea. Yachts report harbour charges and fees being quoted in the thousands of dollars or euros. This treatment is not unique to foreign-flagged yachts. Owners of local yachts have become so frustrated with the procedures, or lack thereof, that they advise against visiting Russia by yacht.

Some yachtsmen report that the experience was similar to that of arriving in Yalta without an agent; however, unlike the Ukraine, it is thought that no privately owned foreign yachts have received permission to visit Black Sea Russia in recent years. The only accounts of yachts visiting this part of Russia are from those who participated in the KAYRA rallies and those who attempted to visit but chose to leave in the face of the above-mentioned hassles. Despite their own extensive network of personal and professional contacts in Russia, *Gyatso* was not successful in finding a local agent or representative who was willing to handle the clearance formalities in 2010.

Until Russia develops formalities for visiting yachts or a reputable agent is found to handle this, Russian ports will remain off-limits for all practical purposes. This is why Russian ports and territorial waters are included in a 'yachting caution zone' (see Chapters 1 and 5).

Russia is the only country on the Black Sea coast where a visa must be obtained in advance. This is best done in your home country; however, the process requires identifying specific dates. For some nationalities, including Americans and many Europeans, a Russian visa can be obtained from the Russian Consulate in Istanbul or Trabzon, Turkey, but the process will likely require the use of an agent or rush service which can be considerably more expensive. Consult the Russian consulate in your home country for information about obtaining travel visas.

### Ports of Entry

At present, there are no reliable ports of entry for yachts. Commercial ports of entry include: Sochi, Tuapse and Novorossiysk.

### An alternative for visiting the Russian Black Sea coast

While cruising on the Black Sea, the crews of foreign yachts have an alternative way of visiting Sochi: by overnight ferry from Trabzon, Turkey.

## HARBOURS AND ANCHORAGES

### SOCHI and SOCHI YACHT CLUB

Sochi 43°34'·6N 39°43'·0E
Sochi Yacht Club 43°33'·7N 39°45'·2E

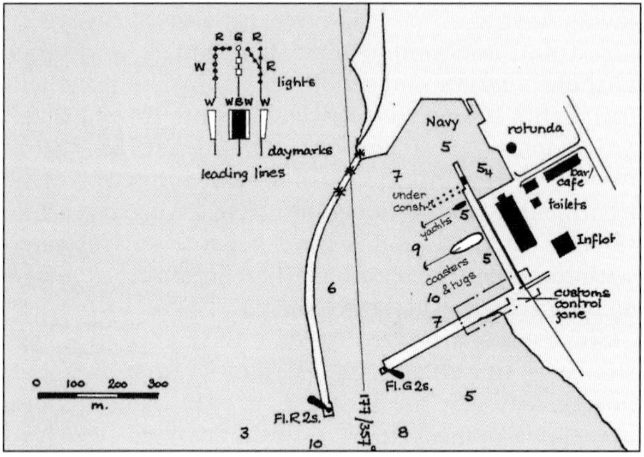


SOCHI

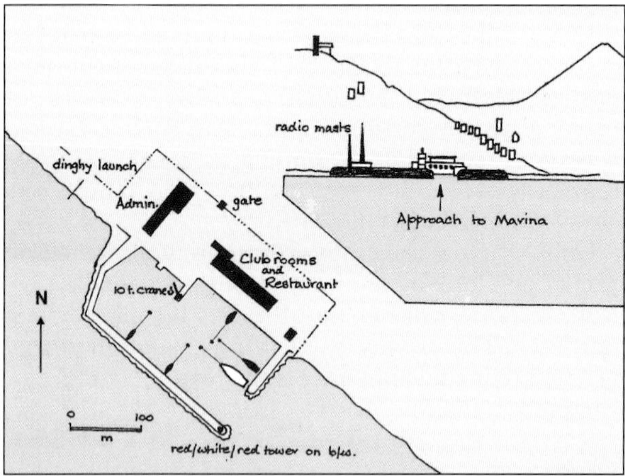


SOCHI YACHT CLUB

The Annans visited Sochi aboard their yacht *Okura* in 2001. They wrote:

> '*Okura* had a multiple entry visa and had previously had agreement it would be possible to cruise the coast visiting Sochi Yacht Club, Sochi, Tuapse, Gelendjik, Novorossiysk 7 Feets Yacht Club and Anapa but on arrival at Sochi were told by Border Police it would not be possible. *Okura* could sail along the coast to Anapa to check out but could not go ashore anywhere else except Anapa. After many phone calls and being held in Customs for several days *Okura* was held with several Ukrainian yachts at the ferry terminal. Once cleared into Sochi there seemed to be no restrictions on personal movement. When the yacht was finally allowed to depart *Okura* went directly to Sulina in Romania.'

A German-flagged yacht attempted to visit Sochi in 2010 but was turned away.

Sochi Commercial Harbour is the southernmost port of entry. The breakwaters with buildings behind are easily seen in the approaches. The Sochi Yacht Club is 1M S of the commercial harbour but difficult to distinguish amongst other jetties and groynes. The Annans advise:

> [Yachts are advised to] call Sochi Traffic Control on VHF 16 when 5 miles off; however, this attracts Patrol Boat of 35m length who may insist in boarding at sea. Suggest approach harbour from seaward, not along the coast and call control when ½ M off.

On arrival and departure, go alongside the customs quay. After clearing in, yachts are usually directed to anchor and tie stern-to the quay used by tugs and small freighters in 5m with good holding of thick mud. There is constant movement of commercial traffic in the harbour. In 2001, harbour charges were reported at $100 per day plus agent fees but are negotiable for as little as $20 per day plus agent fees (to be paid in US dollars). More recently, harbour charges were quoted at much higher rates.

### TUAPSE

44°05'·15N 39°04'·15E

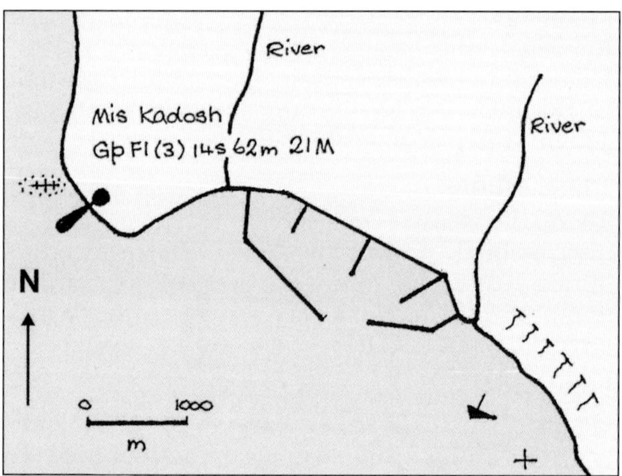


TUAPSE

### GELENDJIK (GELINCIK)

44°30'·0N 38°02'·0E

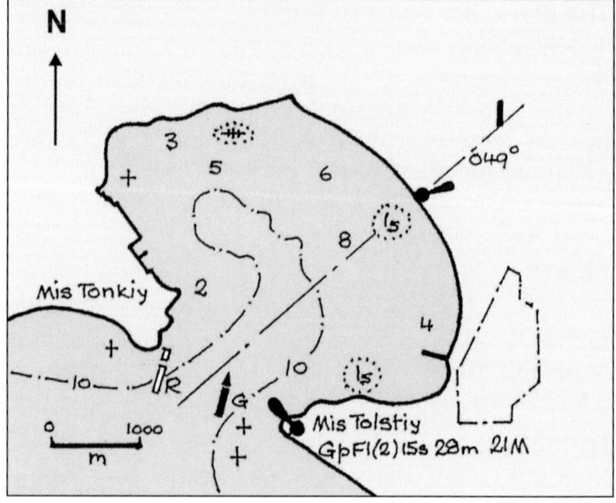


GELENDJIK (GELINCIK)

## NOVOROSSIYSK

44°39'·8N 37°49'·5E for Sudhuskiy Lighthouse
44°41'·7N 37°47'·58E for Yacht Club Seven Feets

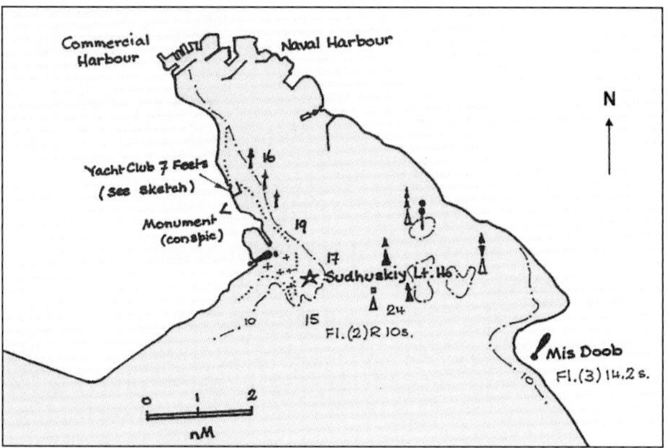


**NOVOROSSIYSK HARBOUR**

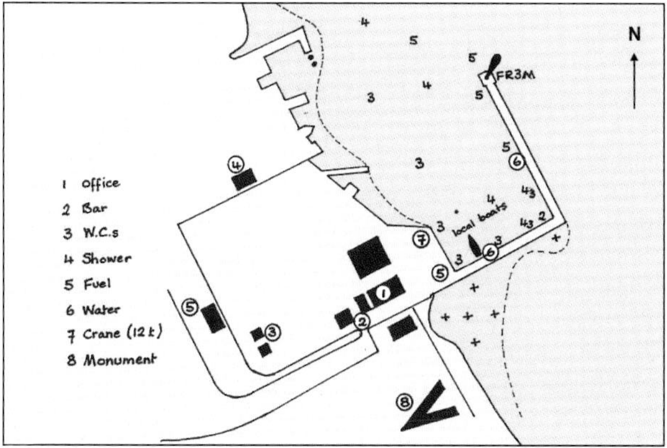


**NOVOROSSIYSK YACHT CLUB 7 FEETS**

Rick and Sheila Nelson visited in 1993. The KAYRA Rally visited Novorossiysk in 1999.

Doreen and Archie Annan were not permitted to visit in 2001. A German-flagged yacht attempted to visit Novorossiysk in 2010 but was turned away.

The commercial harbour is a large oil distribution base and offers nothing for visiting cruising yachts; however, a small yacht club is reported on the left side near the entrance to Novorossiysk Bay. Yachts should approach the 'Yacht Club 7 Feets' first for a berth and to see if clearance formalities can be arranged.

## ANAPA

44°54'·0N 37°18'·4E

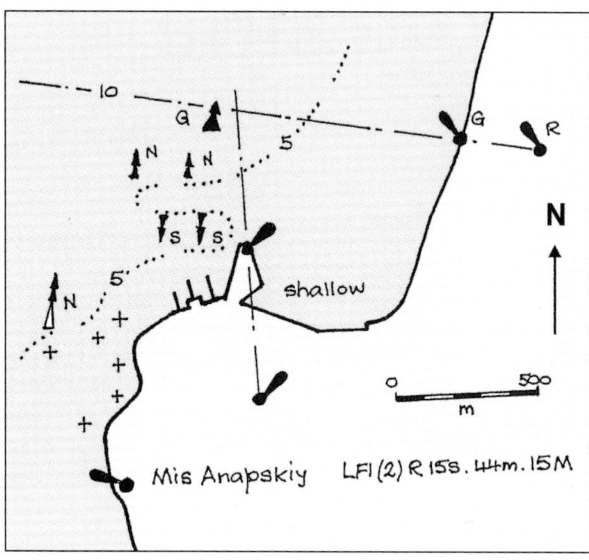


The crew of *Gyatso* were not able to identify any foreign yachts that have written about visiting Anapa.

# 7. Ukraine

The name 'Ukraine' means 'frontier' or 'borderland' in Russian, a term which came into use during the time of the Christian Byzantine Empire, which sustained long and successful missionary activities among the Slavic principalities of Kiev, and, farther north, Moscow. The irony is that although Russians refer to Ukrainians as 'little Russians', it was from the Ukrainian capital of Kyiv ('Kiev' in Russian) that Russia began to come into existence. Volodymyr the Great's embrace of Christianity in 989 established Kyivan Rus as a Christian state, rather than Muslim.

Ukraine is the largest country that is entirely in Europe, stretching some 2,000km from E to W and 1,000km from N to S. Nearly all of the country is flat steppe, and there are mountains only in the far west and on the Crimean Peninsula. The country shares borders with Moldova, Romania, Slovakia, and Poland on the west, Belarus on the north, and the Russian Federation on the north and east. The Crimean Peninsula extends south into the Black Sea and sets off the Sea of Azov, which is separated from the Black Sea by the Kerch Strait.

### History

The modern history of Ukraine can be summarised as the long struggle by Russia to conquer the northern territories of the Ottoman Empire, starting with Peter the Great on the Don River and culminating, in the late 1700s with Catherine the Great's founding of Odessa as the capital of Novorossisk, New Russia. This gave Russia access to the Black Sea. Wars between the Russians and the Ottomans continued every decade or two until November 1853, when the Russian Imperial navy destroyed an Ottoman fleet at Sinop, Turkey. In retaliation, Britain and France joined with the Ottomans to cripple the Russian Black Sea fleet, based at Sevastopol. The Crimean War, 1853–6, was a defeat for the Russians, but within a generation they had rebuilt the fleet and were pressing for access to the Mediterranean through the Turkish Straits.

In the disruption following the collapse of the Russian, Austro-Hungarian and Ottoman Empires following the end of the First World War, the Ukraine was given to the Soviet state, a condition which lasted until 1991. The Second World War was

an especially grim time for Ukraine, which was overrun by Germany and its Romanian allies and re-won by the Red Army. In February 1945, President Roosevelt, Prime Minister Churchill, and General Secretary Stalin met at a conference at the Livadia Palace in Yalta to discuss arrangements for post-war Europe.

The breakup of the Soviet Union in 1991 created many problems for Ukraine, particularly the dispersion of the Soviet Black Sea fleet. The first two post-Soviet leaders, Leonid Kravchuk and Leonid Kuchma, were sympathetic to Communism and pro-Russian, but in 2004 Victor Yushchenko twice defeated Kuchma's designated successor, Viktor Yanukovych, in what became known as the 'Orange Revolution'. Since then, Ukraine has been repeatedly torn between nationalist and pro-Russian sentiments.

### Time

Ukraine Standard Time is GMT +2 hours.

### Communications

Prepaid mobile phones are readily available in Odessa and Yalta. Beeline is a well-established company that provides good voice and data services.

Telephone country code: +380

### Weather

The Summer months are generally very hot along the Black Sea.

### People

*Gyatso* considered the Ukrainian people to be among the most unhappy they had encountered anywhere. Perhaps it was the heat or perhaps the swarms of holidaymakers who flock to the Crimea, but no one seemed to really relax and just enjoy themselves. They found this a surprising contrast to the coast of Romania and Bulgaria, which was just about as hot and crowded but where people were obviously having a good time. *Gyatso* were left with the impression that the people of Ukraine were searching for a non-Russian national identity which still eluded them and that the instruments of state power still engendered widespread fear, especially among officials.

### Food and drink

Ukrainian food provides comfort during frigid winters. Best known is borsch, the national soup of beetroot and salted pork fat. Cabbage rolls, potato pancakes and dumplings are also favourites. Red and white wines are drinkable, plentiful and cheap, as are vodkas and brandies.

### Language

Two languages – Ukrainian and Russian – are commonly spoken in Ukraine. The languages are closely related in grammar and vocabulary, and both use the Cyrillic alphabet, but they are different enough to exacerbate underlying ethnic tensions.

### Travel ashore: taxi, train, plane, road

There are good public transport facilities between just about everywhere on the coast of Ukraine and just about anywhere else. Ukrainians have such a distaste for draughts that even in a heatwave they keep local bus windows closed, without AC.

### Provisions

Basic foods are readily available just about everywhere, in both markets and shops. The concept of 'self-service' has not reached many Ukrainian shops, however, so shopping is likely to require a lot of gesticulation. Labelling is primitive compared to EU standards.

Mis I'li near Feodosia

## Money/ currency

Ukrainian currency is the Grivna, or Hryvnia, abbreviated UAH. In early 2011 the exchange rate was 1.00 UAH = €0.092, and €1.00 = 10.91 UAH. ATMs are locally known as Bankomats and are common in cities, large towns and holiday resorts.

## The Black Sea coast

The 600M Black Sea coastline of Ukraine offers many beautiful and relaxing places to cruise. Balaclava and Chernomorskoe are two of only a handful of natural harbours on the Black Sea. Feodosia, Sevastopol and Odessa are large man-made harbours which offer generally good shelter.

## Charts

There is a small chandlery in Sevastopol that sells old Soviet-era charts, which are 'interesting' to use, but it is best to arrive with Turkish or British Admiralty paper charts, as well as electronic charts.

## Formalities

Ukrainian entry and exit formalities are expensive and range from being merely tedious and annoying to downright scary. The officials who deal with yachts, particularly the Border Police, are trained to view yacht captains with the deep suspicion that comes with the fear of losing their job – or worse – if anything goes wrong. 'Problems' can appear out of nowhere, accompanied by increasing frowns and muttering. Or you may encounter highly aggressive agents, demanding exorbitant fees (say, €400) to straighten things out.

The cost and annoyance of visiting Ukraine by yacht can be minimised by entering and departing through only two ports: Yalta and Odessa. In both places yacht captains can find highly reputable agents who will handle the blizzard of paperwork and greatly reduce the pain. Although Sevastopol is technically a port of entry for yachts, there are numerous recent reports of bureaucratic difficulties there. Other places that previously served as ports of entry for yachts, such as Feodosia, now only handle commercial vessels.

Odessa

Hotel Odessa

Security gate at marina in Odessa

Checking into the Ukraine at Yalta and out at Odessa, or vice versa, makes it inconvenient to visit the lovely spots along the east Crimean coast and south of Odessa, but it nevertheless offers a straightforward opportunity to visit some of the most beautiful cruising sites on the north and west coasts of the Black Sea.

Yachtsmen's experiences of Ukraine appear to range from terrific to terrible. Some said, 'You're crazy to visit the Ukraine by yacht' and others said, 'I'd go back in a minute'. Visiting the Ukraine during a cruise on the Black Sea adds to the richness of the experience. Patience with bureaucracy, some understanding for the culture and preparation will help to reduce the risk of being taken advantage of or having a bad experience with authorities. Once cleared in to the Ukraine, yachts are required to stay within 12M of the shore. Don't take shortcuts. There have been several reports of yachts being stopped by coastguard at sea; one was less than 1M into international waters. Although the 12M rule makes the passage between the Crimea and Odessa slightly longer, stay in Ukrainian territorial waters if you don't want to run the risk of being stopped by the coastguard. In any case, a N route keeps you clear of the oil platforms and fish havens.

Patience is especially important because only very limited English is spoken. There is a culture of extensive paperwork and bureaucracy and lack of respect for private property. Security is important to keep people from boarding yachts, and gates alone do little to deter people from entering restricted areas of marinas or boarding yachts for photo opportunities.

If you visit the Crimea in the summer, you will likely be required to stay two or three miles offshore in the area between Yalta and Sevastopol when the president and other government officials are in residence. When planning your route on the Black Sea, you may want to take into account several reports of hassles and excess fees when clearing *in* at Odessa. Clearing *out* in 2010, *Gyatso* experienced a highly professional operation at a reasonable rate. There are many reports of difficulties for yachts trying to go through Ukrainian border formalities at Izmail, on the Danube.

All the reports of problems in Yalta came from yachts lacking up-to-date information about clearance procedures. By law, clearing into the Ukraine requires an agent, and a fee of $200. Owners and crew are not allowed to leave the yacht until fully cleared in. Arriving on a weekday is better than during the weekend. Move to Balaclava as soon as possible. Yachtsmen run into trouble if they arrive without the name of a reputable agent and are not informed about the required fees. This opens you up to being taken advantage of by customs and immigration authorities, agents looking to drum up business, etc. Clear in with a reputable agent at Yalta and out in Odessa. *Gyatso* recommends Volodymyr R Papakin as agent, whose contact information is in the section on Yalta formalities. For administrative reasons alone, in 2010 a W to E (clockwise) transit of the Ukraine could not be recommended.

Your Transit Log entries will include a list of every place you plan to visit by yacht. *Gyatso* assumed that it was better to be safe than sorry and listed some places that they weren't sure they would visit. Kherson, on the Dnieper River, was one such. When they checked in at Skadovsk, unbeknown to them the Border Police wired the Kherson authorities that *Gyatso* were coming along, and this caused a big row when *Gyatso* sailed directly to Odessa instead.

Tour boat along the Crimean coast between Yalta and Feodosia

Feodosia harbour entrance

The Odessa police initially demanded that they sail to Kherson, 80M away.

The hassle of clearing in has encouraged some yachts to depart from Ukraine without a formal checkout. This is deeply upsetting to officials who have been trained that the borders are sacred. So the system has evolved to make checking out much easier than checking in.

## Ports of Entry

Yalta and Odessa are reliable ports of entry for yachts. Sevastopol is possible but likely to be less straightforward than Yalta. Balaclava is **not** a port of entry.

In this guide the order of harbours and anchorages has been strictly anticlockwise (counterclockwise). For the Ukraine, the order changes. Section 1 jumps to Yalta and moves E from there to Feodosia, before resuming the W course again in Section 2, Yalta to the Romanian border. The first section is much smaller, but this division emphasises the key role of Yalta as the preferred port of entry for yachts into Ukraine, on a par with Odessa. It fails to highlight the geographic limitations of the authority of Crimean officials, which does not extend beyond the Crimea. And it eliminates what is probably a very interesting stretch of coast between Feodosia and the Kerch Strait. No reports have been seen from yachts about conditions at the Kerch Strait.

From a yachting viewpoint, the Crimean Peninsula extends from Feodosia in the east to Chernomorskoe in the west. With endless variations, the Crimean coast is steep-to, with cliffs. Right in the middle is the remarkable indentation at Sevastopol, the shelter of which for a navy is so vastly superior to any other place that the Russians still haven't devised a way to leave. Balaclava is equally attractive for yachts – and preferred by some. It is easy to visit Sevastopol by bus from Balaclava.

From Chernomorskoe to Odessa is a distance of a little over 100M. N of this line, the shoreline is sandy beach and there is motion everywhere, especially in the huge lagoons, known locally by their Turkish name, *liman*.

# Section 1: Yalta to Feodosia

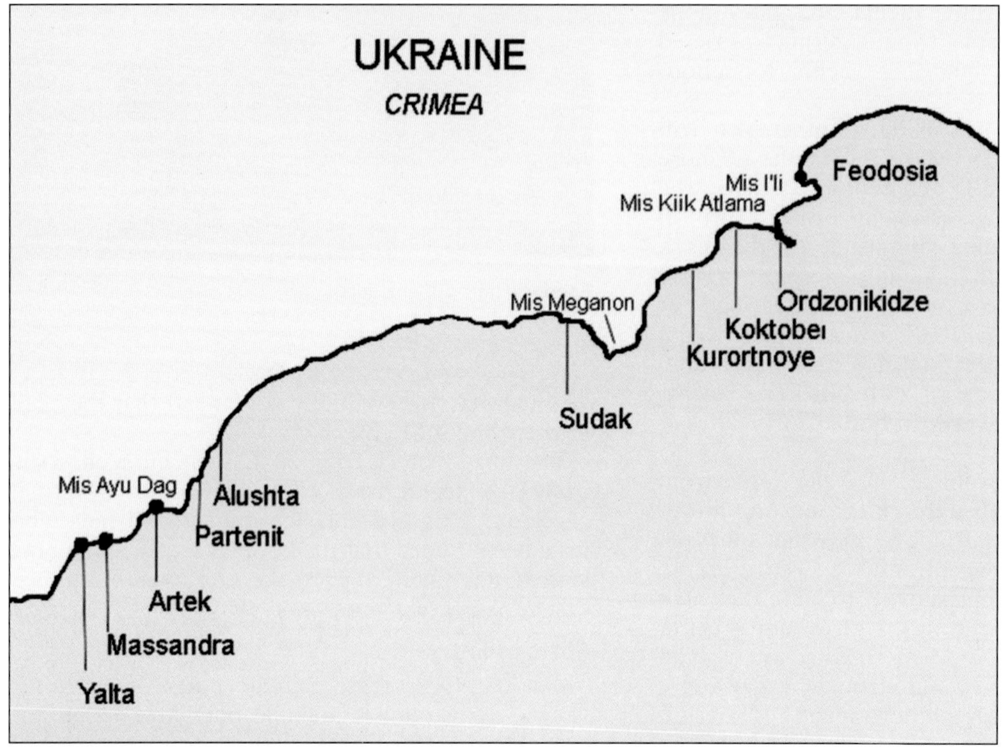


## YALTA PASSENGER PORT

44°29'·4N 34°10'·3E

### Approach

The approach to the Yalta Passenger Port at the N end of a large bay is straightforward. Contact Yalta Port Control in the approach for permission to enter the harbour.

*Conspicuous* The breakwater with a large light on the end is easily seen in front of the spectacular setting of the city.

*VHF* Ch 16 for Yalta Port Control and to report to Lebed (Ukrainian coastguard). VHF Ch 14 for dispatcher to assign mooring position. If there are no answers to your calls, proceed to the customs dock where Border Control police will meet you. Ask them to contact your pre-arranged agent to conduct clearance formalities.

Danger Keep a careful watch for busy and fast-moving ferry and charter boat traffic entering and exiting the harbour.

### Mooring

There are no facilities for yachts in the busy Yalta Passenger Port which is filled with cruise ships, day charter and dinner cruise boats, tugs, Russian-owned motor yachts, etc. Whether arriving from another country or port in the Ukraine, yachts should report first to the customs dock to conduct clearance formalities for the Crimea (a semi-autonomous region) and the Ukraine. You are required to use an agent and pay a fee which is set by law; however, to avoid corrupt agents, be sure to make arrangements with a reputable agent in advance.

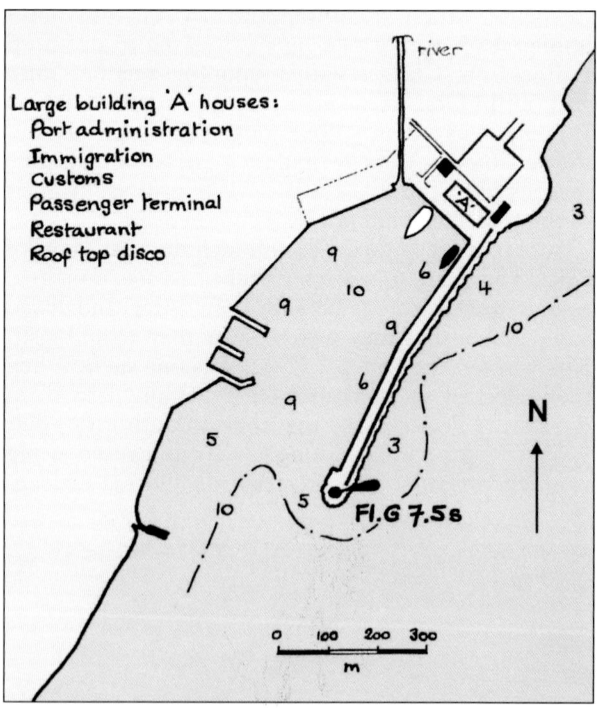


YALTA PASSENGER PORT

*Berth* After completing clearance formalities, it is possible to arrange a berth on the NW quay. Go bow- or stern-to with your own anchor with excellent holding. Because there is no security or services for yachts, very high volumes of foot traffic along the quay and constant swell and surge in the Yalta Passenger Port, a

Yalta Passenger Port customs dock

better option is to move to Balaclava after clearing in and to visit Yalta by bus, rental car or with a guided tour from there.

*Depths* 6m at customs dock and 9–10m in the harbour.

*Shelter* The harbour is subjected to almost constant swell and wash from busy commercial and charter boat traffic. The harbour is open from the SE to SW, and the swell and surge is particularly uncomfortable and can be dangerous from these directions.

*Local Weather Considerations* When clouds gather and fall on the mountains to the NW of Yalta, a NW squall of up to 35 knots can be expected with a duration which seldom exceeds 30 minutes.

*Authorities* Port of entry. All harbour officials can be found in the building and tower in the NE corner of the harbour.

*Charge band* Charges range from $0–50 (prices quoted in USD) for a 12m yacht, apply for overnight stays and are negotiated by your agent (yet another reason to be sure you have a good one lined up in advance). *Gyatso* was permitted to spend two nights at the customs dock for free (without water and electricity) but had to leave the dock twice when river cruise ships arrived or departed.

*Contact information* To arrange for an agent to handle clearance formalities and berthing in Yalta Passenger Port contact Volodymyr R Papakin. Previously the Technical Director of Yalta Port, Papakin has started an agency, Yalmara, which has an excellent reputation for the quality and integrity of its work. Contact him in advance if at all possible so that he can begin preparations for the yacht to berth at the Customs dock. ✆ (business): +38 (065) 432 8289. *Mobile* +38 (050) 347 5833 *Email* Papakin@isd.com.ua and yalmara@ukrpost.ua.

## Facilities

*Services* None.

*Fuel* By jerry can and taxi (can be arranged through your agent). If you have enough fuel to reach Balaclava, it is much more convenient to refuel there.

*Repairs* Repairs can be arranged through your agent but likely to be expensive.

*Provisions* Small supermarkets and local market selling speciality products in the several block area outside the customs dock gate.

*Eating out* Numerous restaurants, bars and cafés in this large city which serves as a major tourist destination.

*Other* Banks, ATMs and shops catering to tourists abound along with internet cafés and gambling casinos. Buses, hire cars and international airport.

## General

Yalta is the Crimea's major Black Sea resort port. It is a major stop for cruise lines of all sorts, and the city seems to be gaining a more cosmopolitan flavour. In the 19th century it was developed as an aristocratic resort which attracted many artists such as Tolstoy, Chekhov and Rachmaninov. A new elite class is continuing the tradition of Yalta as an exclusive hideaway for the rich and powerful. Unfortunately for visiting yachts, the harbour can be uncomfortable due to the swell and surge and even dangerous in strong S winds. Throngs of tourists walk along the lengthy promenade throughout the day and evening hours.

Sites of interest include: Livadia Palace, Vorontsov Palace, Alupka Palace, Botanic Gardens, Chekhov Museum.

A good system of public transport makes it easy to visit popular tourist sites. A visit to the famous Massandra Vineyards wine factory can be arranged. The wine tasting centre is located 50m from the bus stop for Alupka. Swallows Nest sits precariously atop Avrorina rock, jutting 38m out over the sea, built by a Russian architect for an industrialist in 1912. The summit of Mt Ay-Petri (1,233m) can be reached by a two-stage cable car or by mountain road, walking and horse riding expeditions. Unfortunately for those visiting by private yacht in July and August it is a requirement to remain 2–3M off the coast when travelling along the S coast of the Crimea (see clearance formalities regarding these restrictions). The mountainous landscape is dramatic nonetheless and much can still be seen with good binoculars.

7. UKRAINE

## MASSANDRA (YALTA COMMERCIAL PORT)

44°29'·8N 34°12'·0E

Massandra, Yalta's commercial port located just E of Yalta Passenger Port, has no facilities for visiting yachts. Yachts must report to the Yalta Passenger

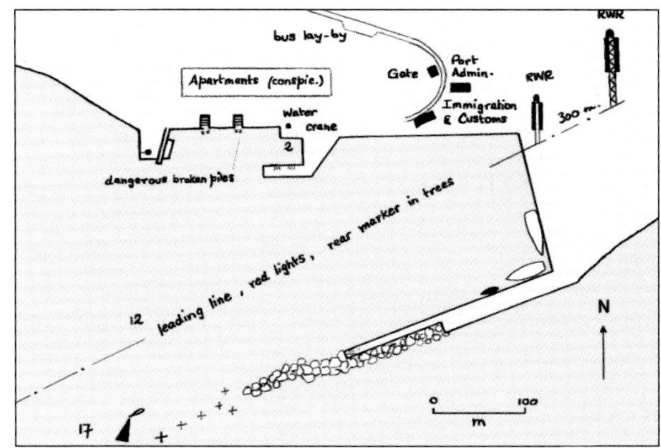


MASSANDRA (YALTA COMMERCIAL PORT)

Coastline between Yalta and Feodosia

Port and can only move to Massandra if instructed to do so by Yalta Port Control. Owners of local yachts with good connections moor their yachts here along with commercial vessels. The small basin previously identified as a yacht harbour is no longer in use. Massandra is no longer a port of entry nor is it the harbour authorities' preferred harbour for yachts.

In the approach, leave the green buoy to starboard to avoid rocks and debris that extend to the SW of the breakwater. Moor alongside the concrete quay with plenty of fenders. Swell from the SE or SW works its way into the harbour and can be quite uncomfortable. The commercial harbour is open to the W.

A minibus leaves from outside the harbour gate for the 30-minute ride into Yalta.

## ARTEK

44°33'·07N 34°18'·21E

Artek was an All-Union and international Young Pioneer camp in the Soviet Union. It was established in 1925 near the Black Sea in the town of Gurzuf located on the Crimean peninsula, near Medved Mountain, Ukraine. The camp first hosted eighty children but it grew rapidly. In 1969 it had an area of 3·2km²; there were 150 buildings, including three medical buildings, a school, film studio, three swimming pools, a 7,000-seat sports stadium and playgrounds for other activities. Unlike most of the young pioneer camps, Artek was a year-round camp, thanks to the climate.

Destination Artek was considered to be an honorable award for Soviet children as well as internationally. During its heyday, each year Artek gave 27,000 children vacations. Between 1925 and 1969 the camp hosted 300,000 children including more than 13,000 children from seventy foreign countries. In 2010 Artek was closed, but a public campaign is underway to reopen it.

When the camp was open, a small private marina was filled with local yachts and welcomed visitors. The entry is straightforward after rounding the rocky islets at 44°29'·6N 34°17'·9E. Ballasting of the breakwater extends 30m beyond the SE corner. There are also two metal posts to the S of the breakwater and shallow water near the entrance is marked with a red buoy. Depths of 6m at the harbour entrance decrease to 3–5m inside. Check the current status of the facility before planning a visit here.

It is possible to visit Botanic Gardens of Yalta and the nearby village of Gurzuf, 3km from here (long walk or dinghy ride through the rocky islets). It is also possible to visit the Gagarin Centre, where astronaut training is explained.

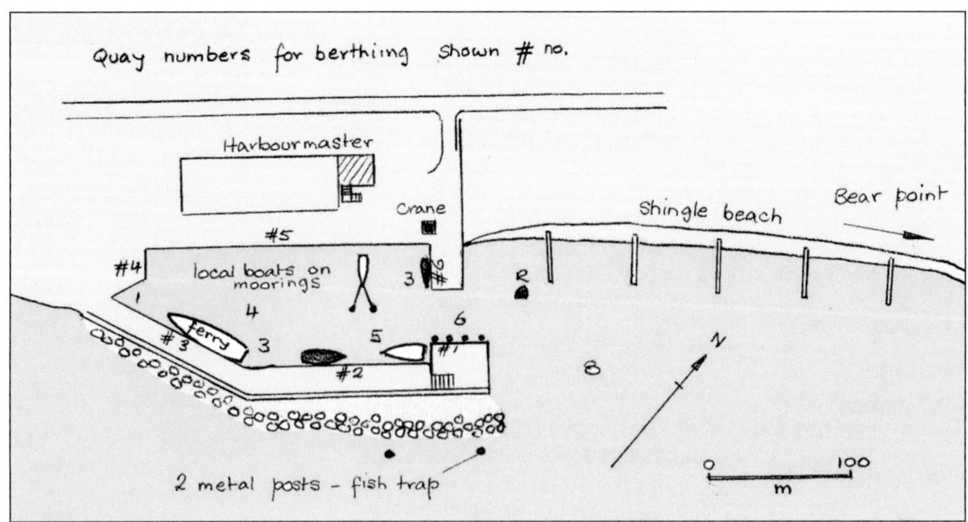

ARTEK

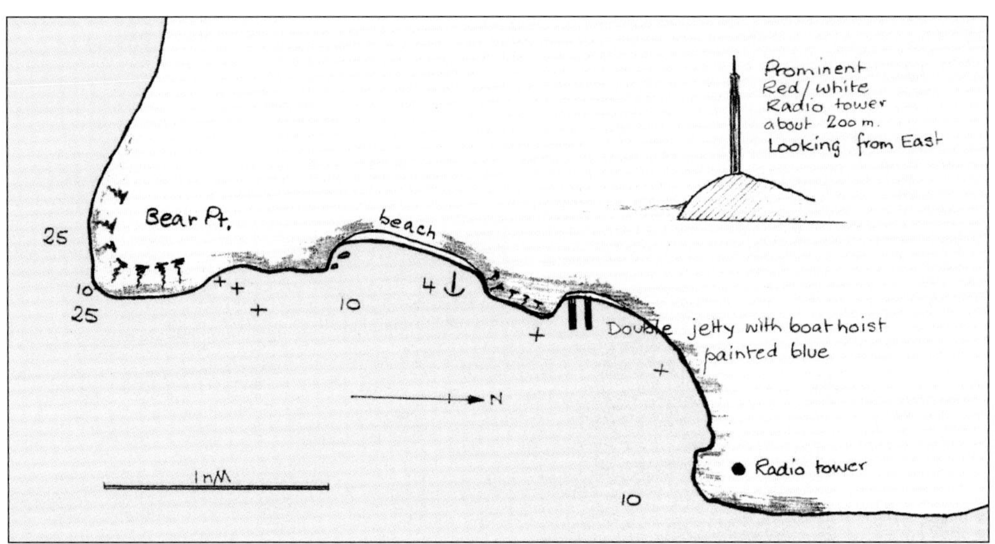


PARTENIT

## PARTENIT

44°34'·32N 34°20'·94E

Partenit is a seaside resort village in the S part of the Crimean peninsula, situated between Alushta and Yalta and about 75km from the international airport at Simferopol. Population is up to 8,000 inhabitants. The name has its origins in the Greek 'Parthenon'. Partenit lies just near the bottom of Bear Mountain (Ayu Dag). Ayu Dag mountain can be seen in many guide books relating to the Crimean peninsula. The beach of Partenit is pebbled, like those in most other resorts on the S coast of Crimea.

Partenit is on a fairly flat coastal plot of land, although the elevation quickly rises the farther away one goes from the sea. Much of the architecture of the city is in the 'Soviet Realist' style. The current permanent population is largely Ukrainian, with a significant influx of Tatars and Armenians.

Partenit has two beaches. One is the public beach, which is free. The other is on the property of the military resort and much bigger. Most tourists rent an apartment from a local landlord, and the going rate in recent years has been about €15/day for an apartment within a 10-minute walk of the beach.

There are several businesses set up for tourists between the bazaar and the beach, offering excursions to different parts of Crimea, including to Massandra and Livadia, as well as waterfalls. A local tour goes through Ayu Dag, tracing its history through earthquakes and past ruins of ancient churches of the Goths. One of the first national parks in Ukraine was established to protect Ayu Dag.

In settled weather, anchor in 5m where suitable, taking care to avoid above-water rocks. The anchorage is sheltered from the N and NE but open to the S. VHF Ch 16 for harbourmaster and to report to Lebed (Ukrainian coastguard).

## ALUSHTA

44°40'·49N 34°25'·35E

Alushta is a large town spread long the bay of the same name.

After Yalta, Alushta is the second largest town on Crimea's S shore, between Sevastopol and Feodosia, and it is one of Crimea's major recreation centres. It is just an hour's drive by taxi or minibus to Simferopol, with its busy train station and airport.

A partially constructed marina is located at the N end of town and offers some shelter. It is open to the E. Plans to complete a 300-berth marina have not materialised. Use VHF Ch 16 for Alushta Marina and to report to Lebed (Ukrainian coastguard).

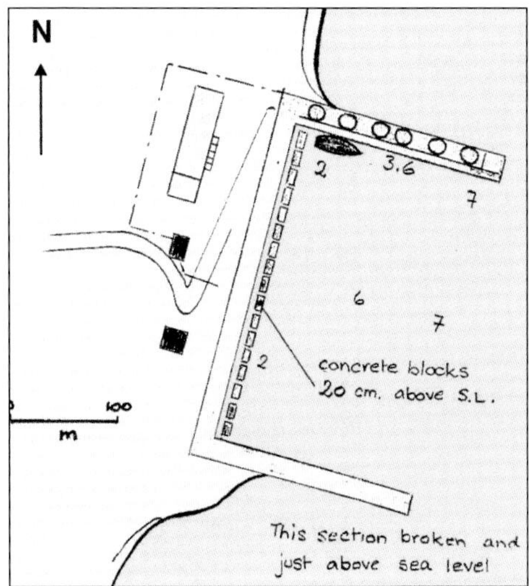


ALUSHTA

7. UKRAINE

SUDAK

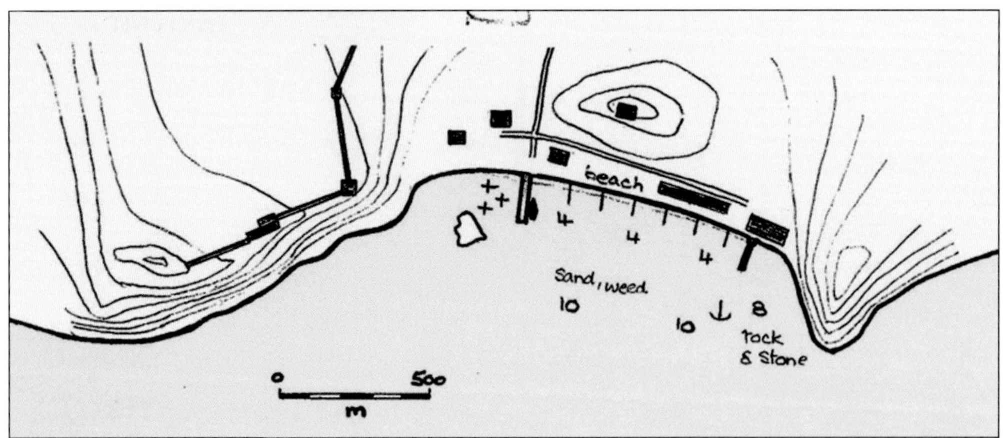


## SUDAK

44°50'·4N 34°57'·85E

In the 13th century the Genoese built a series of fortresses along Crimea's S shore before losing their lands in the Turkish invasion of 1475. The fortress of Sudak is the largest and best preserved of these. Anchor in 5–10m with good holding, or in settled weather it is possible to lie alongside the rusted and broken piles and decked jetty in 4m for easy access to the fortress. This is potentially dangerous with any swell. There may be a small charge for tying to the jetty. VHF Ch 16 for harbourmaster and reporting to Lebed (Ukrainian coastguard). The bay is open to the S.

Sudak

## KURORTNOYE

44°54'·4N 35°11'·6E

In settled weather, this daytime anchorage provides convenient access to the Dolphinarium and the Flora and Fauna Museum associated with the Karadag Nature Reserve. It is also the start of an organised walking tour around the nature reserve. Sally Humphries reported on her 2010 visit,

KURORTNOYE

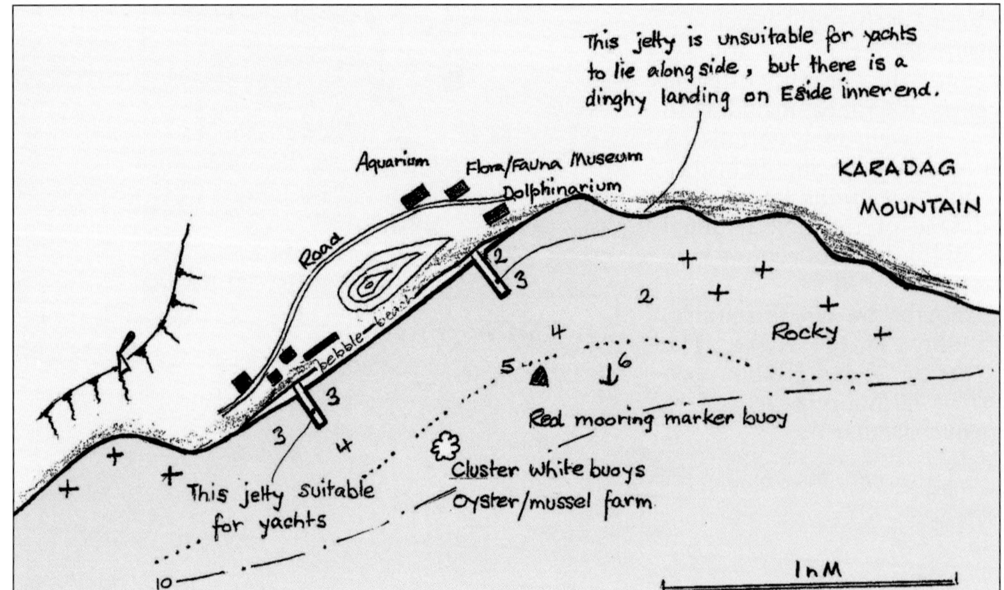

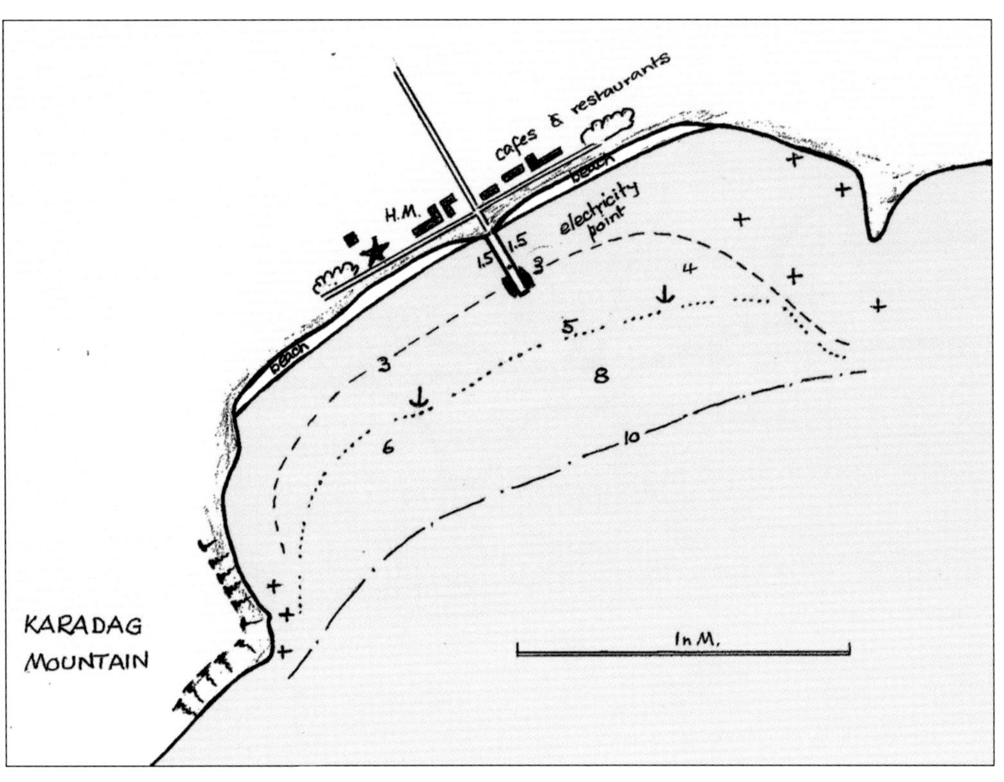


**KOKTOBEL (KOKTEBEL)**

'We anchored off the village and went ashore but discovered that the aquarium and dolphinarium were on the Karadag peninsula by a jetty. We moved there, anchoring outside the prohibited nature zone as shown on the GPS, and landed by dinghy. GPS exaggerated the extent of prohibited zone, including villages with anchored boats. We had trouble getting onto the jetty to rejoin our yacht; only tourist boats with licenses are allowed to use it, but when the guards saw our dinghy they dropped objections.'

## KOKTOBEL (Koktebel)

44°57'·64N 35°15'·34E

Koktobel is a resort village located under Karadag Mountain and at the edge of the Karadag Nature Reserve, with a choice of anchoring in the sandy bay or mooring along the outer half of an open steel and concrete jetty. There is clear water for swimming and a lively village ashore.

### Approach

There is a reef in the approach at position 44°57'·55N 35°18'·7E.

### Mooring

Anchor or go alongside the end of the jetty in 3–5m. Several Ukrainian charter sailing yachts use this bay as their base. In the summer, you can expect calm nights with a S wind starting about 1000 veering during the day and falling again in the evening. This is a suitable day or overnight anchorage in settled weather. The bay is open to the NE. With a fresh N wind, better shelter can be found at Ordzhonikidze.

### Facilities

Minimal harbour charges may apply if tied to the jetty where water and electricity may be available upon request. Local produce, cafés and restaurants are located at the end of the jetty. Local specialities include Koktobel wine and brandy available in the local market located on the main road to Feodosia W of the junction with the road leading from the jetty. Flights by micro-aircraft, gliders and small planes can be arranged from the Glider and Aeroplane Museum several kilometres away. A nudist beach is located on the E side of the bay.

### General

Karadag is the ruins of an ancient Jurassic volcano which was active nearly 150 million years ago. Karadag Nature Reserve occupies the area of 2,874ha. It is a unique haven of landscape and biological diversity, with 2,870 species of flora and 5,350 species of fauna, a gene pool of rare plants and animals. It is an important refuge of Mediterranean fauna in the Crimea.

Passage between Yalta and Feodosia

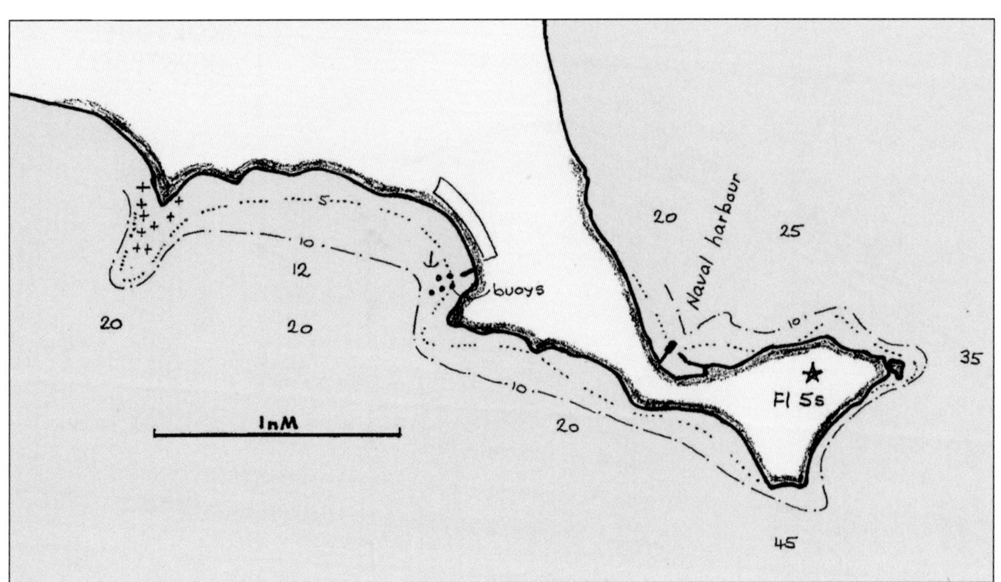


ORDZHONIKIDZE

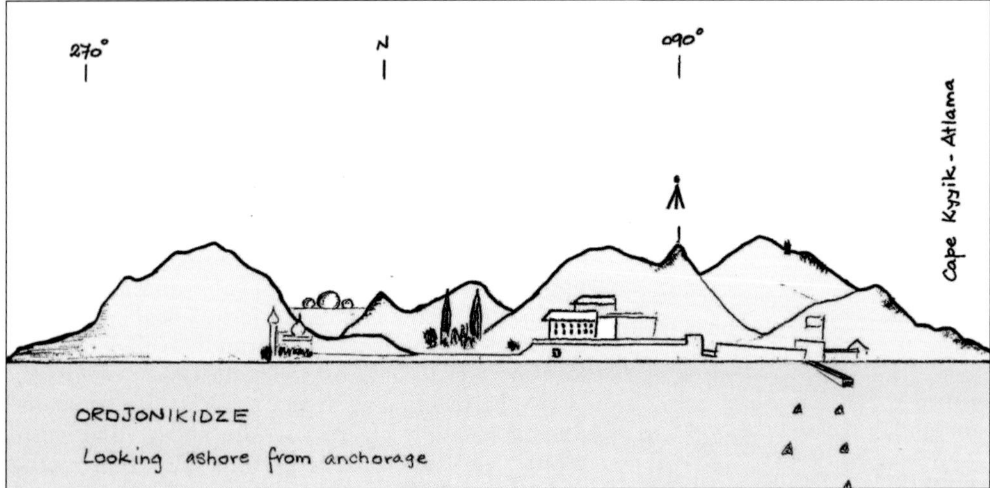


## ⚓ ORDZHONIKIDZE

44°57'·7N 35°21'·1E

### Ordzhonikidze Former Naval Harbour

Located on the coast between Dvuyakornaya Bay and the Koktobel Gulf is the village of Ordzhonikidze, where there is a former naval harbour on the N side of Cape Kyyik-Atlama. It is protected by a long breakwater with entry at the W end and provides shelter. A safe approach point is 44°57'·7N 35°22'·7E. The sea here is claimed to be one of the cleanest stretches of the Black Sea in the whole of the Crimea. Plans to privatise the port were reported in 2000, but this had not materialised as of 2010. There is no current information about the port.

### Ordzhonikidze Bay

About 1·5km W of the naval harbour, a jetty extends SW from the cape. It is not suitable for yachts, and the bay itself is suitable for overnights only in settled weather. Sally Humphries reported in 2010:

> 'Now has about 12 mooring buoys. We anchored in 8m clear of them; they seemed to be in use. Best shelter is in E corner of the bay, but it may be shallow.'

## FEODOSIA

45°02'·4N 35°25'·0E

Feodosia is the most important commercial and naval port in the E half of the Crimean peninsula. It is a Port of Entry for cargo vessels, but in 2010 foreign yachts were not permitted to clear in or out of this port. This is an important change from 2001, when it was reported that this would be possible and that yachts were welcomed. If a yacht has cleared into the Ukraine in Yalta and obtained advance permission to visit Feodosia, then it is possible to visit. However, there are only limited facilities for visiting yachts.

### Approach

The approach is straightforward.

### Mooring

Contact Feodosia Port Control dispatcher VHF Ch 14 upon arrival for permission to enter the harbour and for instructions on where to berth.

Sally Humphrey reported in 2010:

> 'the ex-naval inner harbour is now open to private craft but plans for a marina seem to have been

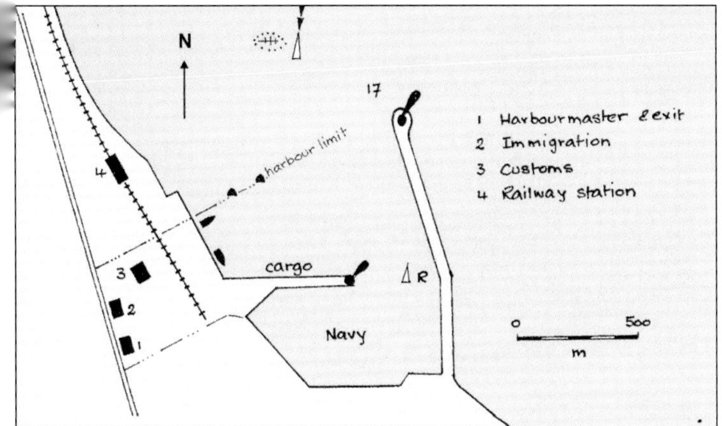


## FEODOSIA

Freighter ashore in Kerch Strait storm, November 2007
*Dumitru Bucureştanu*

abandoned after provision of a set of unconvincing and unoccupied pontoons in the SW corner. There are local boats on moorings along part of the breakwater forming the S side of this inner harbour, but there was room to anchor and take stern lines between them and the pontoons. There is a guard on the inner end of the breakwater, but commuter-boats land passengers on it. No other facilities, although we were charged $20 for mooring. Small shops 10 minutes' walk away.'

### General

Founded by the Greeks in the 6th century BC, the ancient Greek name Theodosiya means 'gift from the gods'. Today it has few amenities for yachts arriving by sea, but with a population of about 85,000, Feodosia offers something for yachtsmen once ashore, including an old town and a waterfront promenade lined with numerous cafés and restaurants. The long stretch of beach in the bay to the N of the port makes this a popular summer resort. All provisions can be found in the city, and a daily market with a good selection of fresh produce and other supplies is located W of the harbour gate. Ferries and tour boats shuttle swimmers to nearby beaches. A waterfront railway station connects Feodosia with Kiev and Moscow. Sites of interest include a museum of artist Ivan Ayvazovsky, a man of Armenian descent who spent most of his life in Feodosia. There is also an Archeological Museum. Although not as grand as the one in Sudak, Feodosia's citadel serves as a reminder of past Genoese control of the city. There is considerable evidence that the bubonic plague spread into Europe from Asia through Feodosia in the 14th century. The terrified Genoese fled back to Italy when Mongols arrived from the Asian steppes, carrying the disease with them.

### *Passage note: Ukraine. Feodosia to Kerch Strait*

It is expected that Ukraine will continue to grant permission for yachts to sail within Ukrainian territorial waters as far E as Feodosia. Although Feodosia is no longer a port of entry for yachts, there appears to be no prohibition for yachts to visit here as long as the visiting yacht had already cleared into Ukraine.

This leaves about a 50M stretch of coastline along the easternmost portion of the Crimean Peninsula, separated from the Russian Federation by the Kerch Strait, connecting the Black Sea and the Sea of Azov. *Gyatso* learned of no reports of visits by foreign yachts at the straits or in the Sea of Azov.

Disputes between Russia and Ukraine over the Kerch Strait are not as obvious as those between Russia and Georgia over Abkhazia, but they do exist and could affect yachts in unpredictable ways. One of the worst shipwrecks on the Black Sea in modern times occurred in the Kerch Strait on 11 November 2007. The Russian-flagged oil tanker *Volgoneft-139* sought shelter in the strait, but it broke apart and released more than 2,000 tonnes of fuel oil. The Russians complained that the Ukrainian authorities had failed to permit the Russian ship to gain shelter.

Feodosia

# Section 2: Yalta to the Romanian border

W of Yalta there are three main sections in the passage to the Romanian border:

1. The Crimean Peninsula extending to Chernomorskoe
2. Passage S of the Bug and Dnieper estuaries
3. Odessa and the W coast

Highlights of the W Crimea are Balaclava, Sevastopol, and Yevpatoria. A stop in Yevpatoria may be required to get a transit log for places outside of the Crimea.

From Chernomorskoe direct to Odessa is a distance of a little over 100M, but it takes you through an area of shallows, oil wells, and fish havens, so it is preferable to swing well N of the rhumb line. N of this line, the shoreline is sandy beach. *Gyatso* enjoyed several hours of rest, anchored NW of Djarilgach Island light and had some of the best sailing all summer, bound for Odessa.

Odessa is the best that Ukraine has to offer on the Black Sea. There are some places along the coast south of Odessa where a yacht might find shelter, but most chose to make the overnight passage to Sulina or points further south.

The Crimean coastline between Yalta and Laspi

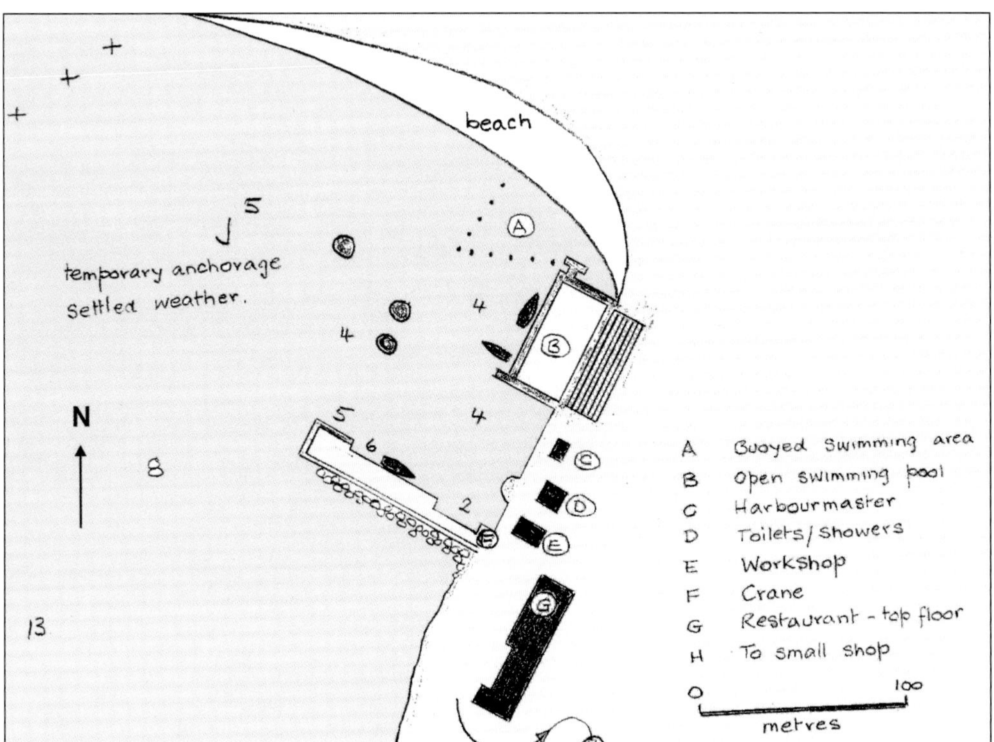


LASPI



## LASPI

44°25'·1N 33°42'·5E

The Annans reported this children's camp to have a slightly broken-down appearance in 2001, with few children. Many of the houses appeared to be converted to holiday homes. In 2010, Sally Humphries reported Laspi to be an attractive bay, but chock full of jellyfish.

## BALACLAVA

44°29'·2N 33°35'·9E

Balaclava, also spelled Balaklava, is by far the best of the three natural harbours in the Black Sea (the other two being Gideros and Akliman, in Turkey). It offers virtually complete shelter, good depths for yachts of all sizes and freedom from underwater obstructions. In addition to being an attractive harbour, all facilities are within easy walking distance of the marina, making Balaclava a convenient and pleasant place to stop over and to use as a base for visiting the Crimea.

The English will know of Balaclava from remembered history of the Crimea war, of the dreadfull health conditions of the allied troops and Florence Nightingale's developments in nursing care, and of the 'Charge of the Light Brigade' into the 'Valley of Death' immortalised in Tennyson's poem. The valley is now covered in vines. If touring from Balaclava a visit to the Panorama of the 1854–5 defence of Sevastopol is worth a visit – the canvas is 115m long by 14m high and is outstandingly well presented.

### Approach

The harbour entrance is difficult to see at a distance. Follow the buoyed passage and watch for busy local boat traffic near the harbour entrance.

*VHF* Ch 16 to report to Lebed (Ukrainian coastguard). Upon arrival to or before departing from the harbour, contact Balaclava Port Control dispatcher or Golden Symbol Marina on Ch 16 (not likely to answer radio calls). Proceed to marina for further instructions.

Danger Rocks extend 0·5M from the shore 1·5M to the SE of the harbour entrance.

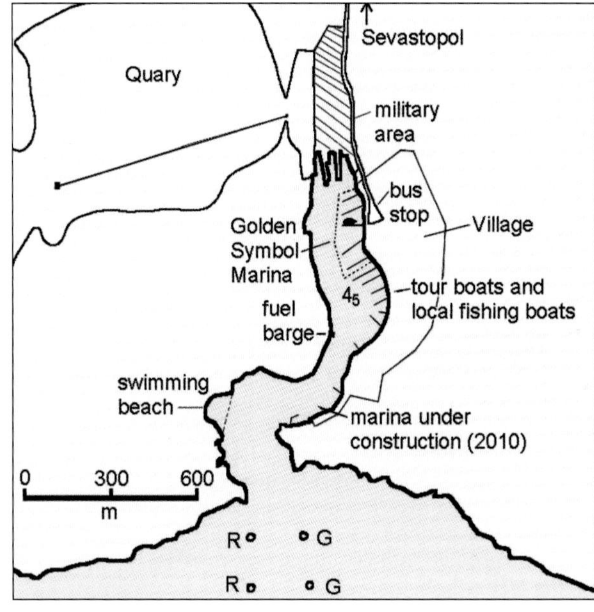


BALACLAVA

Entance to Balaclava harbour

Tower ruins and white building E of the entrance to Balaclava harbour

## Mooring

Where directed alongside one of the floating pontoons. If marina staff do not meet you at the dock, go alongside the outer end of the first floating pontoon to arrange for your berth. The port dispatcher is located on the ground floor of the building at the base of the third pontoon, next to the marina gate. The marina office is located in the same building with an entrance facing the harbour.

*Berth* Where directed alongside one of the floating pontoons.

*Depths* 4·5–6m in the marina.

*Shelter* Excellent all-round shelter.

*Authorities* Balaclava is not a port of entry. It is recommended that yachts clear-in at Yalta first (see clearance procedures for the Ukraine). Marina staff are available to assist you with berthing.

*Charges* Eight nights were charged as 1,324 UAH, equivalent to €110.

*Contact information* Golden Symbol Marina, Sevastapol Balaklava 99042. ✆ +38 0692 637 224 or 353, *Fax* +38 0692 455 334 *Email* goldensymbol@gmail.com. In 2010 Natasha in the office spoke English and was very helpful in assisting the owners of foreign yachts.

## Facilities

*Services* Water and electricity at every berth (a long hose and cable required at some berths). Sometimes the government limits the supply of fresh water, so it may only be available in low volumes or not at all during certain times of the day. Well-maintained toilets and showers located next to the office are managed independently and may require a small fee. As long as the water supply is not interrupted, the marina office can arrange laundry service (wash or wash/dry/fold).

*Fuel* Fuel dock on floating pontoon to the left as you enter the main harbour area (local cash currency only).

*Repairs* Emergency haul-out and repairs arranged through marina office.

*Provisions* Basic provisions can be found in the supermarket across the street from the marina entrance gate. Other small but good supermarkets and produce stands one block from the waterfront promenade. A busy outlet selling bulk and bottled local wine (sparkling, sweet and dry varieties) is conveniently located across the street from the marina entrance gate.

*Eating out* The marina operates a restaurant onsite which serves good fried local fish and local wines. Another restaurant with an excellent view, and worth noting for

Golden Symbol Marina, Balaclava

Balaclava. Cossack Bay 1855–6

its local specialities, is located upstairs from the marina office on the N end of the same building. Many other restaurants, bars, and cafés catering to tourists, including a popular seafood restaurant at the S end of the promenade, are located near the waterfront or on the main road toward Sevastopol.

*Other* An internet café (for use with their terminals only) is located behind the supermarket across the street from the marina entrance gate. Wi-Fi internet available at waterfront bars for a fee (look for signs advertising Wi-Fi). Post office, mobile phone store and ATM across the street from the marina. Buses to Sevastopol and onward to Yalta every 30 minutes from square outside marina gate (get instructions from marina office about transferring to a local bus or long distance bus at the '5km' bus station on the outskirts of Sevastopol).

## General

The former military harbour was home to the Russian nuclear submarine fleet and now has an excellent marina suitable for visiting yachts and another private marina under construction in 2010. The Ukrainian coastguard operates from a base and training facility in the N end of the harbour.

One of the monuments in Balaclava is an underground, formerly classified, submarine base that was operational until 1993. The base was said to be virtually indestructible and designed to survive a direct atomic impact. During that period, Balaclava was one of the most secret residential areas in the Soviet Union. Almost the entire population of Balaclava at one time worked at the base; even family members could not visit the town without a good reason and proper identification. The base remained operational after the collapse of the Soviet Union (in 1991) until 1993, when the decommissioning process started. This process saw the removal of the warheads and torpedoes. In 1996 the last Russian submarine left the base, which is now open to the public for guided tours around the canal system, the base, and a small museum, which is now housed in the old ammunition warehouse deep inside the hillside.

## ⚓ GEORGIEVSKIY

44°30′·14N 33°30′·41E

This is a beautiful bay set off by steep cliffs and offering a daytime anchorage. But swimming is compromised by the jellyfish.

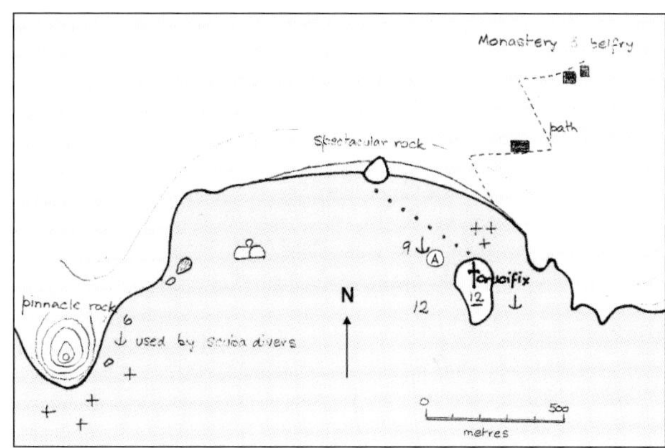


GEORGIEVSKIY

7. UKRAINE

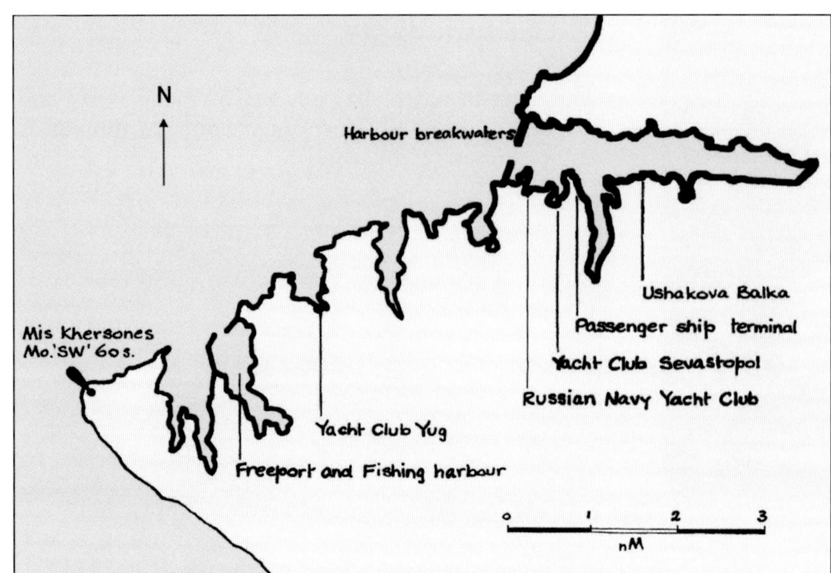


APPROACHES TO SEVASTOPOL

## SEVASTOPOL

44°37'·3N 33°30'·5E

### Approach

After rounding Mis Khersones from the S and W, take care to avoid a reef area and submarine exercise area as noted below. The approach is straightforward from the N.

*Conspicuous* The large breakwaters are easily seen from a distance.

*VHF* Ch 16 for Sevastopol Port Control. On approach to Sevastopol, call *Sevastopol Port Control* on VHF Ch16 and report your intended destination in the harbour. If arriving from outside the Ukraine, yachts must first report to the Passenger Ship Terminal to clear customs and immigration before moving to another location.

Dangers (1) In the approach to Sevastopol from the SW, a yellow and black small pole buoy in position 44°36'·98N 33°27'·83E marks a dangerous reef which is reported to have less water than shown on the charts. Pass the buoy on the N side leaving it at least 20m to the S. (2) Outside of the large Sevastopol breakwaters, four yellow buoys mark a submarine exercise area centred on position 44°37'·2N 33°29'·0E. Pass to the N of two conical buoys or to the S of two pole buoys with an x topmark. Do not enter the restricted area in between. (3) Yachts are not allowed to enter the Freeport and Fishing Harbour located 2M NE of Mis Khersones. (4) Yachts are forbidden on the N side of Sevastopol Harbour, which is controlled by the Navy.

*Authorities* Port of Entry. See information regarding Ukraine and Crimea clearance procedures. If using Sevastapol as a port of entry, report to the Passenger Ship Terminal first.

### Mooring

Visiting yachts have several berthing options within Sevastopol's main harbour and one anchorage in the approaches as noted below.

Sevastopol waterfront in the city centre

## Sevastopol Yacht Club Yug

44°36'·46N 33°26'·33E

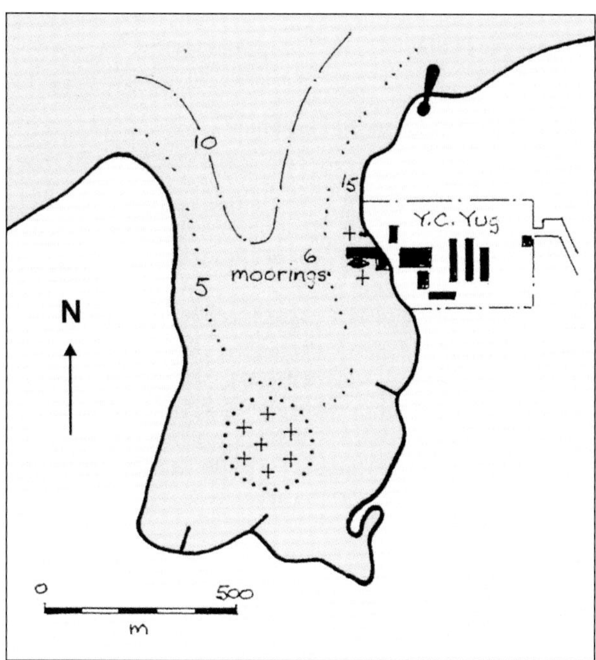


SEVASTOPOL YACHT CLUB YUG

In the approaches to Sevastopol from the S and W, the first anchorage suitable for yachts is the Yacht Club Yug in Omega Bay. However, the bay is completely open to the N, and a NW swell enters the bay. Dangerous rocks lie off the headlands on both sides as you enter the bay, and a shallow patch in the middle of the bay lies just S of the yacht club moorings and jetty. With permission, it is possible to lie alongside the club's jetty or to pick-up one of their moorings in the bay.

The Yacht Club Yug supports a competitive youth sailing programme and club members are reported to be helpful and friendly. They have a swimming area and bar which serves meals. Sevastopol is reached by taxi, and provisions are found in a suburb 1km from the Yacht Club.

## Sevastopol Russian Yacht Club

44°37'·07N 33°30'·8E

The Russian Yacht Club is located on the S side just after entering the large Sevastopol breakwaters and is suitable for smaller yachts. Go alongside the floating pontoon with permission. Local yachts use moorings tied back to the pier and one of these may be available. Members are friendly and the Yacht Club offers the best shelter in Sevastopol harbour. Sally Humphries reported in 2010:

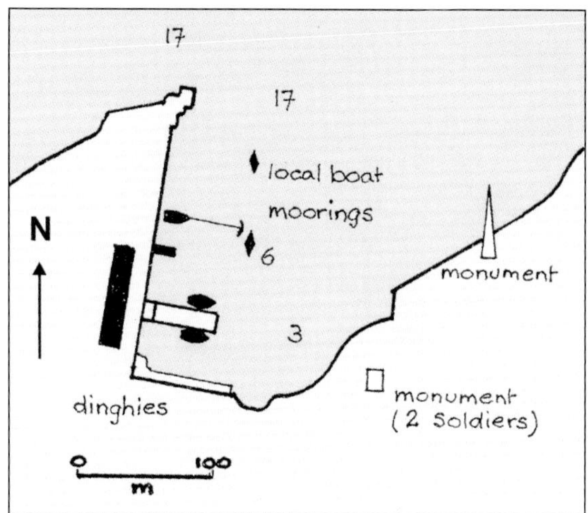


SEVASTOPOL RUSSIAN YACHT CLUB

'We picked up a mooring at the Russian Navy Yacht Club but the owner returned, helped us to arrange to take a vacant mooring on pontoon. Friendly, interested fellow-yachtsmen, especially helpful over propane gas (needed new fitting). No sign of toilets or showers at the club, but Wi-Fi, phone for taxis. Bay OK for swimming. Superb fireworks display from Russian fleet last weekend in July.'

## Yacht Club Sevastopol

44°36'·95N 33°31'·25E

There is a small mooring area in front of the Dolphinarium and close to the city centre with depths ranging from 1–4m. Crowded with local boats, busy with foot traffic and subjected to considerable wash from passing boats and ferries, the Yacht Club is not suitable for visiting yachts.

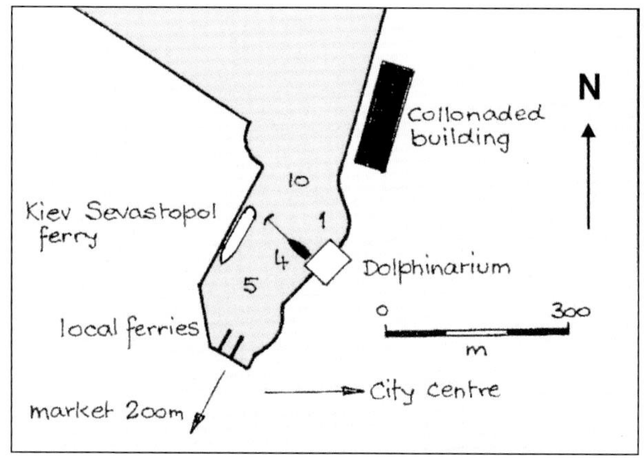


YACHT CLUB SEVASTOPOL

7. UKRAINE

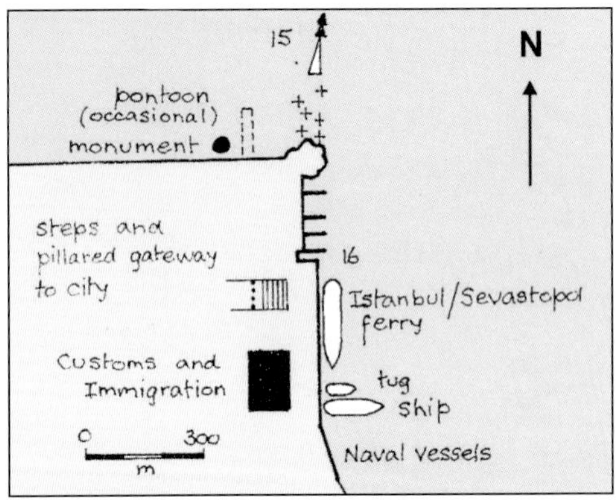


SEVASTOPOL PASSENGER SHIP TERMINAL

## Sevastopol Passenger Ship Terminal

44°36'·94N 33°31'·63E

A N cardinal buoy in the approach to the Passenger Ship Terminal marks rocks which extend to the buoy and should be left to starboard. Yachts entering the Ukraine should report here to conduct clearance formalities before moving to one of the other moorings. The location provides convenient access to the Sevastopol waterfront and city centre but is subjected to wash from passing tour boats, ferries and naval ships.

## Sevastopol Ushakova Balka

44°37'·0N 33°32'·78E

The Ushakova Balka Yacht Club is located E of the bustling part of Sevastopol harbour. Visiting yachts anchor and tie back to the dock, lie alongside the jetty (shallows to less than 2m) or anchor out in 13m. Security is reported to be good. Water and electricity are available. Small shops selling basic provisions are just a short walk up the hill where buses into the city centre can also be found.

### Facilities

*Fuel* By jerry can and taxi from all locations in the harbour.
*Repairs* Arrange repairs through the yacht clubs.
*Provisions* All provisions can be found in the city. Vendors sell fresh produce from a small market close to the waterfront.

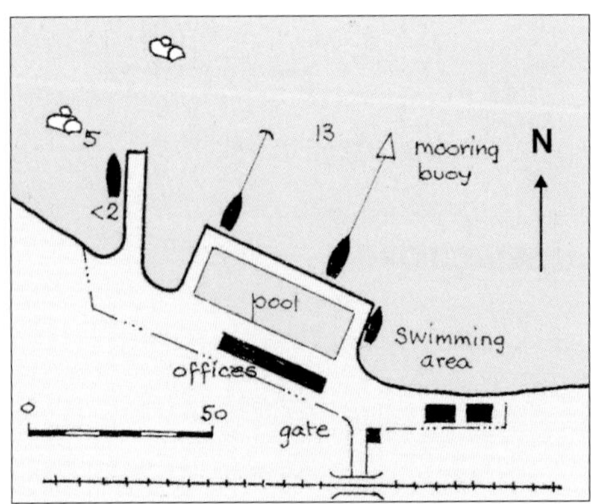


SEVASTOPOL USHAKOVA BALKA

*Eating out* Numerous restaurants, cafés and bars along the waterfront promenade and in the city.
*Other* ATMs along the waterfront and banks with ATMs throughout the city. A small yacht chandler selling locally made boat fittings and Russian charts is located near the Dolphinarium. Trolley buses and inexpensive taxis make it easy to travel within the city centre. Numerous travel agencies to assist with travel and tours in the Crimea and beyond.

### General

Until 1996 Sevastopol was a closed city run entirely by the Soviet, then the Russian, navy. It exhibits a certain Neoclassical grandeur in its overlooks, and it escaped the miles of dreary apartment blocks that make so many Russian cities look so forlorn. It still carries a whiff of Peter the Great and Catherine the Great; Sevastopol was entirely the Tsars' vision. Beneath its architectural presence, this city of 330,000 has an edginess to it, amplified by the heat and the crowds of August. Perhaps change is coming quicker than people can handle.

As everywhere on the Black Sea, Sevastopol's development is based on its geography. In this case, it is the best place to house a naval fleet, and really the only place with enough room. This led directly to its destruction, twice. The first time was during the Crimean War of 1854–6, when it was besieged and heavily shelled by Britain, France and the Ottoman Empire. The second was when it fell to the Nazi German army in 1942. Many buildings have been restored to their former glory. The last Sunday in July is the Black Sea Fleet Review.

The State Historical and Archeological Museum of Khersones, site of the ancient Greek town of Chersonesus (422 BC) is located 3km from the city centre. At the entrance to the harbour and surrounded by sandy beaches, it makes for a pleasant day outing. The Cathedral of Peter and Paul is being restored as a Palace of Culture on the site of the first Russian Orthodox church.

## ⚓ NIKOLAEVKA

44°57'·6N 33°36'·2E

This sanitorium resort spread along a sandy beach offers little shelter but can be used as a lunch stop or an overnight anchorage in settled weather. The jetty is reported to have over 4m alongside but is not recommended due to the large number of swimmers in the area. It is preferable to anchor out in 5–6m. A partially built breakwater lies off the jetty.

NIKOLAEVKA

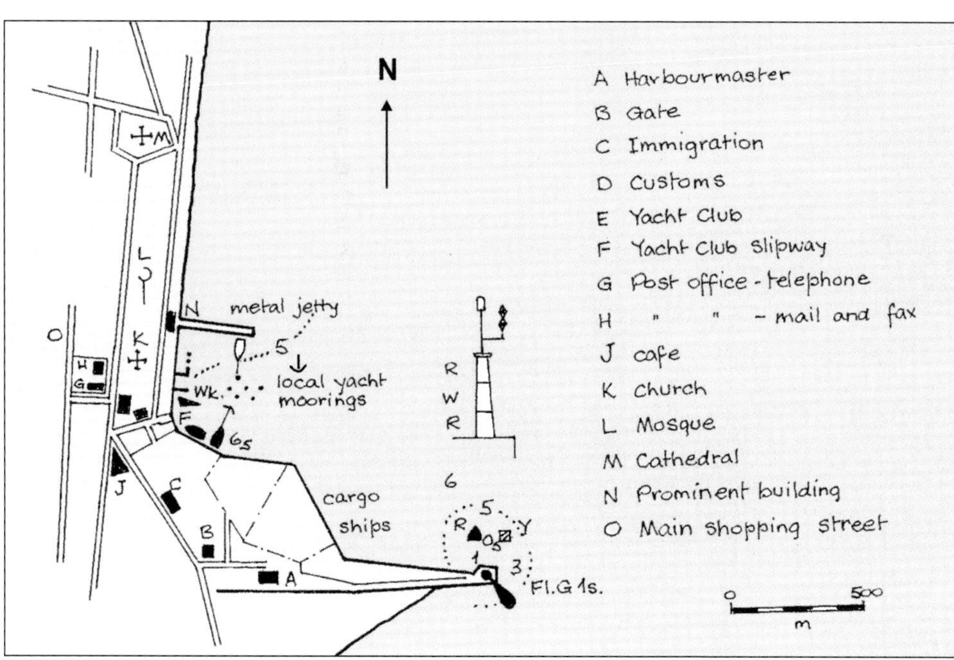


YEVPATORIA

## YEVPATORIA

45°11'·2N 33°22'·8E

### Approach

Situated in a bay on the W coast of the Crimea, Yevpatoria offers some shelter from prevailing winds and is commonly used by local sailors to break up the passage to Odessa. From the W, a safe point of approach is an E cardinal buoy at location 45°10'·6N 32°22'·95E.

*Conspicuous* Large radar towers in the vicinity of Mis Karantinniy are visible from a distance. Closer in, a long commercial pier indicates the location of the harbour.

*VHF* Ch 16 to report to Lebed (Ukrainian coastguard) and Ch 14 for Yevpatoria Harbour (do not expect answer to your calls).

Dangers (1) A wreck with 1·5m over it reported near Mis Karantinniy at position 45°06'·6N 33°16'·4E. Yachts are advised to enter the bay close to Mis Karantinniy. (2) Upon entering the harbour, a yellow buoy in position 45°11'·29N 32°22'·79E and a red buoy mark an obstruction off the pier with 0·5m of water over it. Leave to port.

### Mooring

Going alongside the inner portion of the commercial pier can be uncomfortable with the constant wash of boats or if a swell enters the bay. It is preferable for visiting yachts to anchor in 5–6m just outside the area where local yachts are moored, or with permission, to pick up one of the moorings. The metal jetty is used by swimmers and local yachts when the NE wind makes the yacht club quay untenable. Less than 2m depths are reported near this quay. In NE wind, it is possible to anchor off the opposite shore of the bay.

*Shelter* The harbour is open from the NE to S but offers good shelter from the NW and W. The wind tends to blow off the land during the day and onshore at night.

*Authorities* Port of Entry. Yachts with prior permission from Yalta to clear out in Yevpatoria must report to the Border Police in the harbour office building to provide copies of the crew list and an itinerary for passage to Odessa. The Harbourmaster and all other authorities are located in the same building. Upon departure from Yevpatoria, contact Lebed (Ukrainian coastguard) to report your position and inform them of your sailing plans.

*Charges* None

Yevpatoria

### Facilities

Yevpatoria offers limited facilities for visiting yachts, but most needs can be met in the busy resort community.

*Fuel* By jerry can and taxi.
*Repairs* Minor repairs can be arranged through the harbourmaster.
*Provisions* Small supermarkets located on main road, two blocks in from the harbour. Daily market operates in park along waterfront promenade.
*Eating out* Numerous restaurants, cafés and bars along the waterfront promenade. (See *Lonely Planet* for further descriptions).
*Other* Bank and ATM in the town centre. Post office behind the harbour.

### General

Although a faded example of the Crimea's multi-cultural past, Yevpatoria is today a somewhat charming and busy summer resort. A waterfront promenade and park stretch along the bay toward beaches crowded with swimmers. The city was a major health resort for children during the Soviet era but now caters to Ukrainian and Russian families on summer holiday. A range of architectural styles in the ancient city represent the diverse cultures of the Crimea.

When visiting by yacht, the old town is easily accessible from the harbour area making this a pleasant stop on passage from the Crimea to Odessa. Two cathedrals, both modelled after the Hagia Sophia in Istanbul, dominate the view of Yevpatoria's waterfront, the domes of St Nicholas Cathedral and the minarets of Dzhuma-Dzhami Mosque, the largest in the Ukraine. An 18th-century prayer house of the Karaite Jewish Sect is also located in the city with small restaurant serving Karaite food. The main gate of Medieval Keslev (the Crimean Khanate name for Yevpatoria) is located across the road from the dilapidated, former Dervish Monastery.

## ⚓ OLENEVKA

45°22'N 32°30'E

A sandy bay to the N of Mis Tarkhankut lighthouse should be entered from the W to avoid rocks off the lighthouse. The bay is exposed to prevailing winds and is only suitable for a lunch stop in settled weather. Anchor 200–300m offshore in 5m wherever you can find the least swell. Campers line the shore.

**OLENEVKA**

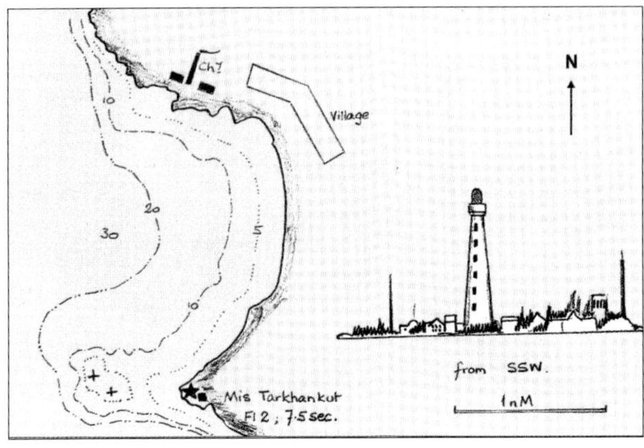

Mis Tarkhankut lighthouse

### *Passage note: Lake Donuslav*

Lake Donuslav is a naval base and forbids foreign vessels. A small commercial harbour is reported on the W side of the entrance, but it should not be entered.

## ⚓ CHERNOMORSKOE

45°32'·0N 32°41'·4E

Chernomorskoe is the final port on the W shore of the Crimea where yachts on passage to Odessa can find good to excellent shelter at anchor in the open bay or the former naval harbour.

### Approach

Safe approach is made from 45°32'·0N 32°41'·4E entering on a course of about 131° and passing NE of the lighthouse and buoy (see dangers below).

*VHF* Ch 16 for Naval Base Commander and to announce location to Lebed (do not expect to receive an answer to your call).

Danger A buoy in position 45°31'·47N 32°41'·94E marks rocks extending offshore from the SW entrance to the bay.

### Mooring

Anchor inside the former naval harbour, taking care to set the anchor; there are heavy weeds and rocky patches. A private pontoon has been installed on the N side of the naval harbour, but it is not suitable for visiting yachts. The bay is busy with swimmers and holidaymakers who like to be towed on floating toys at high speed behind jet skis and small speed boats.

*Depths* 6m at anchor in the former naval harbour and 4m at the anchorage in the outer bay.
*Shelter* Excellent shelter in the inner harbour. Anchorage offers good shelter but is open to the NW. The prevailing summer wind is S, and the shape of the harbour tends to accelerate the wind.
*Authorities* None observed.
*Charges* None.

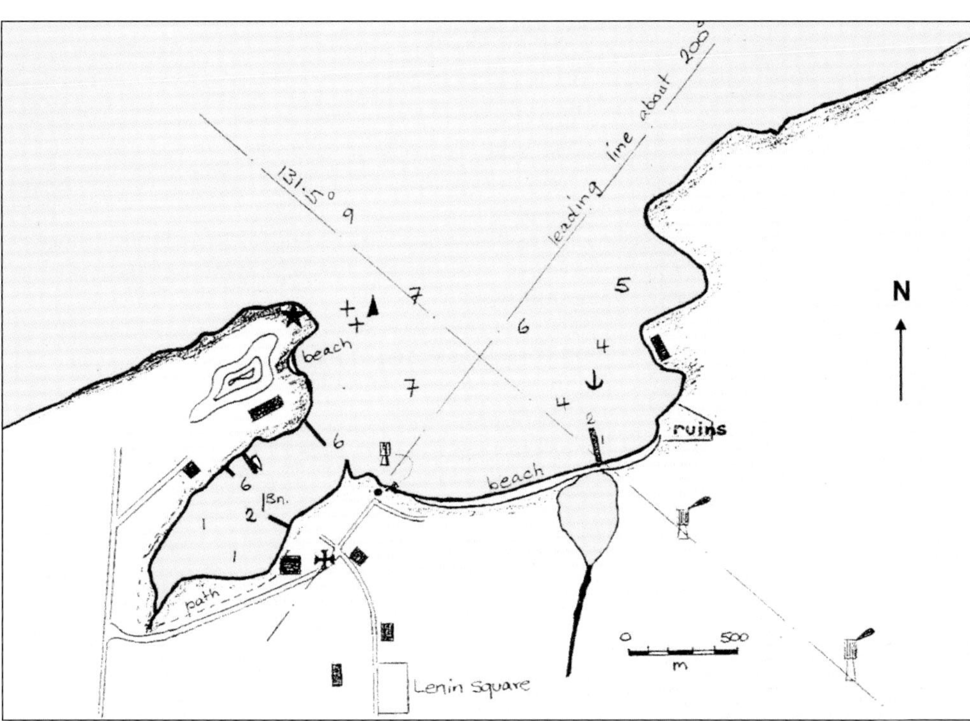


CHERNOMORSKOE

Chernomorskoe beach

Chernomorskoe beach

## Facilities

Chernomorskoe offers limited facilities for visiting yachts.

*Services* None.
*Fuel* By jerry can and taxi but not very convenient.
*Provisions* Local market located close to the harbour and a larger regional market with good selection and reasonable prices is reported to be a 30-minute walk from the harbour.
*Eating out* A waterfront restaurant on the SE shore of inner harbour is convenient for keeping an eye on your yacht while at anchor. Draught wine can be purchased from streetside cafés.
*Other* ATM in town.

## General

The settlement along the shore of the small bay is completely oriented toward resort living. Moving inland, the town quickly changes character, becoming normal with its multi-story apartments. There are ancient Greek ruins right up to the shoreline at the NE end of the long beach. Presumably they were a fortification guarding the excellent sheltered landing which the bay offered.

# ⚓ DZHARILGACH ISLAND

46°01′·0N 33°04′·15E

Dzharilgach Island, approximately 45km E–W and 6km N–S, shelters Dzharilgach Lagoon, on which Skadovsk is the only large community. The maximum depth of the lagoon is about 8m. Formerly, the lagoon was open at both ends, but in the past few decades the W end has silted up. *Gyatso* wanted to see what a big lagoon looked like, but were unhappy with what they saw: massive eutrophication. The water was bright green, almost iridescent algae green, and it was just packed with the huge *Rhizostomo pulmo* jellyfish, strong swimmers looking like a jet engine the size of a dinner plate. We suspected that superphosphate fertiliser runoff might be a culprit. No one seemed worked up about it, and it did not seem unusual.

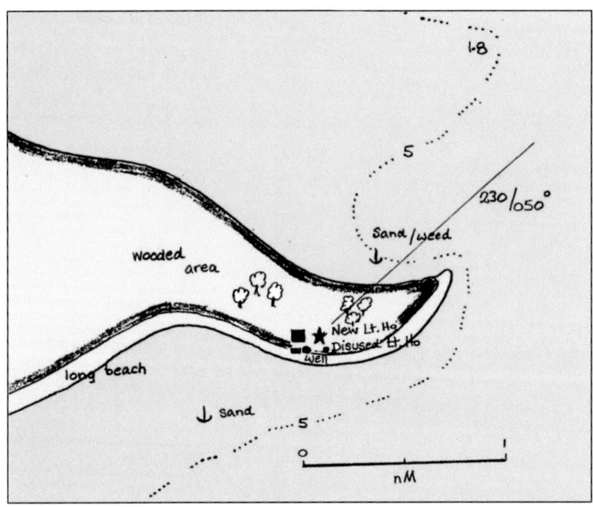


DZHARILGACH ISLAND

Dzharilgach Island lighthouses

There is a wee bit of shelter from S winds, enough to anchor N of the island in a few metres of sand and weed. *Gyatso* had a relaxing few hours here before the wind came up out of the NE providing a glorious sail to Odessa.

## SKADOVSK

46°06'·25N 32°54'·6E

### Approach

Skadovsk is located 9M W of the entrance to Dzharilgach Bay and is protected to the S by Dzharilgach Island. After passing the two lighthouses marking the end of the island, a buoyed passage leads to Skadovsk. Suggested waypoints are as follows:

SE of Island 46°00'·0N 33°05'·5E
NE of Island 46°03'·0N 33°05'·5E
Fairway buoy 46°04'·6N 32°54'·0E

Harbour entrance buoys are as follows:

R and G 46°05'·83N 32°54'·53E
G 46°06'·11N 32°54'·61E
Harbour entrance 46°06'·25N 32°54'·60E

*VHF* Ch 16 for *Skadovsk Radio*. Call when you reach the Fairway buoy. Do not expect a reply.

*Note* A RoRo ferry uses the commercial port several times a week. The harbour should not be entered when the ferry is expected to arrive or depart. Yachts may be asked to anchor off when ferries are expected in port.

### Mooring

Skadovsk is the first port in Ukraine after leaving the Crimea, but it is not a port of entry for yachts. Customs and immigration officials are on site for commercial traffic and will visit your yacht if you enter the commercial harbour. Contrary to reports in earlier guides, visiting yachts are now not welcome in the commercial harbour of Skadovsk. Even if a yacht is cleared into the Ukraine and has permission to visit Skadovsk, the harbour authorities will require paperwork, create administrative problems or levy harbour charges as if you are fully loaded cargo vessel in an effort to extract unnecessary fees. Proceed at your own risk into the commercial harbour and tie alongside the cement quay on the

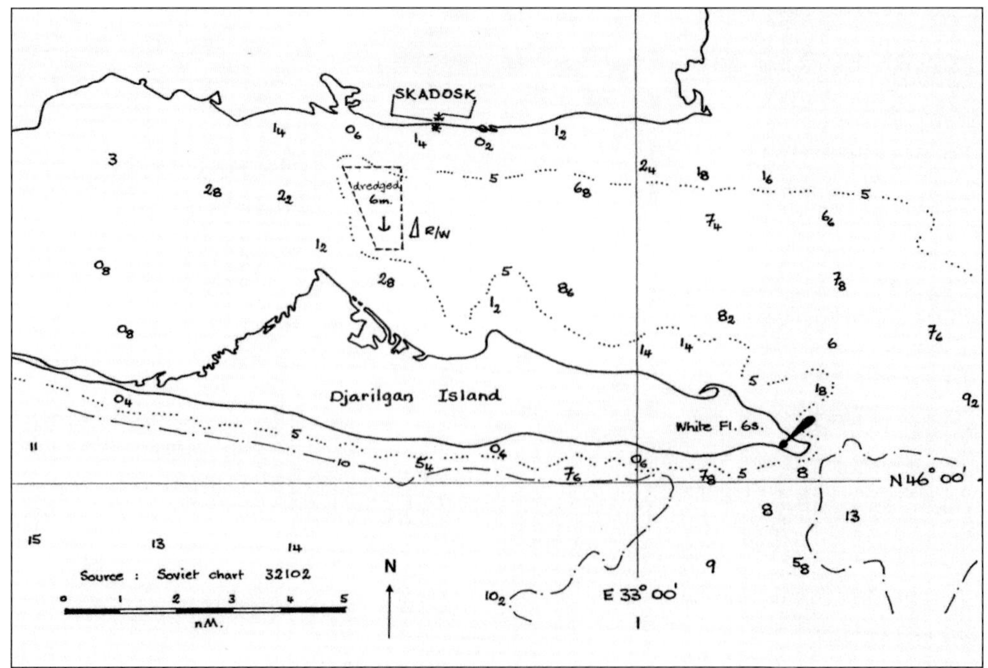


APPROACHES TO SKADOVSK

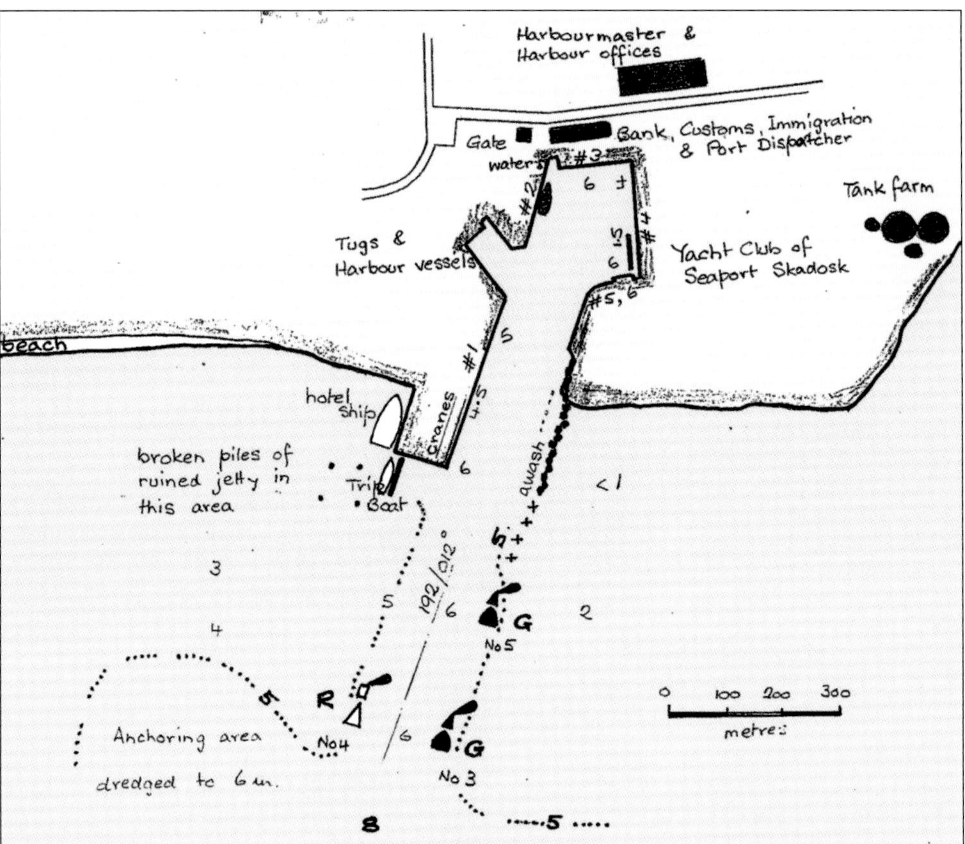


SKADOVSK

right after entering the small basin or alongside the high wall near the harbour offices in the NW corner. It may be possible to avoid these hassles by anchoring outside the harbour W of the buoyed area in 4–6m. The beach resort is busy with swimmers and local boats. The Yacht Club of Seaport Skadovsk is located E of the harbour and is used by local yachts.

### Facilities

Electricity may be available in the commercial harbour. Basic provisions can be found ashore in the small resort town.

### General

Skadovsk is a small town, so stores can be reached by easy walk from the harbour.

Skadovsk commercial harbour

## ⚓ MIS TENDROV

46°21'·9N 31°32'·0E

A long, low-lying sand spit stretches for 90km from Dzharilgach Island to its NW-most point at Mis Tendrov. In settled conditions, a yacht can anchor in shallow water on either side of the narrow peninsula depending on the wind direction.

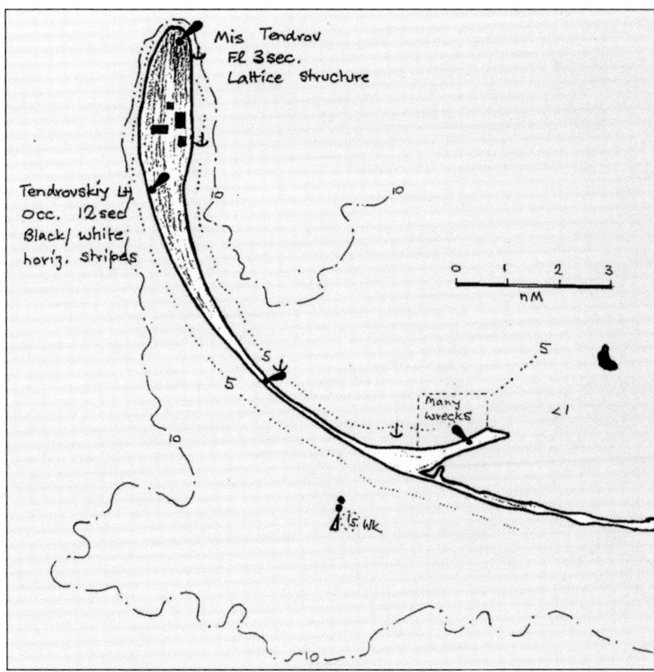


MIS TENDROV

## ODESSA

46°29′·63N 30°44′·95E

A modern marina suitable for yachts of all sizes is located in a yacht harbour within the larger Odessa commercial port.

### Approach

The safe approach point is off Varonkovskiy Lighthouse at position 46°29′·87N 30°45′·6E.

*Conspicuous* The large commercial port is easily seen from a distance. The white Voronovskiy Lighthouse on the N end of the E breakwater is conspicuous as is the large Hotel Odessa which is located on the same Passenger Terminal pier as the marina.

*VHF* Ch 16 for Lebed (Ukrainian coastguard), Ch 14 for Odessa Port Control and Ch 84 for Odessa Yacht Club. When arriving in Odessa, contact Lebed at 5M out. At 1M out, contact Odessa Port Control dispatcher to receive permission to enter the commercial harbour and instructions regarding which entrance to use. After receiving permission and instructions, contact Odessa Yacht Club on VHF Ch 84 (**not** 73) to arrange a mooring (if no answer to calls, ask dispatcher to contact them for you). Upon departure, you must clear Immigration and then contact the Odessa Port Control dispatcher to request permission to leave the marina before casting off your dock lines.

Dangers (1) Beware of anchored ships and busy shipping traffic entering and exiting the harbour. (2) Beware of vessels and tour boats which may be hidden behind the breakwater leaving the harbour at high speed.

Varonkovskiy Lighthouse at the entrance to Odessa commercial harbour and yacht marina

### Mooring

The Yacht Club Odessa -2009 (formerly TCF Nautical Club Marina) is a modern marina with floating pontoons situated in a yacht harbour within the larger Odessa Commercial Port which can accommodate visiting yachts of all sizes.

*Berth* Where directed by marina staff who are onsite 24 hours a day.

*Depths* 10m at mooring position.

*Shelter* Excellent.

*Authorities* Port of entry. Clearance formalities are handled by marina staff and an agent is not required. All authorities are located in the same building as the marina office.

*Charges* $3.00 per metre per day (prices quoted by marina in US$). The actual charges were equivalent to €23.75 per night. The Harbourmaster Services Fee to check out in 2010 was 121UAH, equivalent to approximately €10.12. He arranged for the various officials to come to his office to process the paperwork: Health inspector, Customs, and Border Police.

*Contact information* Yacht Club Odessa-2009, 65026 Ukraina, Odessa, Vul Primorska, 6.

### Facilities

*Services* Water and electricity at each berth. Toilets and showers inside building where Yacht Club office is located. When ships are unloading and the wind blows in an E direction, coal dust and other particulates can accumulate on decks, which is one of the few downsides of an extended visit to the yacht club.

*Fuel* Arrange with yacht club staff to visit fuel dock. There are reports that it is sometimes not available for yachts.

*Repairs* Haul-out by crane can be arranged for smaller yachts. Arrange repairs, including sail repairs, through the marina staff.

*Provisions* A mini-supermarket and vendors selling fresh produce are located near the top of the Potemkin Steps. A larger supermarket is located in the Galereya Afina (Gallery Athena) shopping mall in the city centre. Pryvoz Market, a large open-air farmer's market located next to the Railway Station on the S side of the city centre, is recommended by some tourist guides as a sightseeing stop. Beware of sophisticated pickpockets in the Ukraine, especially at tourist sites such as the Pryvoz Market.

*Eating out* Many options for eating out in Odessa, including places for sampling local Ukrainian,

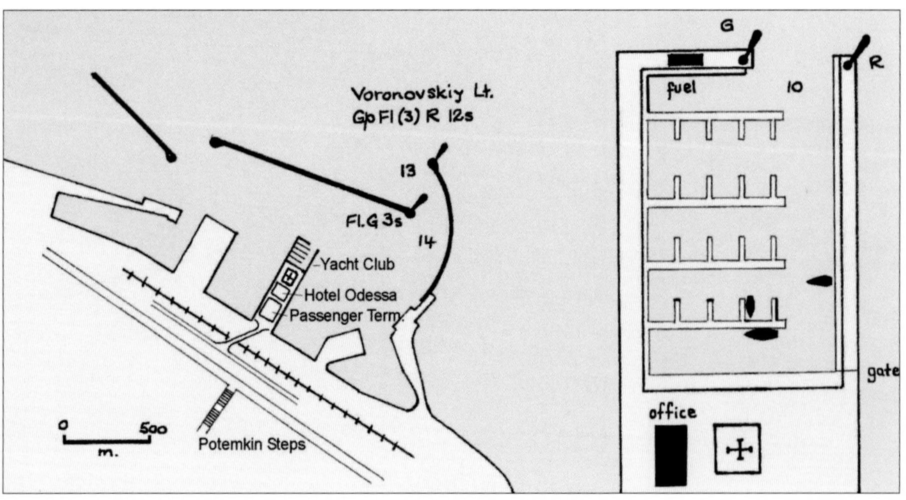


**ODESSA COMMERCIAL HARBOUR AND YACHT HARBOUR DETAIL**

Odessa Marina

Georgian and Turkish specialities, as well as the usual range of international cuisines including Italian and Chinese. Many options to join holidaymakers sipping champagne or vodka and enjoying a light meal at one of the streetside cafés. The food court in the basement of the Galereya Afina shopping mall is popular among locals, reasonably priced and convenient if provisioning at the supermarket.

*Other* ATM in the Hotel Odessa lobby and free Wi-Fi in their bar. Other ATMs and banks around the city centre. Hire cars are not recommended for foreign tourists in this part of Ukraine. Local trolleybuses operate in the city. Taxis tend to be more expensive for tourists, especially if you take them from a hotel or the train station; however, the Hotel Odessa is a convenient place to arrange for a taxi. An alternative is to hail a taxi on the street or ask a restaurant to call a taxi for you. The bus station near the train station and Pryvoz Market is for shorter trips and other domestic and international buses leave from the long-distance bus station 3km from the train station. Trains to Kiev as well as all major Ukrainian, Russian and E European cities. In summer, you can take ferries to Istanbul and Varna and river cruise ships from Kiev to Odessa and then Sevastopol. Ferries and local tour boats to nearby beaches leave from outside the marina gates.

## General

Known as the 'Pearl of the Black Sea', Odessa was founded in 1794 by Russia's Catherine the Great. She invited immigrants from all over Europe to settle the city. The French, Italian and Spanish heritage and active Greek, Armenian, Georgian and Bulgarian communities give the cosmopolitan city a truly European feel. Walking around the city, you will hear many languages being spoken, including more English than in other Ukrainian cities on the Black Sea.

Odessa at night

With a modern marina near the base of the Potemkin Steps, the vibrant city centre is easily accessed and especially nice to visit in your own yacht. The main pedestrian area begins at the top of the famous Potemkin Steps and is lined with parks and sweeping views of the Black Sea and the Ukraine's largest commercial port. Odessa's main commercial street, vul Derybasivska, runs E–W and is just a few blocks S of the top of the steps with the City Garden at its W end. There is much to see and do in Odessa, and a travel guide to the Ukraine or one specific to Odessa is recommended for those wishing to get the most out of their visit to this vibrant city. In addition to the beaches, nightclubs, and casinos at this popular summer holiday destination, sites of interest include visits to the Archaeology Museum, Museum of Maritime History, Museum of Western and Eastern Art, the Odessa Fine Arts Museum, City Hall (formerly the Stock Exchange) and the Pushkin statue in the square in front of city hall, Opera and Ballet Theatre (better yet, catching a performance there) which re-opened after extensive renovations in 2007, and the newly rebuilt Probrazhensky Cathedral.

As former residents of the Washington, DC area the *Gyatso* crew were struck by the similarities between Odessa and the US capital. The designs of both cities were intended to be political statements by countries that were in the midst of establishing themselves (US) or rapidly expanding monarchies (Russia). The gridded street pattern laidout by French city planners with tree-lined streets, parks and sightlines to public monuments and the Neoclassical architecture are reminiscent of the American capital of about the same age.

Southwards from Odessa the coast becomes low-lying again, passing the large commercial port of Ilyichevsk.

## ILYICHEVSK

46°17'·28N 30°39'·94E

The commercial port of Ilyichevsk does not welcome yachts, which will be directed to the yacht club harbour, located 1·5M S of the commercial harbour. This harbour is not considered suitable for foreign yachts for several reasons. Yachts clearing in or out of Ukraine in Odessa are not allowed to stop in this harbour before or after clearance procedures are conducted. The area to the S of the entrance is silted and very shallow, and the breakwater has offlying rocks which can make the entrance even more tricky with a NE through S swell. Depths of 5·4m reported at the entrance decrease rapidly to less than 1m once inside the harbour. The status of dredging in the harbour is unkown.

### *Passage note: Belgorod-Dnestrovsky*

The Dnestrovskiy Liman is a lagoon with a narrow entrance to the Black Sea crossed by a railway and road bridge which opens for commercial traffic at fixed hours. Passage through a buoyed channel leads to the port town of Belgorod-Dnestrovsky, which is at the limit of navigation of the liman. E of the entrance, 5M offshore, is a long shallow bank marked by N and S cardinal buoys. This area is not suitable for yachts unless already cleared in to the Ukraine and given permission to visit. Yachts cleared in or out of the Ukraine in Odessa, are not allowed to stop in this harbour before or after clearance procedures are conducted.

### *Passage note: Ust-Dunaysk*

The shore continues southwards to Ust-Dunaysk, which is now a silted entrance to the Ukrainian branch of the Danube River delta. The buoyed channel is no longer maintained. A new buoyed channel has been dredged. In former years it was possible for a yacht to motor upstream to the border town of Izmail to clear out from the Ukraine and then continue to the town of Tulcea to clear into Romania, but in 2010 Ukrainian officials strongly advised not to visit Izmail by yacht.

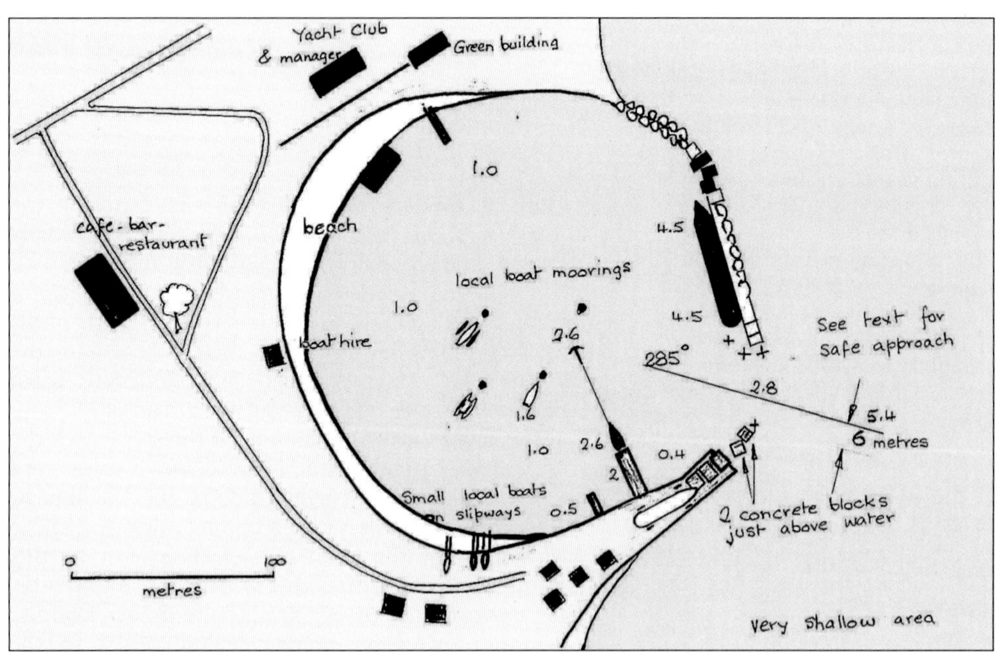


**ILYICHEVSK**
(Note soundings taken from Annans' visit in 2001)

# 8. Romania

Along with Bulgaria, Romania is one of the two former Communist states on the Black Sea which have joined the European Union.

### The Black Sea Coast of Romania

Romania's Black Sea coastline stretches for 225km between Ukraine to the north, and Bulgaria to the south. The country has an area of 238,000km² most of which is quite distant from the coast. The national population is 22·2 million and declining due to out-migration elsewhere in the European Union.

Romania has brought a case against Ukraine before the International Court of Justice (ICJ) in The Hague over the delimitation of the common border in the Black Sea and Snake Island. It also opposes Ukraine's proposal to reopen the navigation canal from the Danube.

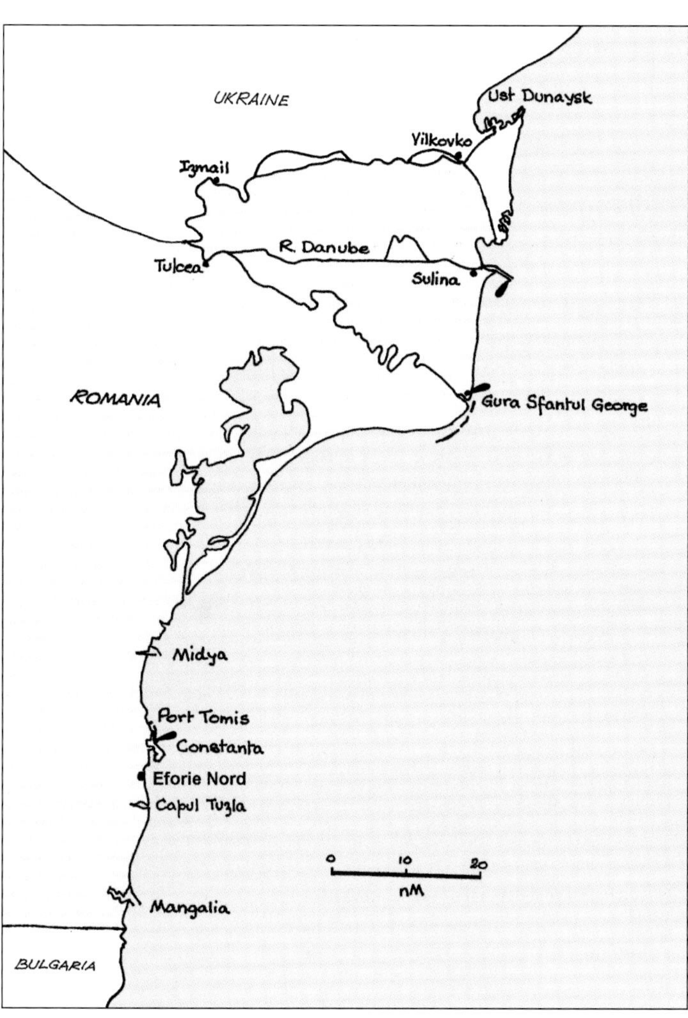


**ROMANIA**

The Romanian coast is made up of three regions. The northern third is the delta of the Danube River, which meets the Black Sea along sandy beaches. The beaches stretch south along a barrier which separates the sea from a sparsely-populated interior of lakes and wetlands. The southern third of the coast is more densely populated, starting at the commercial harbour of Midia and the most important beach resort, Mamaia. The beach resorts of Neptun, Venus, Saturn, Jupiter and Olimp continue down the coast all the way to the village of Vama Veche, near the Bulgarian border.

Unfortunately, there are no secure anchorages anywhere along the coast. Four harbours are suitable for yachts and secure from wind and swell: Sulina, Port Tomis (Constanţa), Eforie Nord and Mangalia. Of these, Eforie Nord is unique in being a purpose-built yacht harbour along a sandy beach. All four are suitable places to leave a yacht while exploring inland, and three offer some security.

### History

The principalities of Wallachia and Moldavia secured their autonomy from the Turkish Ottoman Empire in 1856; they united in 1859 and a few years later adopted the name Romania, which gained recognition of its independence in 1878.

It joined the Allied powers in the First World War and was awarded new territories by the victors following the war. But in 1940, Romania allied with the Axis powers and participated in the 1941 German invasion of the USSR. Three years later it was overrun by the Soviets.

The post-war Soviet occupation led to the formation of a Communist 'People's Republic' in 1947 and the abdication of the king. The rule of dictator Nicolae Ceauşescu lasted from 1965 until 1989, when he was overthrown and executed on Christmas Day. Former Communists dominated the government until 1996 when they were swept from power. Romania became a NATO member in 2004 and a member of the EU on 1 January 2007.

### Time

Romania is GMT +2 hours during the Summer.

### Communications

Telephone country code: +40

### Weather

Winters are cold and cloudy, with frequent snow and fog. Summers are hot and sunny, with frequent rains.

### People: customs, religion, holidays

About 87% of Romanians belong to one of the Orthodox denominations, the religious legacy of the effectiveness of the missionaries of the Byzantine Empire and the church on which it was built. Islam never made much headway here during the four centuries of Turkish rule, from the mid-15th to the mid-19th centuries. What later became Romania was one of the first places to break away from the Ottoman Empire, then already becoming known as the 'Sick Man of Europe'. Protestants and Roman Catholics make up most of the remaining 13% of the population.

### Food and drink

Romanian cuisine maintains its own character while blending dishes from several different traditions: Ottoman, Hungarian and German. Good wine is widely available at relatively low cost. Plum brandy is perhaps the alcoholic drink for which the country is best known.

### Language

The official language is Romanian, which is based on Latin and uses the Latin script rather than the Cyrillic script found to the north (in Ukraine) and south (in Bulgaria). It is quite easy to grasp the meaning of signs. French is more widely spoken than English, but it is not difficult to get by speaking only English.

### Charts

Admiralty chart *2230, Constanţa to Kefken Adası*, was useful. The C-Map *EM-M917* electronic chart proved to be reliable.

### Formalities

Since it joined the EU, Romanian entry and exit procedures for yachts are greatly improved and in 2010 were simple and professionally conducted. At all four Romanian harbours suitable for yachts, either some official will come to the vessel shortly after arrival, or the marina staff direct you to the nearby office of the harbourmaster, the Border Police, Customs, and Health. They will want to receive several copies of the crew list and the General Declaration, with appropriate signatures and the ship's stamp, along with the vessel's registration documents and the passport of each crew member. There is no fee and no agent is required.

### Ports of Entry

The official ports of entry are Sulina, Constanţa and Mangalia. The manager of the Ana Yacht Club marina at Eforie Nord says that he can arrange for officials to come from Constanţa to handle entry or exit.

### Travel ashore: taxi, train, plane, road

Sulina is not connected to the rest of Romania by road or air, only by ferry and hydrofoil to Tulcea, where the road begins and the Danube delta ends. Constanţa is among the five largest cities of Romania, so it is well connected to Europe and Ukraine by rail and highway. Eforie Nord is situated on the coast S of Constanţa, with regular bus service to the city centre. Mangalia is smaller and under Constanţa's transportation shadow.

### Provisions

Provisions can be found in abundance in all four of Romania's ports for yachts. Big European chain supermarkets are appearing throughout the country, and there is a huge Carrefour supermarket on the outskirts of Constanţa. Most shops are closed on Sundays.

### Medical

The Romanian medical system is struggling to grow out of the Communist mould. Although some medical facilities are reasonably good, health care professionals of all sorts still expect cash bribes to provide quality services. As a whole, the country has not reached the standard set by the older EU members.

### Costs

Although it is not in the Euro zone yet, prices in Romania have risen sharply during the past 20 years. Prices of both department store goods and local products such as fruits and vegetables are now generally comparable with those throughout Europe.

### Money/ currency

Romanian currency is called the Leu and is abbreviated RON. In early 2011 the exchange rate was 1.00RON = €0.235 and €1.00 = 4.236RON. Romania would like to join the Euro zone. ATMs, known locally as Bankomats, are common in cities, large towns and resorts.

### *Passage note: Odessa to Sulina*

Southwards from Odessa the coast becomes low-lying again, passing the large commercial port of Ilyichevsk.

The Dnestrovsky Liman is a lagoon with a narrow entrance to the Black Sea crossed by a railway and road bridge which opens for commercial traffic at fixed hours. Passage through a buoyed channel leads to the port town of Belograd Dnestrovsky, which is at the limit of navigation of the *liman*. East of the entrance, 5M offshore, is a long shallow bank marked by N and S cardinal buoys.

The shore continues southwards to Ust-Dunaysk, which is now a silted entrance to the Ukrainian branch of the Danube River delta. The buoyed channel is no longer maintained. A new buoyed channel has been dredged. In former years it was possible for a yacht to motor upstream to the border town of Izmail to clear out from Ukraine and then continue to the town of Tulcea to clear into Romania, but in 2010 Ukrainian officials strongly advised not to visit Izmail by yacht. This was confirmed by several yachts which had difficulties and were required to pay fees in excess of €200 to clear in or out here. It is recommended to continue offshore to enter Romania at the Danube River port of Sulina.

The only island of any real significance in the Black Sea, Zmeiny (Snake) Island, is located just N of the Ukraine-Romania border, about 18M offshore. The island has an area of only 17ha but has been used since antiquity. During the Cold War, the Soviet Union used it as a forward position for radar domes, and most recently it has been at the centre of a dispute between Romania and Ukraine before the International Court of Justice in The Hague over the delimitation of the common border in the Black Sea. Its small size and obscure location have not prevented Snake Island from boasting an illustrious past associated with the Greek hero Achilles. Today it is a Ukrainian border outpost, a bit off the coast of nowhere. But it remains one of the three formerly sacred islands in the Black Sea, along with Kefken Adası and Giresun Adası, both in Turkey.

The sea passage from Ust Dunaysk to Sulina passes many unlit and disused buoys that marked a former entrance, now silted and closed, to the Ukrainian portion of the Danube River system.

Give the low-lying land at the Danube Delta a good offing, particularly in the final approach to the Sulina channel fairway buoy which is located about 2M SE of the conspicuous control tower on the Sulina channel breakwater. There are often large standing waves where the Danube River current meets the Black Sea.

# HARBOURS AND ANCHORAGES

## SULINA

45°08'·0N 29°47'·5E (Danube River mouth)
45°09'·4N 29°41'·0E (Sulina port)

Sulina is a commercial port on the Danube River and the most convenient port of entry for yachts entering Romania from Odessa, Ukraine to the N, or leaving for places S and E.

### Approach

Yachts should follow the buoyed channel of the shipping lane from the fairway buoy (Position 45°08'·0N 29°47'·5E) into the Sulina Channel which is protected by low breakwaters. The channel is dredged regularly and water depths are good throughout.

*Conspicuous* The light and control tower are visible from a distance.

*VHF* Ch 16 for port control and harbourmaster (calls may not be answered until you arrive in Sulina when the harbourmaster will respond and direct you where to go).

Dangers (1) Shallow water extends on either side of the entrance to the Sulina Channel. (2) Standing waves build where the channel meets the sea and can be quite large in strong E winds.

### Mooring

The river is lined with commercial quays for ocean-going ships entering the Sulina Arm and for dozens of small fishing boats, tour boats, ferries and hydrofoils.

*Berth* Contact the harbourmaster on VHF Ch 16 for instructions on available moorings. Yachts are usually told to find a place among the many small tour boats on the town quay, leaving room for the huge incoming ships, to moor long enough to carry out clearance formalities. More spaces are available if you arrive in late morning on an overnight passage from Odessa

Danube control tower

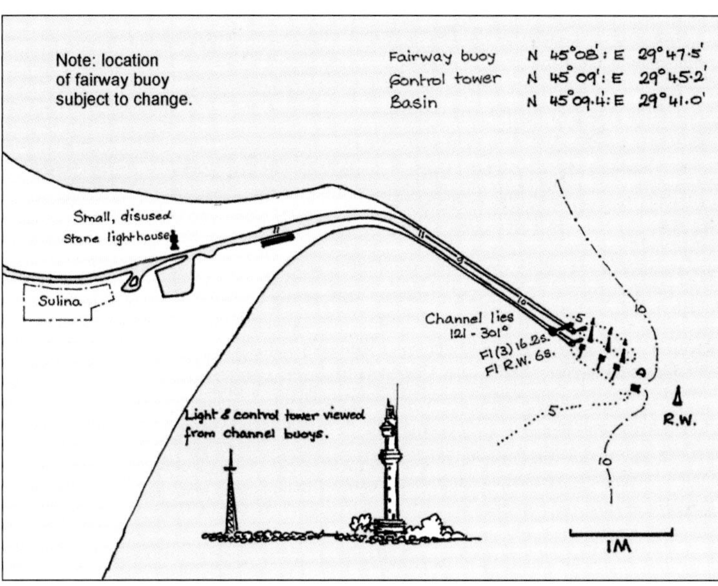


SULINA ENTRANCE

8. ROMANIA

## SULINA TOWN

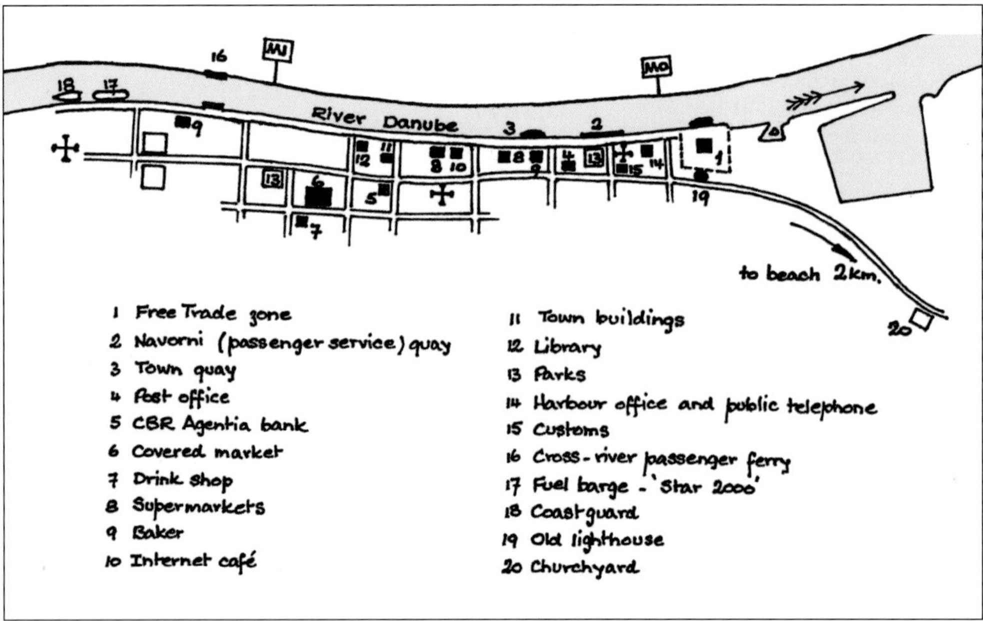

Sulina town quay

than later in the day, when the small tour boats return from their Delta tours.

*Depths* 10m alongside town quay.

*Shelter* Very good shelter, subject to wash from passing ships, ferries and small boat traffic.

*Authorities* Port of entry. Harbourmaster will arrange for authorities to conduct clearance formalities in the harbour office, located W of the commercial quay on the waterfront.

*Charges* The harbourmaster said that he was charging only a modest entry processing fee. Then, in accordance with the visa that we received at the harbourmaster's office, yachts could stay as long as they liked, or at least a couple of days, at no charge.

### Facilities

*Services* Very limited. Water and electricity can be arranged on town quay, charges will apply and long hose and cable may be required.

*Security* No apparent security and lots of foot traffic along the town quay. Although that might seem cause for concern, *Gyatso* was left in the care of the harbourmaster for a day and this proved satisfactory.

*Fuel* Fuel barge located just upstream, immediately W of the town quay (local cash currency only).

*Repairs* Emergency repairs may be arranged through the harbourmaster.

*Provisions* Several small supermarkets along the waterfront street, but prices are higher due to the remote location of the town (everything is brought in by ferry). A local market with fresh produce operates daily during the summer season. Other vendors sell fruits and vegetables from stalls along the quay.

*Eating out* Several good restaurants, bars and cafés, including an Irish pub. Many offer free Wi-Fi internet access to their patrons.

*Other* Post office and ATM in town. Catamaran (fast), hydrofoil (faster) and traditional (slow and infrequent) ferry service to Tulcea and intermediate destinations on the Sulina Arm of the Danube Delta. If interested in exploring the Danube Delta, local boats with guides are for hire in Sulina, Tulcea and intermediate ports. Prices vary and are negotiated directly with boat operators or local tour companies.

### General

Sulina is a pleasant and interesting river port. The Sulina Channel is the largest of the three main Danube River channels, both in terms of the volume of water and the size and number of freighters that clear in along the town wharf. The ceaseless rush of water and the constant coming and going of huge ships create a sense of bustle which belies Sulina's scarcely-hidden character as a sleepy delta town. The tree-lined riverfront promenade changes hour by hour as different elements of the population take over. The Biosphere Reserve museum is worth a visit. There are many opportunities to take guided or unguided river trips, starting from the ferry and hydrofoil docks. A good day trip is to take the ferry to Tulcea and return by hydrofoil. There was a Free Trade Zone at Sulina, but it appeared not to be operating.

Because of the busy shipping traffic, constant shuffling of boats along the town quay and lack of security, this is not recommended as a place to leave your yacht for extended inland travel. It is safe, however, to leave your yacht for day tours to Tulcea and the Danube Delta. The harbourmaster should be notified if you plan to be away from your yacht for more than a few hours. Be prepared for huge ocean-going freighters to pull alongside the pier, just a few metres ahead of or behind you.

## The Danube Delta

The Delta is designated as a Biosphere Reserve and is managed by the Danube Delta Biosphere Reserve Authority (DDBRA). The DDBRA is headquartered in a prominent riverfront office in Tulcea, which serves as the capital of the Romanian portion, which is 82% of the whole delta region; the other 18% of the delta is in Ukraine.

With permission, it is possible for yachts to visit the Danube Delta, including the upstream port of Tulcea; however, many find it easier to travel by ferry from Sulina or to take an inland tour from Constanţa and to explore the delta with a guide in a small boat. The DDBRA maintains a good website in English: www.ddbra.ro/en

The Danube Delta

Yachts arriving by sea at Sulina and yachts arriving down the Danube can find startling differences between their experiences, if they happen to meet in the Danube delta. This meeting place is No.2 among the top five yachting destinations on the W coast of the Black Sea.

### *Passage note: Sulina to Mangalia*

S of Sulina there are three ports on the Romanian Black Sea coast where a yacht may find safe shelter: Constanţa (Port Tomis), Eforie Nord and Mangalia. All three have modern marina facilities at various stages of development. The commercial ports in Constanţa and Midia are not suitable for yachts. Night entry to all four Romanian harbours is possible, but in stormy NE winds it would be better to wait for daylight to enter them.

From Sulina the sandy coast runs S for 20M to the Gura Sf. Gheorghe light, blue tower, 50m in height, GpFl(2)7s19M, located at 44°54′N 29°36′E, yet another mouth of the Danube that is blocked by sand bars.

Two isolated oil and gas pipelines lie 16·5M and 48M SSE of Gura Sf. Gheorghe. They do not pose a special hazard for yachts.

The sandy coast continues for another 50M to Cape Midia, serving as a narrow beach barrier between the sea and a number of lakes. There are a number of fishing stations along this coast, and the numerous fish nets and markers are a hazard.

A charted oil and gas field is located about 22M S of Gura Sf. Gheorghe. There are seven platforms, five of which are connected by submarine pipelines to the main platform, located at 44°31′·5N 29°33′·9E. Submarine oil and gas pipelines connect the main platform to the shore 34M WSW. A mooring buoy at which tankers may load oil is located about 1M SW of the main platform. The platforms, mooring buoy and pipelines are in an area in which anchoring, fishing and dredging are prohibited. The platforms are well lit at night.

Between Cape Singol and Cape Constanţa (44°10′N 27°40′E), 3M S, the coast consists of a steep cliff backed by the N suburbs of Constanţa.

S of Midia the coastline changes to become a succession of large hotels fronted by beautiful sandy beaches for 10M until Constanţa, which has extensive harbour breakwaters and a lighthouse which is 1·5M inland. Yachts should not enter the commercial harbour but go to Port Tomis, about 2M to the N.

There are no significant coastal features in the 23M between Port Tomis and Mangalia.

S toward Mangalia there is a proliferation of tourist resorts, mainly named after the planets. Trees are a backdrop to the tourist hotels and the arcades and stalls on the promenades above the beaches, where there are the tourist restaurants, nightclubs, casinos and discos. There are a number of breakwaters, some illuminated, which will give some protection from N and S winds if there is sufficient depth. There are no places to tie up to any of them.

Cape Tuzla is marked by a light at 43°59′·5N 28°40′·1E with GpFl(2)9·7s62m 20M based on a green metal framework tower with white bands. Beside it is a radio mast painted red and white. A charted E cardinal buoy marks a one mile off-shore wreck, S of the light. A local magnetic anomaly is reported S of Cape Tuzla, at 44°00′N 28°40′E.

The harbour breakwaters of Mangalia are conspicuous, but the light, GpFl(2) is even farther inland than the one at Constanţa.

It is only a short distance to the Bulgarian border, with no remarkable features.

The summer resorts continue until 43°53′N when the scenery changes to low brown cliffs which are only broken by Costinesti. This section of the Romanian coast lacks natural harbours.

## MIDIA

44°19′·2N 28°41′·8E

Midia is a large commercial harbour located 10M N of Cape Constanţa. It handles mainly crude oil, oil products, ammonia natural gas and livestock. It has absolutely no facilities for yachts. For emergency entry, the fairway is marked by a S cardinal buoy located at 44°19′·0N 28°41′·95E. Follow a course of 335° into the harbour between the red and green buoys.

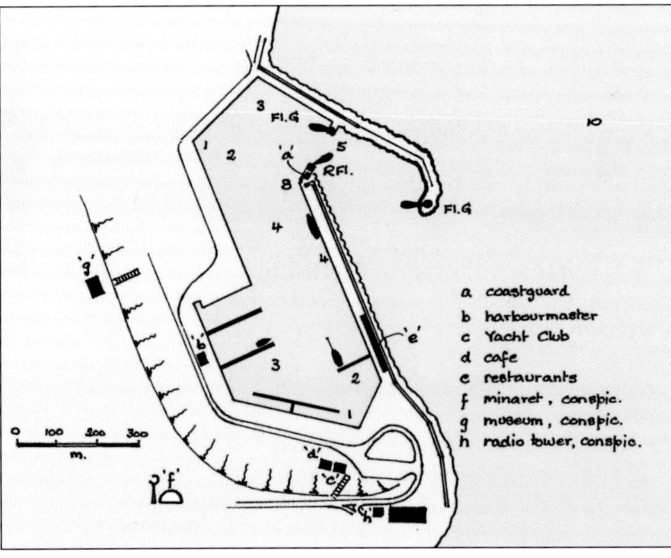


PORT TOMIS

## CONSTANŢA PORT TOMIS

44°10′·6N 28°39′·9E

Port Tomis is a purpose-built yacht harbour with a modern marina which opened in 2008 and is under active construction. The harbour lies just N of the large commercial harbour.

### Approach

The harbour should be approached from an E direction to avoid shallow areas and any other hazards along the coast. The 'rectangular buoy with a yellow topmark' reported in 2001, was not seen in 2010. The outer (N) breakwater was extended in 2007. The new position of the breakwater end is: 44°10′·6N 28°39′·9E. Favour this side on entering to avoid shallow areas S of the entrance. The breakwater extension has greatly reduced the swell entering during sustained SE winds.

*Conspicuous* At night, the harbour entrance lights are difficult to distinguish from other lights on shore until close-in. The old Genoese lighthouse is still in operation and is located on a bluff about 0·5M S of the harbour entrance. In the daytime, the large white naval command centre and a minaret are conspicuous. From the S, yachts should continue past both breakwaters at the entrance to the commercial harbour before turning W towards the Port Tomis yacht harbour. Yachts are not permitted to enter Constanţa commercial port.

*VHF* Ch 16 for port control (call in advance to announce your planned arrival but do not expect to receive an answer). The marina did not monitor VHF in 2010.

Dangers (1) N of the harbour, fixed fishing nets extend up to 1·5M from shore which are difficult to see by day and hazardous at night. (2) A shallow patch with 3m is reported due N of the harbour entrance.

### Mooring

Port Tomis Marina Management began operation in 2008 and is gradually developing the harbour by installing floating pontoons with water and electricity. In 2010, pontoon 'D' extending from the restaurant at the base of the E breakwater, was used for visiting yachts. Pontoon 'A' is used for local yachts, pontoon 'B' is complete but not being used (except by the local gull population) and Pontoon 'C' is used by small boats.

Port Tomis

Constanţa

Port Tomis waterfront looking towards Constanţa commercial harbour

*Berth* Where directed, go bow or stern-to to a floating pontoon with tailed mooring lines. Yachts can moor alongside the currently unused pontoon 'B' on the W side of the harbour if arriving after hours. Alternatively, tie alongside the cement quay on the E side of the harbour (water and electricity not available at these berths in 2010). Additional floating pontoons are planned for this section of the harbour. The marina management does not have VHF radio or staff to assist with mooring lines but may be able to send a security guard to offer limited assistance.

*Depths* 5m at entrance, 3–4m at 'D' pontoon and 4m alongside quay on S breakwater.

*Shelter* Excellent. The breakwater extension has improved the shelter and greatly reduced the swell previously reported in this harbour.

*Authorities* Port of Entry. Border Control police are located in a small building at the end of the inner (S) breakwater. Report (in person) to the border control office after arrival and again before departure. If you have already cleared into Romania, the border police will just document your arrival and departure from the port – no other formalities are required. The marina office is located in a temporary building under the restaurant and tower at the S end of the inner (S) breakwater. A new office, clubhouse, toilets and bathrooms are planned adjacent to the restaurant.

*Charges* Based on 41·3m$^2$, the fee is approximately €18.00 per night. A 10% discount may be offered for stays of three nights or more.

*Contact information* Tomis Marina Management ✆ +40 372 777 169, *Email* office@portultomis.ro Staff member Magdalena Ion speaks good English. Her email is: mion03@yahoo.com and her mobile +40 728 872 887.

## Facilities

*Services* Water and electricity on 'D' pontoon. A locked security gate provides reasonable security and prevents the constant foot traffic found alongside the quay. A security guard is posted 24 hours a day at the marina entrance. Toilet, shower and clubhouse facilities are planned for a future phase. Two restaurants on the quay are not associated with the marina. Marina guests can use the restaurant toilets, but they are heavily used and not well maintained. No convenient laundry services were found in Port Tomis.

*Fuel* By jerry can and taxi.

*Repairs* Hardstanding available with lift. Onsite workshop. All repairs can be arranged with large commercial harbour close by. Diver can be arranged with marina office.

*Provisions* Small supermarkets can be found on the road leading into Port Tomis. A large Carrefour supermarket and shopping mall is located N of the city as well as other large supermarkets in Constanţa.

*Eating out* A casual restaurant/bar, popular among local tourists, is just steps away from pontoon 'D'; however, the quality of the food is mediocre. A more formal restaurant is located upstairs with excellent views and reportedly better quality food. An Italian restaurant located across from Ovidiu Square and the History and Archeology Museum, in Tomis, is a short walk from the marina. A wine bar and restaurant serves excellent steaks and pasta dishes and offers free Wi-Fi to its patrons, and there are many other options in Port Tomis and Constanţa.

*Other* Post office, bank and ATMs on the road leading from the marina to Port Tomis.

## General

With a population of nearly 450,000, Constanţa is one of four Romanian second-tier cities, after Bucharest. The commercial port is located at the crossroads of the trade routes linking the markets of the landlocked countries of Central and Eastern Europe with the Transcaucasus, Central Asia and the Far East. It is the main Romanian port and it ranks among the top 10 European ports. The Port of Constanţa is connected with two Pan-European Transport Corridors: Corridor VII – Danube (inland waterway) and Corridor IV (rail-road). The Romanian Maritime Ports Administration coordinate Constanţa with the satellite ports of Midia and Mangalia.

Constanţa still suffers from the legacy of the Ceauşescu regime, which ended private ownership of real estate. Localities such as Constanţa struggle with establishing new private ownership of fine private houses which are starting to fall apart. But as a yachting destination, the city has a lot of shoreside appeal after you look past the decrepit spots. In Ovidiu Square there is the statue of the poet Ovid, and the old Town Hall, which houses the History and Archaeology Museum. The engaging 1872 statue of the Roman poet Ovid gazes down enigmatically on the traffic of a city which has co-

Histria. Greek and Roman ruins

opted him as its guardian spirit. But Ovid was only in Tomis because he had been banished there by Caesar Augustus, and he hated the place as only a poet in exile could. A huge Roman mosaic still remains, covered, near the square, to suggest what life might have been like in 8–17 AD.

The Port Tomis marina is a good place to leave a yacht for one or several days to visit other places in Romania. It might even be secure for weeks or months.

The best tour guide is Cornel Ciucu, owner of Direct Travel, who can assist with travel needs in Romania, including hire cars or car, minibus or bus with driver and guide. Cornel has been helping yachtsmen since the days when he organised tours for the KAYRA Black Sea rallies. Tours to Histria, Bucharest, the Danube Delta, and 'Dracula Tours', are just some of his offerings. Cornel Ciucu ✆ +40 754 025 698, *Email* cornel@direct-travel.ro www.direct-travel.ro.

Close by Port Tomis, a nice day trip is to the restored archaeological site of Histria. During Greek and Roman times, Histria was a busy port city sheltered behind a barrier beach, but when the whole area filled in with sediment, Histria was cut off from the trade that sustained it, and it was eventually destroyed and abandoned. Its environmental downfall makes it a historical treasure, the only site of its kind around the Black Sea. It has been carefully restored since 1914, and it is substantial enough to explore at length.

There are many buses and trains to destinations in Constanţa and beyond. The airport 15km N of Constanţa services domestic and international charter flights.

## EFORIE NORD

44°03'·8N 28°38'·7E

### Approach

The small purpose-built yacht harbour is located in a beach resort 1·5M S of the base of the Constanţa commercial harbour breakwaters and harbour works and 4M SW of the commercial harbour entrance. The approach is straightforward. Entrance is made from a S direction.

*Conspicuous* The large, greenish Ana (formerly Europa) Hotel and other hotels, including a smaller blue and white hotel with a round front, are conspicuous behind the long stretch of sandy beach. The breakwaters and a white crane can be seen closer in.

*VHF* Ch 67 for Ana Yacht Club. The radio was not working in August 2010 but was to be repaired.

Dangers (1) The approach should be made from an E (seaward) direction to avoid rock groynes and other hazards along the coast. (2) The entrance is narrow and extra caution should be taken if a swell is running as waves break along the beach immediately to the W of the entrance.

### Mooring

The marina accommodates approximately 40 yachts. Max LOA 18m. Space for visiting yachts.

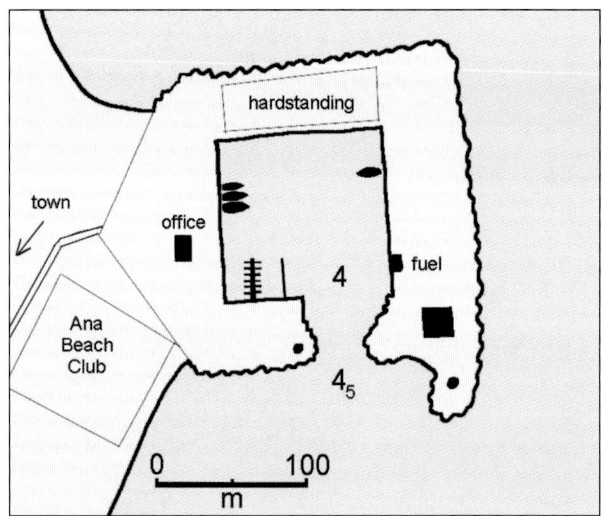


**EFORIE NORD**

Eforie Nord, Ana Yacht Club

Beach at Eforie Nord

*Berth* Bow or stern-to the W quay in 3m with mooring lines tailed to the quay. Staff will assist you if you call ahead. The proximity of the harbour to the beach requires that it be dredged every Spring.

*Shelter* Good shelter from prevailing winds, although some swell works its way in with NE through S wind or swell. The marina often freezes in winter; all yachts are placed on hardstanding.

*Authorities* While this is not an 'official' Port of Entry, the marina staff can telephone Customs and Border Police to come to clear yachts in and out. The marina office is in the buildings on the W side of the yacht basin.

*Charges* €15.00 + €3.60 VAT = €18.60 per night for a 12m yacht.

*Contact information* Ana Yacht Club (formerly Europa Hotel Yacht Club), Lucian Rădulescu, Director
*Mobile* +40 722 803 940
*Email* lradulescu@anayachtclub.ro.
www.anayachtclub.ro
The Ana Yacht Club at Eforie Nord is one of the two Blue Flag marinas on the Black Sea. (The Blue Flag programme for marinas certifies that they meet standards for environmental education and information, environmental management, safety and services, and water quality.)

### Facilities

*Services* Water and 220V electricity at the berth. Toilets and showers near office. Wireless internet at the Ana Yacht Club Restaurant. Ana Yacht Club staff provide 24-hour security.

*Fuel* Diesel and petrol available from the small fuel dock on the E quay.

*Repairs* Hardstanding for 70 yachts available with haul-out by crane. Mechanical and electrical repairs can be arranged through marina office.

*Provisions* A well-stocked City Market supermarket can be found by following the road lined with small kiosks and shops leading away from the beach and harbour area and then turning left on the first main street. Alimentara (minimarkets), bakeries, patisseries and fruit and vegetable stands can be found throughout the town and beach area.

*Eating out* There is a small bar/restaurant at the marina, and there are numerous fast-food stalls, cafés, restaurants and bars throughout the town and beach area. The most popular among summer tourists are the large, cafeteria-style restaurants in town, several of which have live music performances.

*Other* Post office in town. Bank and ATM at the Ana Hotel Europa. Hospital in Constanţa. Hire cars available through the marina manager. Buses to Constanţa and beyond. International airport 15km N of Constanţa.

### General

The yacht harbour of Eforie Nord was originally constructed in 1987 but for years it remained without the final touches that would make it useful. In 2003 the town of Eforie Nord granted a 50-year lease to the owner of the Europa Hotel (now Ana Hotel Europa), who completed the yacht harbour development and opened the marina in 2004.

For yachts heading S from the River Danube-Black Sea Canal, through Constanţa Port, Eforie Nord offers a convenient place to stop-over after reaching the Black Sea. The harbour is located in a beach resort community only about 1·5M SW of the entrance to the Constanţa commercial harbour. During July and August, beaches packed with tourists are located on both sides of the marina, along with carnival stalls and rides. This is an acceptable place to leave a yacht for inland travel, although space is more limited and shelter is not as good as in Port Tomis, just N of the commercial harbour.

For assistance with travel needs in Romania, contact Cornel Ciucu, Direct Travel (see Port Tomis for contact information).

## MANGALIA

43°47'·9N 28°36'·1E

### Approach

Mangalia harbour serves both yachts and large ships, so the approach is straightforward. Ships often anchor off the harbour mouth while awaiting entry, and the harbour breakwaters can be seen from a distance. The Fairway buoy is at position: 43°47'·75N 28°36'·35E. There are no charted dangers. The outer harbour is very large. Observe the red and green buoys in the outer entrance.

There are now separate authorities for the commercial harbour and the 'touristic' harbour. For the commercial harbour, port administration and Customs staff are at the N entrance of the administration building by the control tower, and Immigration staff are at the S end of the same building. The control tower is owned and operated by the Navy.

Yachts should proceed directly to the yacht harbour, which is straight ahead from the entrance to the northern-most of the green buoys and then into the 'touristic harbour'.

*VHF* Ch 67 for Mangalia Yacht Marina (not necessary to call in advance).

Approach to Mangalia

## MANGALIA

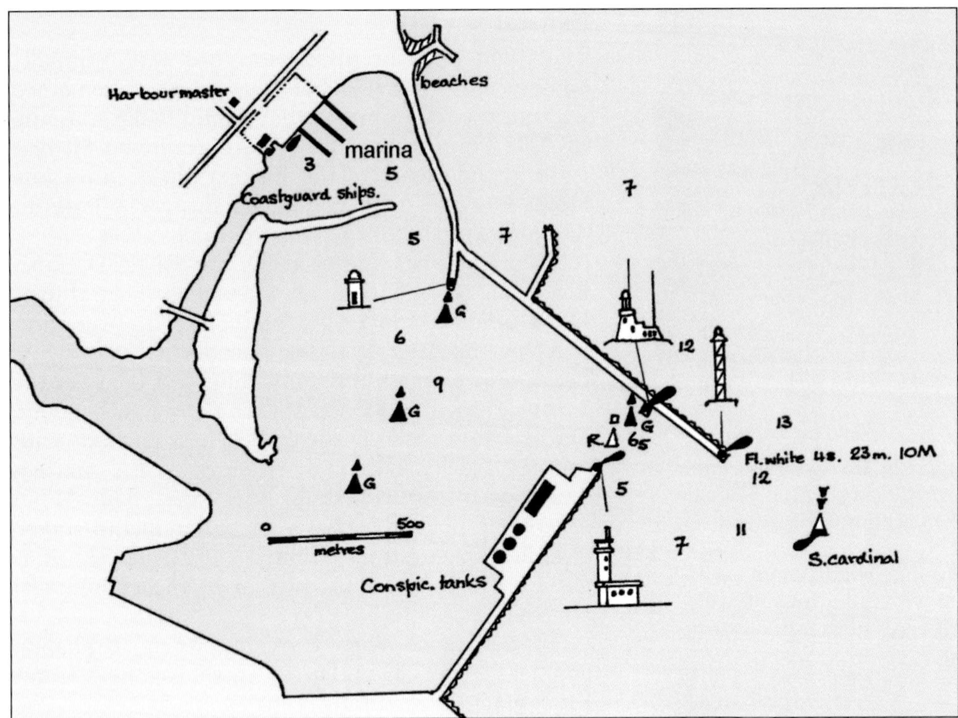


### Mooring

A new marina with floating pontoons is located in the 'touristic' harbour inside the larger commercial harbour. There is room here for up to about 100 yachts of all sizes up to Mega.

*Berth* Marina staff will direct an incoming yacht to one of the floating pontoons with finger piers and will assist in securing the vessel. Depths are 5m.

*Shelter* Excellent all-round shelter.

*Authorities* Port of Entry. Mangalia is the southernmost Port of Entry in Romania for yachts and commercial vessels. Marina staff will arrange for formalities after arriving or before departing from ports outside of Romania. If you have already cleared into Romania, the only required formality is to register with the Border Police upon entry or departure from a Romanian port. The Border Police are located in a small white modular building with a Romanian flag, by the exit from the marina's parking lot. The Border Police officer was professional and efficient in clearing *Gyatso* and its crew out of Romania; no other agencies were involved in the process.

The marina is owned by the Mangalia municipal government, and there is no private component. It was opened for business in July 2008. The harbourmaster reported that the 2010 fees for the marina were set too high and would be lowered by the 2011 season.

*Contact information* Claudiu Terciu, Harbourmaster ✆ 0753 060 628

### Facilities

*Services* Water and 220V 50Hz electricity are available at each berth. The marina claims to have a large collection of adaptors, for all sorts of special electrical connections. It is reported to have toilets and showers and/or laundry. Security is provided with 24-hour watchman and restricted access to the pontoons. The marina intends to install Wi-Fi in the future. Meanwhile, internet access is said to be found nearby.

Mangalia yacht marina

*Fuel* In 2009, there was a fuel station at the marina, but it was out of order during 2010. The marina hopes to restore this service in 2011.

*Repairs* In 2010 there were no facilities for repairs, but the Marina Store in Constanţa will deliver parts and gear.

### General

Mangalia has a year-round population of about 45,000 which swells to several times this number during the summer season, 1 June–15 September. Many seasonal restaurants are located near the yacht marina, and all the other normal facilities are also conveniently located, including ATMs and car rental agencies. There are a number of discos near the marina. The large bandstand on a barge moored along the harbour wall is the venue for the Callatis Festival, held on 8–15 August since 1998. The Muzeul de Arheologie Callatis, named after the 7th century BC Greek settlement, contains a good collection of Roman sculpture.

# 9. Bulgaria

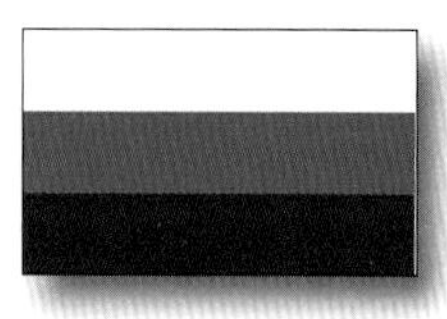

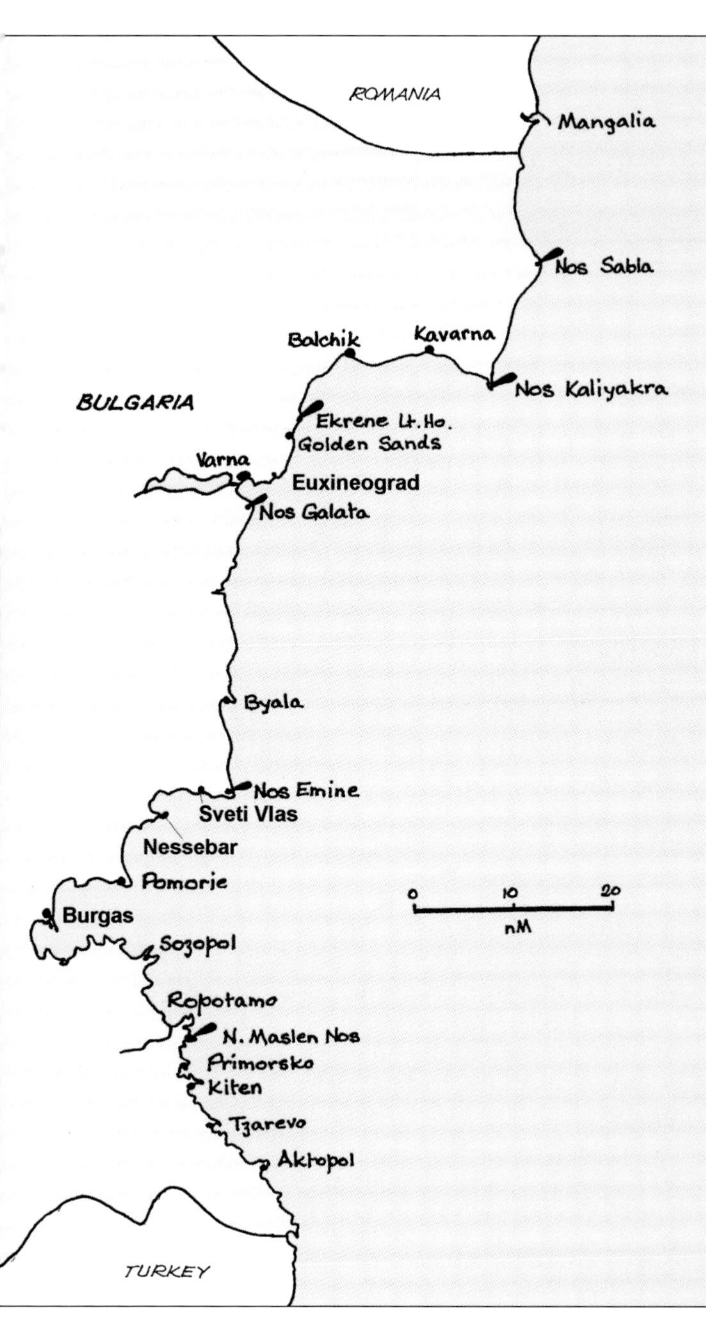


**BULGARIA**

## The Black Sea Coast of Bulgaria

Bulgaria is located on the Balkan Peninsula on the W coast of the Black Sea. The Black Sea coastline is reported to be 354km or 165M. Romania is to the north; Turkey and Greece are to the south; Serbia and Macedonia are to the west. The land area of the country is 110,879km$^2$. Administratively, the country is divided into 28 provinces (*oblasti*). Bulgaria controls key land routes between Europe and the Middle East and Central Asia.

## History

What is today Bulgaria was conquered by the Roman legions and was administered as the Roman provinces of Scythia, Moesia, Thrace, Macedonia and Dacia. After the Roman Empire collapsed in the west, Bulgaria remained among the lands and peoples of the Eastern Roman, or Byzantine, Empire. For a thousand years, centres of power shifted, sometimes favouring the Bulgars, sometimes the Byzantines. The Ottomans began their conquest of Bulgaria in the 14th century, and this was completed following the capture of Constantinople in 1453. Bulgaria remained part of the Ottoman Empire until 1878, when it liberated itself and created an independent kingdom. The country allied itself with Germany in both the First and Second World Wars. The Soviet army drove out the German army in September 1944. Bulgaria became a People's Republic in 1946 and was among the most loyal members of the Warsaw Pact until 1989, when the Soviet system began to collapse. Multiparty elections were held for the first time in 1990, and Bulgaria joined NATO in 2004 and the European Union on 1 January 2007.

## Time

Bulgarian standard time is GMT +2 hours.

## Communications

The telephone country code is +359. There is excellent coverage for wireless internet access.

## Weather

The sailing season extends from May to the end of September, though in both May and September there are often short unsettled periods. June to August is usually very hot, but sea breezes blow during the day. July and September generally have light winds. Strong N winds sometimes blow during August. August is the main vacation month, and all the holiday resorts are filled with families seeking relaxation.

Balchik harbour resort

## People

The population is 7·2 million and falling due to out-migration to other parts of Europe.

## Food and drink

Bulgarian cuisine is an interesting blend of Slav and Ottoman cooking styles. There is much greater use of cabbage than is found in most of Turkey, and there is much more flaked pastry than is found in the Ukraine or Russia. The Bulgarians are proud of their food, especially yoghurt and white cheese, which often accompanies a meal. Dishes are normally cooked slowly over low heat, which they say contributes both to good nutrition and better taste.

Bulgarian wine is not yet well established in the European or world markets, but quality has improved tremendously during the past 20 years, and they now represent excellent value among lower-priced wines. Black Sea Gold, a large winery a short ride out of Pomorie, is a convenient place to sample a wide range of varieties and prices.

Street food is delicious. Smarter are the seasonal restaurants of the older summer resorts, such as Nessebar, Pomorie and Sozopol. Varna and Burgas both have streets with many good restaurants.

## Provisions

Provisions of all sorts are readily available for yachtsmen, who represent only a tiny fraction of the vacationers who flock to the Black Sea coast throughout the summer months. Minimarkets, fast food stalls, vegetable and fish markets and supermarkets are abundant, and Varna has a 'hypermarket'. The minimarkets sell fresh bread.

## Language

Bulgarian is a Slavonic language and uses the Cyrillic alphabet. Russian is also widely spoken, but English-speakers are rapidly growing in number.

## The Black Sea coast

The 165M coast is very important to the national economy. It offers six harbours with facilities suitable for yachts: Varna, Burgas, Balchik, Sozopol, Sveti Vlas and Nessebar. The Bay of Burgas, between Sveti Vlas and Sozopol, holds the only real cruising grounds in the Black Sea, in the sense that a yacht can find relatively isolated anchorages amidst towns offering modern marinas and every tourist amenity. Most Black Sea visitors on yachts say that Bulgaria was their favourite coastal country.

## Charts

*Gyatso* hoped to find good local charts of Burgas Bay, but never found any Black Sea charts anywhere in Bulgaria. In 2010 the C-Map by Jeppesen chart of the Black Sea was particularly weak in its coverage of Burgas Bay.

## Travel ashore: taxi, train, plane, road

Bulgaria has a good public transport system.

## Money/ currency

Although Bulgaria very much wants to join the Euro zone, the currency is still the Leva.

### Ports of Entry

The ports of entry are: Balchik, Varna, Burgas and Tsarevo. The most convenient port of entry depends on the direction from which you are entering Bulgaria. From the south, it is Tsarevo. From the north, it is Balchik. Officials have all the necessary forms. No agent is required for entry or exit.

### Formalities

Bulgaria wins the gold star for the most dramatic improvements in the management of foreign yachts, to the point that the country now sets the standard among the six countries bordering the Black Sea. It is not part of the Schengen zone. A visa is issued on arrival.

All foreign flag private yachts entering in or departing from Bulgarian ports shall follow the same procedure through Bulgarian ports of entry, which on the Black Sea are: Balchik, Varna, Burgas and Tsarevo. Bulgarian ports of entry on the Danube River are: Vidin, Oryahovo, Lom, Somovit-Nikopol, Svishtov, Ruse, Tutrakan and Silistra.

The Certificate is valid for six months on condition that the vessel and the owner/captain does not visit foreign ports. The Certificate consists of:

Form A, in five copies, which should be completed upon entering into Bulgarian ports;

Form B (Change pages) which can be used when alterations are to be made in the lists of yachtsmen, crew members or in case of use by alternate owners of multiple-owner yachts; and

Form C, in four copies, which should be completed on departure from Bulgarian ports to foreign ports, when the ownership of the vessel is changed, or when the validity of this certificate has expired.

Keep this Certificate on board at all times as it might be requested by relevant authorities, since it contains all the necessary information about you and your vessel.

### Entering into Bulgaria

If you are coming from international waters or foreign ports, you will have to communicate with Border Police on VHF Ch 16. Complete Form A and:

1. Apply first to the Coastal Health Control while flying the quarantine flag (i.e. the yellow flag) in accordance with the World Health Organisation procedure and after having declared whether or not there is a case of contagious disease or an incident of death among your crew members or yachtsmen; you can have the pertinent section of your certificate approved by the Health Officer.
2. You should then apply to the Border Police and after having declared the necessary information, you can have the pertinent section of your certificate approved by the Officer in charge.
3. You should then apply to the Customs Officer and after having declared the inventory list of your vessel, you can have the pertinent section of your certificate approved by the Customs Officer.

Cathedral

Roman bath ruins

Pedestrian street

4. You should finally apply to the Maritime Administration Office and after having declared your ports of call within Bulgarian territorial waters, you can have your certificate approved by the Maritime Administration.

### Sailing in Bulgarian territorial waters and between Bulgarian ports

As the owner, you and your guests have the right to sail freely within Bulgarian territorial waters and between Bulgarian ports provided that no commercial activity shall be undertaken by yourself, your crew members, or your guests. In case of a contagious disease, death or any other incident which may occur during your sailing into Bulgarian territorial waters, you should immediately report to MRCC Varna on VHF Ch 16. As long as there is no change of captain, crew members or yachtsmen you can sail into bays or points of interest on your route, provided they are not forbidden zones, without the need to make any further changes in your certificate. If there is a change of captain, yachtsmen or crew members while between intermediate ports, the captain should complete the updated crew list (Form B). Unless there is information relayed to the authorities in due legal process about illegal possession of prohibited goods, no search or inspections of your vessel can be made without your permission. In case goods that are not allowed entry into Bulgaria are declared by yourself or found by authorities after inspection, such goods shall be placed under customs control and will not be returned until your departure from Bulgarian territorial waters. In case the certificate is lost, contact the nearest Maritime Administration Office to renew your certificate. In the course of necessary arrivals or departures due to extraordinary conditions, *force majeur* or obligations set out within the Law on Maritime Spaces, Inland Waterways and Ports of the Republic of Bulgaria, you must submit a statement underlining such conditions to Bulgarian authorities at the first port of call.

### Leaving your yacht in Bulgaria

You can leave your yacht in a yacht harbour or a boat repair yard and leave Bulgaria by alternative means of transportation. Vessels moored in such yacht harbours or laid up in such boat repair yards, if used once in every two years, can remain in Bulgaria up to five years without the need for any further permission.

### Changes to be made in inventory lists

If there is a change to be made in your inventory list because of repairs, assurance or warranty, necessary notes shall be made on your certificate by relevant Customs offices. All spare parts and other materials belonging to your vessel should be kept on board as long as your yacht remains in Bulgaria. It is necessary to record all spare parts that are obsolete or unusable having resulted following maintenance or repair on your vessel. In case you wish to take them out of Bulgarian customs zone, they will have to be noted on your certificate. You can also leave them in specific areas under customs management as per the Customs Law.

### Diving regions

Diving with scuba equipment in Bulgaria territorial waters is subject to permission by the Ministry of Transport, Information Technology and Communications. Necessary information on the subject can be obtained from the Maritime Administration offices.

### Departure from Bulgaria

When sailing from a Bulgarian port to international waters or foreign ports, complete the departure section of the certificate (Form C) and apply to the Border Police office to have the appropriate section of the certificate authorised after having completed the departure procedure at the Maritime Administration office and the Customs office.

### Conditions of expiry

(1) Departure from a Bulgarian port to a foreign port; (2) Changes having occurred in the ownership of the vessel; (3) Six months after the date of authorisation, provided that other conditions have not already caused termination; and (4) Loss of the certificate.

### Please note that you are not to engage in activities described below:

(1) You cannot undertake any commercial activity within or through your vessel. (2) You cannot collect charges or dues from persons declared as guests. (3) You cannot make false declarations.

You cannot transport or take out of Bulgaria any historical objects or objects of cultural value.

You cannot buy or sell any goods or materials from yachts and ships whose customs transactions have not been completed. This is considered as an illegal activity according to the national legislation of Bulgaria and if apprehended, due judicial processes shall be conducted according to the laws of the Republic of Bulgaria.

Burgas Bay is a unique corner of the Black Sea, the only area that might be considered 'cruising grounds', meaning a concentration of secure spots for a yacht to moor in attractive surroundings. Highlighting Burgas Bay means dividing Bulgaria into three areas of greatly different size and interest to yachtsmen. The northern piece, from the Romanian border to Cape Emine, includes a great stretch of coast from Balchik to Varna. Burgas Bay has five diverse yacht-friendly places. South from Burgas Bay to the Turkish border, only Tsarevo offers secure shelter.

## HARBOURS AND ANCHORAGES

### *Passage note: Cape (Nos) Kaliyakra to Cape (Nos) Emine*

Cape (Nos) Kaliyakra is a popular tourist attraction with its dramatic cliffs, scenic views, peaceful nature preserve and historic sites which can be visited from nearby Kavarna or Balchik. Other yachtsmen report spectacular sunsets from the restaurants built into the cliffs, a small museum located in a cave commemorating the Russian defeat of the Turkish Navy in 1791, ruins dating back to the 4th century BC, and a small chapel to St Nicholas, the patron saint of sailors, on the pathway to the very end of the cape. According to local legend, forty girls who were the sole survivors of a Turkish attack jumped to their deaths from the high cliffs to avoid being captured and converted to Islam.

Nos Galata is at the S corner of Varna Bay. From Nos Galata to Nos Emine (42°42'N 27°54'E), a distance of 28M, the coast is backed by wooded hills, rising to over 300m, which slope steeply to the sea.

Cape Kaliyakra

## KAVARNA

43°24'·6N 28°21'·3E

### Approach

Karvarna is located 5·5M NW of Cape (Nos) Kaliyakra and 8·5M E of Balchik in a long bay backed by steep cliffs. The approach is straightforward.

*Conspicuous* A white, cone-shaped hill and large grain silos are visible in the approach.

Dangers (1) Fixed fish nets and traps on either side of the harbour and along the coastline. (2) Ships anchor in the large bay SE of Kavarna, awaiting clearance into or out of commercial ports at Kavarna, Balchik and Varna.

### Facilities

Limited. Not a Port of Entry (see Balchik).

### General

The harbour is part of a beach village about 3km down a steep road from the main hillside village of Kavarna and the port is used to export grain. White cliffs topped with a flat plateau form the backdrop to the harbour and long bays stretching toward Cape Kaliyakra and Balchik. Kavarna is not a port of entry and has limited facilities for visiting yachts but is conveniently located near Balchik which is a Port of Entry and has a secure marina for yachts. Inside the E breakwater, yachts can find good shelter by mooring bow or stern-to among the local boats or by anchoring out in this part of the harbour, taking care to avoid shallow water near the beach. The Annans reported in 2001 that the harbour is prone to silting and the W side of the harbour is shallow and that it is not possible for a yacht to tie to the central mole in the harbour.

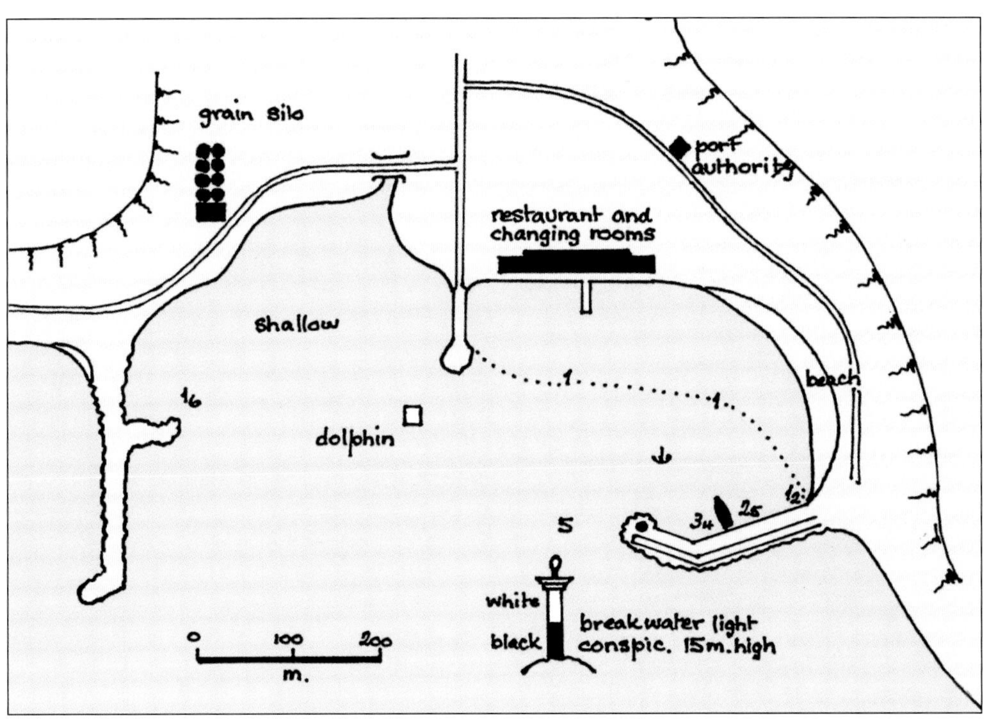


KAVARNA

9. BULGARIA

Local places of interest include: several museums displaying the town's history dating back to the 5th century BC, examples of 19th century Ottoman architecture and a dozen fountains tapping into the fresh spring water for which the main town is famous. Sailing along this coast, you may also notice the professionally designed 18-hole golf courses and associated high-end villa communities (under development in 2010). Another option for visiting this area is to leave your yacht in the secure marina in Balchik and use it as a base for travel to Kavarna and Cape Kaliyakra by bus or rental car.

## BALCHIK

43°24'·0N 28°09'·8E

### Approach

Balchik is located 15·5M W of Cape Kaliyakra and 19·5M NE of Varna. The approach is straightforward. However, contrary to convention, the tower and light on the end of the E breakwater is red. The light on the tower at the end of the inner (S) breakwater is white.

*Conspicuous* The cranes and buildings at the commercial port are obvious in the approaches from all directions. The breakwater is easily seen.

*VHF* Ch 16 for port authorities and Ch 8 marina (calls are likely to go unanswered).

*Note* If arriving in Bulgaria from the N or E, the border police will contact you on VHF Ch 16 from their tower on Cape Kaliyakra. They will then call ahead to notify authorities in Balchik of your planned arrival.

Dangers (1) E of the harbour, some rocks extend from Nos Balchik. (2) Fixed fishing nets are located on either side near the entrance to the harbour. (3) From the S, care should be taken to avoid Monastery Rocks, located E and immediately S of Golden Sands marina (see Golden Sands below).

### Mooring

A modern new marina, with floating pontoons, has been developed within the former fishing harbour since the publication of previous cruising guides. A fleet of mostly small fishing boats still actively use the beach area on the N side of the harbour and a few moorings near the S seawall. The harbour is also used by day charter boats serving the surrounding resort communities.

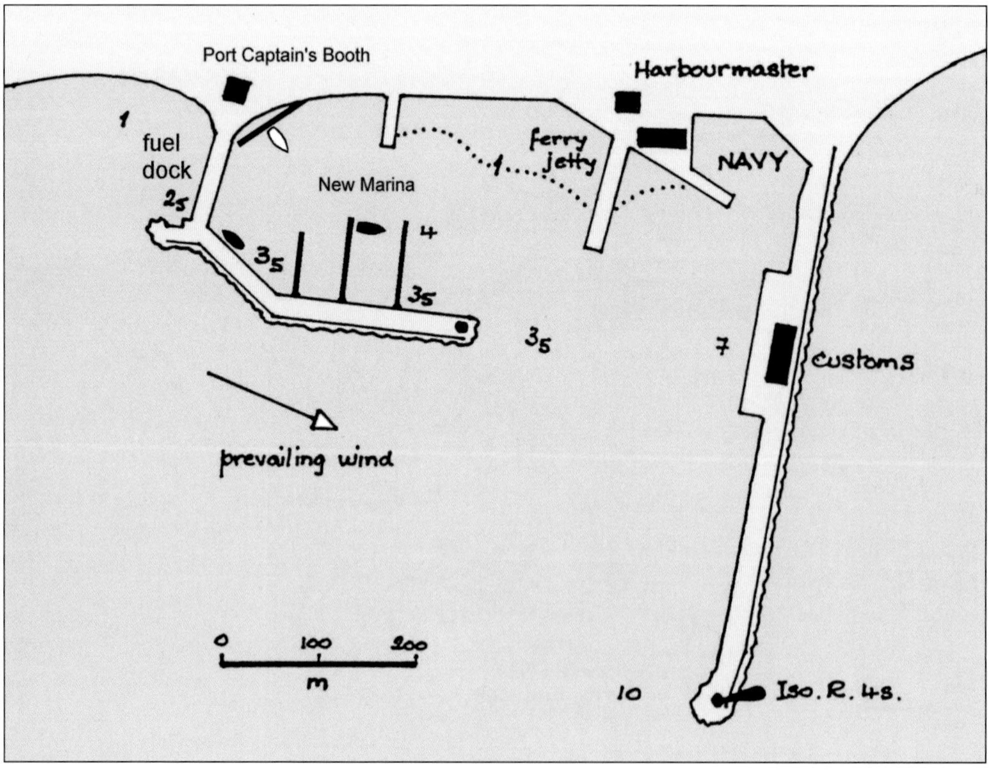


BALCHIK

Balchik

*Berth* Where directed in the marina, either in a slip on one of the floating pontoons with short finger piers extending from the S breakwater, or alongside the inner seawall on the W or S side of the yacht harbour. There are no laid moorings. Many of the finger piers are small and it can be a challenge to secure yachts over 11m. A few spaces which are suitable for larger yachts may be available along the seawall.

*Depths* 3·5m in the marina and 2·5m on W side of fuel dock. Less than 1m depths along N shore of harbour.

*Shelter* Excellent shelter in the marina.

*Authorities* Balchik is a Port of Entry. Upon arrival from ports outside Bulgaria, yachts must report to Customs and Border Police alongside the quay on the commercial dock. If a ship is in port, you may be directed to pull alongside a tug or the outer wall. As of 2010, new procedures are in place for entrance and exit formalities for foreign yachts (see summary in the introduction to this chapter). The customs and immigration process takes about one hour to fill out necessary forms and receive a transit log good for all ports in Bulgaria. Balchik authorities are friendly and professional. An agent is not necessary, and yachts are no longer required to check in/out of each port or to obtain special permissions while cruising in Bulgaria.

*Charges* Approximately €12.00 per day for a 12m yacht.

*Contact information* The Port Captain who manages the marina is called George. His office can be found at the base of the W breakwater.

## Facilities

*Services* Water and electricity at slips in the marina. A laundry with wash/dry/fold service (charged by individual piece or by the kilo) is located in Marina City, the hotel and shop complex adjacent to the marina. Toilets and shower facilities are located across from the laundry. Wi-Fi is available at the waterfront bars and restaurants.

*Fuel* Petrol and diesel is available at the fuel dock in the SW corner of the yacht harbour.

*Repairs* Minor repairs can be arranged through the harbourmaster.

*Provisions* Minimarkets and fruit and vegetable stand near Marina City. Small Sok supermarket one block E of the marina. A bakery and other provisioning options can be found in the main town.

*Eating out* Bars, cafés and restaurants serving Bulgarian, European and pub fare, including fresh seafood, line the harbour-front walkway. Additional options can be found by heading uphill into the main town.

*Other* ATM located once block from marina. Wi-Fi internet access available at Hemingway Bar across from the marina. Buses to Varna where there is an airport with domestic and international flight connections.

## General

Balchik is the main port of southern Dobruja, a region long famous for growing grain. The commercial port of Balchik specialises in the export of wheat, mostly in ships of 3,000–4,000 tonnes. Arriving from Romania, this is the first, and most convenient, port of entry into Bulgaria.

Built on the steep, white cliffs, the scenic port town of Balchik is an interesting case study in resort development. Its year-round population of about 10,000 dramatically increases during the summer with Romanians, Bulgarians and other Europeans on holiday. Until 2005, the main street of the town ran one block inland from the fishing and commercial harbours. Then the Consortium Marina Balchik received a 35-year lease from the municipality and installed pontoons and shore facilities for yachts. Despite the economic difficulties that Bulgaria has experienced since 2007, the marina development resulted in a wholesale migration of restaurants and shops to face the harbour. The new Marina City apartments have been sold to investors in Europe and Russia. The local standard of living has benefitted from the tourism boom while the town has successfully maintained its identity as a 'real' place to live and work.

Sites of interest include the seaside summer palace and surrounding botanical gardens of Queen Marie, a granddaughter of Queen Victoria, which is located W of the harbour.

## GOLDEN SANDS MARINA (ZLATNI PJASCI)

43°18'·0N 28°03'·2E

### Approach

The shoreline near Golden Sands consists of white sand beaches with offlying rocks backed by forested hills. Southerly swell builds at the harbour entrance, but it is not dangerous. Four wave-break jetties are located on the shore to the N of the harbour and are used by local fishermen.

*Conspicuous* Apartment blocks and hotels of the resort community stretch along the shoreline and can make it difficult to see the yacht harbour at the N end of the resort development.

*VHF* Ch 77 or 16 for harbourmaster (not necessary to call)

Dangers (1) Approaching from or departing to the S, take care to pass outside Monastery Reef, marked by a cardinal buoy at 43°16'·6N 28°04'·3E. (2) Fixed fishing net may be found 100m E of the breakwater. (3) Offlying rocks and fixed fish nets along the coast when heading N to Balchik.

### Mooring

Moorings for yachts can be found on the jetties projecting into the harbour from the S seawall. The jetties are concrete slabs on top of pilings that are considerably higher than modern floating docks. The marina is popular, but there is usually an empty space available with a laid mooring tailed to a float. The harbour is used by day charter boats. Fishing boats occupy moorings along the outer breakwater.

*Berth* 50 berths with services and 100 berths without services. Berth where directed by marina staff who will meet you on the jetties, on your left upon entering the harbour.

*Depths* 4m at entrance and 3·5–4m at mooring position.

Golden Sands Marina

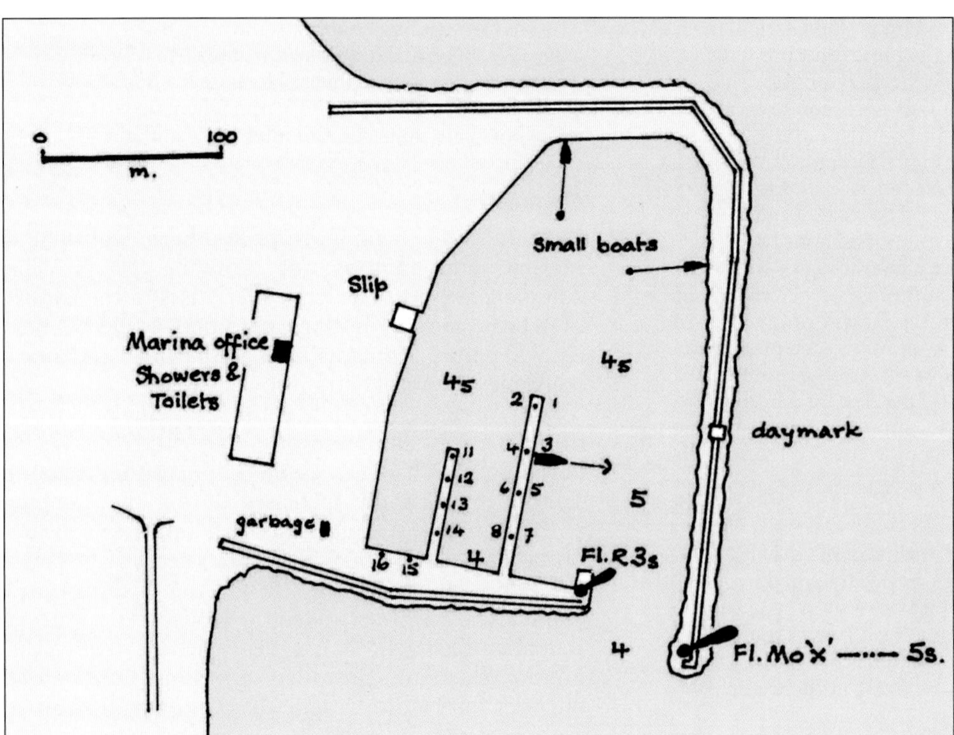


GOLDEN SANDS MARINA

*Shelter* Very good, except reports that S winds push swell into the harbour. Authorities: Golden Sands marina is no longer a port of entry. Yachts entering Bulgaria from the N should use Balchik instead.
*Charges* €1.00 per metre per night
*Contact information* (for marina): None available. Resort website: www.goldensands.bg/yachtport/yahtport.htm.

### Facilities

*Services* Electricity and water on the pontoon. Toilets and showers in marina office building.
*Fuel* Arranged by marina staff (see Balchik for nearby convenient fuel dock).
*Repairs* Minor repairs may be arranged.
*Provisions* Expensive and limited to small kiosks or a small supermarket that caters to the needs of holiday makers.
*Eating out* Numerous restaurants and cafés catering to tourists.
*Other* Bank and ATMs. Buses to Varna and airport.

### General

Golden Sands is a resort of more than 80 hotels fronting a beach of golden sand 17km N of Varna on the Black Sea coast. Construction of the marina began in 1956, at which time it was a major addition to local yachting facilities. Although tetrahedron blocks reinforce the outer breakwater, investment to maintain the marina facilities has not kept pace with normal wear and tear, so it had a somewhat bedraggled air in 2010 that contrasted rather sharply with the fancy yachts moored there and the surrounding resort development. Possible excursions and sites of interest include the grotto of Aladzha Monastery in Hanchuka Forest and the resort's excellent beaches.

## RIVIERA

43°16'·4N 28°02'·7E

A small harbour used by small yachts and day-sailors use this port to get away from the bustle of Balchik. Space for 2–3 boats with silting reported in N corner of the harbour. Buoys laid along adjacent sandy bar are for use by day charter trip boats.

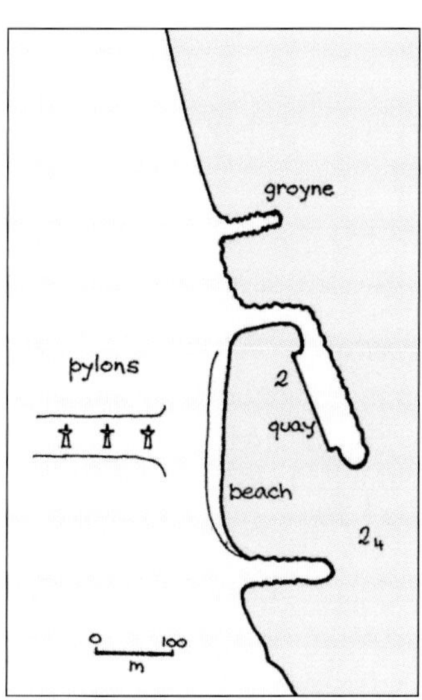

RIVIERA

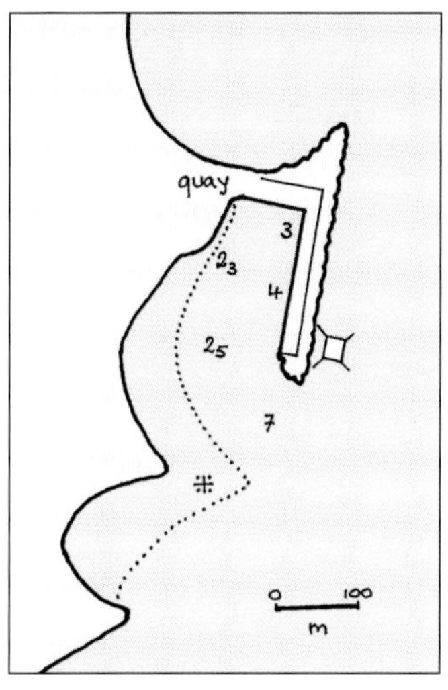

SUNNY BEACH (PISATEL, KABAKUM BISSER)

## SUNNY BEACH (PISATEL, KABAKUM BISSER)

43°14'·8N 28°01'·8E

There is a fish trap tied to the inside of the breakwater or extending out from the breakwater (depending on the time of year) which restricts the room in the harbour, which is mostly used by day charter trip boats to collect passengers from nearby hotels.

## SUNNY DAY (SLÂNCHEV DEN)

43°14'·6N 28°01'·4E

This is a private marina built and maintained by the hotel. The entrance to the marina, marked by red and green buoys, is very badly silted to 1·5m or less and scheduled for dredging. Deeper water can be found inside the harbour. A ship chandler is located on the W side of the road which bypasses the resort.

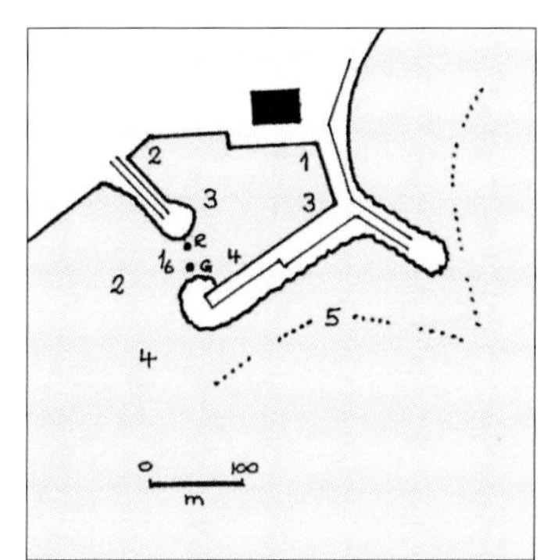

SUNNY DAY (SLÂNCHEV DEN)

## SAINTS KONSTANTIN AND ELENA MARINA (ST ELIA) AND DELFIN MARINA

43°13'·4N 28°00'·7E

The harbour at St Konstantin and St Elena (also referred to as St Elia in previous guides), one of the oldest resorts on the Black Sea coast of Bulgaria associated with the Grand Hotel Varna and located 7km S of Golden Sands Resort, was constructed in 2001. The harbour almost adjoins Delfin Marina,

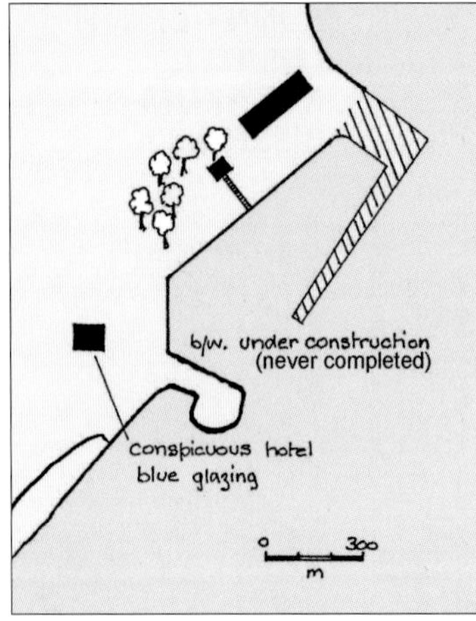


ST KONSTANTIN AND ST ELENA

located immediately to the SW. According to local yachtsman, these harbours are crowded with swimmers and not suitable overnight stops for yachts.

## EUXINEOGRAD (EVKSINOGRAD)

43°13'·0N 27°59'·2E

A breakwater with a light extends W from the shore and protects a bay. Although excellent shelter is reported, use of the harbour is forbidden when the Prime Minister or government officials are in residence. The palace was built for Prince Alexander Battenberg, the first sovereign of Bulgaria, in the 1880s. In Communist times, this place became the home of the Politburo, who built themselves a luxury beach resort. The present government still uses the resort for holidays, especially in summer months. The name *Euxineograd* means 'City on the Black (Euxine) Sea'.

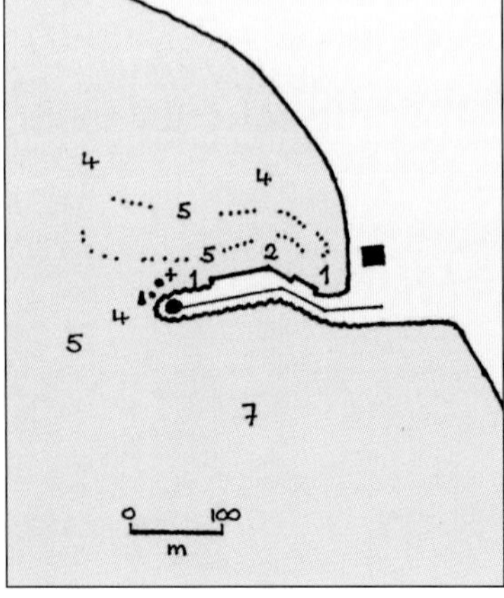


EUXINEOGRAD

### *Passage note: Varna Bay Fishing Harbours*

Four small fishing harbours are located on the N shore of Varna Bay, between Saints Constantine and Elena and Varna commercial harbour, that are not suitable overnight stops for yachts. Consult with local yachtsman regarding the suitability for making a short stop in these harbours.

## VARNA

43°11'·2N 27°55'·4E

The approach is straightforward from Red Buoy No.100 at 43°11'·0N 27°56'·3E.

*Conspicuous* The marina is not visible until inside the large breakwater of the commercial harbour.

*VHF* Ch 16 for port control tower. Contact port control for permission and/or to notify them that you plan to enter the harbour. Shipping traffic uses Ch 26.

Dangers (1) Keep a sharp lookout for shipping traffic. (2) The Annans noted that Turkish chart *18* shows rocks with less than 2m depths on N side of Nos Galata, whereas the local large-scale chart shows 7m over these.

### Mooring

Visiting yachts should contact the port control tower upon arrival in Varna where you will be directed to the Yacht Club Marina Port Varna, immediately to the N (right)of the harbour entrance. The yacht club is operated by Port Varna, which is owned by the Government of Bulgaria.

*Berth* Where directed by yacht club staff. If the Yacht Club does not have space, you may be asked to tie up at the passenger terminal nearby.

*Depths* 10–11m at harbour entrance and 3–6m inside Yacht Club Marina.

*Shelter* Very good, some wash from passing commercial traffic and pilot boats on the outer wall.

*Local weather note* The Annans reported that with high pressure systems, the N wind will blow as an E wind or even SE up to Force 5 in the afternoon and early evening, then falling.

*Authorities* Port of Entry. Note new and improved procedures in place for formalities in Bulgaria. If clearing in or out in Varna, ask Yacht Club or passenger terminal staff to direct you to appropriate authorities or to contact them on your behalf.

*Harbour charges* €10.00 per day for a 12m yacht.

*Contact information* The Yacht Club Marina Port Varna, Toni Karagyozov. Manager ✆ +359 52 69 2434/ 2435/ 2436 *Email* portvarna@bulsaf.bg http://yachtclubportvarna.com

Adjoining the Yacht Club Marina Port Varna is the Seaport Varna Yacht Club, which has docks for about 20 motor yachts owned by local people. The office of this yacht club also has a small chandlery selling clothing, with some lines and Harken blocks.

*Contact information* Seaport Varna Yacht Club/Yacht-Office Ltd., Alexey Minkov, Manager, ✆ +359 (52) 69 1110, *Fax* +359 (52) 69 1110 *Email* office@yacht-office.com www.yacht-office.com

Another marine chandlery, Marina Store, is located between the Yacht Clubs and the passenger terminal. It is a retail outlet for Lalizas Marine Bulgaria, 7, Al. Dyakovich, 9000 Varna, ✆ +359 52 616 695 *Fax* +359 52 604 284 *Email* lmbg@lalizas.com

Other marine businesses are located on the second floor of the passenger terminal, including:
Yacht Shop, ✆ +359 52 692 299
www.yachtshopbg.com

Additional yacht clubs are based in Varna Lake and may be possible to visit now that new yachting regulations are place. A buoyed channel under a

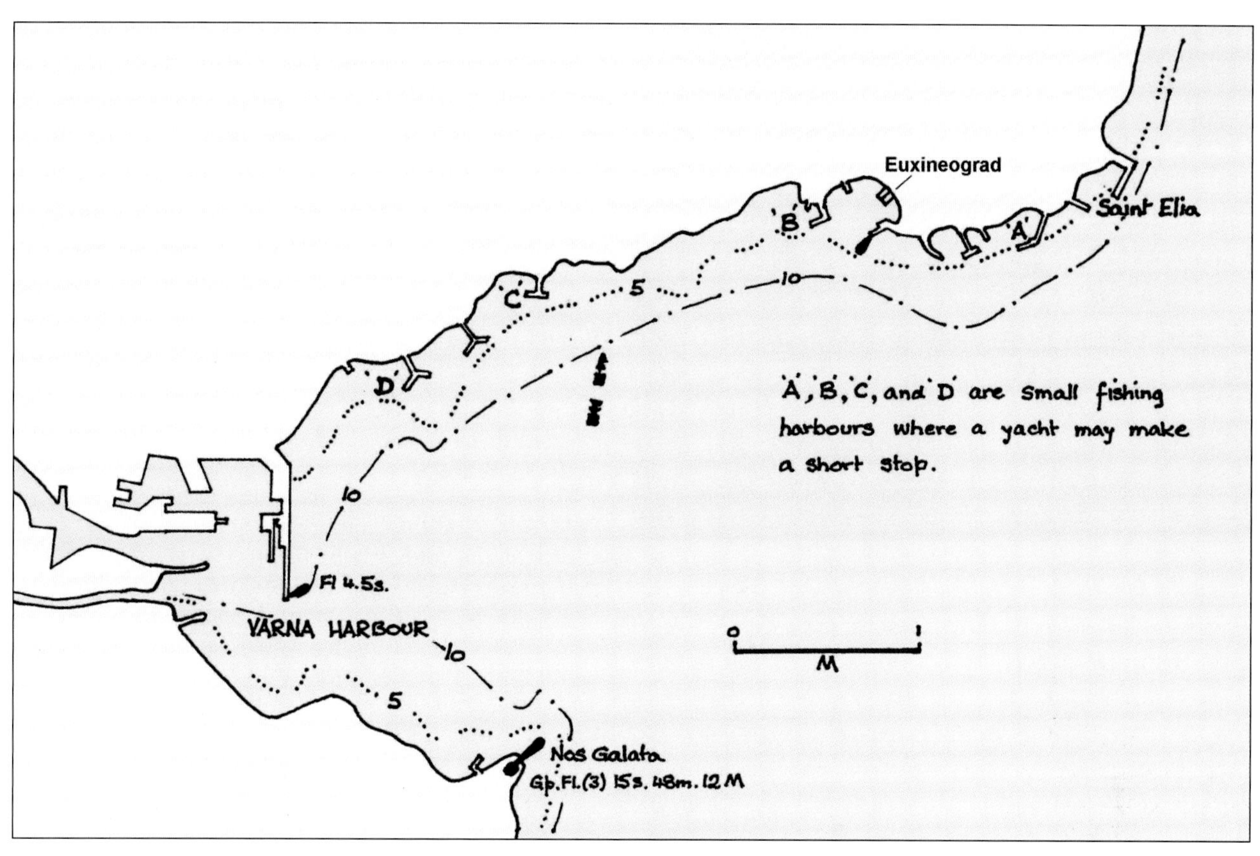
Euxineograd
Saint Elia
A
B
C
D
5
10
A, B, C, and D are small fishing harbours where a yacht may make a short stop.
Fl 4.5s.
VARNA HARBOUR
10
5
0
1
M
Nos Galata
Gp.Fl.(3) 15s. 48m. 12M

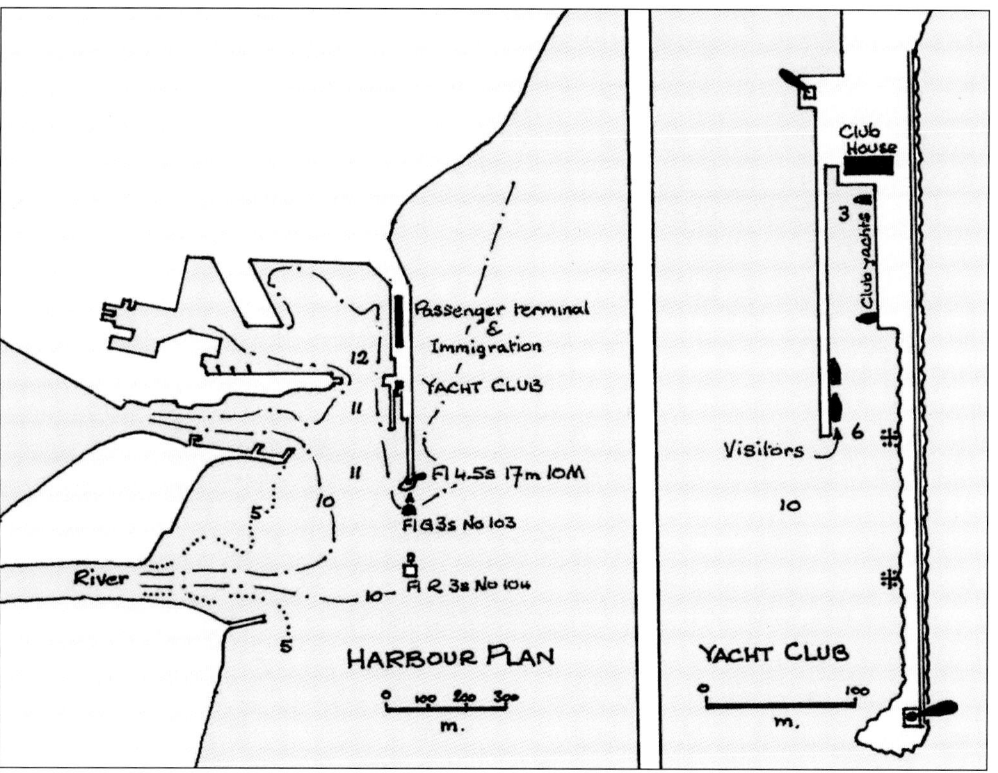
Passenger terminal & Immigration
YACHT CLUB
12
11
11
10
5
Fl 4.5s 17m 10M
Fl G 3s No 103
Fl R 3s No 104
River
10
5
HARBOUR PLAN
0 100 200 300
m.
Club House
3
Club yachts
Visitors
6
10
YACHT CLUB
0
100
m.

VARNA

Varna Yacht Club

Varna Yacht Club

bridge with 50m clearance leads to the lake. Consult local yachtsman or the Yacht Club for further details.

### Facilities

*Services* Water and electricity at slips inside the yacht club basin. A long cable is required at some slips. Toilets and showers in clubhouse. Public telephone at passenger terminal adjacent to the marina.

*Fuel* By tanker truck or jerry can and taxi.

*Repairs* Most repairs are possible and can be arranged by the Yacht Club manager.

*Provisions* Minimarkets, fruit and vegetable stands and a small Sok supermarket in the neighbourhood near the harbour. Large Metro supermarket located 7km out of town.

*Eating out* The upmarket Captain Cook seafood restaurant is located in the passenger terminal adjacent to the yacht club. There are many choices for eating out in the old town neighbourhoods near the port and even more options in the main pedestrian area of the city.

*Other* Two marine chandleries are conveniently located near the Yacht Club (see above). Post office located behind the cathedral and next to the flower market. Banks, ATMs and internet cafés in the city centre. Travel to domestic and international destinations is possible by bus from one of two bus terminals, by train from Varna Railway station, and by plane from Varna International Airport. Hire cars available in the city centre and at the airport. Buses to nearby resort beaches depart from in front of the cathedral.

### General

Varna, population 365,000, is the third largest city in Bulgaria and the largest city and the largest port on the Bulgarian Black Sea coast. The modern port opened in 1906 and handled eight million tonnes in 2010.

To reach the town, walk along the breakwater to the end of the commercial quay. A short walk through the old town brings you to the main pedestrian streets and shopping area where there is a lively café scene in the summer. Local sites of interest include: the Opera House, Old Clock Tower, domed Cathedral of the Assumption, Museum of History and Art, and the Naval Museum set amidst the seaside Marine Gardens. Varna is a good place to leave a yacht for inland tours in Bulgaria.

## ⚓ BYALA

42°51'·2N 27°53'·7E

The harbour is not visible until after rounding Nos Sveti Atanas when approaching from the N. A prominent modern house on the shore indicates the harbour which is located S of the town with the same name. Care should be taken of fish traps off the breakwater (see plan). Anchor where shown in settled weather. Good shelter from prevailing N to E winds. Water is available from a tap on the quay. Plans for a small marina have not materialised. Silting with less than 1m depths is reported near the end of the breakwater – leave it at least 50m to starboard upon entering.

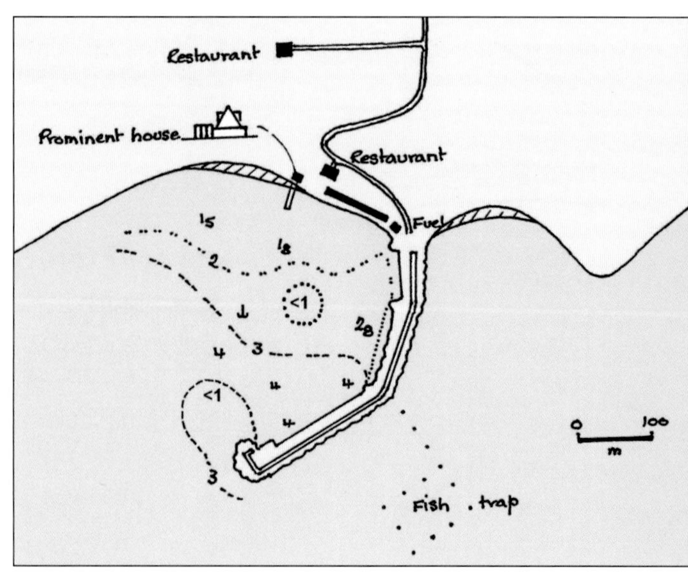

**BYALA**

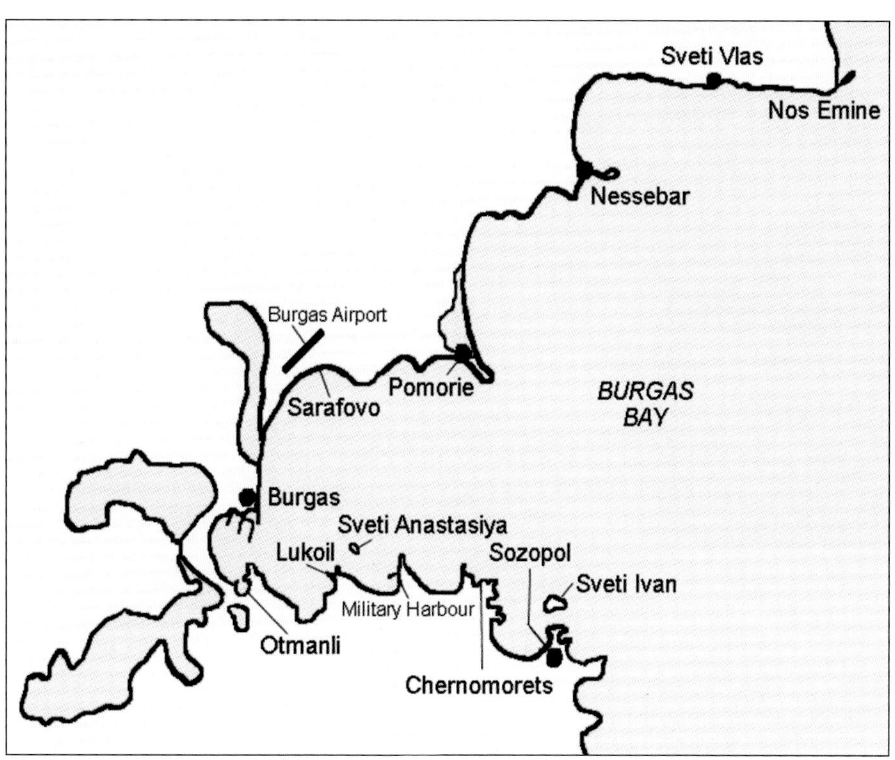

BURGAS BAY

## BURGAS BAY

Burgas Bay, as defined here, extends from Cape (Nos) Emine in the N to the town of Sozopol in the S. Burgas, the smaller rival of Varna, is an attractive small city at the end of a deep Bay. Sozopol came out as *Gyatso*'s top spot on the whole Black Sea for its blend of ancient architecture, congenial people and summer resort atmosphere. Nessebar is a UNESCO World Heritage site.

## SVETI VLAS

42°42'·3N 27°46'·0E

### Approach

The approach is straightforward. The harbour entrance is 6M W of Cape Emine. When approaching from the S, care should be taken to avoid offlying rocks E of Nessebar.

*Conspicuous* The breakwater is easily seen in front of the Spanish-style resort development.
*VHF* Ch 73 for marina.

Dangers None.

### Mooring

A modern new marina was constructed in 2006 in the resort town of the same name.

*Data* 300 berths.
*Berth* Contact marina office on VHF Ch 73. They will send a RIB to guide you to a slip and help with tailed mooring line.
*Depths* 3·5m at visitors' berth along seawall inside of S breakwater and 2m at floating pontoons.
*Shelter* Excellent. Reported that some swell works into the harbour with strong S winds.

SVETI VLAS

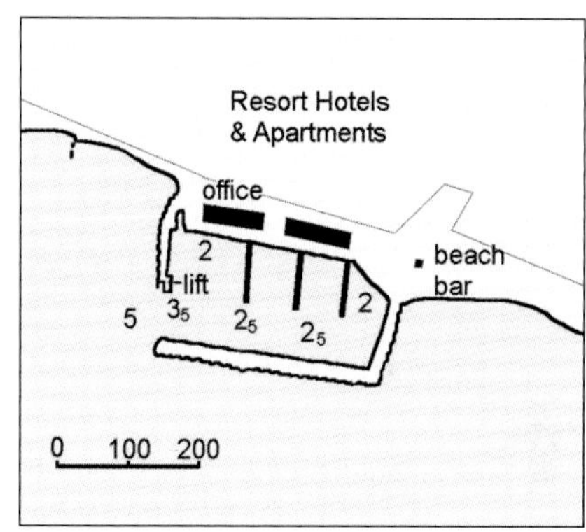


*Authorities* Marina staff.
*Marina charges* €25.00 per night for a 12m yacht
*Contact information* Kolyu Marinov, Manager, Dinevi Marina, ✆ +359 554 64018, *Mobile* +359 885 285294, *Fax* +359 554 64019, *Email* marina@dineviandco.com www.dinevimarina.com

### Facilities

*Services* Water, electricity, digital TV, telephone, and Wi-Fi internet access at every slip. Toilets, showers and laundry with wash/dry/fold service located near marina office. 24-hour security.
*Fuel* Available from tanker truck parked onsite.
*Repairs* Hardstanding with 50-tonne travel-lift and slipway to the left as you enter the harbour. Onsite repair shop where all mechanical and electrical repairs can be arranged.
*Provisions* Supermarkets catering to holiday makers in the resort community.
*Eating out* A variety of waterfront restaurants in the marina with diverse cuisines, including Bulgarian, Italian, Chinese and Armenian.
*Other* Buses to Burgas and Burgas airport. Water taxi to Nessebar.

Marina Dinevi

## General

For yachts, the resort town of Sveti Vlas (Saint Blaise) is dominated by the 300-berth Marina Dinevi, built by the Dinevi brothers, who are among the most prominent of Bulgaria's upmarket resort developers. The marina is one of only two on the Black Sea to be designated as a Blue Flag marina for environmental education and management, safety and services, and water quality. It forms the centrepiece of a huge Spanish-style beach resort and offers visiting yachts almost everything imaginable in terms of services. This is the preferred resort for the wealthy jet-set with the 5-star Palace Hotel, limousine service, and pricey clubs, bars and restaurants.

### *Passage note: Sunny Beach Resort*

Sunny Beach, the largest Bulgarian seaside resort, is located on the shoreline between Sveti Vlas and Nessebar.

## NESSEBAR

42°39'·2N 27°43'·7E

### Approach

Care should be taken of the extensive rocks lying E of Nessebar. The Annan's reported the following local lore when approaching from the E: '... if the cross on the church cannot be seen, you are too close. Which one is not known – there are 41 churches in the town.'

*Conspicuous* Nessebar appears like an island from a distance. Closer in, the churches and historic town are seen. Sandy beaches and high rise resort development line the shore to the W.

*VHF* Ch 16 and 11 for Port Control (not necessary to contact in advance and not likely to respond to calls).

Dangers (1) Rocks extend some distance E of Nessebar. This area should be avoided. (2) If entering the Yacht's Port marina, stay within 10m of the end of the marina NE mole to avoid the rock in the bay which forms part of the marina. Small floats mark the rock.

### Mooring

There are two places at Nessebar where yachts can moor securely. To the E of the causeway, near the cruise ship dock (passenger terminal), a berth can usually be found, though it is likely to be noisy and to have quite a lot of wash from day-tripper boats going to and fro. A better alternative with less foot traffic is Yacht's Port marina, at the W end of the causeway. This marina was constructed about 1990, and Rosco, the harbourmaster, says that there's been

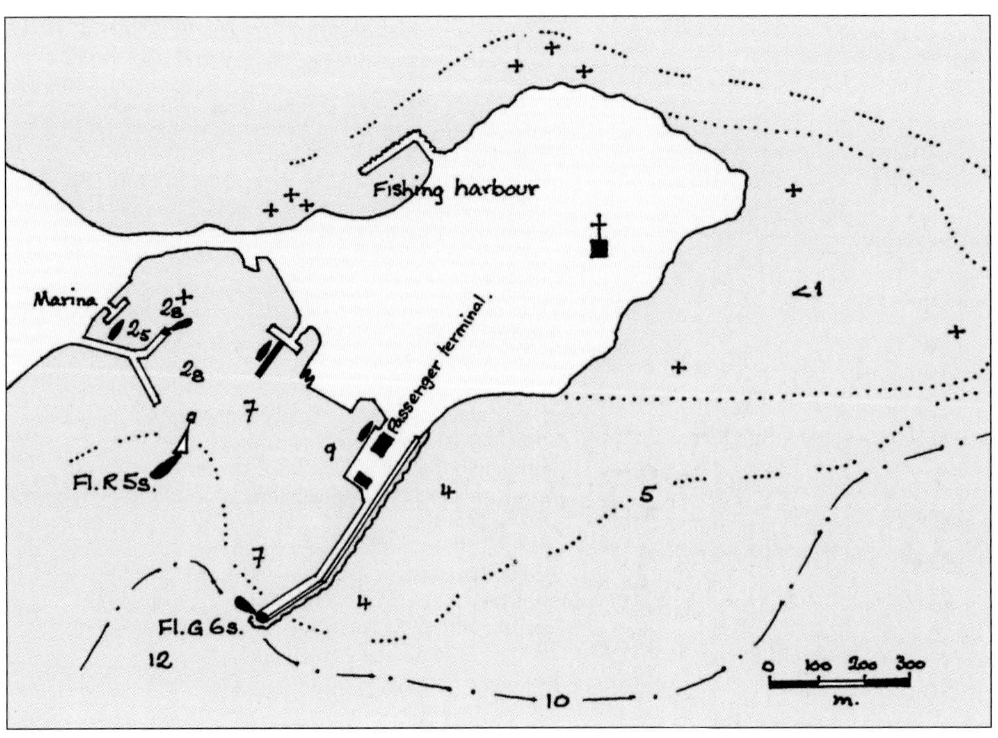


NESSEBAR

Nessebar. Yacht's Port

no change in the place since then. It is a friendly and remarkably laid-back place considering the tourist bustle just down the road. A new marina has been constructed near the E end of the breakwater where a yacht may be able to arrange for a short-term berth.

*Berth* At Yacht's Port, go where directed, bow or stern to the floating pontoon. Tailed mooring provided.
*Depths* 9m at Passenger Terminal and 2·8m in Yacht's Port marina.
*Note* See 'dangers' noted above about rocks in marina.
*Shelter* Good in the marinas, but swell works its way into the harbour. During strong wind events, yachts moored along the breakwater wall are better off moving to anchor.
*Local weather note* Typically, the wind blows from the NW in the morning, veering to the NE or E by evening, and then falling away.
*Authorities* Port of Entry. Report to the passenger terminal in the main harbour first if arriving from a port outside Bulgaria.
*Harbour charges* €12.00 per day for 12m yacht.

## Facilities

*Services* Water, electricity and Wi-Fi provided at each slip in Yacht's Port marina.
*Fuel* Fuel berth at NE end of Yacht's Port marina with 1·8m reported alongside. Keep close to the end of the marina's E pier in the approach to the fuel dock, as the water shallows to the NE.
*Repairs* None.
*Provisions* Larger supermarket catering to the resort community in the new section of town (the centre road of the three leading away from the causeway).
*Eating out* Simple bar and restaurant at Yacht's Port marina. Many other options in the old and new sections of town.
*Other* Post office in old Nessebar. ATMs and internet cafés in old and new sections of the city. Buses to Burgas and airport which is 21km to the W.

## General

Nessebar is the only UNESCO World Heritage cultural site on the coast of the Black Sea. Nowadays the town occupies two distinct areas. 'Old Nessebar' is built on what may have originally been a small rocky promontory that was connected to the nearby peninsula by a 300m isthmus. The island afforded a natural defence for the original Thracian settlement called Menembria. During the 6th century BC, colonists from Megara, on the Greek mainland, settled on the island and renamed it Messembria. The Greeks constructed a defensive wall on the landward side of the causeway and established a marketplace (*agora*) and a temple to Apollo at the E end of the peninsula. Roman, Byzantine, and Turkish occupation have all left their marks on the site. UNESCO describes the town as 'a unique example of a synthesis of centuries-old human activities ... a location where numerous civilizations have left tangible traces in a single homogeneous whole.'

Fast forwarding to 1983, the Communist government headed by Todor Zhivkov welcomed Nessebar as the fifth of what eventually became nine World Heritage sites in Bulgaria. But such designations have their own pitfalls, and by the Summer of 2010, Nessebar was being overwhelmed by tourists arriving by both land and sea. Landward, hotels and vacation rental developments extend for miles. By sea, cruise ships arrive at the Passenger Terminal to disgorge 2,000 or more passengers for a few hours or a day of sightseeing. As worthy as they might be, the remnants of ancient civilizations in Nessebar are smothered by tourists wandering among the hundreds of souvenir stalls.

## POMORIE

42°33'·6N 27°38'·3E

### Approach

The approach is straightforward. Yachts should pass outside Pomorie Bank. The breakwater is easily seen from a distance. Conspicuous: There is a big hotel in the shape of a ship which juts out into the sea next to the harbour. Radio VHF Ch 16 for harbourmaster (not necessary to call ahead). In 2010 the harbourmaster's VHF radio was broken, and he seemed to feel no great urgency to repair it, though he said that he used it when it was working.

Dangers Pomorie Bank is marked with a light tower. It is not recommended to pass between Pomorie Bank and the mainland.

### Mooring

Visiting yachts are welcomed in Pomorie, either along the breakwater or anchored among moored boats. A preliminary study has been conducted for expanding the harbour to include a modern marina and passenger port. The local fishermen's coop is located in a shed near the outer end of the seawall. There are approximately 50 small fishing boats on shore and moored along the seawall. There are also several medium-size fishing boats and day charter boats moored along the outer end of the seawall, and a large, Russian-owned power boat at the end.

*Berth* Where directed by the harbourmaster. If there is an empty space along the seawall, visiting yachts are welcome to tie up. If fishing boats and day charter cruise boats have taken all the prime spots, yachts should anchor among the local yacht moorings.

*Depths* 5m alongside the outer end of the seawall and 3m further in.

*Shelter* The harbour consists of a large seawall jetty that extends S and then W from the Pomorie peninsula. The peninsula and the jetty give the harbour fairly good protection from winds from the N and E but none from the W and NW.

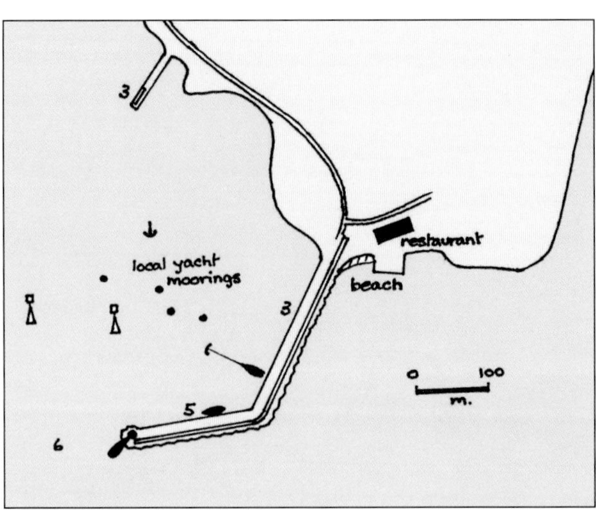


**POMORIE**

*Authorities* Not a port of entry. Harbourmaster can be found in the building on the jetty (phone number posted if he's away).

*Harbour charges* Visiting yachts are not usually charged.

*Note* An expanded harbour with modern marina is planned for Pomorie (date uncertain).

### Facilities

*Services* Water and electricity on the quay can be arranged through the harbourmaster.

*Fuel* By tanker truck, on the quay. Contact the harbourmaster to make arrangements.

*Repairs* Basic carpentry, mechanical and electrical.

*Provisions* Several minimarkets and one supermarket in town.

*Eating out* Numerous small restaurants, bars and cafés in town.

*Other* Internet cafés. Several ATMs. There is a hospital in town. Burgas Airport is 12km.

Pomorie harbour

Pomorie. Fishing boats on the beach

### General

The town of Pomorie, population 14,600, is located at the end of a narrow peninsula which extends in a SE direction and forms the NE point of the Bay of Burgas. North of town, a 7km beach, the longest in Bulgaria, is dotted with hotels that make almost the entire Bay of Burgas a major Bulgarian summer resort. Pomorie has 60,000 hotel rooms.

Peter, the harbourmaster, has for more than a decade been an active cheerleader for yachts visiting his town. He notes with pride that the harbour, lined with colourful fishing boats, is at the centre of the town and that two museums have opened during the past decade: a museum of Pomorie artifacts and a salt museum. In town you will find a pleasant tree-lined pedestrian street with shops, cafés and local women selling lace items which they hang from the trees. A long, sandy beach stretches along the shoreline north of town.

Pomorie is known for its Black Sea Gold Winery, located 3km outside of town, just off the road to Nessebar. The winery has a shop and tasting room. Tours can also be arranged. The famous wine and brandy can also be purchased from shops in the town centre.

www.bsgold.bg.

## ⚓ SARAFOVO

42°33'·4N 27°31'·4E

Sarafovo is a small town at the NW corner of Burgas Bay, located between Burgas Airport and the bay shore. Seven groynes provide a place for small local fishing boats to be hauled out of the water, but the place offers minimal shelter. Although convenient to the airport and suitable for a daytime stop, yachtsmen are likely to prefer Pomorie or Burgas.

## BURGAS

42°29'·9N 27°29'·0E

### Approach

The approach to this large commercial harbour is straightforward. Care should be taken to avoid a rock marked by a S cardinal buoy (see below), but the red and green channel buoys can be ignored by a yacht. The breakwater to the W of the main harbour entrance has been extended to the S to protect expanded commercial harbours to the W, but this does not affect entrance to the Yacht Club.

*Conspicuous* The harbour and city are easily seen from a distance. Many ships are anchored off the harbour entrance.

*VHF* Ch 16 and 11 for *Traffic Control* and Ch 73 for *Yacht Club Port Burgas* (not necessary to call in advance).

Dangers A rock with 2·3m over it is located 1M E of the commercial harbour's E breakwater. The rock is marked by a S cardinal lit buoy, Q6+LFl.15s, horn and is not shown on Turkish chart *18*.

### Mooring

The Yacht Club Port Burgas is located just inside the outer end of the E breakwater for the commercial harbour. The Ports of Burgas and Varna were designed by the same person and built according to almost identical plans, starting in the 1890s. Since the layout of the Port of Burgas is virtually identical to that of Varna, the location of the Burgas yacht club is, as at Varna, at the inner end of the breakwater that forms the E port. The main difference between the two clubs is that the outer breakwall extends beyond the yacht harbour and a long concrete quay has been built at Varna which provides additional shelter and space for yachts to tie up; this is absent at Burgas.

*Berth* Where directed by Yacht Club staff. Space is limited, especially for yachts over 12m. Customs, Border police and Port Control are located inside the commercial harbour on Pier 6 (see plan). Yachts should berth here to conduct clearance formalities before moving to the Yacht Club or departing Bulgaria.

BURGAS

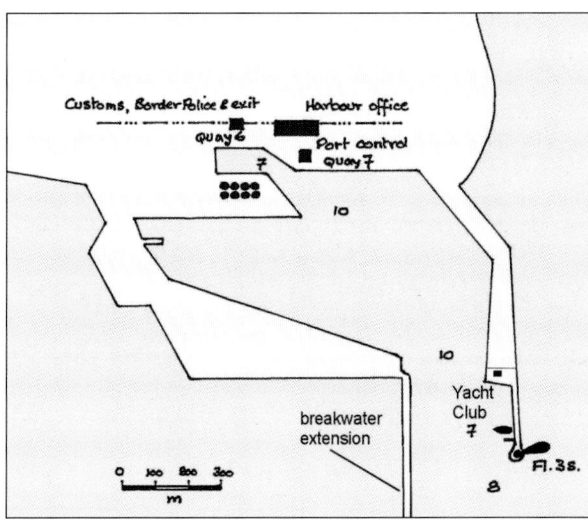

Yacht Club Port Burgas

*Depths* 6–7m at Yacht Club visitors' moorings.
*Shelter* Good, except in strong E winds when the swell causes a surge in the Yacht Club moorings.
*Authorities* Port of Entry (see berthing instructions above).
*Note* If heading S, Tsarevo is another option for clearing out to Turkey where officials are now stationed to process yachts. Special arrangements to have an official come down from Burgas are no longer necessary. This allows for a stop in Sozopol.
*Charges* A cruiser reported a charge of €12 for three nights in 2005.
*Contact information* Yacht Club Port Burgas, 1, Alexander Battenberg Street, Burgas 8000, Bulgaria ✆ +359 56 822302, *Fax* +359 56 822302; 840124 *Email* office@yachtclubportbourgas.org www.yachtclubportbourgas.org/

Several ship chandleries are located in Burgas. Ask at Yacht Club for current locations and contact information.

### Facilities

*Services* The Yacht Club Port Burgas was created in 1976 by a group of sailing enthusiasts and has a clubhouse with toilets, showers and a lounge and occasional social events. The Yacht Club actively promotes yachting and dinghy racing. They hosted a large, international youth regatta in September 2010. Water and electricity are available.
*Fuel* By jerry can and taxi.
*Repairs* Minor repairs can be arranged.
*Provisions* Small supermarket near the harbour entrance. A large Carrefour supermarket is located N of the city centre, reachable by bus or hire car (follow signs).
*Eating out* Numerous cafés, fast food stalls and restaurants line the pedestrian street leading to the seaside park.
*Other* Banks and ATMs near the railway station. Hire cars can be arranged across the street at the Hotel Burgas or from the airport. Buses to Burgas International Airport depart every 30 minutes from the bus terminal next to the railway station.

### General

With a population just under 200,000, Burgas is the second largest city on Bulgaria's Black Sea coast and an important commercial port. The port and the train station opened together in 1903, with the station located at the gates to the port. From a large square adjoining the train station, inter-city buses arrive and depart for Sofia and the resort towns along the coast. The upmarket quarter of the city begins right at the port. A few blocks inland is the main E–W street, Aleko Bogoridi Boulevard, a pedestrian thoroughfare with trendy shops, restaurants offering a wide range of European cuisine, and an ambiance which blends modernity with a very traditional European feel.

As the facilities for visiting yachts are currently quite limited in Burgas, and it is quite a long walk from the Yacht Club into the city, another option for visiting this interesting city is by bus (departing every 30 minutes) from Sozopol where there is a modern and secure marina facility. Nearby sites of interest include salt lakes which are good for bird watching.

## OTMANLI

42°26'·3N 27°31'·6E

Until recently, Otmanli was a fishing village with a harbour formed by two breakwaters at the mouth of a small river. Many modern vacation homes have been built along the beach. The harbour has silted to the point of being unusable by yachts, and the S breakwater is now in very bad condition.

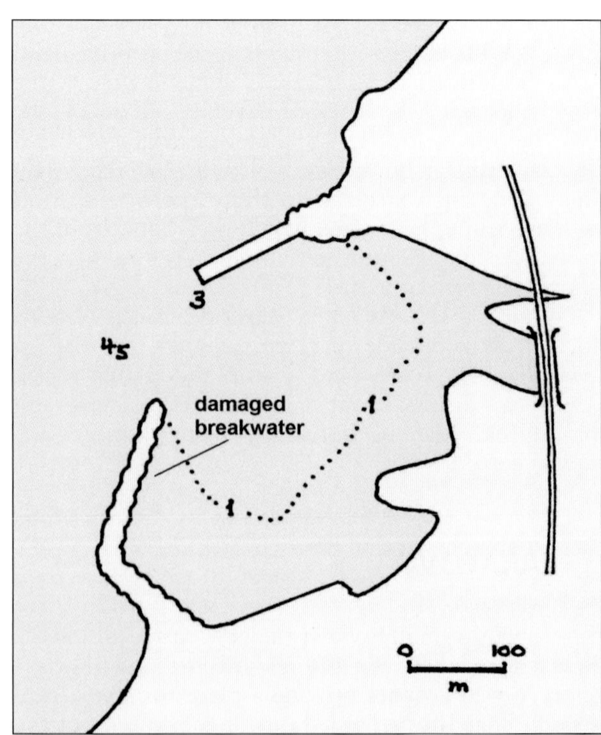


OTMANLI

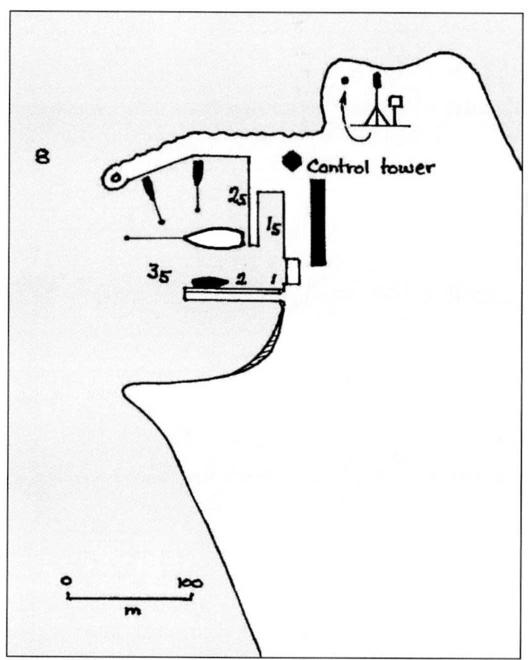


LUKOIL (NEFTOCHIM) MARINA

Sveti Anastasiya

## LUKOIL (NEFTOCHIM) MARINA

42°27′·45N 27°32′·2E

Lukoil is the largest oil company in the Russian Federation, and Lukoil's Neftochim Burgas refinery is the largest oil refinery in SE Europe and the largest industrial enterprise in Bulgaria, employing 8,500 people. The company has created a very small marina for employees' yachts, with water and electricity on pontoons.

## SVETI ANASTASIYA

42°28′·85N 27°33′·15E

This small, rocky island with a light structure and several buildings and surrounded by rocks and shallow patches in the Bay of Burgas, is only suitable as a daytime stop in settled weather. Yachts can anchor stern-to a small jetty on the S side of the island. The area inside the jetty is reserved for day charter trip boats from nearby resorts. Sveti Anastasiya is famous for the white rabbits that thrive on the island. A small church and simple restaurant are found ashore.

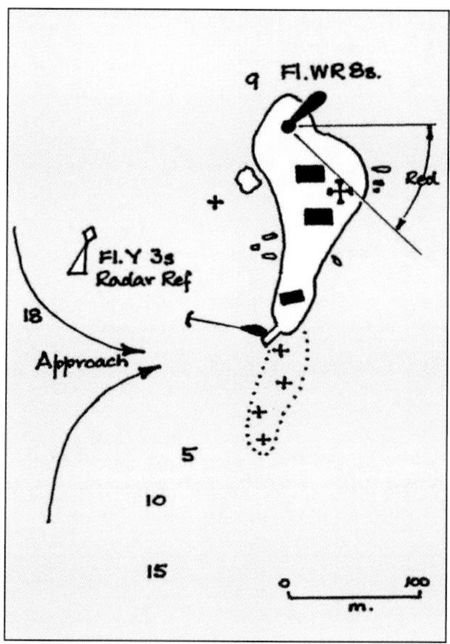


SVETI ANASTASIYA

## ⚓ CHERNOMORETS

42°27′·0N 27°38′·7E

A bay with a sandy beach and surrounded by a resort village. Two small quays are used by small fishing boats. Not a suitable overnight anchorage. Chernomorets can be visited conveniently by bus from Sozopol.

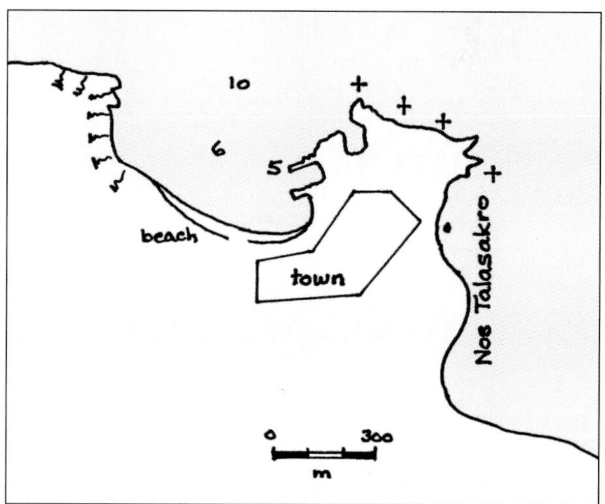


CHERNOMORETS

## SOZOPOL

42°25'·3N 27°41'·0E

### Approach

Located on the S side of the Bay of Burgas, the harbour is entered from the W, and the marina is located on the right as you enter the harbour.

*Conspicuous* The large building of the former naval college is easily seen as well as the breakwater extending to the SW.

*VHF* Ch 88 for Marina Port Sozopol

Dangers (1) St Ivan Island is located 0·5M N of Sozopol. Yachts can pass between the island and the mainland. (2) Fixed fishing nets outside the harbour in Sozopol Bay.

### Mooring

Marina Port Sozopol is a newly constructed, modern marina with floating pontoons which occupies the SW portion of this previously restricted military harbour. It is a safe place to leave a yacht and a relatively easy place to exchange crew (regular buses to Burgas where there are regular buses to the airport). Yachts can anchor to the SW of the inner breakwater, just outside the harbour with good shelter from prevailing wind and swell.

*Berths* 330 berths. The marina can accommodate vessels up to 25m. Berth where directed after contacting the marina office on VHF. Floating pontoons with tailed moorings.

*Depths* 6m in the marina.

*Shelter* Excellent.

*Authorities* Not a Port of Entry. Yachts should use Tsarevo if departing or arriving from the S. Marina staff available 24 hours a day.

*Marina charges* €21.00 per day for a 12m yacht.

*Contact information* Marina Port Sozopol, Stoyan Penev, Manager, ✆ +359 550 24033, +359 888 804674
*Fax* +359 550 22484
*Email* stoyan.penev@marinasozopol.com or info@marinasozopol.com
www.marinasozopol.com

### Facilities

*Services* Water and electricity at each slip. Toilets and showers in building near entrance gate to the marina. Public telephones at town square. Off-site laundry with wash/dry/fold service (ask for directions at marina office).

*Fuel* Available by tanker truck at the fuel dock to the right after entering the marina.

*Repairs* Hardstanding with crane. Mechanical and electrical repairs can be arranged. Small chandlery onsite.

*Provisions* Daily market with fresh vegetables in the town square. Minimarkets with speciality items (butcher, produce, deli, beer/wine/spirits, etc.) in market area on left as you walk into town from the marina. Other minimarkets and small supermarkets in historic district (old town) and modern section (new town) of the small city.

*Eating out* There is a simple café on the premises of Marina Sozopol, with a greater variety in the old and new sections of town. Fish restaurants and bars on the waterfront near the fishing harbour. There are also several restaurants on the peninsula, perched on the cliffs above the beach with excellent views.

*Other* PO, Bank and ATM in modern town. Cooking gas refills from station at the S end of the beach area in the modern town. Hire cars available from tour office on main street in modern town or in Burgas. Buses depart from the town square every 30 minutes to Burgas with connections to Burgas airport and other resort towns. The bus to Burgas stops in Chernomorets along the way.

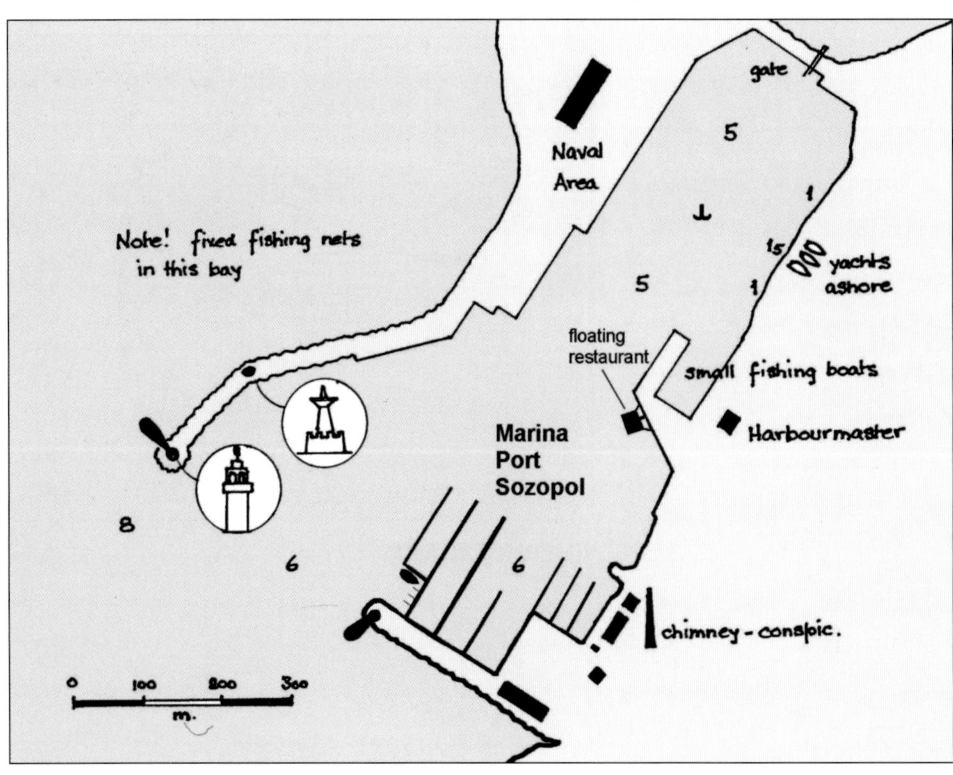


SOZOPOL

Sozopol Marina looking toward the former Naval Academy

Sozopol shoreline

Beach near Sozopol

## General

Like Balchik, Nessebar, and Pomorie to the N, Sozopol is a popular tourist destination and resort town with a long history. A tree-lined square connects the old town on the peninsula with the modern town on the hillside. A public park opens onto the beach. A pedestrian walkway, lined with small cafés and restaurants, follows the cliffs above the beach. The old town starts at the fountain where the three roads diverge, each leading to the far end of the peninsula. One passes along the fishing harbour where there are many choices for eating out. The Bulgarian Naval Academy, once located here, now sits abandoned on the hillside across the harbour from the old town. Many old Ottoman-style wooden houses can be seen on a walk around the peninsula.

The modern town has numerous hotels, holiday apartments, fast food stalls, restaurants and tour agencies catering to the booming tourist industry here. Although busy in summer months, the combination of a secure, full-service marina and the historic resort town make this a favourite stop among cruising sailors on the Black Sea.

***Passage note: Sozopol to the Turkish Border***

Along the coast from Sozopol to the Turkish border, Tsarevo is the only harbour offering secure shelter. Tsarevo is a Bulgarian port of entry whose officials are exceptionally friendly and efficient.

## DUNE (DUNI, DYUNI)

42°22'·2N 27°42'·8E

A jetty offers good shelter at the N end of a long bay. An all-inclusive resort, set amidst a nature reserve, is found ashore. The resort staff may allow you a short visit, but this is not a suitable overnight stop for foreign yachts.

## ⚓ ROPOTAMO

42°20'·0N 27°45'·1E

The Annans reported that there is a wonderful anchorage at the mouth of the River Ropotomo at the S end of a long sandy bay. The anchorage is difficult to spot but a monument on the headland is easily seen. Shelter is better than it first appears. Entrance is tricky due to rocks and underwater training wall for the river. Do not attempt to go alongside the small jetty, as it is very shallow. The river mouth is very shallow, but once over the bar, a dinghy can travel several miles upstream to a lake with giant water lilies. The area is a nature reserve and overnight restrictions may be in place for visiting yachts. The reserve's warden limits the number of small craft using the river but it may be possible to take a tourist boat trip upstream.

The reserve and protected area was extended to 5,500ha in 2002. The river was named after the Greek Goddess Ro and *potamo* (river). She is reputed to have charmed the pirates with her song, who in turn agreed to leave the area in peace.

## ⚓ ST PALASKEVA (ANGELICA)

42°19'·3N 27°47'·0E

Open to the east, this anchorage is considered dangerous in NE winds, and with uncertain holding, it is only suitable for a daytime stop for one yacht at anchor, or more if tied back to the shore, in settled or light SE winds. The remote setting in a rocky cut surrounded by cliffs is unique along this coast of the Black Sea.

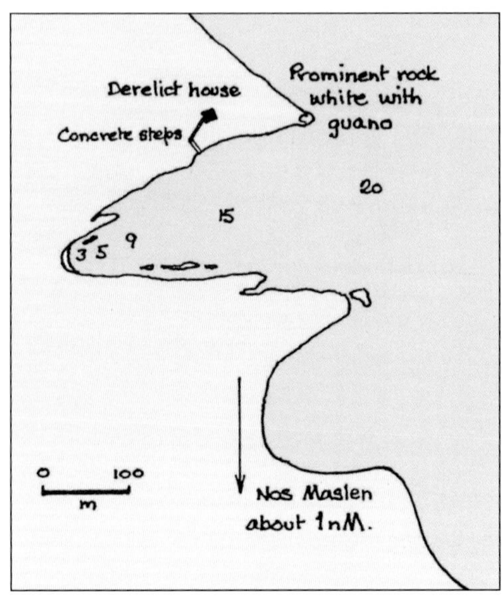


ST PALASKEVA (ANGELICA)

## ⚓ PRIMORSKO

42°15'·8N 27°45'·5E

An attractive spot, but there is no space to tie alongside the breakwater as this is used by day charter boats to pick up and drop off passengers. No

ROPOTAMO

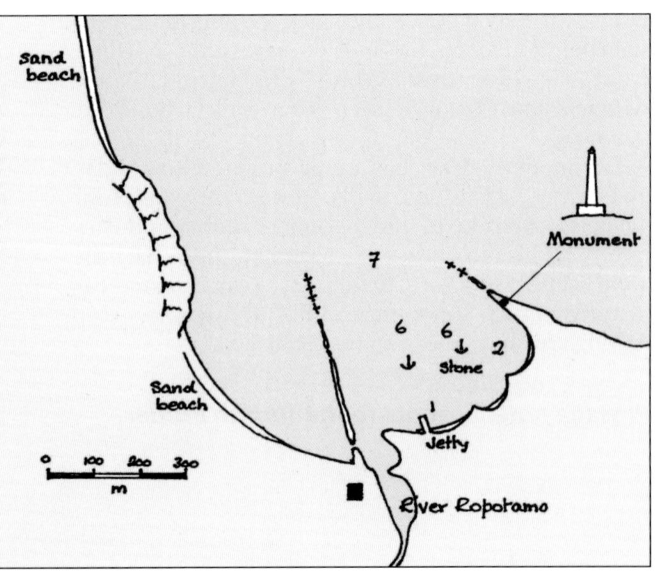


PRIMORSKO

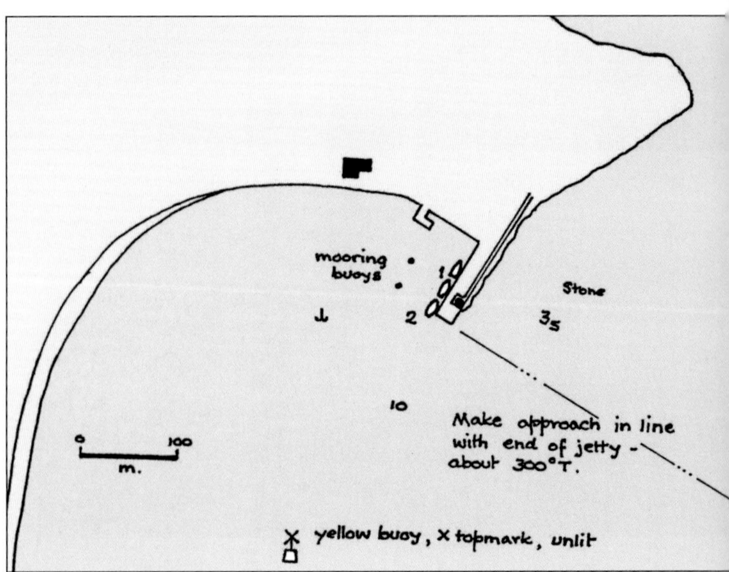

shelter from wind or waves. This is not suitable for overnight stops except in settled conditions. There are no services available. However, it is reported that the harbourmaster operates a hoist here and speaks German. Local yachtsmen recommend anchoring in the bay and taking a dinghy ashore to visit the town and beach.

## KITEN

42°14'·0N 27°46'·85E

A small harbour lies behind the breakwater and is easily seen in front of the hotels and apartment buildings on the hillside. The harbour is very crowded with local boats with no spaces set aside for visiting yachts. There is a small yacht club with a clubhouse, restaurant and friendly staff which may be able to accommodate a small yacht. They will indicate where to moor.

Dangers (1) The Annans reported a very dangerous rock with less than 1m over it in position 42°13'·5N 27°47'·8E. In calm weather, it cannot be seen. With fresh winds and swell, it breaks but not heavily. The rock is located 0·85M SE of the harbour. (2) Fixed nets are in place E of the breakwater.

### KITEN

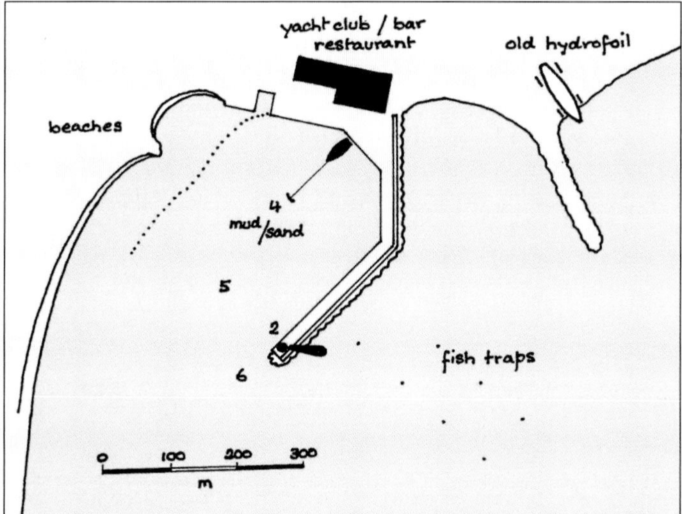

Approach to Tsarevo

## TSAREVO (CAREVO or MIČURIN)

42°10'·15N 27°51'·6E

### Approach

This harbour is the most convenient port of entry when arriving from the S.

*Conspicuous* A yellow and black beacon with a light marking rocks to SE of harbour entrance and a red-roofed church on the headland can be seen in the approaches.

*VHF* Ch 16 for harbourmaster and port authorities (not necessary to call in advance)

Dangers (1) Rocks SE of the harbour in position 42°10'·1N 27°52'·1E are not shown on charts. The rocks extend from a beacon E of the harbour in a SE direction toward shore. (2) Offlying rocks along shore on headland NE of harbour entrance.

### Mooring

Several berths are set aside for visiting yachts along the N quay of this excellent harbour.

*Berth* Where directed by the harbourmaster, usually beneath the large sign. Tailed moorings.

*Depths* 5m at the mooring position.

*Shelter* Good.

*Authorities* Port of Entry. Harbourmaster.

*Contact information* None available.

Tsarevo harbour

Welcome to Bulgaria

9. BULGARIA

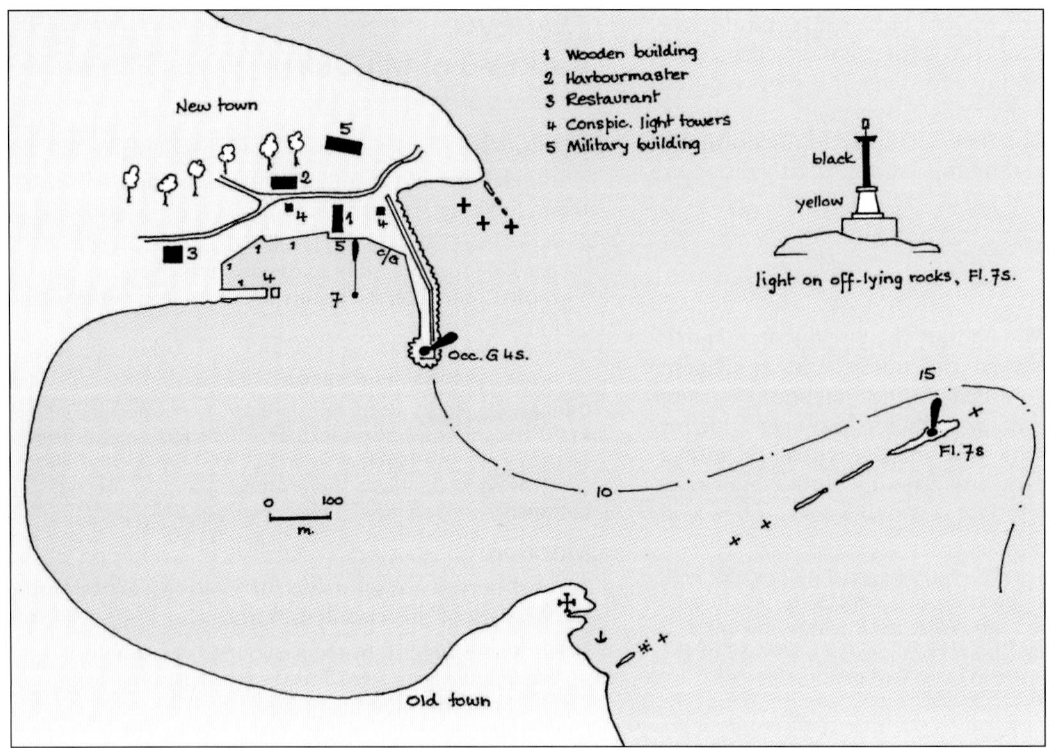

TSAREVO

## Facilities

The yacht harbour is operated by the town where visiting yachts are most welcome. The friendly harbourmaster is helpful and will assist with any of your needs.

*Services* Water and electricity available at visitors' berths on the quay.
*Fuel* By jerry can and taxi.
*Repairs* Minor mechanical repairs can be arranged. A factory producing fibreglass boats is located in the vicinity and may be able to arrange fibreglass repairs.
*Provisions* Small supermarket, minimarket, bakery, and fruit and vegetable stands in the town to the W of the harbour. The fruit and vegetable market offers fresh produce and is situated in the gardens behind the large, blue-domed church.
*Eating out* A small, open-air café located at the end of the harbour is reported to serve good food and local beer.
*Other* Post office, bank, ATM, internet café and bus station in town.

## General

The Tsars Ferdinand and Boris bathed here in the 19th century and the village was called Tsarevo after them. The name may also be in honour of Tsar Boris because he financed the construction of a new wharf in 1927–1937. Between 1950 and 1991, it was known as Mičurin, in honour of the Soviet botanist Ivan Vladimirovich Mičurin.

Steps lead up from the harbour to a small, seaside resort town where many shops are spread between well kept squares and gardens. A pedestrian area runs E–W through the compact town. Several bays near the harbour are used by local yachts for day anchorages.

## AHTOPOL

42°06'·1N 27°57'·1E

A jetty which serves as the only mooring for yachts is in very bad condition and has shallow water alongside. Anchoring is not recommended due to bad holding in stones and rock. No convenient services are available. This harbour is located south of the port of entry in Tsarevo.

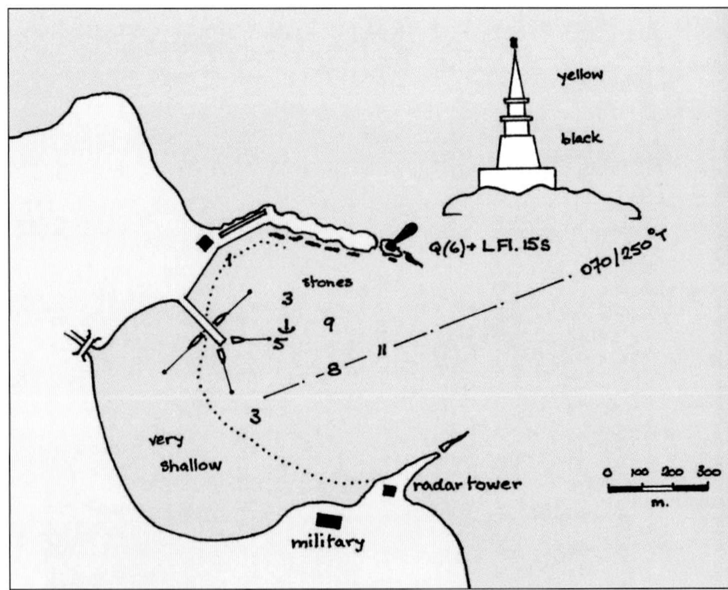


AHTOPOL

# 10. Turkey west of the Bosphorus

### *Passage note: Bulgarian Border to Bosphorus*

This is a lovely coast and should be interesting to explore, but most yachts are in bureaucratic limbo when transiting the Turkish coast between the Bulgarian border and the Bosphorus. Because Iğneada is not (yet) a port of entry for Turkey, yachts that stop in one of the places described below will not have cleared in, if coming from Bulgaria. Likewise, yachts coming from the Bosphorus which have cleared out of Turkey in Istanbul, do not have proper clearance to stop in at ports along this stretch of coast. As long as yachtsmen are following proper clearance procedures by clearing out of Bulgaria or Turkey, port authorities will usually permit a stop at one or more of the ports (including Poyrazköy on the Bosphorus). They should be kept informed of your plans and might not allow you to go ashore, so plan accordingly. Ship's papers may be requested upon arrival in port.

Most southbound yachts can complete the 67M passage from Iğneada to Poyrazköy in a long day with favourable wind and current helping out. The coastline is generally low-lying fronted by attractive beaches with very few houses. During the summer, the wind is generally N, producing a swell which makes all the harbours except Iğneada difficult or untenable for yachts during the day, after the wind picks up. At Dalyan Burnu, 5M W of the Bosphorus, the coast becomes higher. Türklifeneri Light, GpFl(2)12s, marks the NW point of the Bosphorus, near the Clashing Rocks. Poyrazköy is the fishing harbour offering the best shelter for yachts at the mouth of the Bosphorus. The harbour of Rumelifeneri is reserved for fishing boats and does not welcome yachts.

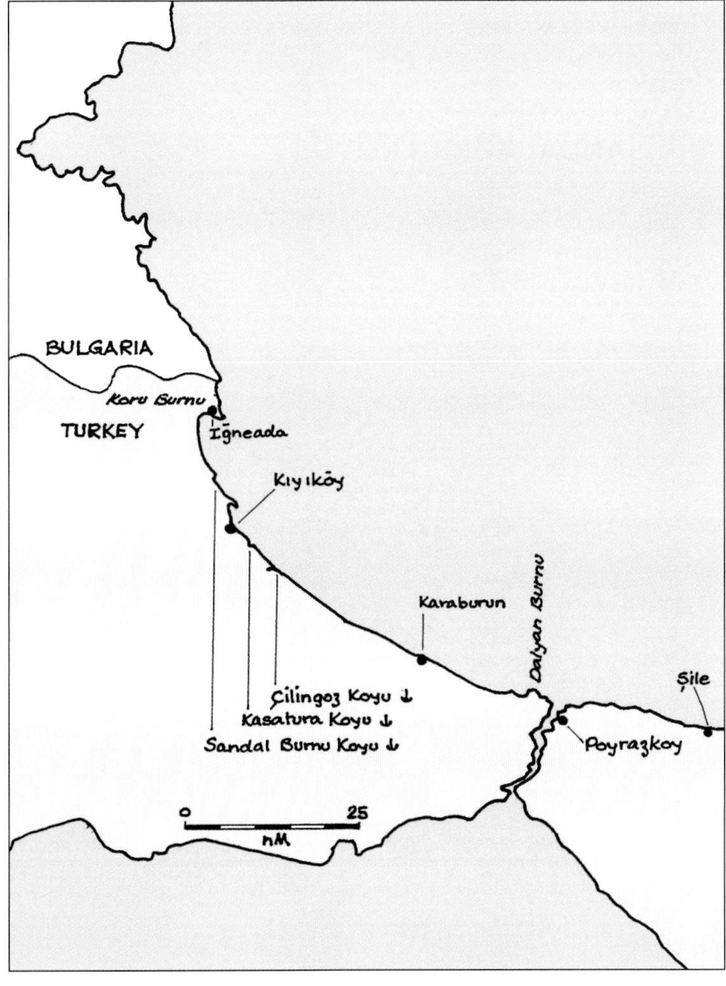


BULGARIAN BORDER TO BOSPHORUS

## IĞNEADA

41°53'·2N 28°01'·2E

### Approach

Iğneada is situated at the NW corner of a S-facing bay created by Koru Burnu sheltering it from the prevailing NE and NW winds. Once rounding Koru Burnu from the N, the breakwaters of the harbour are easily seen. From the S, the harbour is at the N end of a large sandy bay and 1·5M NE of the town of Iğneada. The scar from mining operations on the hillside behind the harbour is conspicuous.

Dangers (1) A wreck with masts and superstructure above the water is located about 1M SE of the end of the main breakwater at a bearing of 160°. The wreck is marked by a yellow buoy with an x topmark and yellow flashing light which lies 0·5M SW of the wreck. (2) Some silting has

Iğneada

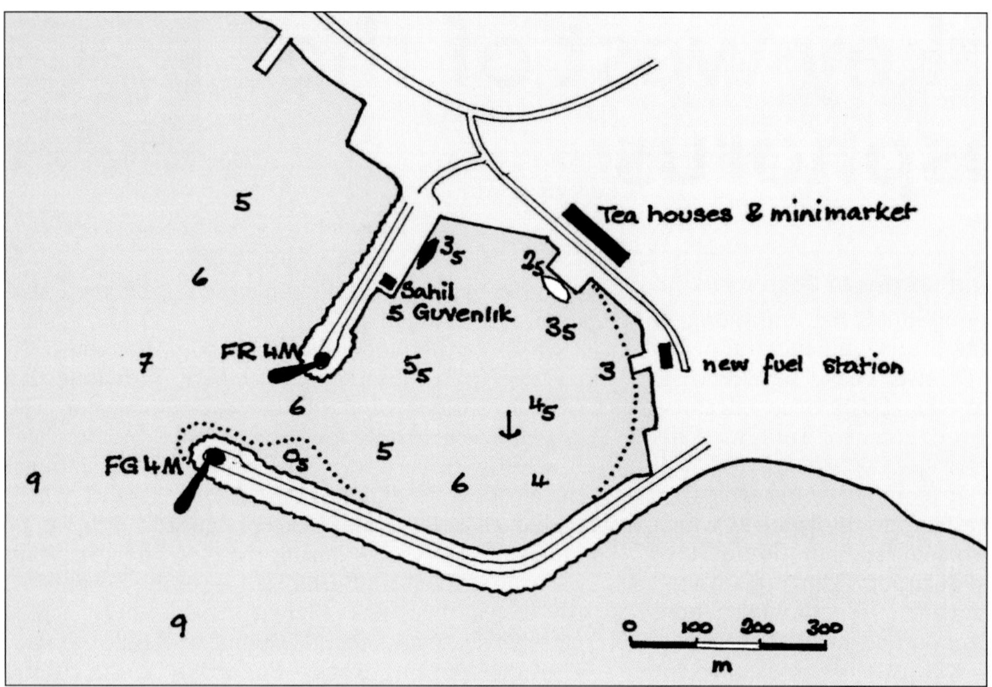


IĞNEADA

occurred inside the main breakwater but is easily avoided by keeping in the middle of the entrance or by favouring the inner breakwater.

### Mooring

The purpose-built fishing harbour provides excellent shelter, either at anchor in 5m or alongside the NW quay, north of the Sahil Güvenlik. The bottom is sand and mud with thick weeds. Whether at anchor or at the quay, the Sahil Güvenlik will visit your yacht and request ship's papers. Iğneada is no longer a port of entry.

### Facilities

The harbourmaster is friendly and welcoming to visiting yachts. Water and electricity is available at the quay by arrangement with the harbourmaster. Petrol is available from the new fuel station. Diesel can be obtained by mini-tanker or jerry can and taxi.

Anchor fouled with seaweed in Iğneada

### General

The busy fishing harbour has several restaurants, a tea house and a small minimarket. The main town is a popular beach resort 5km by road from the harbour. If walking along this road, you will likely be offered a ride into town which can supply all basic needs.

## ⚓ SANDAL BURNU KÖYÜ

41°44'·15N 28°02'·35E

This small bay between Iğneada and Kiyiköy is sheltered by a headland which makes it suitable for a daytime stop in settled weather with W or SW wind.

SANDAL BURNU KÖYÜ

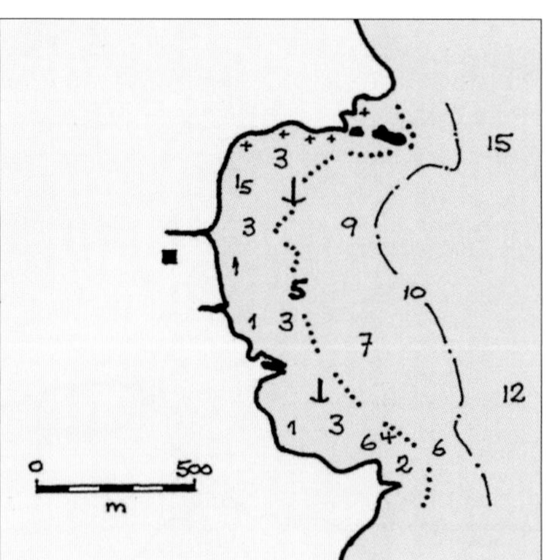

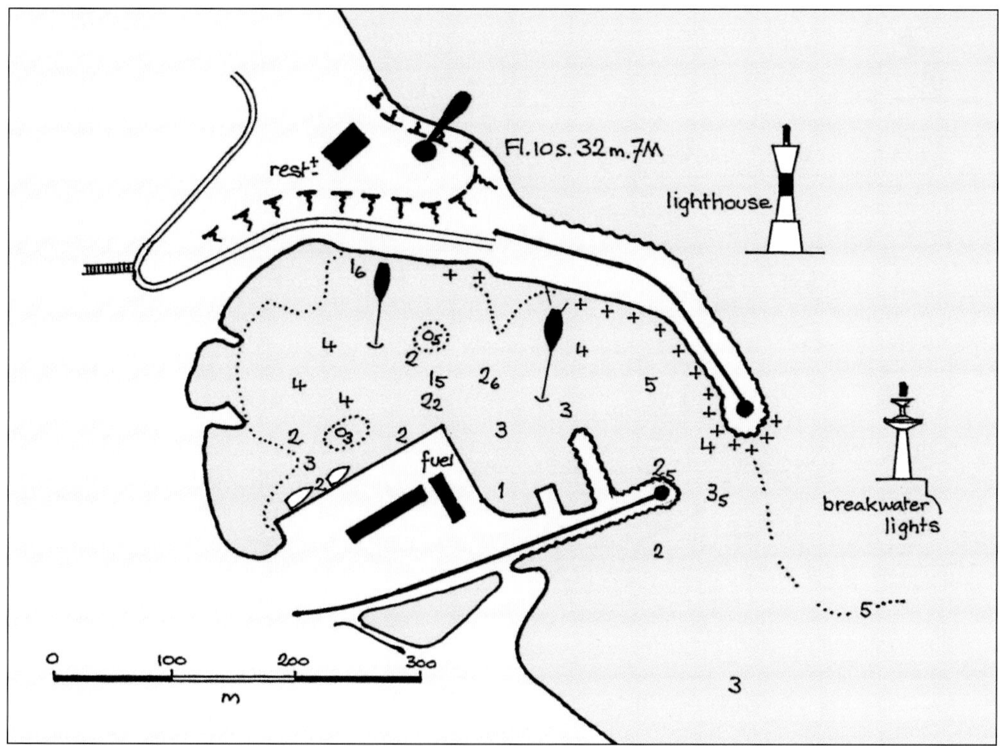


KIYIKÖY (MIDYE)

## KIYIKÖY (MIDYE)

41°38'·0N 28°06'·2E

When approaching from the N, give Kayla Burnu a reasonable offing. Rocks lie off the end of both breakwaters and a shallow patch with 0·5m depths is located in the middle of the harbour with 2m or less extending south toward the quay. A heavy onshore swell would make this harbour hazardous.

There is room to anchor or tie stern-to the N breakwater. The southern breakwater is shallow with rocky patches. Fuel is no longer available at this quay. Steps lead to the town where all provisions can be found. A fish restaurant near the lighthouse above the harbour is popular with people making day trips from Istanbul.

## ⚓ KASTURA KÖYÜ (KASTRO)

41°35'·4N 28°00'·0E

This sandy bay with a small islet at the north end is a popular picnic area and provides a scenic anchorage. An attractive river flows into the bay which can be explored by dinghy or local boats available for hire. The sand beach is reported to be unsafe for swimming due to a dangerous undertow. A restaurant serves simple Turkish meals ashore.

## ⚓ CILINGOZ KÖYÜ

41°31'·4'N 28°13'·5E

This is a small bay with clear water and a golden sand beach lined with some holiday homes. It is suitable for a daytime stop in settled weather.

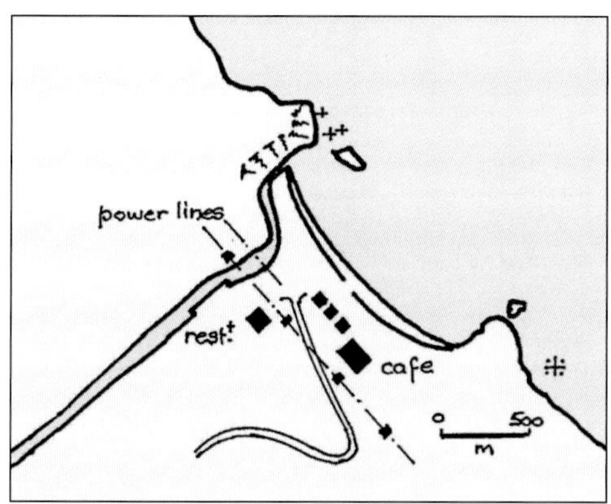


KASTURA KÖYÜ (KASTRO)

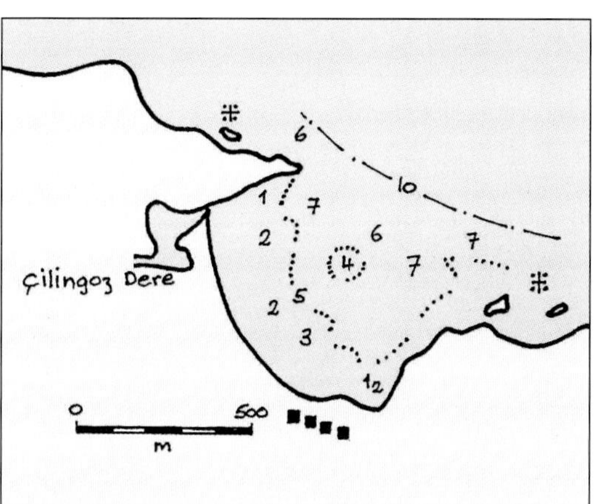


CILINGOZ KÖYÜ

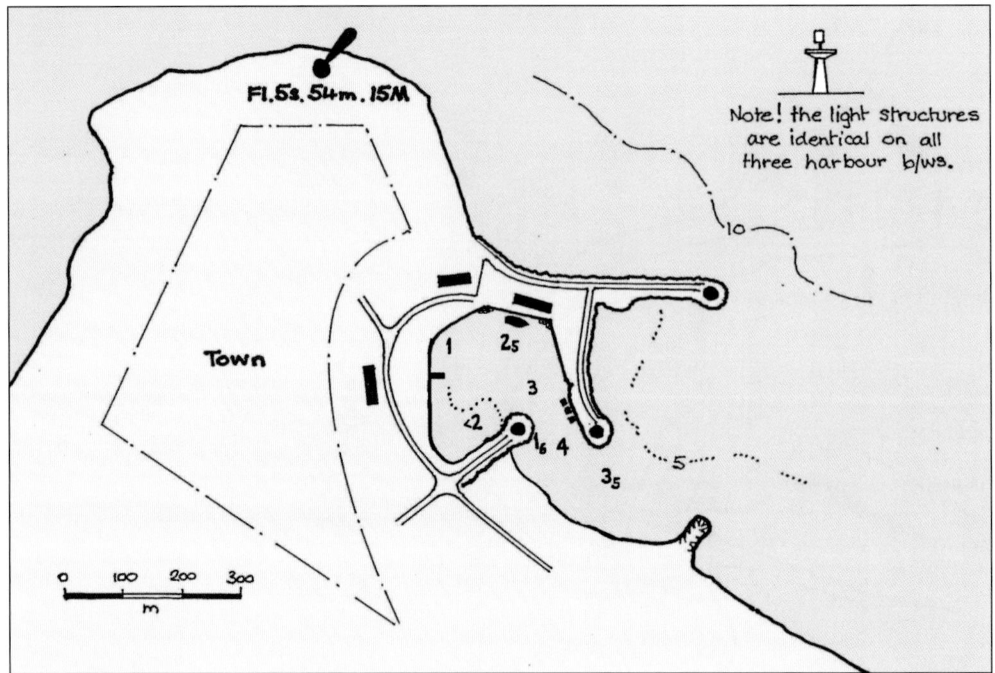


KARABURUN

## KARABURUN

41°20'·6N 28°41'·3E

The three structures seen on the breakwaters are misleading in the approach. From the north, a yacht passes two breakwaters before the entrance is seen. The harbour entrance was dredged in 2008 with 3·5m least depths reported in the centre and is suitable in settled weather. Restaurants serving fish are located at the south end of the harbour.

Southbound in the Bosphorus

Bosphorus from the NW

# Appendix

## I. Suppliers of charts and publications

In the United Kingdom British Admiralty charts are available from:

**BRITISH ADMIRALTY CHARTS**

**United Kingdom Hydrographic Office**

www.ukho.gov.uk – homepage of the United Kingdom Hydrographic Office, including free, downloadable weekly *Notices to Mariners* and the entire Admiralty Chart Catalogue. Orders for UKHO charts and publications must be placed with official agents.

**Imray Laurie Norie & Wilson Ltd**
Wych House, St Ives, Huntingdon
Cambridgeshire PE27 5BT
✆ +44 (0)1480 62114
*Fax* +44 (0)1480 496109
www.imray.com

**RUSSIAN CHARTS**

**RUSSIAN FEDERATION**

**Morintech Ltd**
6 Prospekt Kima,
199155 Saint Petersburg
✆ /*Fax* +7 812 3254048
✆ +7 812 3238528
*Email* support@morintech.ru
www.dkart.com/ & www.morintech.spb.su

**TURKISH CHARTS**

**Seyir Hidrografi ve Oşinografi**
Dairesi Başkanlığı, 34805 Çubuklu, Istanbul
www.shodb.gov.tr

## II. General declaration on arrival and departure

| | | |
|---|---|---|
| YACHT NAME: | LENGTH: | metres |
| TYPE: | BEAM: | metres |
| FLAG: | DRAFT: | metres |

REGISTRATION NO:

PORT OF REGISTRY:

ENTRY/DEPARTURE PORT:
DATE/TIME:

LAST PORT/NEXT PORT:

Items to be declared:

There are no firearms, narcotics or other dangerous or prohibited substances onboard.

There are no stowaways onboard.

There are no pets onboard.

There are no communicable diseases.

There are no rats onboard.

CAPTAIN:
SHIP'S STAMP

SIGNATURE:

ENTRY/DEPARTURE APPROVAL:

## III. Crew list

Yacht Name:
Flag:
Registered Number:

| Family Name | Given Name | Date of Birth | Nationality | Passport Number |
|---|---|---|---|---|

Owner/Captain's Name:

Signature:
Date:

APPENDIX

## IV. Abbreviations used on Russian charts

| | |
|---|---|
| IALA System A | МАМС |
| List of Lights | список маяков |
| Light | свет/огонь |

**Structures**

| | |
|---|---|
| Lighthouse | маяк (Мк) |
| Light vessel | пл. Мк |
| Radiobeacon (RC) | РМк |
| Beacon | зн |
| Column | колонна |
| Framework tower | ажурная установка ферма |
| House | дом |
| Building | здание, домик |
| Hut | будка |
| Mast | мачта |
| Post | столб |
| Tower | башня (бня) |
| Concrete | бетон(ный) |
| Iron | желез(ный) |
| Metal | металл(ический) |
| Stone | камен(ный) |
| Wooden | дерев(янный) |
| Band | горизонтальная полоса |
| Stripe | вертикальная полоса |
| Destroyed | разруш(енный) |
| Occasional | случ(айный) |

**Lights**

| | |
|---|---|
| Temporary | времен(ный) |
| Extinguished | погаш(енный) |
| F | П |
| Oc | Зтм |
| Iso | Изо |
| Fl | Пр |
| Q | Ч. Пр |
| IQ | прер. Ч. Пр |
| Al | пер |
| Oc(...) | Гр. Зтм |
| Fl(...) | Гр. Пр |
| F.Fl | П. Пр |
| FlFl(...) | П. Гр. Пр |
| LFl | Дл. Пр |
| Sec | С |
| Leading light | Ств. |

**Examples**

| | |
|---|---|
| Fl.7s8M | Пр 7С 8М |
| Iso.7M | Изо 7М |
| Fl(3)WR.15s12/10M | Пр(3)15С12/10М |
| Q.5M | Ч. Пр5М |
| Leading light, Q | Ств Ч. Пр |
| Leading light, Iso | Ств Изо |

**Supplementary information**

| | |
|---|---|
| Whistle | (Рев) |
| Horn | (Н) |
| Gong | (гонг) |
| Bell | (К) |
| Explosive | (В) |
| Cannon | (П) |
| Reed | (Г) |
| Siren | (С) |

**Colours**

| | |
|---|---|
| Black | чр. |
| Violet | фл. |
| Blue | сн. |
| Green | зл. |
| Orange | ор. |
| Red | кр. |
| White | бл. |
| Yellow | жл. |
| Brown | кч. |
| Grey | ср. |
| Pale blue | гл. |

Or abbreviated as in:

| | |
|---|---|
| Black/red/black | ч к ч |
| Black/yellow/black | ч ж ч |
| Yellow/black/yellow | ж ч ж |
| Red/white | к б |

**Bottom**

| | |
|---|---|
| Bottom | грунт |
| Broken, cracked | б |
| Pebbles, shingle | гк |
| Clay | гл |
| Gravel, sand with small stones | гр |
| Mud, silt, sludge | И |
| Clay, mud, silt | гл. И |
| Lime | Изв |
| Stone | К |
| Small stones | мК |
| Large stone, boulders | кК |
| Shallow | м |
| Soft | мг |
| Coarse | к |
| Hard, firm | т |
| Sand | П |
| Fine sand | мП |
| Coarse sand | кП |
| Plate, slab | Пл |
| Shells | Р |
| Cliff, rock face | С |
| Medium, average | с |
| Weed | вд |
| Firm, fine sand and mud | тмПИ |
| Magnetic variation | Магн. скл |
| (former) spoil dumping ground | (бывшая) свалка грунта |

# V. Conversion tables

1 inch = 2·54 centimetres (roughly 4in = 10cm)
1 centimetre = 0·394 inches
1 foot = 0·305 metres (roughly 3ft = 1m)
1 metre = 3·281 feet
1 pound = 0·454 kilograms (roughly 10lbs = 4·5kg)
1 kilogram = 2·205 pounds
1 mile = 1·609 kilometres (roughly 10 miles = 16km)
1 kilometre = 0·621 miles
1 nautical mile = 1·1515 miles
1 mile = 0·8684 nautical miles
1 acre = 0·405 hectares (roughly 10 acres = 4 hectares)
1 hectare = 2·471 acres
1 gallon = 4·546 litres (roughly 1 gallon = 4·5 litres)
1 litre = 0·220 gallons

## Temperature scale

t°F to t°C = $\frac{t°F - 32 \times 5}{9}$

t°C to t°F = $\frac{t°C \times 9}{5} + 32$

So:

70°F = 21·1°C    20°C = 68°F
80°F = 26·7°C    30°C = 86°F
90°F = 32·2°C    40°C = 104°F

**WIND SCALES**

| *Beaufort* | *Wind Description* | *Effect on Sea* | *Effect on Land* | *Wind speed (knots)* | *m/sec* |
|---|---|---|---|---|---|
| 0 | Calm | Sea like a mirror | Smoke rises vertically | <1 | – |
| 1 | Light air | Ripples like scales, no crests | Direction of wind shown by smoke | 1–3 | 2 |
| 2 | Light breeze | Small wavelets, crests do not break | Wind felt on face, leaves rustle | 4–6 | 2–3 |
| 3 | Gentle breeze | Large wavelets, some crests break | Wind extends light flags | 7–10 | 3–5 |
| 4 | Moderate breeze | Small waves, frequent white horses | Small branches move | 11–16 | 5–8 |
| 5 | Fresh breeze | Moderate waves, many white horses | Small trees sway | 17–21 | 8–11 |
| 6 | Strong breeze | Large waves form, white crests | Large branches move | 22–27 | 11–14 |
| 7 | Near gale | Sea heaps up, white foam from breaking waves | Whole trees in motion | 28–33 | 14–17 |
| 8 | Gale | Moderately high waves some spindrift. Foam blown with wind | Twigs break from trees, difficult to walk | 34–40 | 17–20 |
| 9 | Strong gale | High waves, dense foam, wave crests topple, spray may affect visibility | Slight structural damage | 41–47 | 20–24 |
| 10 | Storm | Very high waves, sea appears white, visibility affected | Trees uprooted, structural damage | 48–55 | 24–27 |
| 11 | Violent storm | Exceptionally high waves, long white patches of foam, crests blown into froth | Widespread damage | 56–63 | 28–31 |
| 12 | Hurricane | The air is filled with foam, visibility very seriously affected | Widespread structural damage | 64+ | 32– |

# Index


Abana, 68-9
*abbreviations (Russian charts)*, 200
Abkhazia, 3, 8, 10, 29, 31, 129
*Achilles*, 163
*Admiralty Sailing Directions*, 13
Ağva (Yeşilçay), 42-3
Ahtopol, 194
*AIS*, 18
Akçaabat, 103
Akçakale, 11, 102
Akçakoca, 8, 11, 47-8
Akliman, 9, 10, 11, 72-3
Alaçam, 79
Alapli, 48
*alcohol*, 16
*algal blooms*, 20, 22-3, 24
Alushta, 141
Amasra, 9, 10, 11, 56-8
*Amazons*, 85
*Ana YC (Eforie Nord)*, 8, 11, 162, 165, 168-9
Anapa, 133
*Apollonia*, 46
*Apollonius of Rhodes*, 26, 46, 85, 128
Arakli, 108-9
Ardeşen, 115-16
Arhavi, 117
*Arrian*, 10, 17, 27
Artek, 140
*Ataköy Marina YC (AMYC)*, 3, 12, 13
Ayancik, 71
Ayandon Burnu, 69

Baba Burnu (Olüce Burnu), 50
Bafra Burnu, 9, 25, 79-81
Bağirganlik, 43
Bağirganlik Köyü, 43
Balaclava, 10, 11, 147-9
Balchik, 6, 11, 176-8
Balikli, 109
*ballast water*, 22, 23, 24
Bartin Limani, 11, 55-6
*bathymetry*, 21-2
Batumi, 6, 10, 31, 121, 122-5
*beaches*, 6, 15, 32
*Beaufort scale*, 201
Belediye Köyü, 84
Belgorod-Dnestrovsky, 160
Beşikdüzü, 99-100
*Black Sea Commission*, 30
*Black Sea Economic Co-operation (BSEC)*, 31
*Blue Flag Marinas*, 8
Bolaman, 88
*books & guides*, 3, 13-14, 17, 38
*border disputes*, 28-9
Bosphorus, 2, 5, 21, 30
Bozgaca Isklesi/Köyü, 42
*Bucharest Convention*, 30
Bug River, 20
Bulancak, 94
Bulgaria, 2, 3, 6, 29, 31, 171-94
  *cruising routes*, 8, 10
  *harbours suitable for yachts*, 11, 172
  *ports of entry*, 6, 7, 173
Burgas/Bay, 6, 8, 11, 31, 174, 183, 187-8
Byala, 182

Çakraz Burun/Köyü, 58-9
Çam Burnu, 96, 97
Cambu Köyü, 59
Çamburnu, 110-111
Cape Constanţa, 165
Cape Emine, 175, 183
Cape Kaliyakra, 175
Cape Midia, 165
Cape Singol, 165
Cape Tuzla, 165
Çarşibaşi, 100-101
Catalkaya (Gülyali), 93
Çatalkaya Köyü (*near* Amasra), 59
Çatalzeytin (Konakli Liman), 69
Cavusoğlu (Medreseönü), 90
Çayeli, 114
Çaylioğlu, 10, 11, 70-71
Cehan, 31
*cellphones*, 18-19, *see also start of each chapter*
*Certificate of Competence*, 17
*Certificate of Private Yacht Registration (transit log)*, 37, 38, 137
*chartplotter*, 18
*charts*, 18, 199, 200
*chemistry & salinity*, 23
Chernomorets, 189
Chernomorskoe, 11, 154-5
Chilia Channel (Danube Delta), 26
Cide, 10, 11, 63-4
Cilingoz Köyü, 197
Civa Burnu, 84, 85
Clashing Rocks, 39-40
*coastguards*, 29-30
*coastline*, 2-3, 6, 21, *see also start of each chapter*
*commercial fishing*, 32
*commercial harbours*, 11
*commercial shipping*, 30-31
*communications*, 18-19, *see also start of each chapter*
*conflicts*, 28-9
Constanţa, 6, 8, 11, 165, 166-8
*conversion tables*, 201
*Coptic Calendar*, 19
Crimean Peninsula, 2, 6-7, 9-10, 25, 146-55
*cruise ships*, 11
*cruising guides*, 13-14
*cruising routes*, 8-10, *see also start of each chapter*
*cultures*, 28, *see also start of each chapter*
*currency*, 15, *see also start of each chapter*
*currents*, 5, 22, 23

Danube Delta, 3, 8, 25, 26, 160, 162, 163, 165
*Danube Delta Biosphere Reserve Authority (DDBRA)*, 26, 164, 165
Danube River, 5, 20, 21, 23
Değirmenağzi Köyü, 51
Delfin Marina, 179-80
Dereköy, 81-2
Derepazar (Iyidere), 111-12
Dikili Köyü, 59
Dinevi Marina (Sveti Vlas), 8, 11
*diving*, 174
Dnevstrovskiy Liman, 160, 162
Dnieper River, 11, 20, 25
Dniester River, 20, 25
*documentation*, 17-18, 199, *see also start of each chapter*
Doğancilar, 53
Doğanyurt, 10, 11, 64-6
*dolphins*, 24-5
Don River, 21, 25
Donuslav, Lake, 154
*dress*, 15-16
Dune (Duni, Dyuni), 192
Dzharilgach Island, 2-3, 20, 155-6

Eferli (Ordu), 91-2
Eforie Nord, 8, 11, 165, 168-9
*entrance, travel & exit formalities*, 17-18, *see also start of each chapter*
*environment & pollution*, 22-3, 30-31
*equipment*, 12-15
Ereğli, 6, 8, 9, 11, 49-50
*European Union*, 6, 31
*eutrophication*, 22-3, 24
Euxineograd (Evksinograd), 180

Fatsa, 87-8
Feodosia, 6, 10, 144-5
*ferries*, 30
Filyos, 9, 10, 11
Filyos (Hisarönü), 53-4
*fish*, 23-4, 25
*fishing, commercial*, 32
*fishing harbours*, 11
*flags*, 17-18
*food & drink*, 16, *see also start of each chapter*
*formalities*, 17-18, 199, *see also start of each chapter*
*fuel*, 15
Fyndykly, 116

*gales*, 19
Garipçe, 39-40
Gelendijk (Gelencik), 132
Gemiciler, 68
*geography*, 20-21
*geology*, 21
Georgia, 3, 29, 30, 31, 119-29
  *climate*, 6
  *cruising routes*, 10
  *harbours suitable for yachts*, 10
  *ports of entry*, 6, 120-21
Georgievskiy, 149
Gerze, 11, 76-7
Gideros Limani, 9, 62
*gifts*, 16-17
Giresun, 6, 9, 10, 11, 94-6
Giresun Adası (Island), 96
*Global Environment Facility (GEF)*, 23
Göktepe, 48
Golden Sands Marina (Zlatni Pjasci), 178-9
Golden Symbol Marina (Balaclava), 148
Görele, 99
*GPS*, 4, 18
*Greeks, ancient*, 26-7
Gülyali (Catalkaya), 93

Gündoğdu Shipyard, 47
Gürgenlik Liman (Zarbana), 66
Güzelce Hisar Köyü, 55

Hamsilos (Hamsi Cove), 71-2
*harbours & marinas*, 4, 6, 10-11, *see also start of each chapter*
*health & medical*, 16, *see also start of each chapter*
Helaldi (New Harbour), 70
Hisarönü (Filyos), 53-4
*history*, 26-7, 28, *see also start of each chapter*
*holiday resorts*, 6, 15, 30, 32
*Homer*, 26
Hopa, 6, 7, 11, 117-18, 121
*hydrology*, 22-3

Iğneada, 6, 7, 195-6
Iliksu Köyü, 51
Ilyichevsk, 160, 162
Imrenli Köyü, 42
Inebolu, 6, 9, 10, 11, 66-7
*international organisations*, 30-31
*international relations*, 28-9
Işikli Burnu Liman, 101-2
Istanbul, 30, 31
Iyidere (Derepazar), 111-12
Izmail, 6, 160, 162

*Jason & the Argonauts*, 26, 85, 90
Jason's Cape (Yasun Burnu), 9, 90
*jellyfish*, 24, 155

Kabakum Bisser (Sunny Beach), 179
Kakoren/Yakaören, 68
Kapan Burnu Köyü, 55
Kara Burnu (Karaburun), 41
*Kara Burnu (Karaburun (placename)*, 41
Karaburun (Turkey W of Bosphorus), 7, 198
Karadag Nature Reserve, 143
Karasu (Sakarya) Shipbuilding Harbour, 47
Kastura Köyü (Kastro), 197
Kavarna, 175-6
*KAYRA Rallies*, *vii*, 3, 5, 12-13
Kedi Adası Köyü, 55
Kefken, 8, 9, 11, 44-5
Kefken Adası, 45-6
Kemelpaşa, 118, 121
Kerch Strait, 3, 10, 21, 145
Kerempe Burnu, 64
Kerpe, 44
Kiev, 11
Kilimli (E of Zonguldak), 53
Kilimli Köyü (E of Yeşilçay), 43
Kişlaönü (Perşembe), 91-2
Kiten, 193
Kiyiköy (Midye), 197
*Kizil Burnu (placename)*, 41
Kizilirmak River & Delta, 9, 25, 80
Kobuleti Reserves, 26
Koktobel, 143
Kolkheti National Park & Wetlands, 25, 26, 128
Konakli Liman (Çatalzeytin), 69
Köşeağzi Köyü, 50
Kozlu Zonguldak, 51
Kuban River, 21, 25
Kulevi, 31, 129
Kumbaşi (Ordu), 9, 11, 91-2
Kurotnoye, 142-3
Kurucaşile, 11, 60-61

Lake Donuslav, 154
Lake Paleostomi, 26
*languages*, 28, *see also start of each chapter*
Laspi, 147
*laundry*, 15
*local currency*, 15, *see also start of each chapter*
*local customs*, 15-16
*local weather lore*, 19
Lukoil (Neftochim) Marina, 189

Mangalia, 6, 11, 165, 169-70
*marinas* see *harbours & marinas*
*marine life*, 2, 20, 23-5
*Marmara Offshore YC*, 3, 12
Massandra (Yalta Commercial Port), 139-40
*medical & health*, 16, *see also start of each chapter*
Medreseönü (Cavusoğlu), 90
Mersin Perşembe, 90-91
Midia, 165, 166
Midye (Kiyiköy), 197
*military exercises*, 18, 29
Mis Tendrov, 157
*mobile phones*, 18-19, *see also start of each chapter*
*money*, 15, *see also start of each chapter*
*Montreux Convention*, 28, 30
Mount Kaçkar, 115

*NATO*, 29, 31
*natural history*, 2, 20, 23-5, 143
*naval operations*, 29
*navigation*, 18
*Navtex*, 18
Neftochim (Lokoil Marina), 189
Nessebar, 11, 184-5
*Noah's Ark*, 21, 26
Nos Emine, 175
Nos Galata, 175
Nos Kaliyakra, 175
Novorossiysk, 6, 133
*Novorossiysk YC 7 Feets*, 133
*nutrient overload*, 22-3, 24

Odessa, 6, 8, 11, 158-9
Of, 111
*oil & gas*, 30, 31, 129, 165, 189
Olenevka, 154
Olüce Burnu (Baba Burnu), 50
Omega Bay (Sevastopol), 151
Ordu (Eferli/Kumbaşi), 9, 11, 91-2
Ordzhonikidze, 144
Otmanli, 188
Ovaköy (Tekkeönü), 60

Paleostomi, Lake, 26
*paperwork*, 17-18, 199, *see also start of each chapter*
Partenit, 141
Pazar, 11, 114-15
*people*, 28, *see also start of each chapter*
*Periplus Ponti Euxini*, 10, 17, 27
Perşembe, 90-92
*pets*, 38
*pharmacies*, 16
Piraziz, 93-4
Pisatel (Sunny Beach), 179
*plans*, 4
*pollution*, 22-3, 30-31
Pomorie, 11, 186-7
Port Tomis (Constanța), 6, 8, 11, 165, 166-8
*ports of entry*, 6-7, *see also start of each chapter*
Poti, 6, 8, 10, 26, 125-9
*Poti Sea Port YC*, 125, 126-7
Poyrazköy, 5, 7, 39-41
*prescriptions*, 16
Primorsso, 192-3
*provisions*, 16, *see also start of each chapter*

*radar*, 18
*radio*, 18
*rainfall*, 21
*Ramsar Convention*, 25, 26
*religions*, 28
*resorts*, 6, 15, 30, 32
Rioni River Delta, 25, 26
Rize, 6, 11, 112-14
*Roman Empire*, 28
Romania, 3, 6, 29, 161-70
  *cruising routes*, 8, 10
  *harbours suitable for yachts*, 11, 161
  *ports of entry*, 6, 7, 162
Ropotamo, 192
Rumelifeneri, 195
Russian Federation, 2, 3, 5, 29, 130-33
  *chart abbreviations*, 200
  *ports of entry*, 6, 7, 131
*Russian YC (Sevastopol)*, 151

St George (Sf. Gheorghe) Channel (Danube Delta), 26, 165
St Konstantin & St Elena Marina (St Elia), 179-80
St Palaskeva (Angelica), 192
Sakarya River, 46
*salinity & water chemistry*, 23
Samsun, 6, 9, 10, 82-4
*Samsun YC*, 9, 82
Sandal Burnu Köyü, 196
Sarafovo, 187
*scuba diving*, 174
*sea*, 21-5
Sea of Azov, 3, 10, 21, 25, 145
*seals*, 24
*seamanship*, 18
Sevastopol, 6, 7, 11, 29, 150-52
*Severin, Tim*, 62
Seyrek Köyü, 44
Sf. Gheorghe (St George) Channel (Danube Delta), 26, 165
*ship's papers & stamp*, 17
*shoreline*, 2-3, 6, 21, *see also start of each chapter*
Şile, 8, 11, 41-2
Sinop, 6, 7, 9-10, 11, 73-6
Skadovsk, 157-8
Slânchev Den (Sunny Day), 179
Snake (Zmeiny) Island, 163
Sochi, 6, 131, 132
*Sochi YC*, 132
South Ossetia, 29, 31
Soviet Union, 29
Sozopol, 11, 183, 190-91
*storms*, 19
Sudak, 142
Sukhumi, 10
Sulina, 3, 5, 6, 10, 162, 163-5
Sulina Channel (Danube Delta), 26
Sunny Beach (Pisatel, Kabakum Bisser), 179
Sunny Day (Slânchev Den), 179
Supsa, 31, 125
Sürmene, 109
Sveti Anastasiya, 189
Sveti Vlas, 8, 11, 183-4
*swell*, 5-6

Tarlaağzi Köyü, 56
Tekkeönü (Ovaköy), 60
*telephones*, 18-19, *see also start of each chapter*


APPENDIX

*temperature scale*, 201
Terme, 11, 85
*time* see *start of each chapter*
Tirebolu, 11, 97-9
*tour guides* see *books & guides*
Trabzon, 6, 7, 9, 10, 104-7
*Trabzonspor YC*, 9, 10, 105-6
*transit log*, 37, 38, 137
*travel* see *start of each chapter*
Tsarevo (Carevo, Mičurin), 6, 193-4
Tuapse, 6, 132
Tulcea, 6, 26, 160, 162
Türkeli, 69-70
Turkey, 33-118, 195-8
*cruising routes*, 8, 9
*harbours suitable for yachts*, 10, 11
*navy & coastguard*, 29-30
*ports of entry*, 6, 7, 37

Ukraine, 2-3, 6, 29, 31, 134-60
  *cruising routes*, 8, 9-10
  *harbours suitable for yachts*, 11, 135
  *ports of entry*, 6-7, 137

*UNESCO World Heritage Site*, 185
*United Nations Globallast Programme*, 23
'Unye, 11, 86-7
Ust Dunaysk, 160, 162, 163

Varna, 6, 11, 180-82
Varna Bay, 175
Varna Bay Fishing Harbours, 180

*wars*, 28-9
*weather*, 2, 19, *see also start of each chapter*
*weather forecasts*, 19
*wetlands*, 25-6
*WGS84*, 4
Wi-Fi, 18, 19
*wildlife*, 2, 20, 23-5, 143
*winds*, 5-6, 19, 201

*yacht & equipment*, 12-15
*Yacht Club Odesa*, 158
*Yacht Club Port Burgas*, 187-8
*Yacht Club Sevastopol*, 151
*Yacht Club Yug (Sevastopol)*, 151
*Yachting Caution Zone*, 3, 8, 10, 29, 129
Yacht's Port Marina (Nessebar), 11, 184-5
Yakakent, 9, 11, 77-8
Yakaören/Kakoren, 68
Yaliköy, 11, 89
Yalta, 2, 6-7, 9-10, 11, 138-40
Yasun Burnu (Jason's Cape), 9, 90
Yeniay, 109-110
Yeşilçay (Ağva), 42-3
Yeşilirmak River, 9, 81, 84
Yevpatoria, 11, 153-4
Yomra, 108
Yukari Mescit, 64

Zarbana (Gürgenlik Liman), 66
Zlatni Pjasci (Golden Sands Marina), 178-9
Zmeiny (Snake) Island, 163
Zonguldak, 6, 11, 51